Falsifying the Fathers

How Pre-Tribulationists pervert the Apostolic End-times Teaching

By Nathanael Lewis

McKnight & Bishop Ltd
Inspire

About The Publisher

McKnight & Bishop are always on the look-out for new authors and ideas for new books. If you write or if you have an idea for a book, please e-mail: **info@mcknightbishop.com**

Some things we love are undiscovered authors, open-source software, Creative Commons, crowd-funding, Amazon/Kindle, social networking, faith, laughter and new ideas.

Visit us at **www.mcknightbishop.com**

About The Author

By day Nathanael Lewis is chained to desk and PC as a mild-mannered office-worker, by night..... he's in about the same condition at home, doing lots of reading and research. He has an Honours Master of Theology Degree from St Andrews University, the oldest university in Scotland, with a world-class Theology faculty. He also writes poetry, composes music - when he has the time - and plays improvisational piano. He is co-author of 'The Targeting of Minority Others in Pakistan' - a seminal work on the human rights situation of minorities in Pakistan. He wrote the section on Christians, which makes up about a third of the book. His work on the Pakistani Christian situation has been cited by official government reports from both the UK and Canada. For more on this, see:

http://www.britishpakistanichristians.co.uk/blog/the-targeting-of-minority-others-in-pakistan-pakistan

If you want to sign up for news and updates from Nathanael Lewis, including exclusive snippets of his poetry, music and other creative endeavours, email info@melodyofthemind.com with the heading NEWSLETTER in the subject.

ISBN 978-1-905691-37-1

A CIP catalogue record for this book is available from the British Library

First published in 2015 by McKnight & Bishop Inspire, an imprint of:

McKnight & Bishop Ltd. | 28 Grifffiths Court, Bowburn, Co. Durham, DH6 5FD
http://www.mcknightbishop.com | info@mcknightbishop.com

This book has been typeset in Garamond-Normal, Eskapade Fraktur and Museo Sans.

Printed and bound in Great Britain by Lightning Source Inc, Milton Keynes.
The paper used in this book has been made from wood independently certified as having come from sustainable forests.

Contents

Introduction......6
Didache......9
Dead Sea Scrolls......10
Justin Martyr......12
Shepherd of Hermas......13
Epistle of Barnabas......17
Barnabas......18
Papias......19
Clement of Rome......20
Ignatius of Antioch......25
Polycarp......26
Cyprian......28
Irenaeus......39
Tertullian......51
Hippolytus (and 'Pseudo-Hippolytus')......54
Origen and Clement of Alexandria......75
Lactantius......76
Commodianus......82
Methodius......87
Victorinus......88
Macarius, and a change of situation......97
Athanasius......98
(The Real) Ephrem the Syrian......98
Basil 'the Great' and the two Gregory's......99
Cyril of Jerusalem......101
Jerome......108
Rufinus......111
Ambrose......113
Sulpitius Severus......114
Hilary of Poitiers......117
The Apostolic Constitutions......117
Revelation of Esdras......118
The (Second) Revelation of St John......119
Apocalypse of Elijah......121
John Chrysostum......130
Augustine......151
John Cassian......158
John of Damascus......159
Abbot Ceolfrid's Latin Codex Amiatinus and the Venerable Bede......161
Pseudo-Ephraem......171
Pseudo-Methodius......184
Joachim of Fiore, Brother Dolcino and beyond......185
Conclusions and Applications......188

Appendix 1: Reclaiming Clement from the Clutches of Jason Hommel...........200
Appendix 2 : The Confusion of Pastor Bob and the Five Doves Website..........207
Appendix 3 : John 14 and the early church fathers - a Heavenly Home?..........218
Appendix 4 : Irenaeus - a Dispensationalist out of time?....................................231
Appendix 5 : Commodianus' 'Carmen Apologeticum' on the end times..........243
Appendix 6 : Hildegaard of Bingen on the Antichrist..249
Appendix 7 : Fraudulent misrepresentation of Seventeenth Century Puritans and their contemporaries..257
Appendix 8 : It's the UFO's wot dun it, honest - because the 'Queen of Heaven' says so and related issues...284
Appendix 9 - Help! So what do I do about it?...287
Great News for Imperfect people in Terrible Times..291
Other books by Nathanael Lewis..295

Introduction

My earlier book, 'Rapture Rupture!' has shown how Pre-Tribbers invariably distort scripture, usually by taking little snippets out of context. As I was preparing to make some corrections and improvements in the book, I came across a number of extremely deceptive claims from the Pre-Tribulation proponents that the early church fathers taught some form of Pre-Tribulation rapture. They do this to try and refute basically correct claims that the Pre-Tribulation wasn't taught in the church until the 1820's. I saw these distortions and slanders again and again, and got very very angry at the lies, and so decided to write another appendix for the updated 'Rapture Rupture!' book, but it grew and grew, until it became clear that it would need to be a book in its own right, and this is that book.

For those who don't know, I include here at the start a brief explanation of the issue and terms, and encourage you to buy 'Rapture Rupture!' for a much fuller examination. The bible teaches that in the seven years before Jesus' returns, there will be a terrible time on earth, especially for God's people, with a mix of persecution by the forces of the anti-Christ, plus disasters that are the judgement of God on a wicked world. This is often referred to as 'The Tribulation' or 'the Great Tribulation'. In the last 200 years or so, a doctrine has arisen, primarily starting with the founder of the Brethren churches, an Irish preacher called Darby, in large parts of the evangelical and fundamentalist Protestant church movements that teaches that the true church will be 'raptured' before the start of this terrible period - that is, they will vanish from earth to go to be with Jesus who comes to meet them in the air and takes them back to heaven to sit out the seven years of suffering. This is known as the 'Pre-Tribulation' position, or 'Pre-Trib' for short. In 'Rapture Rupture!' I show how this is emphatically not what Jesus and his apostles taught, and that in fact they consistently warned that the church would go through the Tribulation and that the rapture-event would happen as Jesus returned to earth to destroy evil and bring in His kingdom rule on earth (something that is called a 'Post-Tribulation' or 'Post-Trib' view). The reason that the views of the earliest church fathers are important is because they were writing in the generations immediately after the apostles, and therefore could be expected to teach about the issue very close to what the apostles taught, since the early church had a huge emphasis on maintaining what they called 'the apostolic tradition' or teaching. Thus, if the Pre-Tribulation view is the one that the New Testament writers taught (who were either the apostles, or those close to the apostles), then we would expect to find the same being taught in the early church writings.

There are hundreds of videos and articles on the internet which claim that a long swathe of early church fathers taught the Pre-Tribulation rapture. Some of the more cautious will issue caveats to say only that the early church fathers had concepts that are consistent with such a position. Either way, these articles and videos pretty much invariably follow the same basic pattern, which is to say that actually there are loads of church fathers who taught the Pre-Tribulation view, and then cite a few snippets from one or two church fathers, and then list a whole load of other figures who allegedly taught a Pre-Trib rapture (and guess what, when you look at 'Post-Tribulation' sites they will list pretty much exactly the same authors as teaching a Post-Trib view!). You will usually see the same few names and quotes over and over again. I am sure that in many cases people are honestly parroting what they have taught, but sometime, someone has to have known that they were deceiving people with these dishonest tactics. In this book, I will carefully examine each quote in context and show that the Pre-Tribulationist teachers are distorting and perverting the early Church Fathers in exactly the same way they do the New Testament, taking little snippets out of context, when the context shows that either they are explicitly what we would call 'Post-Tribulationist, or that they were teaching that we must endure suffering, something totally anti-thetical to the Pre-Tribulationist teaching that Jesus loves his church too much to let her suffer greatly.

Another tactic is to associate the Pre-Trib position with a particular concept - usually 'imminence' - a concept they falsely claim is used in the New Testament and which I have exposed and refuted in 'Rapture Rupture!' (A brief recap - Pre-Tribbers take 'imminence' as meaning that Jesus' return will be sudden and without warning. Since the bible teaches a set of events that happen in the 7 years leading up to the visible return of Jesus, they believe that any passage that they deem teaches 'imminence' must therefore be describing Jesus somehow coming before the start of this seven year Tribulation period, hence their belief in the 'Pre-Tribulation' rapture.) When an early church writer is deemed to have displayed belief, however vaguely expressed, in 'imminence' in relation to the return of Jesus, suddenly they are claimed as somehow supporting a Pre-Trib rapture, even if they weren't aware of it. You usually see this in the more scholarly articles from the 'Pre-Trib Research Centre', a major source of deception on this issue. In one article, I found a particularly interesting footnote, tucked away at the bottom of the article where they admit that the concept of what they call imminence appears in writers who taught that certain events must happen before Jesus' return. Rather than revisit the issue and realize that their concept of imminence is what is at fault, they blithely go on claiming as one of their own, it seems, any writer in whom they see any expression of 'imminence'. I examine the footnote in more detail further below in the section on Hippolytus. This is an example of a pervasive pattern in Pre-Tribulation argument which I exposed in 'Rapture Rupture!' - that of continually assuming the very position you are trying to 'prove', otherwise known as 'circular argument'.

Another rhetorical tactic is to - usually correctly - claim that a particular church father held to particular beliefs about the Tribulation events and the earthly rule of Jesus in the Millenium, and then associate that solely with the Pre-Trib position and hint that they really must have believed in something like the Rapture. And if there is any fragment that could be taken to support that position, lo and behold, it becomes 'proof' that the church father taught the full panoply of Pre-Trib positions, or at least was well on the way to doing so.

A number of early Pre-Tribulationist writers frankly and freely admitted that the doctrine was new (Darby apparently boasted of it being totally new) and a few still do, noting that the early church consistently held what is usually termed the 'Historic Pre-Millenial' view, which is Post-Tribulation. However, a good many - and again, the Pre-Tribulation Research Centre are among the chief culprits here - deliberately try and imply that the early church fathers were vague and unformed in their views so as to try and make room for a Pre-Tribulation teaching. On the face of it, this is rather extra-ordinary, since the early church was ferocious in guarding its deposit of apostolic teaching, including detailed teaching on the end times. Doubtless some writers could be vague (or non-specific, because the rapture-timing date was a non-issue for them - they had other issues to focus on), but what is consistent whenever issues of the Tribulation are taught, is that they were Post-Tribulation, but they believed that God would preserve many righteous saints through it, often by gathering them to a particular place of safety in some way (they are often a bit vague about this last part).

If you want an example of how such writers deliberately muddy the waters to try and prise open room for a Pre-Tribulation teaching in the early church, then this quote is typical :

> 'As was typical of every area of the early church's theology, their views of prophecy were undeveloped and sometimes contradictory, containing a seedbed out of which could develop various and diverse theological viewpoints. While it is hard to find clear pretribulationism spelled out in the fathers, there are also found clear pre-trib elements which if systematized with their other prophetic views contradict posttribulationism but support pretribulationism.
>
> Since imminency is considered to be a crucial feature of pretribulationism by scholars such as John Walvoord, it is significant that the Apostolic Fathers, though posttribulational, at the same time just as clearly taught the pretribulational feature of imminence. Since it was common in the early church to hold contradictory positions without even an awareness of inconsistency, it would not be surprising to learn that their era supports both views. Larry Crutchfield notes, "This belief in the imminent return of Christ within the context of ongoing persecution has prompted us to broadly label the views of the earliest fathers, 'imminent intra-tribulationism.'"

Weasel-worded indeed! What they usually mean is that because there is some element of 'imminence', therefore they contradict Post-Tribulationism, a basic argument I have shown in 'Rapture Rupture!' to be utterly false as applied to the New Testament. The same applies to the church fathers too, as we shall see. As we shall also see, it is not at all true to say that these writers held 'contradictory positions without even an awareness of inconsistency': in fact there is a remarkable consistency across these writers, let alone within each individual's writings. What utter arrant and arrogant condescension, what an insult to the intelligence and integrity of holy church fathers, to assert that they were utterly and blithely inconsistent in their teachings. This is almost as stupid as those liberal scholarly idiots who teach that there are contradictions in the Laws of Moses because it is allegedly woven together from different accounts by an editor who was so dumb he couldn't see the contradictions in what he was writing (sorry, irritation from university days there, rant over. For those of you who don't understand what I mean, well, don't worry, you're not missing much!).

Although there are a few medieval and later examples cited, it is the early church fathers that I am chiefly interested in.

Didache

Let's start with the easiest of all to refute, and my favourite non-biblical source from the early church, the Didache, whose full title is 'The Teaching of the Twelve Apostles of the Lord to the Gentiles', and which was basically a church manual for non-Jewish churches and was immensely popular in the early church, deemed the official teaching of Jesus' Twelve disciples. I see repeated claims from Pre-Tribbers that the Didache (which I cited several times in 'Rapture Rupture!') teaches a 'Pre-Trib rapture'. Let's be blunt here. It doesn't. How they claim it does is, as usual, by citing a fragment out of context, and then because it teaches 'imminence' go 'There, it teaches a pre-Trib rapture'. The teaching about the end times comes right at the end of Didache, and it starts as follows :

> 'Watch for your life's sake. Let not your lamps be quenched, nor your loins unloosed; but be ready, for you know not the hour in which our Lord will come.'

And this is all that they quote. Because it says we won't know the hour Jesus returns, they say, therefore it must be teaching a Pre-Trib rapture. This is profoundly dishonest. It's not like there is much material in the final chapter, and the rest makes it quite clear that they didn't teach anything of the sort. Yet we get claims that the Didache clearly teaches a rapture and then persecution of a separate group of Tribulation saints under the antichrist. I will quote the whole passage, and remember that it is written exclusively to Gentile Christians, a group that to Pre-Tribbers, who are almost always dispensationalist, believe will be raptured out of the way before the Anti-Christ comes to power.

> 'Watch for your life's sake. Let not your lamps be quenched, nor your loins unloosed; but be ready, for you know not the hour in which our Lord will come. But come together often, seeking the things which are befitting to your souls: for the whole time of your faith will not profit you, if you are not made perfect in the last time. For in the last days false prophets and corrupters shall be multiplied, and the sheep shall be turned into wolves, and love shall be turned into hate; for when lawlessness increases, they shall hate and persecute and betray one another, and then shall appear the world-deceiver as Son of God, and shall do signs and wonders, and the earth shall be delivered into his hands, and he shall do iniquitous things which have never yet come to pass since the beginning. Then shall the creation of men come into the fire of trial, and many shall be made to stumble and shall perish; but those who endure in their faith shall be saved from under the curse itself. And then shall appear the signs of the truth: first, the sign of an outspreading in heaven, then the sign of the sound of

> the trumpet. And third, the resurrection of the dead – yet not of all, but as it is said: "The Lord shall come and all His saints with Him." Then shall the world see the Lord coming upon the clouds of heaven.'

Do you see any sign of the apostles teaching that the believers will be raptured out of the way, and escape the Tribulation? Do you see any mention of a separate group of 'Tribulation Saints'? I don't. The apostles here warn that 'the whole time of your faith will not profit you, if you are not made perfect in the last time.' The reason? 'For in the last days, false prophets...' etc, etc. The apostles were warning their readers that they and not some separate group of 'Tribulation Saints' could face this. The apostles here teach exactly what the New Testament and Jesus taught. In the last days the church will be beset by false teachers and corrupters, leading to great wickedness inside and outside of the church, with loving unity turned to hatred and persecution, and this paves the way for the anti-Christ to appear. (Jesus warned what will happen if 'salt loses its saltiness' – it is only fit to be thrown into the fire. When the church as a whole loses integrity, then the restraints on the anti-Christ coming to power will be lifted.) Specifically, when lawlessness increases – and by this, the apostles meant not just general violence or anything like that, but the abandoning of the precepts and teachings of God's law as found in the Old Testament, something we see rife in the church today with the abandoning of the teaching about creation, marriage, the sanctity of life and the promises to Israel – then shall the hatred and persecution of each other come. The apostles warn their Gentile readers that they will have to undergo this if they are alive at that time. Many shall perish and fall away from the faith, but those who remain and endure in their faith will be saved. (As Jesus said, 'When the Son of Man comes, will he find faith in the earth?') It is only then, after the deception of the anti-Christ and the false prophets, that the signs of truth appear, after the Tribulation, as Jesus says in Matthew 24. The heavens are opened, the trumpet sounds and there is the resurrection of the dead believers (aka the rapture) who then return with Jesus followed by those still alive. At that point the whole world will see His return in glory. This is quite clearly a Post-Tribulation teaching about the rapture.

If ever anyone tells you that the Didache preaches a Pre-Tribulation rapture, they are lying to you, no matter how sincerely they believe it.

Dead Sea Scrolls

I am absolutely gobsmacked to be writing this, but whilst researching the church fathers I found the claim, which I have since found it is relatively common in some Pre-Tribulationist circles because it apparently comes from a popular bible teacher, Jack van Impe (and my already low opinion of him has gone rather lower now!), that a Scroll had been found among the Dead Sea Scrolls (DSS) which taught the rapture. For those of you who don't know, the DSS are a large number of scrolls and similar ancient documents found preserved in jars in caves near the Dead Sea in Israel from around the time of Jesus – dating from c 200BC to AD70 when the Romans destroyed the nearby site from where the scrolls are presumed to have originated. The DSS are the library of this community, which most scholars believe to be the HQ of a Jewish sect called the Essenes, and the DSS are largely either copies of Old Testament books, or the sects' own documents, such as their rule of conduct and the teachings of their founder. Anyway here is the relevant quote in full :

> "A Newly Discovered Dead Sea Scroll Has Revealed Who Will be Left Behind When the Rapture Comes a Leading Scholar Reports" from the journalist David Augustine. (Jack van Impe Ministries, June 16, 2005)
>
> In this article Dr. William Harold, professor of Canon Law, at the Theological Seminary of Essex, GB wrote:
>
> "Without doubt, this is the most important discovery in the history of Biblical archaeology. The scroll, written in Aramaic, the language spoken in the Holy Land during Jesus time on earth, was found in a cave on the shores of the Dead Sea by geologists conducting a survey for the Israeli government."
>
> The scrolls read:
>
> "The Rapture will occur suddenly. And countless thousands will vanish from the earth. Swept up to heaven to live with Jesus and escape the torment of the Tribulation, the others will be left behind."

I knew as soon as I saw it this had to be some sort of out and out fraud, but at first I thought it likely that a genuine scholar had been quoted over some Dead Sea Scroll issue and then contents of the scroll misquoted. The alleged quote from a non-Christian Jewish document somehow manages to mention 'Jesus', the 'rapture' and modern fundamentalist populist notions of thousands vanishing from the earth to be with Jesus and escape the torment of the Tribulation, and using the iconic words 'Left Behind'. Look, even the most hick of hick-town bible teachers should have smelt a rat there, but some are still gullible / desperate enough to proclaim it as evidence on their websites!

But then I considered further. A theological seminary in the UK large enough to have a professor of Canon Law, I would, as a UK theologian, surely heard of? Maybe, maybe not. But why would a professor of Canon Law, which usually indicates Anglican, Orthodox or Catholic seminaries, be supporting an obscure (to them) fundamentalist evangelical doctrine? I searched and searched and could find no such 'Professor', no such Theological seminary and no such quote other than on sites that contained the above fraudulent declaration. Also the article doesn't mention precisely which Dead Sea Scroll - which are meticulously logged down to the very smallest fragment - that this allegedly amazing quote comes from.

I did find just one website that claimed to have found out just which scroll fragment was meant - '4Q521' - and it goes on in very sarcastic and strident tones to proclaim triumphant vindication against people who must have called out this fraud, but in the body of the article admitted that the scroll doesn't mention the rapture at all, but mentions 'resurrections of the dead' (presumably by this the article writer means that because there is more than one resurrection, it allegedly supports the rapture as one resurrection, and the final resurrection too - which, as we shall see is a total misrepresentation of the fragment and the scholarly article). He quoted a scholarly article in full, but ironically, it comes from a notoriously anti-Christian scholar called James Tabor and for anyone who knows anything about the Dead Sea Scrolls and early Christianity it is interesting, as Tabor notes, because it provides a parallel with Jesus' teaching that he, as Messiah, would raise the dead, but absolutely zip, nada on resurrections plural, at the end times. You can read it here - http://www.freerepublic.com/focus/religion/2672877/replies?c=828 - if you want.

So we can absolutely and categorically say that if ever anyone tells you that the Dead Sea Scrolls taught a Pre-Tribulation rapture, they are lying to you, no matter how sincerely they believe it. I would go further and point out that they have fallen for the most blatant of blatant frauds.

Justin Martyr

You fairly often see his name cited as a teacher of Pre-Tribulation rapture, but I have yet to find a single citation of his work to back this up. I searched the Pre-Tribulation Research Centre and they at least, don't cite him once in this regard, although they do repeatedly mention him for other reasons. They also appear not to mention the passage where he makes it quite clear his position was what we would today call 'Post-Tribulation'. In Dialogue with Trypho chapter 110 (You can read it at http://www.newadvent.org/fathers/01288.htm) he makes clear reference to Christians suffering under the anti-Christ (in this work Trypho is a Jew, and Justin is having a religious debate with him to try and convert him to Christianity). Notice how there is not even a hint of some separate future 'Tribulation saints' or similar that Pre-Tribulation positions require - Justin makes it crystal clear that the Christians he is referring to is the body of people he belongs to - 'us Christians'. Here is the quote :

> '....two advents of Christ have been announced: the one, in which He is set forth as suffering, inglorious, dishonoured, and crucified; but the other, in which he shall come from heaven with glory, when the man of apostasy, who speaks strange things against the Most High, shall venture to do unlawful deeds on the earth **against us the Christians**, who, having learned the true worship of God from the law, and the word which went forth from Jerusalem by means of the apostles of Jesus, have fled for safety to the God of Jacob and God of Israel; and we who were filled with war, and mutual slaughter, and every wickedness, have each through the whole earth changed our warlike weapons,–our swords into ploughshares, and our spears into implements of tillage,–and we cultivate piety, righteousness, philanthropy, faith, and hope, which we have from the Father Himself through Him who was crucified;'

And having just declared that the persecution in the last days under the anti-Christ against Christians would be horrific, Justin goes on to note the terrible persecutions

Christians were already enduring in his own time - torture, beheadings and crucifixions, being thrown to the lions and so on :

> 'Now it is evident that no one can terrify or subdue us who have believed in Jesus over all the world. For it is plain that, though beheaded, and crucified, and thrown to wild beasts, and chains, and fire, and all other kinds of torture, we do not give up our confession; but the more such things happen, the more do others and in larger numbers become faithful, and worshippers of God through the name of Jesus. For just as if one should cut away the fruit-bearing parts of a vine, it grows up again, and yields other branches flourishing and fruitful; even so the same thing happens with us. For the vine planted by God and Christ the Saviour is His people. But the rest of the prophecy shall be fulfilled at His second coming. For the expression, 'He that is afflicted [and driven out],' i.e. from the world, [implies] that, so far as you and all other men have it in your power, each Christian has been driven out not only from his own property, but even from the whole world; for you permit no Christian to live.'

If ever anyone tells you that the Justin Martyr preaches a Pre-Tribulation rapture in which the church escapes suffering, they are lying to you, no matter how sincerely they believe it.

Shepherd of Hermas

This is a kind of mystical work in which the author has a number of visions which he recounts, in some ways a bit like Pilgrims Progress. Hermas was an early Jewish Christian, and in these visions he is guided firstly by a woman representing the church, and then secondly by a shepherd who is the angel of repentance, in which he is given a detailed picture of how God is building his church, and how different levels of unrepented sinfulness can affect an individual's inclusion in the final Kingdom of God. (I took the time to read the entirety of the book to make sure I wasn't taking anything out of context). The book is frequently mentioned as supporting Pre-Tribulation rapture and usually a particular fragment of text is cited. Interestingly, I found two different approaches by the same author, Dr Thomas Ice, a prominent contributor to Pre-Tribulation Research Centre. In the first, he precedes the quote by stating unequivocally 'The Shepherd of Hermas speaks of the pretribulational concept of escaping the tribulation.' He then goes on to cite the fragment :

> 'You have escaped from great tribulation on account of your faith, and because you did not doubt in the presence of such a beast. Go, therefore, and tell the elect of the Lord His mighty deeds, and say to them that this beast is a type of the great tribulation that is coming. If then ye prepare yourselves, and repent with all your heart, and turn to the Lord, it will be possible for you to escape it, if your heart be pure and spotless, and ye spend the rest of the days of your life in serving the Lord blamelessly'

But even with such a short quote, it is quite clear that something is wrong for the Pre-Tribulationist position. Pre-Tribulationists teach that if you are a believer in Christ, you will escape the Tribulation, period. However, this passage talks about preparing yourself through repentance and holy living as the means to escape the Tribulation.

In another more 'scholarly' article, Ice is rather more circumspect. He quotes the whole vision, not just a part, but precedes it by saying 'The post-apostolic writing known as The Shepherd of Hermas (ca. a.d. 140) speaks of a possible pretribulational concept of escaping the tribulation' and after simply quoting the entire vision then concludes by saying 'While Hermas clearly speaks of escaping the tribulation, pretribulationists and non-pretribulationists tend to agree that he does not articulate a clear message similar to modern pretribulationism. Pre-trib scholar, John Walvoord argues that the central feature of pretribulationism is the doctrine of imminency and that is a prominent feature of the doctrine of the early church.' Notice how after admitting that this is not really pre-tribulational, he then muddies the water by the usual Pre-Trib hand-waving about 'imminence'.

Before I go on to examine in detail the alleged teaching of escape from the rapture, I should note that it comes from the fourth vision in the book. What these Pre-Tribulation 'scholars' so carefully don't tell you is that there is another passage in the second vision that very clearly teaches a Post-Tribulation position, as follows. The context is that Hermas is being rebuked for the sinfulness of his family and warned there is one last chance for repentance. He is then told :

> 'So speak, therefore, to the officials of the church, in order that they may direct their ways in righteousness, in order that they might receive the promises in full with much glory. You, therefore, who work righteousness must be steadfast, and do not be double-minded, in order that you may gain entrance with the holy angels. Blessed are those of you who patently endure the coming Great Tribulation and who will not deny their life. For the Lord has sworn by his Son that those who have denied their Lord have been rejected from their life, that is, those who now are about to deny him in the coming days.'

Notice that Hermas is commanded to speak to the officials of the church about the need for righteous living, including faithfulness during the Tribulation. There is not one hint that there is a separate body of Tribulation saints or any similar Pre-Tribulational concept. Rather, it is clear that it is the church that will undergo the Tribulation. This is consistent with the teaching of Jesus and the apostles, who as I showed in 'Rapture Rupture!' taught that righteous and faithful living is key to retaining salvation in the Tribulation, and that to those who live righteously, the day of the Lord won't come as a 'thief in the night'.

So, if this is the case, how are we to interpret the vision that is claimed to teach that the church will escape the Tribulation? The full passage reads as follows:

> The Fourth vision which I saw, brethren, twenty days after the former vision which came unto me, for a type of the impending tribulation. I was going into the country by the Campanian Way. From the high road, it is

about ten stades; and the place is easy for travelling. While then I am walking alone, I entreat the Lord that He will accomplish the revelations and the visions which He showed me through His holy Church, that He may strengthen me and may give repentance to His servants which have stumbled, that His great and glorious Name may be glorified, for that He held me worthy that He should show me His marvels. And as I gave glory and thanksgiving to Him, there answered me as it were the sound of a voice, 'Be not of doubtful mind, Hermas.' I began to question in myself and to say, 'How can I be of doubtful mind, seeing that I am so firmly founded by the Lord, and have seen glorious things?' And I went on a little, brethren, and behold I see a cloud of dust rising as it were to heaven, and I began to say within myself, 'Can it be that cattle are coming, and raising a cloud of dust?' for it was just about a stade from me. As the cloud of dust grew greater and greater, I suspected that it was something supernatural. Then the sun shone out a little, and behold, I see a huge beast like a sea-monster, and from its mouth fiery locusts issued forth. And the beast was about a hundred feet in length, and its head was as it were of pottery. And I began to weep, and to entreat the Lord that He would rescue me from it. And I remembered the word which I had heard, 'Be not of doubtful mind, Hermas.' Having therefore, brethren, put on the faith of the Lord and called to mind the mighty works that He had taught me, I took courage and gave myself up to the beast. Now the beast was coming on with such a rush, that it might have ruined a city. I come near it, and, huge monster as it was, it stretched itself on the ground, and merely put forth its tongue, and stirred not at all until I had passed by it. And the beast had on its head four colours; black, then fire and blood colour, then gold, then white.

Now after I had passed the beast, and had gone forward about thirty feet, behold, there met me a virgin arrayed as if she were going forth from a bride-chamber, all in white and with white sandals, veiled up to her forehead, and her head-covering consisted of a turban, and her hair was white. I knew from the former visions that it was the Church, and I became more cheerful. She greeted me, saying, 'Good day, my good man'; and I saluted her in turn, 'Lady, good day'. She answered and said to me, 'Did nothing meet you?' I said to her 'Lady, such a huge beast, that could have destroyed whole peoples: but, by the power of the Lord and by His great mercy, I escaped it).' 'You did escape it well', she said 'because you cast your care upon God, and opened your heart to the Lord, believing that you can be saved by nothing else but by His great and glorious Name. Therefore the Lord sent His angel, which is over the beasts, whose name is Segri, and shut its mouth, that it might not hurt you. You have escaped a great tribulation by virtue of your faith, and because, though you saw such a huge beast, you did not doubt in your mind. Go therefore, and declare to the elect of the Lord His mighty works, and tell them that this beast is a type of the great tribulation which is to come. If therefore you prepare yourselves beforehand, and repent and turn to the Lord with your whole heart, you shall be able to escape it, if your heart be made pure and without blemish, and if for the remaining days of your life you serve the Lord blamelessly. Cast your cares upon the Lord and He will set them straight. Trust in the Lord, you men of doubtful mind, for He can do all things; Yes, He turns away His wrath from you, and again He sends forth His plagues upon you that are of doubtful mind. Woe to them that hear these words and are disobedient; it would be better for them that they had not been born.

I asked her concerning the four colours, which the beast had upon its head. Then she answered me and said, 'Again you are curious about such matters.' 'Yes, lady,' I said, 'make known unto me what these things are.' 'Listen', she said 'the black is this world in which you dwell; and the fire and blood colour shows that this world must perish by blood and fire; and the golden part are you that have escaped from this world . For as the gold is tested by fire and is made useful, so you also that dwell in it are being tested in yourselves. Then you that endure and pass through the fire will be purified by it. For as the gold loses its dross, so you also shall cast away all sorrow and tribulation, and shall be purified, and shall be useful for building of the tower. But the white portion is the coming age, in which the elect of God shall dwell; because the elect of God shall be without spot and pure unto life eternal. Therefore don't cease speaking into the ears of the saints. You have now the symbolism also of the tribulation which is coming in power. But if you will be willing, it shall be nothing. Remember the things that are written beforehand.' With these words she departed, and I saw not in what direction she departed; for a noise was made; and I turned back in fear, thinking that the beast was coming.'

(Where the woman, the church, in the vision, refers to 'the building of the tower' it is referring to an earlier vision, in which the church is likened to a tower that Jesus is building. The final consummation of all things won't happen until it is completed. Individual saints by their conduct and willingness to repent or otherwise will determine whether they will be fitted into this tower, or if they will be cast off).

Unlike the Pre-Tribulationists, I will actually explore what the vision means. As usual, it is completely consistent with the teaching of the New Testament about the Tribulation. First let's look at the frightening vision. Hermas encounters an utterly huge and terrifying supernatural beast. Terrified, he weeps and asks God to rescue him from it. He is reminded of the word spoken to him earlier about not doubting, and so he took courage and reminded himself of God's power and gave himself to the power of the beast. When he did so, it suddenly stilled, and lay down and let him pass. When he meets the church in the vision, she explains to him that he escaped because he put his trust in and cast his cares on God. He escaped because he had faith enough to face up to the monster. She says it is a type of the coming Great Tribulation, and that similarly the church will escape by being faithful, living holy, and not being of doubtful mind. In other words, the escape is not an escape from Tribulation by any Pre-Tribulation rapture, but it is escape through it. You only escape by living righteously, but if you live double-mindedly or doubtfully and share in the wickedness of the world, you will feel the judgement of God. As I proved in 'Rapture Rupture!' this is the basic teaching of the New Testament also.

Those who live righteously will not be taken by surprise by the last days and the coming of the Lord. However, as Peter says, 'Judgement must start in the household of God', and so God will use tribulation and suffering to separate the true believers from the apostates, and to purify the true believers.

This is the interpretation given to the four colours on the beasts head. The black is the world, the red is the blood and fire through which both the world will be destroyed and the elect purified to be made fit for the final Kingdom of God. Hermas is advised that the vision refers to the coming tribulation which will be intense and powerful and frightening like the beast he saw. But if we face up to it with willing hearts, we will endure for the sake of the joy set before us, as Jesus did on the cross, and it will be as nothing to us because of our faith.

Compare this detailed and faithful and simple explanation of the vision, with the utterly facetious and false and flippant and shallow way the Pre-Tribulationists take it. The escape referred to here is exactly the opposite of the teaching they espouse, and they are encouraging the saints into a false delusion.

If ever anyone tells you that the Shepherd of Hermas teaches a Pre-Tribulation rapture, they are lying to you, no matter how sincerely they believe it.

Epistle of Barnabas

(Almost certainly not written by the Barnabas in the New Testament according to most scholars, by the way.) This is an early work, almost certainly written by a Jewish Christian, and written against unbelieving Jews. It uses an intricate allegorical interpretation of mainly Old Testament passages to make its case. I took the time to read the whole work through when I researched this appendix, and I could find not even a hint of a Pre-Tribulation rapture, and yet it repeatedly appears in lists of allegedly Pre-Tribulationist church fathers. In fact, the issue of Jesus' second coming barely turns up at all in the book. However, I did find several quotes that severely undermine Pre-Tribulation rationales, specifically the belief that a loving Saviour would not let his church go through suffering. Both occur in chapters 7-8 when the author is discussing the ceremony of the Scapegoat during Yom Kippur, the holiest Jewish festival of all, the Day of Atonement - look it up in the bible to find out the basics - and also the sacrificing of a heifer for sins. However, Barnabas knows of extra traditions not commanded in the bible that were practiced by the Jews, and he applies them to Jesus. The goat that was driven into the wilderness as the scapegoat after being spat on - which he takes as a type of Jesus - had scarlet cotton or wool tied between its horns. The man who takes it into the wilderness then takes the red material and puts it on the thorns of the rachia bush. Here is how he applies it :

> 'And what does it mean when the place the wool in the midst of the thorns? It is a type of Jesus, set forth for the church, because whoever desires to take away the scarlet wool must suffer greatly because the thorns are so terrible, and can only gain possession of it through affliction. Likewise, he says, 'those who desire to see me and to gain my kingdom must receive me through affliction and suffering'.

This matches the New Testament teaching in Acts 14.22 that we only enter the Kingdom of God through tribulation and testing.

The writer of this Epistle then goes on to talk about the sacrifice of a heifer for sins. The heifer is sacrificed, then burnt, and then the children of those sinners on whose behalf the sacrifice was made were to put the ashes in containers and tie scarlet wool and some hyssop around a tree, and then the children sprinkle people one by one to ritually purify them from their sins. For the writer, the heifer calf is Jesus, brought to slaughter by the men who had him crucified (the Jewish leaders), and the children who sprinkle the people are the preachers of the gospel about Jesus' death. As usual in Christian thought, the tree is a reference to the cross of Jesus. He then goes on :

> 'And then there is the matter of the wool on the tree: this signifies that the kingdom of Jesus is on the tree, and that those who hope in him will live forever. But why the wool and the hyssop together? Because in his kingdom there will be dark and evil days, in which we will be saved, because the one who suffers in body is healed by means of the dark juice of the hyssop.'

Again, totally contrary to the 'loving God won't let you suffer the Tribulation' mantra of the Pre-Trib false teachers.

If ever anyone tells you that the Epistle of Barnabas teaches a Pre-Tribulation rapture, they are lying to you, no matter how sincerely they believe it.

Barnabas

You sometimes see Barnabas appearing in lists separately from the Epistle of Barnabas. I'm guessing this is partly error because different scholars give different dates for the Epistle of Barnabas, but I'm sure the practice continues in large part from a desperate desire to prop up the case by multiplying the alleged 'Pre-Tribulationist' church fathers. But since the Epistle of Barnabas does not in any way teach such a position, as we have seen, well, let me see, ummm.... zero multiplied by zero is – help me here folks - ummm Zero! Naughty Naughty!

However, I missed a possible relevant reference to Barnabas, so to add some relevant teaching material, let us have a look at it because it teaches plainly something that is taught or implied in the New Testament, but is often missed – what it is that enables the anti-Christ to come to power. (I use the caveat 'possible' because Barnabas uses a term that is probably a reference to the anti-Christ, but could also be a term for Satan and his demonic forces generally – however, these two interpretations are by no means completely incompatible.) In 2 Thessalonians 2, Paul teaches that before the return of Jesus, there will have to be two things happen – that there be a great falling away or apostasy from the faith, and then the lawless one appears. This is a repeated theme throughout the New Testament and the early church writers. The relevant quote is from chapter four of the Epistle of Barnabas, and the context is him warning against hypocrisy – against 'piling up sins' whilst claiming 'that the covenant is irrevocably yours', warning that this is just what Israel did at the incident of the Golden Calf when the tablets of the covenant were smashed. He goes on to apply it as follows :

> 'Consequently, let us be on guard in the last days, for the whole time of our life and faith will do us no good unless now, in the age of lawlessness, we resist as well the coming stumbling blocks, as befits God's children, lest the black one find an opportunity to sneak in. Let us flee from every kind of vanity, let us hate completely the works of the evil way. Do not withdraw within yourselves and live alone, as though you were already justified, but gather together and seek out together the common good. For the Scripture says 'Woe to those who are wise in their own opinion and clever in their own eyes'. Let us become spiritual, let us become a perfect Temple for God. To the best of our ability, let us cultivate the fear of God and strive to keep his commandments, that we may rejoice in his ordinances. The Lord will judge the world without partiality. Each person will receive according to what he has done: if he is good, his righteousness will precede him; if he is evil, the wages of doing evil will go before him. Let us never fall asleep in our sins, as if being 'called' was an excuse to rest, lest the evil ruler gain power over us and thrust us out of the Kingdom of the Lord. Moreover, consider this as well, my brothers : when you see that after such extraordinary signs and wonders were done in Israel, even then they were abandoned, let us be on guard lest we should be found to be, as it is written 'many called, but few chosen'.'

This should be a wake-up call to us all. Even if the terms 'black one' and 'evil ruler' are not references to the anti-Christ, but rather to the Satanic kingdom in general, it fits well with the warning that lawlessness and abandoning the law of God will usher in the anti-Christ - and this is precisely what we see in the church and world today - rejection of the foundational truths of God's law - the goodness of God's creating is abandoned for the evils and cruelty of evolution - the divine plan for marriage is increasingly mocked and sidelined - the sanctity of life annihilated by the holocausts of abortion and euthanasia - the covenant and promises to Israel being denied through the Replacement and so-called Fulfilment theologies and vicious anti-semitism against Israel being displayed through anti-Zionist and pro-Palestinian movements. (As well as a theologian I am a human rights worker who is particularly appalled at the slanders and abuse of human rights in which terms like genocide and apartheid are used against Israel today).

Anyway, if ever anyone tells you that Barnabas taught a Pre-Tribulation rapture, they are lying to you, no matter how sincerely they believe it.

Papias

As I have done for most of these names, I have googled the name with the term 'rapture' and put the name into the search engine of that alleged powerhouse of proofs for the Pre-Tribulation rapture, the Pre-Tribulation Research Centre. I also read every fragment I could find, and, apart from the fact that he taught the Millenium, much to the disdain of later church writers, you know what I found? Zip. Nada. Nothing on the rapture, but lots on how he was Pre-Millenialist. This is a tactic we often see – conflating Pre-Millenial views with Pre-Tribulation views. Well, OK, so I did sort of find something. On the Research Centre site, I found an article which tried to claim that Matthew 24.40-1 doesn't refer to the rapture (kind of true) but that John 14.1-3 does. In it the writer cites another writer who lists Papias along with some others as church fathers who held to a 'heavenly and eschatological' interpretation of John 14.1-3. However, that does not mean that they taught a Pre-Tribulation Rapture, which is what the author is trying to imply. I could be said to hold to a 'heavenly and eschatological' interpretation of the same passage, but I don't believe it refers to the Second Coming, let alone any particular view of the rapture. The reason is that 'eschatological' or 'relating to the last days' doesn't just mean the very end of the age, but can be used to refer to any time after Jesus' first coming, since he was held to usher in the (very long, as it turns out - as Jesus implied in his parables) Last Days. Secondly, 'heavenly' was used in the New Testament and probably in much of the early church to refer to something that is currently found in and comes from, heaven. And when a Pre-Tribulation writer cites another person of the same Pre-Tribulation persuasion, but only the conclusions, not the basis for those conclusions, I smell a rat –and that's usually because there is a rat. Either way, not very convincing.

Papias, by the way, is a very early church writer of whom we only have a few fragments preserved by later church writers, one of whom, Eusebius, really did not like Papias' views on the end times at all and consequently called him a man of 'little intelligence'! Papias spent a lot of time collecting the recollections, teachings and traditions of those who had heard the teaching of the apostles, and also directly from 'the elders' the next generation of leaders after the apostles. Out of these he wrote five volumes, and the third book (or the fourth according to some sources) was apparently devoted in its entirety to the teachings about the Millennium, the 1000 year reign of Jesus on the earth from Jerusalem after he returns. Papias was also said to be the scribe who physically wrote down the original of the Gospel of John (who may not have been the apostle John, but another John, one of the elders). If you want to read translations of what fragments of Papias we do have, you can read them here - http://www.newadvent.org/fathers/0125.htm .

Anyway, the bottom line is – if ever anyone tells you that Papias taught a Pre-Tribulation rapture, they are lying to you, no matter how sincerely they believe it.

Clement of Rome

Just watch out – there is a later church father called Clement from Alexandria. To make things even more confusing, there are actually two documents traditionally linked to Clement of Rome. 1 Clement is a letter, also known as 'the Letter of the Romans to the Corinthians', which the Roman church wrote to intervene in an internal schism in the Corinthian church usually dated about AD97 or so (although a few date it in the late 60's, and I certainly found it intriguing that when it refers to the sacrifices in the Jerusalem Temple, the letter refers to them being offered in the present tense, not the past tense, something that would only be true up until the late 60's). Clement was the man they got to write it. 2 Clement is almost certainly not by Clement, but may possibly have been a sermon by an elder in the Corinthian church after the 1 Clement letter and the mission sent with it successfully resolved the Corinthian schism. Regardless of issues of date or authorship, I have read them both and there is not much teaching about the return of Jesus, let alone a Pre-Tribulation rapture. As anyone familiar with the church fathers would expect, any teaching about Jesus' return is linked almost exclusively with the need for righteous and faithful living so we won't be found wanting on judgement day, a pattern also found in the New Testament.

In 1 Clement there is only one passage that to me could even conceivably be taken as 'proof' of a Pre-Tribulation rapture, even by the most die-hard believer in that position (although I later found out that a particularly creatively ignorant writer added a few more which I deal with later on in an appendix). The passage is from chapter 23, which I will quote in full to give the context :

> 'The Father, who is merciful in all things, and ready to do good, has compassion on those who fear him, and gently and lovingly bestows his favours on those who draw near to him with singleness of mind. Therefore, let us not be double-minded, nor let our soul indulge in false ideas about his excellent and glorious gifts. Let this Scripture be far from us where he says 'Wretched are the double-minded, those who doubt in their soul and say 'We have heard these things even in the days of our fathers, and look, we have grown old, and none of these things have happened to us.' You fools, compare yourselves to a tree, or take a vine: first it sheds its leaves, then a shoot comes, then a leaf, then a flower, and after these a sour grape, and then a full ripe bunch.'. Notice that in a brief time the fruit of the tree reaches maturity. Truly his purpose will be accomplished quickly and suddenly, just as the Scripture also testifies : 'He will come quickly and not delay, and the Lord will come suddenly into his temple, even the Holy One whom you expect'.'

That last sentence is the bit that Pre-Tribulationists clamber all over because, according to them, it is a clear teaching of 'imminence' since it talks of suddenness and quickness with relation to the return of Jesus. This is a typical Pre-Tribulationist stratagem of imposing without consideration their views on the passage, desperately searching for something to back up their position, such is their delusion. Notice that although it talks about the return of Jesus being quick and sudden, it says nothing about there being no signs beforehand, which is what the Pre-Tribulationist position allegedly requires. And consider this : in a Pre-Tribulationist scenario, this can only be referring to a time after the alleged rapture, because it talks of Jesus coming to the Temple, not the church, and in that scenario, this can only refer to his visible Second Coming. The only way around this would be to claim that Clement means the church when he refers to the temple, but in fact Clement consistently uses the Temple to refer to the Jewish Temple in Jerusalem and uses the term 'church' of the church. In this passage he is citing an Old Testament prophecy which specifically refers to the Jewish Temple because it goes on to refer to the Lord cleansing the people until there are Levites fit to serve him (Malachi 3.1-4) and the people of Judah and Jerusalem bring acceptable sacrifices again. The only other time 1 Clement mentions the Temple is in chapter 41.2 which reads :

> 'Not just anywhere, brothers, are the continual daily sacrifices offered, or the freewill offerings, or the offerings for sin and trespasses, but only in Jerusalem. And even there the offering is not made in every place, but in front of the temple at the altar, the offering having first been inspected by the high priest....'

In other words, just like the New Testament passages alleged to teach the Pre-Tribulation rapture but teach the opposite when examined in context, so too, the quite frankly disreputably shallow and dishonest claims by the alleged 'scholars' at the Pre-Tribulation Research Centre that 1 Clement supports the Pre-Tribulation rapture proves on examination to teach precisely the opposite. It does not teach the 'imminence' that they so desperately cling to as only consistent with their position, but instead refers to the visible Second Coming of Jesus.

For completeness' sake, it should be mentioned that there are two other passages in 1 Clement that refer to the Second Coming of Jesus. For the record they are 34.2-3 - 'It is, therefore, necessary that we should be zealous to do good, for all things come from him. For he forewarns us: '*Behold, the Lord comes, and his reward is with him, to pay each one according to his work*'.' - and 50.3-4 which relates the Old Testament saints to the church during the resurrection of the last days : 'All the generations from Adam to this day have passed away, but those who by God's grace were perfected in love have a place among the godly, who will be revealed when the kingdom of Christ comes to us. For it is written: '*Enter into the innermost rooms for a very little while, until my anger and wrath shall pass away, and I will remember a good day and will raise you from your graves*'.' Notice that the dead come to the living on earth, not the other way round, which is what Pre-Tribulationists usually teach - that the living rise to meet Jesus and the dead saints in heaven.

For real completeness' sake, I will also deal with the claims of one internet article-writer named Jason Hommel at www.bibleprophesy.org who is spectacularly creative and inane in his desperate distortion of Clement's writing in search to find support for the Pre-Trib position - he is also the one behind the impressively sly attempt to find the Pre-Trib rapture in Polycarp's letter - see below. However, because there is quite a bit of it, I have set this in an appendix at the end of this work ('Reclaiming Clement from the Clutches of Jason Hommel').

2 Clement has rather more teaching relating to Jesus coming. Again there is one verse that is sometimes cited as evidence of 'imminence' and the Pre-Tribulation position, but again, I will show the context indicates the opposite. It quotes the same teaching we saw early in chapter 11 of 1 Clement about the parable of the tree or vine and double-mindedness, and concludes by saying :

> 'So my brothers, let us not be double-minded, but patiently endure in hope, that we may also receive the reward. 'For faithful is he who promised' to pay each person the wages due his works. Therefore, if we do

> what is right in God's sight, we will enter his kingdom and receive the promises which 'ear has not heard nor eye seen nor the heart of man imagined'.'

It doesn't explicitly mention suffering, but it is implied in the exhortation to patiently endure in hope. Chapter 12 continues the exhortation as follows :

> 'Let us wait, therefore, hour by hour for the kingdom of God in love and righteousness, since we do not know the day of God's appearing.'

This is the bit that the Pre-Tribulationists love to quote, claiming it teaches their beloved 'imminence'. But they never quote to their readers the next bit, which might freak out their evangelical followers:

> 'For the Lord himself, when he was asked by someone when his kingdom was going to come, said: 'When the two shall be one, and the outside like the inside, and the male with the female, neither male nor female'. Now 'the two' are 'one' when we speak the truth among ourselves and there is one soul in two bodies without deception. And by 'the outside like the inside' he means this : the 'inside' signifies the soul, while the 'outside' signifies the body. Therefore just as your body is visible, so also let your soul be evident by good works. And by 'the male with the female, neither male nor female' he means this : that when a brother sees a sister, he should not think of her as female, nor should she think of him as male. When you do these things, he says, the kingdom of my Father will come.'

Whatever you think of this - and this saying of Jesus pops up with variants in a number of places in the early church documents, including the so-called Gospel of Thomas, it is quite clear that the passage is not teaching 'imminence'. There are things that must take place before Jesus' return, even though we don't know the day of God's appearing. Also note that term 'appearing'. It is God's public 'appearing', not the invisible secret rapture of the Pre-Tribulation doctrine. Just like the New Testament and the other early church fathers taught, the key is living continuously in love and righteousness. The passage therefore goes on in later chapters to talk of the need for thorough going repentance, before returning back to Jesus' return in chapter 16 and 17.1 :

> Therefore, brothers, inasmuch as we have received no small opportunity to repent, let us, while we still have time, turn again to God, who has called us, while we still have one who accepts us. For if we renounce these pleasures and conquer our soul by refusing to fulfil its evil desires, we will share in Jesus' mercy. But you know that 'the day' of judgement is already 'coming as a blazing furnace' and 'some of the heavens will dissolve' and the whole earth will be like lead melting in a fire, and then the works of men, the secret and the public, will appear. Charitable giving, therefore, is good, as is repentance from sin. Fasting is better than prayer, while charitable giving is better than both, and 'love covers a multitude of sins' while prayer arising from a good conscience delivers one from death. Blessed is everyone who is found full of these, for charitable giving relieves

> the burden of sins. Let us repent, therefore, with our whole heart, lest any of us should perish needlessly....'

Notice that there is no rapture here. Instead, the church must repent in preparation for the public and visible return of Jesus. Chapter 17 goes on to make this even clearer :

> 'For the Lord said 'I am coming to gather together all the nations, tribes and languages.' .... by this he means the day of his appearing, when he will come and redeem us, each according to his deeds.'

Notice that - it is the day of His appearing, so it can't be the rapture, and yet he comes to redeem 'us'. No sign of a separate group of 'Tribulation' saints inbetween. And according to the Pre-Trib position we, the church, will already have been redeemed. There is a clear and utter refutation of Pre-Tribulation position right there. The passage goes on:

> 'And the unbelievers 'will see his glory' and might, and they will be astonished when they see that the kingdom of the world belongs to Jesus, saying 'Woe to us, because it was you, and we did not realize it, and we did not believe; and we did not obey the elders when they spoke to us about our salvation. And 'their worm will not die and their fire will not be quenched, and they will be a spectacle for all flesh'. He means that day of judgement, when people will see those among us who lived ungodly lives and perverted the commandments of Jesus Christ. But the righteous, having done good and endured torments and hated the pleasures of the soul, when they see how those who have gone astray and denied Jesus by their words or by their actions are being punished with dreadful torments in unquenchable fire, will give glory to their God as they say 'There will be hope for the one who has served God with his whole heart.'

Notice how different this is to most Pre-Tribulation accounts, which say that all of those on earth who do not believe in Jesus will be slain at his Second Coming. The judging of the saints, they believe will already have happened at this point, after the rapture, in heaven. The true church has already been revealed and purified - those who have been raptured. This is not at all the picture that 2 Clement paints here. Instead, at the visible and public Second Coming, those who have been righteous are revealed with Jesus in glory whilst those who have professed the name of Christ but denied him or lived ungodly lives are eternally punished. And notice that one thing that the righteous do is 'endure torments'. In other words, there is not a scintilla of support for the Pre-Tribulation position that God rescues his people from suffering in the Tribulation. After a further passage calling for repentance and right living, the sermon concludes:

> 'Let us, therefore, practice righteousness, that we may be saved in the end. Blessed are they who obey these injunctions; though they may endure affliction for a little while in the world, they will gather the immortal fruit of the resurrection. So, then, the godly person should not be grieved if he is miserable at the present time; a time of blessedness awaits him. He will

> live again with the fathers above, and will rejoice in eternity untouched by sorrow.
>
> 'But do not let it trouble your mind that we see the unrighteous possessing wealth while the servants of God experience hardships. Let us have faith, brothers and sisters! We are competing in the contest of a living God, and are being trained by the present life in order that we may be crowned in the life to come. None of the righteous ever received the reward quickly, but waits for it. For if God paid the wages of the righteous immediately, we would soon be engaged in business, not godliness; though we would appear to be righteous, we would in fact be pursuing not piety but profit. And this is why the divine judgment punishes a spirit that is not righteous, and loads it with chains.
>
> 'To the only God, invisible, the Father of truth, who sent forth to us the Saviour and Founder of immortality, through whom he revealed to us the truth and the heavenly life, to him be the glory forever and ever. Amen.'

Again, this perfectly fits a post-tribulation model, echoing the teaching of Jesus that only those who endure (here endure in righteousness specifically) to the end will be saved. Obedience will mean affliction for a little while, but it should be endured for the resurrection, just as Jesus endured the cross. Hardships are just training for the life to come, and the final hardship of the Tribulation will be the final training.

In short, there is not one jot of support for any part, let alone the whole, of the Pre-Tribulationist position. Therefore, if ever anyone tells you that Clement or any of the documents in his name taught a Pre-Tribulation rapture, they are lying to you, no matter how sincerely they believe it.

Ignatius of Antioch

Ignatius was bishop of Antioch in Syria in the early 2nd Century AD. He was arrested and taken to Rome and martyred. On the way he wrote a few letters, mainly to churches who supported him on the way. I read through all his letters and apart from the one passage below, I don't think I saw a single reference even to the Second Coming, let alone any teaching that hinted at the Pre-Trib rapture position! When I googled the matter, I found that Ignatius is claimed as supporting a Pre-Trib rapture because he allegedly clearly teaches 'imminence', the idea that Jesus could return at any moment. And the evidence for this? One verse in his letter to his fellow bishop Polycarp, (also later martyred) which reads :

> 'Be more diligent than you are. Understand the times. Wait expectantly for Him who is above time: the Eternal, the Invisible, who for our sake became visible; the Intangible, the Unsuffering who for our sake suffered, who for our sake endured in every way.'

Notice that there is not a hint of teaching about 'imminence' here. Yes, it says to wait expectantly for Jesus (in suffering, as we shall see in a moment) but it says nothing at all about there being no signs before he comes again. Any position on

Jesus' return - apart from the claim that it is all mythical and symbolic - could fit this passage. And this is their evidence? This shows the unbelievable amount of demonic delusion there is out there on this subject - desperate desire to cling on to anything, no matter how patently absurd or reed-thin, that could be taken as evidence that the early church fathers taught this perverted doctrine. But wait, there is more. They carefully don't give you the context in the verse before which, while not explicitly Post-Tribulation, makes it quite clear that this waiting expectantly is to be done whilst under great suffering. Given the huge deception from apparently trustworthy sources over this strange doctrine, it is a warning that believers in the Pre-Tribulation rapture should heed. It reads :

> 'Do not let those who appear to be trustworthy yet who teach strange doctrines baffle you. Stand firm, like an anvil being struck with a hammer. It is the mark of a great athlete to be bruised, yet still conquer. But especially we must, for God's sake, patiently put up with all things, that He may also put up with us. Be more diligent than you are. Understand the times. Wait expectantly for Him......'

So we can absolutely and categorically say that if ever anyone tells you that Ignatius of Antioch taught a Pre-Tribulation rapture, they are lying to you, no matter how sincerely they believe it.

Polycarp

This same Polycarp whom Ignatius wrote to also wrote his own letter to the Philippian church soon after Ignatius's martyrdom. You fairly often find claims that he too taught a Pre-Tribulation rapture in his letter. So I read the letter, and couldn't find anything at all that supported such a claim. Apart from the usual listing of Polycarp as someone who taught imminence and so somehow really supports a Pre-Trib rapture, the only actual citation I found was in an article that uses all sorts of rhetorical tricks (as well as the usual ignoring the context) to stretch things just a bit...., like, a million miles from the truth. Here is the quote that allegedly teaches a Pre-Tribulation rapture :

> 'For everyone 'who does not confess that Jesus Christ has come in the flesh is antichrist', and whoever does not acknowledge the testimony of the cross 'is of the devil', and whoever twists the sayings of the Lord to suit his own sinful desires and claims that there is neither resurrection nor judgment - well that person is the first-born of Satan. Therefore let us leave behind the worthless speculation of the crowd and their false teachings, and let us return to the word delivered to us from the beginning; let us be self-controlled with respect to prayer and persevere in fasting, earnestly asking the all-seeing God to 'lead us not into temptation' because, as the Lord said, 'the spirit is indeed willing, but the flesh is weak'.

How, you might ask, does this teach a Pre-Tribulation rapture? Well, this is how the article writer spins it :

> 'It seems to me that Polycarp is refuting those who deny both the coming rapture and tribulation, calling these the resurrection (rapture) and judgment (tribulation). In response, Polycarp appeals to the word of God: the key phrase in the Lord's prayer, "not to lead us into temptation" that refutes these heresies, namely, by showing there is a judgment (temptation), and that there is deliverance from it (resurrection and rapture).
>
> 'Matthew 6:13 : 'And lead us not into temptation, but deliver us from evil: For thine is the kingdom, and the power, and the glory, for ever. Amen.'
>
> 'Does the word "temptation" refer to the tribulation or time of trouble to come? Of course.'

He then goes on – quite correctly – to quote a dictionary definition of the Greek word used for 'temptation' in the Lord's prayer in Matthew 6.13, which shows that the word means time of trial or testing. That is indeed one of its meanings, but this is a classic example of the obfuscation and shifting of terms that Pre-Tribbers routinely use to try and justify their case, so let's dissect the moves he makes to pull off this deception.

Firstly, notice how at the end he uses a rhetorical question to shift from defining the word 'temptation' to saying that therefore this refers to the Tribulation. That is a sneaky one. This is to carry people towards his answer 'Of course'. But just because the Lord's prayer uses the term temptation, it does not mean that it is referring specifically to the Tribulation, just all sorts of temptations and trials that believers face in life.

Secondly, right at the start, he redefines terms, by trying to claim that really Polycarp is talking about rapture and tribulation. He shifts terms again, to make Polycarp say what he never intended. Polycarp's focus is not on beliefs about end times, but immoral living by those who justified it by denying the resurrection at which all people will be judged. You see, in Judaism and Christianity at the time, it was taught, in accord with teaching from both the Old and New Testaments, that the resurrection of the dead was the time of judgement. Polycarp calls for self-control and prayerful lifestyle, and as part of that, we should ask God not to 'lead us into temptation'. What temptation? Immoral living, not wrong beliefs about the timing of an alleged rapture. The theme of resurrection and judgement as motivation to righteous and faithful living pops up over and over in the early fathers. They never meant rapture and Tribulation, so why should Polycarp here? This is a desperate, desperate move to deny the truth. If we look at what Polycarp goes on to say, then we find that, like the Ignatius quote above, whilst not specifically Post-Tribulation in teaching since that issue is not at all his focus here, Polycarp's approach is clearly inconsistent with the Pre-Tribulation mantra that if Jesus loves the church, He will spare it suffering. In fact, it goes on to urge enduring suffering in imitation of Jesus. I will quote the next two chapters of the letter to demonstrate:

> 'Let us therefore hold steadfastly and unceasingly to our hope and the guarantee of our righteousness, who is Christ Jesus, 'who bore our sins in his own body upon the tree' 'who committed no sin, and no deceit was

> found in his mouth'; instead, for our sakes he endured all things, in order that we might live in him. Let us, therefore, become imitators of his patient endurance, and if we should suffer for the sake of his name, let us glorify him. For this is the example he set for us in his own person, and this is what we have believed.
>
> I urge all of you, therefore, to obey the teaching about righteousness, and to exercise unlimited endurance, like that which you saw with your own eyes not only in the blessed Ignatius and Zosimus and Rufus but also in others from your congregation and in Paul himself and the rest of the apostles; be assured that all these 'did not run in vain' but in faith and righteousness, and that they are now in the place due them with the Lord, with whom they also suffered together. For they 'did not love the present world' but Him who died on our behalf and was raised by God for our sakes.'

So we can absolutely and categorically say that if ever anyone tells you that Polycarp taught a Pre-Tribulation rapture, they are lying to you, no matter how sincerely they believe it.

Cyprian

Cyprian was a 3rd Century bishop of Carthage in North Africa, initially at a time when the church there was not persecuted, although it was later swept by several waves of intense persecution where Christians had to make sacrifice to pagan gods or face martyrdom. He is frequently quoted as teaching a pre-tribulation rapture, but did he? In some cases I have seen he is paraphrased with only the odd word here or there in direct quotes - that should be suspicious enough. If you have to paraphrase someone rather than quote directly and fully to get an author to support your position, that rather suggests you are hiding something, as is indeed the case, as we shall find out.

You can find a typical example of how Cyprian's writing (and that of some other fathers) are falsely used here - http://beginningandend.com/what-did-ancient-church-fathers-believe-about-the-rapture/ . The article claims to present the teachings of the early church fathers, and I see this section quoted time and again on pre-trib sites. The section on Cyprian starts

> 'Cyprian was Bishop of the church in Carthage. During his short stint as leader of the church, he guided the flock through intense persecution at the hands of the Roman Empire. In 258 AD after spending seven months of confinement to his home by order of Roman authorities, he was beheaded for his faith. Several of his works still exist today.'

So far so good. Then the lies and twisting starts :

> 'In Treatises of Cyprian he wrote in describing the end times Great Tribulation:

> "We who see that terrible things have begun, and know that still more terrible things are imminent, may regard it as the greatest advantage to depart from it as quickly as possible. Do you not give God thanks, do you not congratulate yourself, that by an early departure you are taken away, and delivered from the shipwrecks and disasters that are imminent? Let us greet the day which assigns each of us to his own home, which snatches us hence, and sets us free from the snares of the world and restores us to paradise and the kingdom."
>
> Again we see use of language commonly found in reference to the Rapture as Cyprian describes the judgments of the end times as "imminent." And he makes his belief on the timing of the Rapture when he wrote that Christians will have an "early departure" and be "delivered" from the devastating global judgments that come during the Day of The Lord.
>
> In line with the Apostle Paul who wrote that "God has not appointed us to wrath, but salvation." Cyprian expressed joy and encourages the believing reader to rejoice that the Church will be "taken away" before the disastrous Great Tribulation. Just as The Lord Jesus Christ in Matthew 24 used the same language of one "taken away" and the other "left." Additionally Cyprian references the mansions which The Lord Jesus Christ promises to come back and take His believers to in John 14.
>
> "Let not your heart be troubled: ye believe in God, believe also in me. In my Father's house are many mansions: if it were not so, I would have told you. I go to prepare a place for you. And if I go and prepare a place for you, I will come again, and receive you unto myself; that where I am, there ye may be also." - John 14:1-3.
>
> .... in both the Matthew 24 passages ("one taken, the other left") and in John 14 ("..receive you unto myself..") the Greek work paralambanō is used for taken and receive. The meaning of that word is "join to one's self" indicating that Jesus is coming to fully unify with His church - which takes place at the Rapture. Clearly Cyprian believed and taught that the Rapture takes place before the Great Tribulation.

For those who have not read 'Rapture Rupture', I should point out that contrary to the claims here, when Paul teaches about being 'not appointed to wrath' it had no reference to escaping the Tribulation, but rather to avoiding eternal punishment on judgement day. But notice how the writer has to do commentary to try and spin this passage. Time and again Pre-Trib writers have to 'explain' the snippets they quote so that readers 'get' the message. Here, the writer has to have a whole four paragraphs to 'explain' how one short paragraph is really talking about the Pre-tribulation rapture. This passage is one of three from Cyprian that are routinely used as 'proof' by Pre-Tribbers. This one comes from his Treatises.

Another typical version that appears often in books and articles combines snippets from several different chapters of this work :

> 'Cyprian speaking of the imminency of the rapture, he wrote, "Who would not crave to be changed and transformed into the likeness of Christ and to

> arrive more quickly to the dignity of heavenly glory." After telling his readers that the coming resurrection was the hope of the Christian, he points out that the rapture should motivate us as we see the last days approaching. Cyprian says that "we who see that terrible things have begun, and know that still more terrible things are imminent, may regard it as the greatest advantage to depart from it as quickly as possible." Referring to his hope of the approaching rapture, he encouraged his readers as follows: "Do you not give God thanks, do you not congratulate yourself, that by an early departure you are taken away, and delivered from the shipwrecks and disasters that are imminent?" Cyprian concludes his comments on the translation of the saints with these words: "Let us greet the day which assigns each of us to his own home, which **snatches** us hence, and sets us free from the snares of the world, and restores us to paradise and the kingdom." (Treatises of Cyprian - 21 to 26?)

Now, you won't be surprised to learn that these passages are very carefully edited so that you don't see the context that demonstrates that they are not talking about the rapture, but something very different indeed. Cyprian wrote quite a lot, so I didn't manage to read everything of his we have, but I read quite a lot of the context, and boy does Cyprian say a lot that puts the lie to the pre-Tribulation position.

The passage that involves 'giving thanks' for an 'earlier departure' comes from Treatise 7 : On Mortality. I don't have the space to quote it in full - you can read it all here -
http://biblehub.com/library/cyprian/the_treatises_of_cyprian/treatise_vii_on_the_mortality.htm - but in it Cyprian writes long about suffering and death in this life, and battle with sin and temptation. The historical context was that a plague was spreading in the region, killing many people, including many Christians, and partly Cyprian was writing to counter some of his flock who were asking why were the righteous dying from the plague just the same as the unrighteous. However, Cyprian also repeatedly emphasises - as the New Testament does - that suffering and enduring tribulations is good, and to embrace it because willingly doing so makes us closer to God, more like Jesus who suffered, and thus sharing in his reward, which is hardly consistent with the message of the 'Pre-Tribulation rapture' crowd, who continually crow that 'a loving groom will not let his bride go through the Great Tribulation'. However, their response to points like the one I have just made is usually to say 'Yes, but suffering in this life is not the same as going through the Great Tribulation'. Since this is the case, I will point out that at several points it is quite clear that Cyprian expected the church to go through the Tribulation under the Antichrist. The first occurs in Treatise 7 chapter 15, where Cyprian is explaining the advantages of dying through illness, and what it brings escape from :

> 'The righteous are called to their place of refreshing, the unrighteous are snatched away to punishment; safety is the more speedily given to the faithful, penalty to the unbelieving. We are thoughtless and ungrateful, beloved brethren, for the divine benefits, and do not acknowledge what is conferred upon us. Lo, virgins depart in peace, safe with their glory, **not fearing the threats of the coming Antichrist,** and his corruptions and his brothels. Boys escape the peril of their unstable age, and in happiness

attain the reward of continence and innocence. Now the delicate matron does not fear the tortures; for she has escaped by a rapid death the fear of persecution, and the hands and the torments of the executioner. By the dread of the mortality and of the time the lukewarm are inflamed, the slack are nerved up, the slothful are stimulated, the deserters are compelled to return, the heathens are constrained to believe, the ancient congregation of the faithful is called to rest, the new and abundant army is gathered to the battle with a braver vigour, to fight without fear of death when the battle shall come, because it comes to the warfare in the time of the mortality.'

Notice the bit in bold. If Cyprian had taught or believed a Pre-Tribulation Rapture, he would have said something different. However, he says that an early *death* means being spared from the threats of the Antichrist, not something he would say if he believed the church would be raptured out before the Antichrist comes to power. Cyprian goes on for several chapters urging Christians not to fear death from illness because it will mean they escape persecution and are ushered into the glorious reward and promise of God, nor to grieve for those believers who have so died. It is in this context that all these passages that allegedly speak of the rapture come.

The quote in the first claim I quoted is from chapter 25, and the second set of claims also cites part of chapter 26 as alleged evidence of a rapture teaching. I quote from the end of chapter 24 and show the full context:

> 'Rather, beloved brethren, with a sound mind, with a firm faith, with a robust virtue, let us be prepared for the whole will of God: laying aside the fear of death, let us think on the immortality which follows. By this let us show ourselves to be what we believe, that we do not grieve over the departure of those dear to us, and that when the day of our summons shall arrive, we come without delay and without resistance to the Lord when He Himself calls us.
>
> And this, as it ought always to be done by God's servants, much more ought to be done now – now that the world is collapsing and is oppressed with the tempests of mischievous ills; in order that **we who see that terrible things have begun, and know that still more terrible things are imminent, may regard it as the greatest advantage to depart from it as quickly as possible. If in your dwelling the walls were shaking with age, the roofs above you were trembling, and the house, now worn out and wearied, were threatening an immediate destruction to its structure crumbling with age, would you not with all speed depart? If, when you were on a voyage, an angry and raging tempest, by the waves violently aroused, foretold the coming shipwreck, would you not quickly seek the harbour? Lo, the world is changing and passing away, and witnesses to its ruin not now by its age, but by the end of things. And do you not give God thanks, do you not congratulate yourself, that by an earlier departure you are taken away, and delivered from the shipwrecks and disasters that are imminent?**

> We should consider, dearly beloved brethren – we should ever and anon reflect that we have renounced the world, and are in the meantime living here as guests and strangers. **Let us greet the day which assigns each of us to his own home, which snatches us hence, and sets us free from the snares of the world, and restores us to paradise and the kingdom.** Who that has been placed in foreign lands would not hasten to return to his own country? Who that is hastening to return to his friends would not eagerly desire a prosperous gale, that he might the sooner embrace those dear to him? We regard paradise as our country – we already begin to consider the patriarchs as our parents: why do we not hasten and run, that we may behold our country, that we may greet our parents? There a great number of our dear ones is awaiting us, and a dense crowd of parents, brothers, children, is longing for us, already assured of their own safety, and still solicitous for our salvation. To attain to their presence and their embrace, what a gladness both for them and for us in common! What a pleasure is there in the heavenly kingdom, without fear of death; and how lofty and perpetual a happiness with eternity of living! There the glorious company of the apostles – there the host of the rejoicing prophets – there the innumerable multitude of martyrs, crowned for the victory of their struggle and passion – there the triumphant virgins, who subdued the lust of the flesh and of the body by the strength of their continency – there are merciful men rewarded, who by feeding and helping the poor have done the works of righteousness – who, keeping the Lord's precepts, have transferred their earthly patrimonies to the heavenly treasuries. To these, beloved brethren, let us hasten with an eager desire; let us crave quickly to be with them, and quickly to come to Christ. May God behold this our eager desire; may the Lord Christ look upon this purpose of our mind and faith, He who will give the larger rewards of His glory to those whose desires in respect of Himself were greater!

Thus the context is quite clear that these passages are not talking about the rapture or the second coming, but occur in a treatise exclusively devoted to the issue of dying, not escaping the Tribulation. It is profoundly dishonest to claim otherwise, as these Pre-Tribbers do. The same applies to the other earlier fragments quoted – for instance, where it says 'Who would not crave to be changed and transformed into the likeness of Christ and to arrive more quickly to the dignity of heavenly glory?' the context is the same – death. It comes in chapter 22, and I will quote the context with the quote in bold to show how it too does not refer to the rapture or the second coming:

> 'That in the meantime we die, we are passing over to immortality by death; nor can eternal life follow, unless it should befall us to depart from this life. That is not an ending, but a transit, and, this journey of time being traversed, a passage to eternity. Who would not hasten to better things? **Who would not crave to be changed and renewed into the likeness of Christ, and to arrive more quickly to the dignity of heavenly glory**, since Paul the apostle announces and says, "For our conversation is in heaven, from whence also we look for the Lord Jesus Christ; who shall

> change the body of our humiliation, and conform it to the body of His glory?" Christ the Lord also promises that we shall be such, when, that we may be with Him, and that we may live with Him in eternal mansions, and may rejoice in heavenly kingdoms, He prays the Father for us, saying, "Father, I will that they also whom Thou hast given me be with me where I am, and may see the glory which Thou hast given me before the world was made." He who is to attain to the throne of Christ, to the glory of the heavenly kingdoms, ought not to mourn nor lament, but rather, in accordance with the Lord's promise, in accordance with his faith in the truth, to rejoice in this his departure and translation.

Because Cyprian quotes John 14, which Pre-Tribbers falsely believe refers to the rapture, they rush to claim this passage as proof when it is anything but.

In fact, in his last and longest treatise, Treatise 11 : Exhortation to Martyrdom, Cyprian makes it clear again that he believed the church would go through the Tribulation under the anti-Christ. He is explicit about it right from the start, stating that this whole Treatise is designed to strengthen believers to face the persecution that we will face under the Antichrist:

> 'You have desired, beloved Fortunatus that, since the burden of persecutions and afflictions is lying heavy upon us, and in the ending and completion of the world the hateful time of Antichrist is already beginning to draw near, I would collect from the sacred Scriptures some exhortations for preparing and strengthening the minds of the brethren, whereby I might animate the soldiers of Christ for the heavenly and spiritual contest. I have been constrained to obey your so needful wish, so that as much as my limited powers, instructed by the aid of divine inspiration, are sufficient, some arms, as it were, and defences might be brought forth from the Lord's precepts for the brethren who are about to fight. For it is little to arouse God's people by the trumpet call of our voice, unless we confirm the faith of believers, and their valour dedicated and devoted to God, by the divine readings.'

If he believed in the Pre-Tribulation rapture, he would have no need to say such things. All he needed to have said was something like 'Times might be tough, but don't worry about the worst under the Antichrist, because we won't be there to endure it'. Instead, he devotes long chapter after chapter specifically strengthening his flock by warning them against returning to pagan idolatry and to live righteously in the face of the Antichrist. He urges his flock again and again to remain strong in faith during trial, quoting Jesus as saying that 'Only those who endure to the end shall be saved', and quoting the very scripture passages in support of this need to endure that Pre-Tribulationists claim are talking of the imminent rapture : 'Let ... your lamps burning, and be men who wait for their master when he shall return from the wedding, that when he comes and knocks they may open the door to him. Blessed are those servants whom their Master, when he comes, shall find ready and watchful' (Treatise 11 chapter 8).

Chapter 11 of Treatise 11 is particularly telling, because - and remember that the whole purpose of this Treatise is to prepare and arm Christians to face the anti-

Christ - he quotes several key bible passages fully. He quotes virtually all of Matthew 24 and applies all of it to Christians and the church, contrary to the Pre-tribulation position which teaches that at least some of it must apply to their mythical 'Tribulation Saints'. Cyprian quotes Matthew 24 right up until when it tells of the visible return of Jesus and then says:

> 'And these are not new or sudden things which are now happening to Christians; since the good and righteous, and those who are devoted to God in the law of innocence and the fear of true religion, advance always through afflictions, and wrongs, and the severe and manifold penalties of troubles, in the hardship of a narrow path.'

He then goes on to cite many Old Testament examples of the righteous suffering persecution and Tribulation, ending up with an account from the apocrypha (writings held to be Scripture by the Roman Catholic and Orthodox churches over and above the books used in most Protestant bibles) of a Jewish mother who saw all seven of her sons brutally tortured to death whilst remaining true to the God of Israel before she two was martyred, under the pagan king Antiochus, whom Cyprian labels 'Antiochus Antichrist' to make the relevance absolutely clear. Cyprian then cites Revelation 7.9-15, which Pre-Tribbers either claim are the mythical 'Tribulation Saints' because the passage makes it quite clear that these martyrs have come out of the Tribulation, or claim that they are the church raptured into heaven because it says they have 'come out of' the Tribulation (ie escaped it). That's not how Cyprian saw it, since he both prefaces and ends the quote by saying that these innumerable martyrs are 'Christian martyrs'. In doing so, he rules out either of the Pre-Tribulation positions, and instead shows that it is the church that suffers under the Antichrist.

In chapter 12, Cyprian makes it quite clear that the church will stand up against their persecutors during the reign of the Antichrist:

> '"Then shall the righteous stand in great constancy before such as have afflicted them, and who have taken away their labours; when they see it, they shall be troubled with a horrible fear: and they shall marvel at the suddenness of their unexpected salvation, saying among themselves, repenting and groaning for anguish of spirit, These are they whom we had sometime in derision and as a proverb of reproach. We fools counted their life madness, and their end to be without honour. How are they numbered among the children of God, and their lot is among the saints! Therefore have we erred from the way of truth, and the light of righteousness hath not shined unto us, and the sun hath not risen upon us. We have been wearied in the way of unrighteousness and perdition, and have walked through hard deserts, but have not known the way of the Lord. What hath pride profited us, or what hath the boasting of riches brought to us? All these things have passed away like a shadow."

At the end of chapter 12 he again makes it quite clear that all who stood firm during the age of the Antichrist were given the same reward, to live and reign with Jesus.

The treatise ends in Chapter 13, and quite frankly, I am surprised that a bit from this passage hasn't been taken out of context and used to 'prove' the rapture, since it talks of 'suddenly being taken from the earth'. Maybe it has been, and I haven't seen it, but as we shall see from the quote as Cyprian wraps up his treatise about the church under the Antichrist, the context is all wrong. Pre-Tribulationists claim that the church will not be on earth during God's judgements, nor will she undergo the Tribulation, but Cyprian says just the opposite, ending his treatise in a much more biblical way:

> 'Who, then, does not with all his powers labour to attain to such a glory that he may become the friend of God, that he may at once rejoice with Christ, that after earthly tortures and punishments he may receive divine rewards? If to soldiers of this world it is glorious to return in triumph to their country when the foe is vanquished, how much more excellent and greater is the glory, when the devil is overcome, to return in triumph to paradise, and to bring back victorious trophies to that place whence Adam was ejected as a sinner, after casting down him who formerly had cast him down; to offer to God the most acceptable gift – an uncorrupted faith, and an unyielding virtue of mind, an illustrious praise of devotion; to accompany Him when He shall come to receive vengeance from His enemies, to stand at His side when He shall sit to judge, to become co-heir of Christ, to be made equal to the angels; with the patriarchs, with the apostles, with the prophets, to rejoice in the possession of the heavenly kingdom! Such thoughts as these, what persecution can conquer, what tortures can overcome? The brave and steadfast mind, founded in religious meditations, endures; and the spirit abides unmoved against all the terrors of the devil and the threats of the world, when it is strengthened by the sure and solid faith of things to come. In persecutions, earth is shut up, but heaven is opened; Antichrist is threatening, but Christ is protecting; death is brought in, but immortality follows; the world is taken away from him that is slain, but paradise is set forth to him restored; the life of time is extinguished, but the life of eternity is realized. What a dignity it is, and what a security, to go gladly from hence, to depart gloriously in the midst of afflictions and tribulations; in a moment to close the eyes with which men and the world are looked upon, and at once to open them to look upon God and Christ! Of such a blessed departure how great is the swiftness! You shall be suddenly taken away from earth, to be placed in the heavenly kingdoms. It behoves us to embrace these things in our mind and consideration, to meditate on these things day and night. If persecution should fall upon such a soldier of God, his virtue, prompt for battle, will not be able to be overcome. Or if his call should come to him before, his faith shall not be without reward, seeing it was prepared for martyrdom; without loss of time, the reward is rendered by the judgment of God. In persecution, the warfare, – in peace, the purity of conscience, is crowned.

One more passage from Cyprian to finish the point is his 55th Letter. At least one very prominent Pre-Tribulation proponent, the late Grant Jeffrey, has claimed this teaches the Pre-Tribulation rapture, in his book 'Apocalypse'. Here is what he claims:

> 'Cyprian lived from A.D. 200 to 258, and wrote extensively on Christian doctrine. In his Epistle 55, chapter 7, he wrote about the belief in Christ's ability to deliver the Church from the Antichrist's tribulation.
>
> > 'Nor let any one of you, beloved brethren, be so terrified by the fear of future persecution, or the coming of the threatening Antichrist, as not to be found armed for all things by the evangelical exhortations and precepts, and by the heavenly warnings. Antichrist is coming, but above him comes Christ also. The enemy goeth about and rageth, but immediately the Lord follows to avenge our sufferings and our wounds. The adversary is enraged and threatens, but there is One who can deliver us from his hands.'
>
> Cyprian's declaration that Christ 'is One who can deliver us from his [Antichrist's] hands' suggests the possibility of the Church being raptured before the Tribulation period. It is significant that he did not write about enduring the persecution of the Antichrist. Rather, Cyprian promised that Christ 'is One who can deliver us from his hands.'

You can read a translation of the whole original letter online here :
http://www.ccel.org/ccel/schaff/anf05.iv.iv.lv.html .

Even if you can't read the rest, just looking at this snippet of a quote from Cyprian logically will debunk Jeffrey's claim. If Cyprian really was teaching the Pre-Tribulation rapture of the church, he would not have said 'but immediately the Lord follows to avenge our sufferings and our wounds' because the church wouldn't be wounded at all by the anti-Christ since they would be safely up in heaven.

But let us look at the wider context. This letter was specifically written, like the passages from the Treatises, to exhort the church to man up to face the anti-Christ. After his initial greetings, Cyprian sets out the purpose of his writing the letter in chapter 1:

> For you ought to know and to believe, and hold it for certain, that the day of affliction has begun to hang over our heads, and the end of the world and the time of Antichrist to draw near, so that we must all stand prepared for the battle; nor consider anything but the glory of life eternal, and the crown of the confession of the Lord; and not regard those things which are coming as being such as were those which have passed away. A severer and a fiercer fight is now threatening, for which the soldiers of Christ ought to prepare themselves with uncorrupted faith and robust courage, considering that they drink the cup of Christ's blood daily, for the reason that they themselves also may be able to shed their blood for Christ. For this is to wish to be found with Christ, to imitate that which Christ both taught and did, according to the Apostle John, who said, "He that saith he abideth in Christ, ought himself also so to walk even as He walked." Moreover, the blessed Apostle Paul exhorts and teaches, saying, "We are God's children; but if children, then heirs of God, and joint-heirs with

> Christ; if so be that we suffer with Him, that we may also be glorified together."

Once again, not a hint of the Antichrist only afflicting some mythical future separate 'Tribulation saints', but rather that the church is to face the Antichrist. Cyprian continues in chapter 2:

> 'Which things must all now be considered by us, that no one may desire anything from the world that is now dying, but may follow Christ, who both lives for ever, and quickens His servants, who are established in the faith of His name. For there comes the time, beloved brethren, which our Lord long ago foretold and taught us was approaching, saying, "The time cometh, that whosoever killeth you will think that he doeth God service. And these things they will do unto you, because they have not known the Father nor me. But these things have I told you, that when the time shall come, ye may remember that I told you of them." Nor let any one wonder that we are harassed with constant persecutions, and continually tried with increasing afflictions, when the Lord before predicted that these things would happen in the last times, and has instructed us for the warfare by the teaching and exhortation of His words. Peter also, His apostle, has taught that persecutions occur for the sake of our being proved, and that we also should, by the example of righteous men who have gone before us, be joined to the love of God by death and sufferings. For he wrote in his epistle, and said, "Beloved, think it not strange concerning the fiery trial which is to try you, nor do ye fall away, as if some new thing happened unto you; but as often as ye partake in Christ's sufferings, rejoice in all things, that when His glory shall be revealed, ye may be glad also with exceeding joy. If ye be reproached in the name of Christ, happy are ye; for the name of the majesty and power of the Lord resteth on you, which indeed on their part is blasphemed, but on our part is glorified." Now the apostles taught us those things which they themselves also learnt from the Lord's precepts and the heavenly commands, the Lord Himself thus strengthening us.....'

In chapter 4, Cyprian writes about 'those days' - in other words, the church under the Antichrist:

> Wherever, in those days, each one of the brethren shall be separated from the flock for a time, by the necessity of the season, in body, not in spirit, let him not be moved at the terror of that flight; nor, if he withdraw and be concealed, let him be alarmed at the solitude of the desert place. He is not alone, whose companion in flight Christ is; he is not alone who, keeping God's temple wheresoever he is, is not without God. And if a robber should fall upon you, a fugitive in the solitude or in the mountains; if a wild beast should attack you; if hunger, or thirst, or cold should distress you, or the tempest and the storm should overwhelm you hastening in a rapid voyage over the seas, Christ everywhere looks upon His soldier fighting; and for the sake of persecution, for the honour of His name, gives a reward to him when he dies, as He has promised that He will

> give in the resurrection. Nor is the glory of martyrdom less that he has not perished publicly and before many, since the cause of perishing is to perish for Christ. That Witness who proves martyrs, and crowns them, suffices for a testimony of his martyrdom.

After further exhortations to imitate both Jewish and Christian earlier saints in faithfulness under suffering, we come to the bit that Jeffrey claims is teaching the Pre-Tribulation rapture. I will quote the chapter in full:

> 'Nor let any one of you, beloved brethren, be so terrified by the fear of future persecution, or the coming of the threatening Antichrist, as not to be found armed for all things by the evangelical exhortations and precepts, and by the heavenly warnings. Antichrist is coming, but above him comes Christ also. The enemy goeth about and rageth, but immediately the Lord follows to avenge our sufferings and our wounds. The adversary is enraged and threatens, but there is One who can deliver us from his hands. He is to be feared whose anger no one can escape, as He Himself forewarns, and says: "Fear not them which kill the body, but are not able to kill the soul; but rather fear Him which is able to destroy both body and soul in hell." And again: "He that loveth his life, shall lose it; and he that hateth his life in this world, shall keep it unto life eternal." And in the Apocalypse He instructs and forewarns, saying, "If any man worship the beast and his image, and receive his mark in his forehead or in his hand, the same also shall drink of the wine of the wrath of God, mixed in the cup of His indignation, and he shall be tormented with fire and brimstone in the presence of the holy angels, and in the presence of the Lamb; and the smoke of their torments shall ascend up for ever and ever; and they shall have no rest day nor night, who worship the beast and his image."

The protection that Cyprian is talking about is a protection from denying Christ under Tribulation. Again, notice that he specifically starts by talking to the church, the 'beloved brothers' and applies to them the passage that teaches about damnation for those who take the mark of the Antichrist. Again, no sign - unsurprisingly - of the Pre-Tribbers imaginary 'Tribulation Saints'.

Finally, given that Pre-Tribbers routinely claim that the Day of the Lord is always one to be feared, not welcomed, it is instructive to notice that Cyprian at the start of chapter 10 has completely the opposite attitude:

> 'Oh, what and how great will that day be at its coming, beloved brethren, when the Lord shall begin to count up His people, and to recognise the deservings of each one by the inspection of His divine knowledge, to send the guilty to Gehenna, and to set on fire our persecutors with the perpetual burning of a penal fire, but to pay to us the reward of our faith and devotion.'

And Cyprian goes on for some time in this vein.

So, in the light of all this, if anyone tells you that Cyprian taught the Pre-Tribulation rapture, they are absolutely lying to you, no matter how sincerely they may believe it.

Irenaeus

Irenaeus was a church leader from southern France from the late 2nd Century, somewhat earlier than Cyprian. He wrote several influential works, two of which have survived – 'Against Heresies' which mainly attacked the heresy of Gnosticism, which was very common at the time, and 'On the Apostolic Preaching' which appears to be teaching for new converts. He was brought up in a Christian family, and as a boy living in Turkey he listened to the preaching of Polycarp, whom we covered earlier. In other words, he was within about two, or at most, three generations removed from the apostles and their teaching and was born of parents who might well have heard the apostles preach, and so can reasonably be expected to be very well informed about the true teaching of the apostles.

You often find him quoted as someone who taught the Pre-Tribulation rapture. Possibly the most cited passage is from 'Against Heresies' book 5, chapter 29. Interestingly, the Pre-Tribulation Research Centre actually say this *isn't* teaching a Pre-Tribulation, so I'll give them one thumbs up for some actual honesty on the point (but I have to wonder, did they get burned and exposed, hence the caution?), and a thumbs down for the rather weasel way they downplay the actual post-tribulation message of this passage. Here is what they say:

> Some have thought that Irenaeus (c. 180) could be a pre-trib rapture statement since he actually speaks of the rapture: 'the Church shall be suddenly caught up from this [the tribulation]', as noted below:
>
> > 'And therefore, when in the end the Church shall be suddenly caught up from this, it is said, 'There shall be tribulation such as has not been since the beginning, neither shall be. For this is the last contest of the righteous, in which, when they overcome they are crowned with incorruption.'
>
> However, the very next statement speaks of believers in the tribulation. When taken within the context of all of Irenaeus' writings on these subjects, it appears that he was not teaching pretribulationism.

'It appears he was not teaching' is rather a weasel worded way of presenting the reality. They carefully don't quote what he says next, only paraphrase it. But to be fair, that is rather better than a very commonly repeated assertion about this passage that quotes the entire context but claims that it 'clearly' teaches a Pre-Tribulation rapture:

> On the subject of the Rapture, in Against Heresies 5.29, he wrote:
>
> > "Those nations however, who did not of themselves raise up their eyes unto heaven, nor returned thanks to their Maker, nor wished to behold the light of truth, but who were like blind mice concealed in the depths of ignorance, the word justly reckons "as waste water from a sink, and as the turning-weight of a balance – in fact, as nothing;" so far useful and serviceable to the just, as

> stubble conduces towards the growth of the wheat, and its straw, by means of combustion, serves for working gold. And therefore, when in the end the Church shall be suddenly caught up from this, it is said, "There shall be tribulation such as has not been since the beginning, neither shall be." For this is the last contest of the righteous, in which, when they overcome they are crowned with in-corruption."

> Irenaeus in this passage describes the church leaving the sinful world just before unprecedented disasters. Note his use of the term "caught up" which is Rapture terminology as that is the meaning of harpazo, the term for "caught up" in the King James Bible describing the Rapture in 1 Thessalonians 4. He then quotes Matthew 24:21 where The Lord Jesus Christ says: "For then shall be great tribulation, such as was not since the beginning of the world to this time, no, nor ever shall be." And it is during this time that those who convert to Christianity during the final years will receive the incorruptible crown mentioned by the Apostle Paul in 1 Corinthians 9:25. In Irenaeus' belief, the Rapture took place prior to the end times Great Tribulation.'

But just have a look at that quote. What, exactly, is the church suddenly caught up from? It is not from persecution, but rather from the rebellion against God that the nations indulge in, refusing to acknowledge God. Ireneaus actually goes on to suggest that such useless wickedness will be used to be of service to the righteous, saying that stubble helps wheat to grow and that straw can be burned to purify and work gold. Ireneaus seems to imply that the church will have been somehow initiallycaught up *in* this rebellion against God, but will after a time suddenly be caught up *from* it. This is consistent with a stream of thought that stretches from the New Testament in 2 Thessalonians 2 through to several of the church fathers, which teaches that the rise of the Antichrist is enabled at least in part by a great 'falling away' or rebellion or 'apostasy' from the faith on the part of God's church. So here, it seems that the true church, which has been caught up in worldliness and the rebellion is restored by God to purity, and it is this restoration that happens at the time of Tribulation. It is correct that Ireneaus is quoting Matthew 24.21, *but he is applying it to the church.* He is not teaching that the church escapes *from* the Tribulation, but that it is purified *by* the Tribulation. Thus, we can discount the absurd claim that he is teaching a rapture before the Tribulation by which the church escapes, and that the 'last contest of the righteous' is speaking of some separate group of 'Tribulation saints'. Ireneaus makes no such distinction. Instead, just like all the other church fathers, he is teaching that it is the church that goes through the Tribulation, in the final and greatest test of loyalty, after which those who are faithful and, as Jesus says, 'endure to the end' will be saved and given immortality. The language of 'overcoming' and 'contest' is completely alien to the escapism of the Pre-Tribulation rapture teaching.

However, we can say a lot more, because if we look at the wider context Ireneaus' position becomes even clearer. His teaching on the end times comes towards the end of the final book of his work 'Against Heresies'. Like all the church fathers, he repeatedly emphasizes that he is careful to continue in the teaching and traditions of the apostles. They were not inventing new things, but passing on the teaching that the apostles had originally given. In book 4, among other things, he emphasises the unity of the Old and New Testaments and the applicability of the Old Testament to the church. He does this because he is opposing the teachings of heretics who made great division between the Old and New Testaments, which is interesting, because this is strongly paralleled by the way that dispensationalists (a doctrine whose climactic point is the Pre-Tribulation rapture) similarly make strong divisions between Israel and the church, with some even declaring that the Gospels were written for the Jews, not the church (which is a truly absurd argument, given that they contain the teaching of Jesus primarily to his disciples, not Israel per se). In the first part of book 5, he focuses mainly on heresies that denied the Incarnation of Jesus into human flesh, and he emphasized the physicality of the resurrection of the dead. In chapter 24 of this final book, Ireneaus talks about how God instituted nations and kings and rulers primarily to provide a replacement for the fear of God - fear of man, of human rulers who can kill - to provide some measure of order and respite from violence. However, he also says that some bad rulers are given to a nation that deserves them 'for deception, disgrace, and pride; while the just judgment of God, as I have observed already, passes equally upon all.' He goes on to note that Satan is at work like one of these rulers given for deception - he can only 'deceive and lead astray the mind of man into disobeying the commandments of God, and gradually to darken the hearts of those who would endeavour to serve him, to the forgetting of the true God, but to the adoration of himself as God. (chapter 3). Chapter 4 continues:

> 'Just as if any one, being an apostate, and seizing in a hostile manner another man's territory, should harass the inhabitants of it, in order that he might claim for himself the glory of a king among those ignorant of his apostasy and robbery; so likewise also the devil, being one among those angels who are placed over the spirit of the air, as the Apostle Paul has declared in his Epistle to the Ephesians, becoming envious of man, was rendered an apostate from the divine law: for envy is a thing foreign to God. And as his apostasy was exposed by man, and man became the [means of] searching out his thoughts, he has set himself to this with greater and greater determination, in opposition to man, envying his life, and wishing to involve him in his own apostate power. The Word of God, however, the Maker of all things, conquering him by means of human nature, and showing him to be an apostate, has, on the contrary, put him under the power of man. For He says, "Behold, I confer upon you the power of treading upon serpents and scorpions, and upon all the power of the enemy," in order that, as he obtained dominion over man by apostasy, so again his apostasy might be deprived of power by means of man turning back again to God.'

It is after this, that Ireneaus turns to the doctrine of the end times, and the rule of the Antichrist in chapter 25, arguing that the Antichrist is a manifestation and culmination of apostasy and rebellion - in other words, a deceitful ruler who is given to a world that deserves such a ruler, or, as Paul puts it in 2 Thessalonians 2.9-12:

> The coming of the lawless one will be in accordance with how Satan works. He will use all sorts of displays of power through signs and wonders that serve the lie, and all the ways that wickedness deceives those who are perishing. They perish because they refused to love the truth and so be saved. For this reason God sends them a powerful delusion so that they will believe the lie and so that all will be condemned who have not believed the truth but have delighted in wickedness.

In fact, in the third paragraph of chapter 25, Ireneaus quotes this very passage. In the fourth paragraph he turns to the prophet Daniel's predictions concerning the Antichrist, saying that Daniel 'points out the time that his tyranny shall last, during which the saints shall be put to flight, they who offer a pure sacrifice unto God: "And in the midst of the week," he says, "the sacrifice and the libation shall be taken away, and the abomination of desolation [shall be brought] into the temple: even unto the consummation of the time shall the desolation be complete."

I would like to draw your attention to several things here. At the point that Ireneaus was writing, the Jewish Temple had been completely destroyed, yet he clearly believed that it would be rebuilt for the fulfilment of this prophecy. The passage he is quoting is one much beloved of those who take the Pre-Tribulation position. However, what is interesting is how Ireneaus takes it. He says that '*the saints shall be put to flight, they who offer a pure sacrifice unto God'*, and to demonstrate this he cites a passage that clearly involves sacrifices at the Jerusalem temple. Now, how are we to take this? It cannot be metaphorical - talking about spiritual sacrifices by the church, because earlier Ireneaus has gone to great pains to emphasize that where Paul talks about the Antichrist in the Temple in 2 Thessalonians 2, he is talking about the Jerusalem temple, not the church. Therefore, when Ireneaus is talking about saints, he must mean either faithful Jews in general, or specifically Jewish believers in Jesus who offer sacrifices at the temple but refuse to participate in the bastardized sacrifices of the Antichrist. What we would expect to see, if Ireneaus held a Pre-Tribulation position, is some sign that these saints are somehow different to or separate from the church saints, but, as we shall see, there is no such sign. In later chapters he quotes Revelation which talks of the saints being persecuted under the Antichrist. He also applied the term without distinction to those dead 'saints' from before Jesus' time who were raised from the dead when Jesus was crucified. He also uses the term several times to mean those raised from the dead at the end of the age. In other words, Ireneaus makes no distinction between the righteous from Old Testament times and the church, whether now, or during the Tribulation. Instead he uses the term for all of them. There is not even a hint of a separate set of 'Tribulation saints'. I will cover the passages in more detail as we work through the context of Ireneaus' teaching on the last days.

Back to chapter 25. After talking about the Antichrist and his actions in Jerusalem, Ireneaus starts chapter 26 with a statement that is utterly contrary to a Pre-Tribulation point of view, and is clearly Post-Tribulation, since it teaches explicitly that the Antichrist will put the church to flight during the Tribulation by means of the rulers who are under him. (And again, throughout Ireneaus, the church is the church - there is no room for some special group of 'Tribulation Saints'.) Here is what he says:

> 'In a still clearer light has John, in the Apocalypse, indicated to the Lord's disciples what shall happen in the last times, and concerning the ten kings who shall then arise, among whom the empire which now rules [the earth] shall be partitioned. He teaches us what the ten horns shall be which were seen by Daniel, telling us that thus it had been said to him: "And the ten horns which you saw are ten kings, who have received no kingdom as yet, but shall receive power as if kings one hour with the beast. These have one mind, and give their strength and power to the beast. These shall make war with the Lamb, and the Lamb shall overcome them, because He is the Lord of lords and the King of kings." It is manifest, therefore, that of these [potentates], he who is to come shall slay three, and subject the remainder to his power, and that he shall be himself the eighth among them. **And they shall lay Babylon waste, and burn her with fire, and shall give their kingdom to the beast, and put the Church to flight. After that they shall be destroyed by the coming of our Lord.**

You can't really put it clearer than that. Although it is not directly relevant to the issue of the timing of the rapture, the last sentences of chapter 26 are illuminating, as they show that the early church fathers predicted the exact dynamic in the world today, where people are abandoning God's righteous laws and starting to portray and imagine 'some other Father... one who even approves of all sins':

> For [Satan] did not venture to blaspheme his Lord openly of himself; as also in the beginning he led man astray through the instrumentality of the serpent, concealing himself as it were from God. Truly has Justin remarked: That before the Lord's appearance Satan never dared to blaspheme God, inasmuch as he did not yet know his own sentence, because it was contained in parables and allegories; but that after the Lord's appearance, when he had clearly ascertained from the words of Christ and His apostles that eternal fire has been prepared for him as he apostatized from God of his own free-will, and likewise for all who unrepentant continue in the apostasy, he now blasphemes, by means of such men, the Lord who brings judgment [upon him] as being already condemned, and imputes the guilt of his apostasy to his Maker, not to his own voluntary disposition. Just as it is with those who break the laws, when punishment overtakes them: they throw the blame upon those who frame the laws, but not upon themselves. In like manner do those men, filled with a satanic spirit, bring innumerable accusations against our Creator, who has both given to us the spirit of life, and established a law adapted for all; and they will not admit that the judgment of God is just. Wherefore also they set about imagining some other Father who neither cares about nor exercises a providence over our affairs, nay, one who even approves of all sins.

In Chapter 27, Ireneaus does something very telling, when he quotes a passage also much-beloved of Pre-Tribulationists, the teaching that when Jesus comes 'one shall be taken and the other left'. Pre-Tribulationists continuously clamour that this must refer to a rapture where God takes the righteous away and leaves the wicked to be 'left behind' to face the Tribulation. Ireneaus however - and remember that he was careful to follow closely the teaching of the apostles - says that this refers to the actual second coming of Jesus and judgement day. (You need to understand this is part of an argument where Ireneaus is saying basically that God sends no-one to hell, but rather people send themselves there by their clinging to wickedness and refusal of God's love, and this is what the end-days judgement of the Son confirms). He says:

> 'If the Father, then, does not exercise judgment, [it follows] that judgment does not belong to Him, or that He consents to all those actions which take place; and if He does not judge, all persons will be equal, and accounted in the same condition. The advent of Christ will therefore be without an object, yea, absurd, inasmuch as [in that case] He exercises no judicial power. For "He came to divide a man against his father, and the daughter against the mother, and the daughter-in-law against the mother-in-law; " and when two are in one bed, to take the one, and to leave the other; and of two women grinding at the mill, to take one and leave the other: [also] at the time of the end, to order the reapers to collect first the tares together, and bind them in bundles, and burn them with unquenchable fire, but to gather up the wheat into the barn; and to call the lambs into the kingdom prepared for them, but to send the goats into everlasting fire, which has been prepared by His Father for the devil and his angels. And why is this? Has the Word come for the ruin and for the resurrection of many? For the ruin, certainly, of those who do not believe Him, to whom also He has threatened a greater damnation in the judgment-day than that of Sodom and Gomorrah; but for the resurrection of believers, and those who do the will of His Father in heaven. If then the advent of the Son comes indeed alike to all, but is for the purpose of judging, and separating the believing from the unbelieving, since, as those who believe do His will agreeably to their own choice, and as, [also] agreeably to their own choice, the disobedient do not consent to His doctrine; it is manifest that His Father has made all in a like condition, each person having a choice of his own, and a free understanding; and that He has regard to all things, and exercises a providence over all, "making His sun to rise upon the evil and on the good, and sending rain upon the just and unjust."

(By the way, I also find it interesting that Ireneaus states that those who escape ruin and are resurrected are not just the believers, but also 'those who do the will of His Father in heaven', which he seems to imply are a separate category who will be resurrected. I have noticed that when Jesus talked in Matthew 25 about Judgement day, the criteria was not belief in him, but care for the poor and afflicted among his 'brothers and sisters', which may mean the poor generally, or specifically how they treated his bride, the church, or indeed, Israel. After all, Jesus did say in Matthew 10.41 that 'Whoever welcomes a prophet as a prophet will receive a prophet's reward, and whoever welcomes a righteous person as a righteous person will receive a righteous person's reward.' Similarly, and I know this will upset many evangelicals - but I must go with the word of God - Paul in Romans notes that eternal life comes to those who 'persist in doing good'. He says this in Romans 2.5-11, a passage that the so-called 'Romans Road' to eternal life conspicuously overlooks:

> 'But because of your stubbornness and your unrepentant heart, you are storing up wrath against yourself for the day of God's wrath, when his righteous judgment will be revealed. God "will repay each person according to what they have done." To those who by persistence in doing good seek glory, honour and immortality, he will give eternal life. But for those who are self-seeking and who reject the truth and follow evil, there will be wrath and anger. There will be trouble and distress for every human being who does evil: first for the Jew, then for the Gentile; but glory, honour and peace for everyone who does good: first for the Jew, then for the Gentile. For God does not show favouritism.')

What is also interesting - and scary - is that Ireneaus seems to imply that this judgement especially applies to the church. Rather than teaching the fundamentalist false doctrine of 'once saved, always saved', he followed Jesus who warned in Matthew 24.10-13 that in the last days:

> '... many will turn away from the faith and will betray and hate each other, and many false prophets will appear and deceive many people. Because of the increase of wickedness, the love of most will grow cold, but the one who stands firm to the end will be saved.'

In paragraph 2 of chapter 27, Ireneaus applies this judgement day as follows :

> 'And to as many as continue in their love towards God, does He grant communion with Him. But communion with God is life and light, and the enjoyment of all the benefits which He has in store. But on as many as, according to their own choice, depart from God. He inflicts that separation from Himself which they have chosen of their own accord. But separation from God is death, and separation from light is darkness; and separation from God consists in the loss of all the benefits which He has in store. Those, therefore, who cast away by apostasy these forementioned things, being in fact destitute of all good, do experience every kind of punishment. God, however, does not punish them immediately of Himself, but that punishment falls upon them because they are destitute of all that is good. Now, good things are eternal and without end with God, and therefore the loss of these is also eternal and never-ending. It is in this matter just as occurs in the case of a flood of light: those who have blinded themselves, or have been blinded by others, are forever deprived of the enjoyment of light. It is not, [however], that the light has inflicted upon them the penalty of blindness, but it is that the blindness itself has brought calamity upon them.....'

He continues this theme into chapter 28:

> 'Inasmuch, then, as in this age some persons betake themselves to the light, and by faith unite themselves with God, but others shun the light, and separate themselves from God, the Word of God comes preparing a fit habitation for both. For those indeed who are in the light, that they may derive enjoyment from it, and from the good things contained in it; but for those in darkness, that they may partake in its calamities. And on this

> account He says, that those upon the right hand are called into the kingdom of heaven, but that those on the left He will send into eternal fire for they have deprived themselves of all good.
>
> And for this reason the apostle says: "Because they received not the love of God, that they might be saved, therefore God shall also send them the operation of error, that they may believe a lie, that they all may be judged who have not believed the truth, but consented to unrighteousness." For when he (Antichrist) is come, and of his own accord concentrates in his own person the apostasy, and accomplishes whatever he shall do according to his own will and choice, sitting also in the temple of God, so that his dupes may adore him as the Christ; wherefore also shall he deservedly "be cast into the lake of fire: , God by His prescience foreseeing all this, and at the proper time sending such a man, "that they may believe a lie, that they all may be judged who did not believe the truth, but consented to unrighteousness....'

After discussion the meaning and significance of the 666 'mark of the beast', Ireneaus ends chapter 28 as follows:

> 'And therefore throughout all time, man, having been moulded at the beginning by the hands of God, that is, of the Son and of the Spirit, is made after the image and likeness of God: the chaff, indeed, which is the apostasy, being cast away; but the wheat, that is, those who bring forth fruit to God in faith, being gathered into the barn. And for this cause tribulation is necessary for those who are saved, that having been after a manner broken up, and rendered fine, and sprinkled over by the patience of the Word of God, and set on fire [for purification], they may be fitted for the royal banquet. As a certain man of ours said, when he was condemned to the wild beasts because of his testimony with respect to God: "I am the wheat of Christ, and am ground by the teeth of the wild beasts, that I may be found the pure bread of God'

Just as the New Testament taught - for instance in Acts 14 'We must go through many trials and Tribulations to enter the Kingdom of God' - Ireneaus taught that tribulation is 'necessary for those who are saved'. Now it is technically true that here Ireneaus doesn't refer to '*The* Tribulation' or 'the Great Tribulation', but remember that for chapter after chapter, he has explicitly been discussing the Antichrist and the church suffering under him, as well as the great apostasy that prepares the way for the Antichrist. The context shows that when he talks about the 'apostasy' and 'tribulation' here, he is talking about *the* apostasy predicted in the bible, and about *the* Tribulation. And thus we come back to where we started, the first paragraph of chapter 29. It follows on immediately from chapter 28, where, as we have seen, Ireneaus not only taught that the church *would* go through the tribulation, but that the tribulation is *necessary* for those who are being saved!

Now we can see the true context of chapter 29 and appreciate how it cannot possibly be teaching a Pre-Tribulation rapture of the church:

> 'In the previous books I have set forth the causes for which God permitted these things to be made, and have pointed out that all such have been created for the benefit of that human nature which is saved, ripening for immortality that which is [possessed] of its own free will and its own power, and preparing and rendering it more adapted for eternal subjection to God. And therefore the creation is suited to man; for man was not made for its sake, but creation for the sake of man. Those nations however, who did not of themselves raise up their eyes unto heaven, nor returned thanks to their Maker, nor wished to behold the light of truth, but who were like blind mice concealed in the depths of ignorance, the word justly reckons "as waste water from a sink, and as the turning-weight of a balance-in fact, as nothing; " so far useful and serviceable to the just, as stubble conduces towards the growth of the wheat, and its straw, by means of combustion, serves for working gold. And therefore, when in the end the Church shall be suddenly caught up from this, it is said, "There shall be tribulation such as has not been since the beginning, neither shall be." For this is the last contest of the righteous, in which, when they overcome they are crowned with incorruption.

So, to recap, Ireneaus taught that there would be great apostasy in the church, that this would make way for the rise of the Antichrist, that the church would go through the Tribulation and be purified it, and the escape mentioned here, was the escape from the apostasy and worldliness that results in eternal damnation.

I should at this point touch on one other issue. Many Pre-Tribulationists argue that only their position explains how there could be people to repopulate the earth after Armageddon. They believe that there will be a separate group of 'Tribulation Saints' and a newly believing Israel, and that those who survive until Jesus' return will not be resurrected but will survive to repopulate the earth. This belief that everyone who is not a Christian will be slain by or at the Second Coming of Jesus can easily refuted from the teaching of Jesus on the end days. As I noted earlier, in Matthew 25, Jesus talks of the judgement at his return and those who take their inheritance, the kingdom prepared from before the start of the world, saying that it is those who have been kind to the poor / the suffering church / Israel who inherit the kingdom'. As an aside, I should also note that at the end of Matthew 25, Jesus told a parable that warns that church leaders who failed to look after their flock but instead abuse them and engage in debauchery will be taken unawares by Jesus' return and will be cut to pieces and assigned to the place of weeping and gnashing of teeth. In addition, in Matthew 24, when talking of the Great Tribulation, Jesus said that if the days were not cut short, no-one would be left alive, but that the days would be cut short 'for the sake of the elect', meaning that others too would survive because of God's mercy to his own people.

However, what is of specific interest here is how Ireneaus handles this question of the repopulation of the earth after the return of Jesus. He does this in chapters 33 and especially 34 and 35. Chapter 33 is mainly taken up with showing how God will make the earth extremely fruitful, a restoration of the garden of Eden. Ireneaus takes pains to point out at the end of the chapter that his teaching on the last days comes from Papias, who was a disciple of John who wrote Revelation and the

Gospel of John. Chapter 34 is doubly interesting because according to many Pre-Tribulationists, there will be a strict division between the church and the restored Israel in the time after Jesus has returned. This is not how Ireneaus approaches such matters - he quotes many passages and prophecies about Israel and explicitly applies them to the church as being one with Israel, as well as New Testament passages about the resurrection of the righteous. For instance, after quoting many Old Testament promises, he says 'the promises were not announced to the prophets and the fathers alone, but to the Churches united to these from the nations,' We also find that Ireneaus repeatedly condemns views which held that the church had a 'super-celestial' destiny in heaven, rather than an earthly one, which is interesting since many forms of Dispensationalism similarly teach that the destiny of Israel is to rule from an earthly Jerusalem under Jesus as Davidic King, but the church will reign with Jesus from some heavenly position.

One of the main groups of heretics that Ireneaus opposed were a group called Gnostics, from gnosis, the ancient Greek word for 'knowledge'. This was a movement a little like the New Age movement of today, in that it had a great many variants, some even contradictory on details, but with a common core ideology. In the case of Gnosticism, one main driver was the idea that the physical world is evil, that human beings were little bits of the divine spiritual world trapped in evil physical bodies, who could escape by means of learning secret knowledge that would enable them to escape, rising through various realms of the spirit world to find ultimate release and escape from the evils of the physical world. Some groups preached a Christianized version of this in which Jesus was sent from the spirit world to give a key to this knowledge, and never really had a physical body, but only appeared to be physical. They had their own gospels and other documents that invented teachings of Jesus, or distorted real ones. It is highly likely that some of the letters of the New Testament, such as John's letters or 1 Timothy and Titus, were the apostles' reactions to early forms of this heresy in the church.

In my previous book, I noted that an even earlier church father, Justin Martyr, whose teaching on the church in the Tribulation I have dealt with earlier in this book, said that those in his day who taught that the church had a separate heavenly destiny to Israel on earth were 'blasphemers against the God of Abraham, Isaac and Jacob' and not true Christians at all, something very similar to what Ireneaus is teaching here. It was quite likely that Justin too was referring to a teaching at least influenced by Gnostic doctrines. However, Dispensationalism today maintains just such a distinction, with its proponents often boasting of how their view is the only one that 'keeps separate what the bible teaches are separate', meaning Israel and the church. I showed in my previous work how this is flatly untrue, and in fact they are dividing what the bible teaches should be kept together in shared destiny - an organic unity between Israel and the church.

It is for reasons such as this that I am becoming convinced that the teaching of Dispensationalism and the associated Pre-Tribulation rapture is in fact a kind of attenuated Gnosticism, or at least one of its spiritual heirs, so to speak. As well as this false distinction and the idea of two separate and different destinies for God's peoples, just like Gnosticism, Dispensationalism has an escape from the world to the heavenly realms, just in a different form to Gnsoticism - the 'secret rapture'.

Now, Dispensationalism blatantly isn't Gnosticism per se, despite these parallels, so I don't believe that people who hold to this false teaching are heretics in the way Gnostics were. It certainly isn't heresy in the sense that denial of the Trinity, or of Jesus' divinity or of his atoning sacrifice and resurrection are. Many sincere believers hold to this teaching, but this does not make it any less of a false teaching, any less deceptive or destructive, or any less a dangerous delusion. But in one sense I think it would be helpful to call it a heresy, because when a view so utterly circumvents and undermines the teaching of our Saviour and the apostles on an issue as this does, I don't know what else to call it, to make the severity and danger clear. The dispensationalist doctrine, particularly over the issue of the end times, has the effect of inoculating believers against taking seriously the very practical warnings of Jesus and the apostles because they can say 'Oh, that just applies to the Tribulation Saints, it's not for us'. Jesus' warnings in Matthew 24 that only those who endure to the end will be saved utterly lose their force in a Pre-Tribulation teaching. It also leads to breathtakingly stupid and dangerous beliefs about what parts of the bible apply to the church. As I was writing this book, I came across an article on one of the most prominent and popular end-times websites entitled 'Five top reasons why Matthew 24 isn't talking about the church' and it actually ended with the statement that the Gospels weren't written for the church, but for the Tribulation saints! And this guy thought he was being biblical! If a teacher went into the early churches and told them that the gospels weren't written for the church, what do you think they would say? I think the word 'Heresy' would be uttered very early on, and yet this perversity is accepted as sound biblical reasoning and teaching in too much of the allegedly bible-believing evangelical church today.

Coming back to Ireneaus, we see an example of how the early church fathers took the exact opposite approach to dispensationalists over the issue of Israel and the church, as well as again making it very clear that the church would go through the Tribulation in chapter 35, paragraph 1:

> 'If, however, any shall endeavour to allegorize [prophecies] of this kind, they shall not be found consistent with themselves in all points, and shall be confuted by the teaching of the very expressions [in question]. For example: "When the cities" of the Gentiles "shall be desolate, so that they be not inhabited, and the houses so that there shall be no men in them and the land shall be left desolate." "For, behold," says Isaiah, "the day of the Lord cometh past remedy, full of fury and wrath, to lay waste the city of the earth, and to root sinners out of it." And again he says, "Let him be taken away, that he behold not the glory of God." And when these things are done, he says, "God will remove men far away, and those that are left shall multiply in the earth." "And they shall build houses, and shall inhabit them themselves: and plant vineyards, and eat of them themselves." For all these and other words were unquestionably spoken **in reference to the resurrection of the just, which takes place after the coming of Antichrist**, and the destruction of all nations under his rule; in [the times of] which [resurrection] the righteous shall reign in the earth, waxing stronger by the sight of the Lord: and through Him they shall become accustomed to partake in the glory of God the Father, and shall enjoy in

> the kingdom intercourse and communion with the holy angels, and union with spiritual beings; **and those whom the Lord shall find in the flesh, awaiting Him from heaven, and who have suffered tribulation, as well as escaped the hands of the Wicked one. For it is in reference to them that the prophet says: "And those that are left shall multiply upon the earth,"** And Jeremiah the prophet has pointed out, that as many believers as God has prepared for this purpose, to multiply those left upon earth, should both be under the rule of the saints to minister to this Jerusalem, and that [His] kingdom shall be in it, saying, "Look around Jerusalem towards the east, and behold the joy which comes to thee from God Himself. Behold, thy sons shall come whom thou hast sent forth: they shall come in a band from the east even unto the west, by the word of that Holy One, rejoicing in that splendour which is from thy God. O Jerusalem, put off thy robe of mourning and of affliction, and put on that beauty of eternal splendour from thy God. Gird thyself with the double garment of that righteousness proceeding from thy God; place the mitre of eternal glory upon thine head. For God will show thy glory to the whole earth under heaven. For thy name shall for ever be called by God Himself, the peace of righteousness and glory to him that worships God. Arise, Jerusalem, stand on high, and look towards the east, and behold thy sons from the rising of the sun, even to the west, by the Word of that Holy One, rejoicing in the very remembrance of God. For the footmen have gone forth from thee, while they were drawn away by the enemy. God shall bring them in to thee, being borne with glory as the throne of a kingdom. For God has decreed that every high mountain shall be brought low, and the eternal hills, and that the valleys be filled, so that the surface of the earth be rendered smooth, that Israel, the glory of God, may walk in safety. The woods, too, shall make shady places, and every sweet-smelling tree shall be for Israel itself by the command of God. For God shall go before with joy in the light of His splendour, with the pity and righteousness which proceeds from Him

I have put in bold the relevant bits that are explicitly post-Tribulation. The resurrection of the just (the rapture) happens after the time of the Antichrist. From this resurrection on, the righteous will 'reign in all the earth, waxing stronger' - the exact opposite of what happens in a Pre-Tribulation scenario where they are in heaven from before the time of the Antichrist. Although I don't have space to go into it or quote it in full - just go online and google the book, it is there to be read - the very next paragraph follows Revelation in talking about the 'general resurrection' after the 'time of the Kingdom', meaning the Millennium of Revelation. Thus Ireneaus, like the 'Teaching of the Twelve Apostles' we talked about earlier, has a post-Tribulation rapture - the resurrection of the righteous when Jesus returns, and only later a general resurrection of the dead at the final judgement of Christ.

In short, if anyone tells you that Ireneaus taught the Pre-Tribulation rapture, they are absolutely lying to you, no matter how sincerely they may believe it.

Sometimes Ireneaus will be quoted as teaching dispensationalism generally, so I will deal with this in an appendix.

Tertullian

Tertullian was a church father roughly contemporary with Ireneaus, but based in North Africa, and was a mentor for Cyprian, whom I covered earlier. He was the first major Christian writer we know of to write in Latin rather than Greek, and is famous for his quote 'What has Jerusalem to do with Athens?' warning against the influence of pagan Greek philosophy on Christian doctrine. In fact, given the way that Gnostic concepts have got into evangelical doctrinal teaching by way of Dispensationalism, it might even be useful to quote him in full:

> What indeed has Athens to do with Jerusalem? What has the Academy to do with the Church? What have heretics to do with Christians? Our instruction comes from the porch of Solomon, who had himself taught that the Lord should be sought in simplicity of heart. Away with all attempts to produce a Stoic, Platonic, and dialectic Christianity! We want no curious disputation after possessing Christ Jesus, no inquisition after receiving the gospel! When we believe, we desire no further belief. For this is our first article of faith, that there is nothing which we ought to believe besides.

(Unfortunately, Tertullian became strongly sympathetic to, if not a member of, a group called Montanists who rather went off the rails a bit, and believed that the Heavenly Jerusalem would descend in their day at a particular point in Turkey. It was perhaps the first of many examples in church history of date setting, and the disappointment when it didn't happen was huge. It was a major impetus for the later rejection of the belief in the Millennium as a literal 1000 year reign of Christ, and as a result the book of Revelation, which is the only book of the bible that teaches this explicitly, was nearly rejected as Scripture by large chunks of the church.)

You often see Tertullian quoted as an early church father who taught a Pre-Tribulation rapture, usually in lists of names on youtube videos. Actual evidence, though? That is another matter. Search for him on the Pre-Tribulation Research Centre site and you get lots of mentions of him as teaching Premillenialism, which is true, but then it seems that all too often, that website's strategy is to quote lots of Premillenialist church fathers in their campaign against Post and A-Millenial positions, but then leave you the impression that the Premillenial position of the church fathers was pretty much the same as their own Dispensationalist and Pre-Trib position, even though they hadn't quite 'got' the wonderful concept of the Pre-Tribulation rapture. However, at least, as far as I can see, the Pre-Trib Research Centre doesn't outright claim he taught a Pre-Trib rapture, although they do in one article make quite a bit of the fact that he alluded several times to the teaching about many rooms in the Fathers house from John 14 being in heaven, and as it is explicit that it is trying to provide support for views fundamental to Pre-Tribulation belief, I will deal with it in an appendix.

More broadly, a quick google search reveals 'proofs' that are anything but. For instance, this line is quite typical:

> 'Some will argue that the Pre-Tribulation Rapture view is just "too new" to be considered viable. Critics will point to the origin of the modern Pre-Tribulation view and credit John Nelson Darby (1800-1882) with its founding. But, is that assessment historically accurate? Indeed, it is not.
>
> The Early Church fathers' such as Barnabas (ca.100-105), Papias (ca. 60-130), Justin Martyr (110-195), Irenaeus (120-202), Tertullian (145-220), Hippolytus (ca. 185-236), Cyprian (200-250), and Lactantius (260-330) wrote on the imminent return of Jesus Christ, the central argument for the Pre-Tribulation Rapture view.'

http://www.lamblion.com/articles/articles_rapture7.php

In other words, they must have taught it because they talked about Jesus return being 'imminent', but as usual the actual context of these alleged teaching of imminence is not actually given, and as we have seen, the Pre-Trib concept of 'imminence' is problematic at best. Or, for another example:

> Post-trib believers are the most vocal in their claim that the concepts of imminency and the pre-trib rapture only date back to the early 1800s. For several years, their charges went unanswered, but recently a number of men have dusted off old manuscripts and found several early Church fathers who were clearly looking for an imminent return of the Lord Jesus......
>
> "But what a spectacle is that fast-approaching advent of our Lord, now owned by all, now highly exalted, now a triumphant One!" (Tertullian)

http://www.raptureready.com/rr-imminency.html

It gives no explanation, this being, apparently so clear a teaching of a pre-Tribulation rapture!

So, let's look at context. That last quote comes from the climax of Tertullian's work 'The Shows' or 'The Spectacles' in which he condemned the watching of pagan Roman games and festivals by Christians. In chapter 29, he notes that the church has hymns, songs, music enough, and fighting - of goodness over evil, and if people want blood, they have the blood of Jesus, he said. Then at the start of the final chapter comes the quote, saying how Jesus' return will be the greatest spectacle of all - but I will give the full context:

> 'But what a spectacle is that fast-approaching advent of our Lord, now owned by all, now highly exalted, now a triumphant One! What that exultation of the angelic hosts! What the glory of the rising saints! What the kingdom of the just thereafter! What the city New Jerusalem! Yes, and there are other sights: that last day of judgment, with its everlasting issues; that day unlooked for by the nations, the theme of their derision, when

the world hoary with age, and all its many products, shall be consumed in one great flame!'

Notice that there is not a single hint of a Pre-Tribulation rapture here, but instead this 'fast-approaching advent' - which is apparently what makes 'Pre-Trib' advocates claim it as support, since they believe this is teaching 'imminence' - is all about Jesus as highly exalted and triumphant, something that is revealed only at his actual Second Coming. Similarly, it talks of the glory of the angelic hosts and the saints as they are resurrected, with the kingdom of the just and the New Jerusalem immediately following, along with the last day of judgement, and the whole world consumed in flame. It is very difficult to square this with an allegedly 'secret' Pre-Tribulation rapture, but very easy to square with a Post-Tribulation position in which the resurrection (rapture) happens at Jesus' visible return.

However, there is at least one other place in Tertullian's writing that gives even more decisive evidence that he took what we would call a 'Post-Tribulation' position, and that is in his work 'On the Resurrection of the Body' (or Flesh as it is traditionally translated). In that work he is countering the views of heretics (probably Gnostics or at least Gnostic-influenced groups who denied the doctrine of the resurrection of the body because the body was physical and therefore evil). In chapter 25, commenting on the book of Revelation and the resurrection, Tertullian casually in passing drops in a reference that explodes all possibility that he believed in a Pre-Tribulation rapture (and it is especially interesting in that Revelation is a book that Pre-Tribulationists often claim only makes sense with their interpretation). Here is what he says, with the context:

> 'In the Revelation of John, again, the order of these times is spread out to view, which "the souls of the martyrs" are taught to wait for beneath the altar, whilst they earnestly pray to be avenged and judged: (taught, I say, to wait), in order that the world may first drink to the dregs the plagues that await it out of the vials of the angels, and that the city of fornication may receive from the ten kings its deserved doom, and **that the beast Antichrist with his false prophet may wage war on the Church of God;** and that, after the casting of the devil into the bottomless pit for a while, the blessed prerogative of the first resurrection may be ordained from the thrones; and then again, after the consignment of him to the fire, that the judgment of the final and universal resurrection may be determined out of the books. Since, then, the Scriptures both indicate the stages of the last times, and concentrate the harvest of the Christian hope in the very end of the world, it is evident, either that all which God promises to us receives its accomplishment then, and thus what the heretics pretend about a resurrection here falls to the ground.....'

What is especially relevant, given the elaborate timing of Pre-Tribulation schemes, that Tertullian explicitly has 'the order of these times' 'spread out to view'. He makes it clear the martyrs of Revelation are the church, and that whilst the angels pour out the vials of judgement in the tribulation, the Antichrist is waging war on the Church of God, not some mythical 'Tribulation Saints'. When the devil is bound and cast into a bottomless pit, then the 'blessed prerogative of the first resurrection' (which has evidently already happened) 'may be ordained from the thrones'. This 'first resurrection' is the 'resurrection of the righteous' that we have seen is the 'rapture' of the church along with all God's dead saints. Since Tertullian taught that, consistent with the teaching of the bible and the other church fathers, that the church suffered under the Antichrist, then this must mean a Post-Tribulation position. (I suppose technically it could allow a Mid-Tribulation or Pre-Wrath position, since the church would have suffered some of the time, but there is not a hint of such a distinction here; what it emphatically rules out is a Pre-Tribulation position. Not only that, these alternative midway positions seem particularly unlikely in light of the fact that many early church fathers - see later - seemed to teach that the persecution of the church was really only a big issue in the last half of the final seven years.)

The passage continues with Tertullian's teaching against the heretics. I have ended it where I have, because we can usefully paraphrase him at this point - because what the Pre-Tribulationists pretend about the rapture-resurrection here falls to the ground.

Thus, if anyone tells you that Tertullian taught the Pre-Tribulation rapture, they are most assuredly lying to you, no matter how sincerely they may believe it.

Hippolytus (and 'Pseudo-Hippolytus')

Hippolytus was a disciple of Ireneaus and an important teacher in Rome, roughly contemporaneous with Tertullian. He may have been a bishop of Rome at a time when there were rival bishops - he opposed easing of rigorous rites of penitence to accommodate a flood of new pagan converts to Christianity. However, it appears that he and one of the later rival bishops were exiled together and reconciled, and it is believed they were martyred together - at the least, their bodies were brought back to Rome together and buried. We mostly only have fragments of his written works, unfortunately, but apparently they were many and varied. However, we do have some rather longer sections of works that are relevant to the issue we are dealing with here.

As usual, I checked out the Pre-Trib Research Centre site, and Hippolytus gets a lot of mentions, but again, not a single citation shows he took a Pre-Trib position. One of the reasons Pre-Tribbers get so excited about Hippolytus is that in his commentary on the book of Daniel he clearly teaches that the final week in Daniel's prophecy of 70 weeks is separate from the rest, and future. (For those who don't know, in Daniel chapter 9, Daniel had a visitation from an angel who conveyed a message to him about Jerusalem and Israel which involved 70 'weeks' or 'sevens' of years, split into parts; at the end of 69 'weeks' of years, the Messiah would be killed. Then there is a detailed outline of events in the 70th 'week' in which Israel and a 'ruler who is to come' sign a peace treaty, but the ruler breaks it and defiles the temple after 3 ½ years.) Since this concept is so central in their elaborate doctrine of the end times, this they take as affirmation of their position. However, given that people who don't hold their Pre-Tribulation position also interpret Daniel's 70 'weeks' in this way, it is hardly evidence that Hippolytus taught a Pre-Tribulation rapture. At least the Pre-Trib Research Centre doesn't claim outright he does, although to a casual reader, the impression might be left that he did.

We have seen how, for the first two centuries of the church at least, the writings we have speak with one voice on the issue of the church in the end times, all explicitly stating that the church goes through the time of the Antichrist, and are raptured at the visible Second Coming of Jesus. It is fair to ask how on earth the Pre-Trib Research Centre avoids this crucial fact. The answer is found tucked away in two footnotes in their article on Pre-Darby Rapture Advocates, and - inevitably perhaps, comes in a section headed 'Imminency'. The main body of the passage reads :

> 'Pretribulationists, such as Charles Ryrie define imminency as an event that is "impending, hanging over one's head, ready to take place.' An imminent event is one that is always ready to take place.' Some have recognized that it is common for ante-Nicene writers to speak of an imminent return of Christ, especially during the first century after the Apostles. Patristic scholar Larry Crutchfield argues that the early church fathers believed in what he calls 'imminent intratribulationism.' He summaries the views of pretribulational scholars on this issue as follows:
>
> *'In sum, with few exceptions, the premillennial fathers of the early church believed that they were living in the last times. Thus they looked daily for the Lord's return. Even most of those who looked for Antichrist's appearance prior to the second advent, saw that event as occurring suddenly and just as suddenly being followed by the rescue and rapture of the saints by Christ. . . . This belief in the imminent return of Christ within the context of ongoing persecution has prompted us to broadly label the views of the earliest fathers, imminent intratribulationism. . . .*
>
> *It should be noted that dispensationalists have neither said that the early church was clearly pretribulational nor that there are even clear individual statements of pretribulationism in the fathers. As Walvoord says, 'the historical fact is that the early church fathers' view on prophecy did not correspond to what is advanced by pretribulationists today except for the one important point that both subscribe to the imminency of the rapture.' This view of the fathers on imminency and in some the references to escaping the time of the tribulation constitute what may be termed, to borrow a phrase from Erickson, 'seeds from which the doctrine of the pretribulational rapture could be developed . . .' Had it not been for the drought brought by Alexandrian allegorism and later by Augustine, one wonders what kind of crop those seeds might have yielded–before Darby and the nineteenth century.'*

Since we have already covered many early church fathers from the first century of the church, we are in a position to evaluate these claims. It is certainly true that the early church fathers talked much on the return of Jesus. It was, if nothing else, a major motivation for urging on the church the need for continued holy and faithful living. However, the deception comes in the weasel words in the second paragraph. '*Even most of those who looked for Antichrist's appearance prior to the second advent'* - implying that some didn't, when in fact, as we have seen, they all were pretty explicit about the role of the Antichrist - *'saw that event as occurring suddenly and just as suddenly being followed by the rescue and rapture of the saints by Christ...'* Again, this is rather craftily worded - for someone already imbued with a belief in a sudden rapture that rescues the church from tribulation, this makes it look like somehow the early church fathers taught the church would be rescued by rapture from the Antichrist, when in fact they held no such thing. To a man, they held that the church would be oppressed and suffer under the Antichrist, although some, as we shall go on to see, held that there would be elements of supernatural *preservation* on earth. Because they have an incorrect belief about the meaning of 'imminence', they then have to muddy the waters to explain what to them is a contradiction, and so we have the confusing term 'imminent intratribulationism', whatever that means.

We are then told that '*the early church fathers' view on prophecy did not correspond to what is advanced by pretribulationists today except for the one important point that both subscribe to the imminency of the rapture.'* Again, this implies that those poor confused early fathers believed in a rapture that could be imminent in a way similar to that of Pre-Tribulationists today, but as we have seen, to a man, they held a Post-Tribulationist position. We have also seen how the alleged references to 'escaping the Tribulation' in the early church fathers are precisely not teaching that at all, but rather escaping the apostasy that the Tribulation pushes believers towards by remaining faithful and fearless in the face of the fury of the Antichrist. But instead, these misappropriated out of context quotes are claimed as *'seeds from which the doctrine of the pretribulational rapture could be developed . . .'* This wishful thinking is expressed fully in the final sentence. Because a rival school of interpretation came to dominate biblical interpretation that abandoned belief in a Millennium and the contextual interpretation of church fathers such as those we have been looking at, they imagine that the teaching of the earliest church fathers would somehow have metamorphosed into the Pre-Tribulation position long before the 19th Century rise of such beliefs. Since this is based on a grave misinterpretation of the early church fathers, this is desperate hoping indeed. And it is in this context that the two quotes that further illuminate the lengths Pre-Tribulationists must go to to avoid the force of the clear testimony of the earliest church fathers, by quoting mainly two Pre-Tribuationist scholars, Larry Crutchfield, and Walvoord.

I will avoid all the detailed citations and just quote the relevant text from the footnotes. The first footnote reads:

> 'Larry Crutchfield says, 'Many of them, especially in the first century, did indeed make explicit statements which indicated a belief in the imminent return of Christ. The doctrine of imminency is especially prominent in the writings of the apostolic fathers. It is on the basis of Christ's impending return (e.g., Didache) and on the strength of the literal fulfillment of past prophecy (e.g., Barnabas), that they exhorted the Christian to live a life of purity and faithfulness.' Crutchfield supports this statement with the following: 'See for example Clement of Rome (I Clement XXIII; XXXIV-XXXV); Ignatius (Epist. to Polycarp I and III); Didache (XVI, 1); Hermas

> (Shepherd: Similitudes IX, Chaps. V, VII and XXVI); Barnabas (XXI). For fathers of the second century see Tertullian (Apology XXI); and Cyprian (Treatises I, 27). There are expressions of imminency even in those who expected certain events to occur before the end, as in Hippolytus (Treat. On Christ and Antichrist 5); and Lactantius....'

We have already examined most of these early fathers and shown how this totally twists what the early church fathers said. They did not have the concept of 'imminency' in the sense that Pre-Tribulationists would have us believe. The return of Jesus might have been believed to be close at hand, but they all taught that the Antichrist must come first and afflict the church. However, to an unsuspecting reader who doesn't know this, then it might seem, with all these apparently scholarly citations, that the reality is rather different to what it is. '*There are expressions of imminency even in those who expected certain events before the end....'* This implies that those not cited in this sentence didn't believe that there were certain things that must happen before the end, which is false, as we have seen. The Didache for instance, clearly taught the Antichrist must come before the 'rapture' and return of Jesus. Again, to someone who does not know the facts, this creates a gravely misleading impression. This isn't necessarily deliberate deception on the part of Larry Crutchfield, or those citing him here - it just means that they are so constrained by false beliefs about 'imminency' that such vain strugglings are inevitable as they try and reconcile what is contradictory to their viewpoint. Because of their commitment to the core elements of Pre-Tribulationism, they don't see the fact that they have to go to fantastic lengths to avoid a clear teaching of the early church fathers, something which *should* set them to wondering if there is something profoundly wrong in their beliefs that so constrains them to perform such energetic exegetical contortions.

The second footnote is similar:

> 'Crutchfield adds: 'Some of the fathers like Hippolytus, Tertullian, Lactantius, and others, clearly had posttribulational elements in their views concerning the end times. But we have been unable to find an instance of the unequivocal classic posttribulationism taught today. Walvoord's assessment of the fathers' views on the tribulation is essentially correct. He says, 'The preponderance of evidence seems to support the concept that the early church did not clearly hold to a rapture as preceding the end time tribulation period. Most of the early church fathers who wrote on the subject at all considered themselves already in the great tribulation. Accordingly Payne, as well as most other posttribulationists, takes the position that it is self-evident that pretribulationism as it is taught today was unheard of in the early centuries of the church. Consequently the viewpoint of the early church fathers is regarded by practically all posttribulationists, whether adherents of the classic view or not, as a major argument in favor of posttribulationism. However, the fact that most posttribulationists today do not accept the doctrine of imminency as the early church held it diminishes the force of their argument against pretribulationism'

They are forced to admit the truth, but qualify it as only 'posttribulational elements'. I am unsure what is meant by 'classic posttribulationism', but it introduces the notion that somehow any post-tribulation teaching today is different to that taught by the early church fathers. This is a master-class in how to obfuscate the reality. So are Walvoord's comments. *'The preponderance of evidence seems to support the concept that the early church did not clearly hold to a rapture as preceding the end time tribulation period.'* It is all so wordy and seemingly judicious, but it serves to introduce elements of doubt all over the place, when the reality can be much more simply put. I shall not be so judicious. **There is not a shred of evidence that the early church ever taught anything even remotely resembling a Pre-Tribulation rapture, but overwhelming evidence that it very clearly and explicitly taught the opposite position.** I don't think it is accurate, either, to say that most of the early church fathers believed they were already in the Great tribulation, and I think that this fancy is probably a construct arising from the situation of comfortable Western scholars situated in places far from persecution. Some of the fathers clearly did mention the horrific persecution going on in their own day, but that does not mean they believed they were in the Great Tribulation, particularly since most, if not all of them taught that the Antichrist had to come to power before things reached that stage. Thinking that it might be near is not the same as thinking they were in it (although it is quite possible that at some stage Tertullian believed he was in it due to his connections to the bizarre Montanist belief-system). The footnote then goes on to try and evade the clear force of the fact that the early church fathers were all explicit Post-tribulationists whenever they touched on the issue by claiming that they all taught 'imminence'. Again, this is only works if we accept that the early church father's understanding of 'imminence' was the same as today's Pre-Tribulationists, but given they were all explicitly Post-Tribulation, this is just not possible, whatever Walvoord and co might wish to believe.

Anyway, back to Hippolytus. What did he have to say, other than that the 70th week of Daniel was detached from the rest and still to come? Intriguingly, some of the clearest evidence of Hippolytus' Post-Tribulation position is to be found in another article on the Pre-Tribulation Research Centre website entitled 'The Understanding of the Church Fathers Regarding the Olivet Discourse and the Fall of Jerusalem'. I rather suspect the author of the article doesn't even realize the implications of what he quoted, probably because the article is not focused on the timing of the Rapture, but rather the teaching of an opposing interpretative position on the end times called 'Preterism' and is set on showing how the early church fathers' interpretation precluded Preterism (the view that pretty much all the prophecies about the end times were fulfilled by AD70). Here is the quote - I have removed one or two explanatory edits which I have marked with () and slightly updated old English:

> Hippolytus, likely a disciple of Irenaeus–who himself was in succession from Tatian and Justin, was a disciple of Polycarp, a direct disciple of the Apostle John–in a treatise on Christ and the antichrist said,
>
> 'And the blessed Apostle Paul, writing to the Thessalonians, says: '*Now we beseech you, brothers, concerning the coming of our Lord Jesus Christ,*

and our gathering together at it (), that you won't be shaken in mind, or be troubled, neither by spirit, nor by word, nor by letters as from us, as that the day of the Lord is at hand. Let no man deceive you by any means; for (that day shall not come) except there come the falling away first, and that man of sin be revealed, the son of perdition, who opposes and exalts himself above all that is called God, or that is worshipped: so that he sits in the temple of God, showing himself that he is God. Don't you remember, that when I was still with you, I told you these things? And now you know what restrains, that he might be revealed in his time. For the mystery of iniquity is already at work; only he who now lets (will let), until he be taken out of the way. And then shall that wicked be revealed, whom the Lord Jesus shall consume with the Spirit of His mouth, and shall destroy with the brightness of His coming: (even him) whose coming is after the working of Satan, with all power, and signs, and lying wonders, and with all deceivableness of unrighteousness in them that perish; because they received not the love of the truth. And for this cause God shall send them strong delusion, that they should believe a lie: that they all might be damned who believed not the truth, but had pleasure in unrighteousness. [2 Thess 2:1-11] And Isaiah says, *'Let the wicked be cut off, that he behold not the glory of the Lord.'* [Isa 26:10]

These things, then, being to come to pass, beloved, and the one week being divided into two parts, and the abomination of desolation being manifested then, and the two prophets and forerunners of the Lord having finished their course, and the whole world finally approaching the consummation, **what remains but the coming of our Lord and Saviour Jesus Christ from heaven, for whom we have looked in hope, who shall bring the conflagration and just judgment upon all who have refused to believe on Him**. For the Lord says, *'And when these things begin to come to pass, then look up, and lift up your heads; for your redemption draweth nigh.'* [Luke 21:28] *'And there shall not a hair of your head perish.'* [Luke 21:18] *'For as the lightning cometh out of the east, and shineth even unto the west, so shall also the coming of the Son of man be. For wheresoever the carcase is, there will the eagles be gathered together.'* [Matt 24:27, 28]

Hippolytus quotes at length 2 Thessalonians 2, a passage that Pre-Tribulationists believe teaches that the church will be raptured out of the way before the Antichrist arises. Aside from the fact that Hippolytus takes it to mean that the church is 'gathered together' at the visible second coming of Jesus, as shown by a slight variation he uses at the start, it is clear that he cannot be teaching a Pre-Tribulation rapture, because the events of Daniels 70th week that he refers to, including the desecration of the Jewish Temple, the two witness of Revelation who were forerunners of Jesus' return, and the fact that the complete consummation of all things was at hand, are those that Pre-Tribulationism teaches are after the rapture of the church. Yet, Hippolytus addresses his church readers, saying that when these things have come to pass, all that remains is the return of Jesus form heaven, for whom **we** (no sign of or room for those mythical Tribulation saints) have looked in hope. And he goes on to quote passages such as Luke 21.18 and Matthew 24.27-8 that are so beloved of many Pre-Tribulationists as evidence that the church is going to escape the Tribulation, but Hippolytus never gives a hint that that was how he took these passages.

Now the passage quoted there comes from a work by Hippolytus entitled 'On Christ and the Antichrist', which is directly relevant to our subject, from chapters 63-4, near the end of the work. Since the entire work is on a subject very pertinent to our topic, I took the time to read through the whole work, and unsurprisingly it very much undermines the Pre-Tribulation position, but one of the ways it does so is perhaps rather surprising. I will summarize somewhat, but you can read the entire thing online here : http://www.newadvent.org/fathers/0516.htm . He is writing for Theophilus (almost certainly a pseudonym to help protect a wealthy patron from persecution, much as Luke used the same pseudonym in his gospel for the same reasons - Theophilus means 'lover of God') who wanted teaching on the topic written down. After the usual introductory remarks and general comments on the topic, about the nature of prophecy and of Jesus Christ who calls all the saints to one perfect man (chapter 3), he sets out in chapter five the subject of the work, which is to find out from the bible *'what, and of what manner, the coming of Antichrist is; on what occasion and at what time that implores one shall be revealed; and whence and from what I tribe (he shall come); and what his name is, which is indicated by the number in the Scripture; and how he shall work error among the people, gathering them from the ends of the earth; and (how) he shall stir up tribulation and* ***persecution against the saints;*** *and how he shall glorify himself as God; and what his end shall be; and how the sudden appearing of the Lord shall be revealed from heaven; and what the conflagration of the whole world shall be; and what the glorious and heavenly kingdom of the saints is to be, when they reign together with Christ; and what the punishment of the wicked by fire.'*

Now the first point is that just a paragraph or so earlier, Hippolytus has clearly defined what he meant by the term 'saints' - Christians, those who are part of the body of Christ, the church, and that is the meaning he is using it here. Thus he is here taking an absolutely explicitly Post-Tribulation position. The Pre-Tribulation position says that those whom the Antichrist persecutes are the Jews, plus the purported 'Tribulation Saints', but Hippolytus will have none of that because, as he goes on in chapter after chapter to elaborate, he believes that the Antichrist will be a Jew, specifically from the Israelite tribe of Dan, one who restores the Temple in Jerusalem and gathers the Jews from the nations back to the land of Israel, and then sends out emissaries to persecute the Christians (chapter 6 onwards). The gymnastic exegetical exertions he uses to try and prove this point are rather reminiscent of those of the Pre-Tribbers, and not very convincing to us, but it does serve to show that when he refers to the persecutions of the Antichrist, he does not mean persecution of the Jews. Whether Hippolytus was correct or not in his assertions on this point (and I believe not, although it does seem he was part of a long, though not unanimous tradition on this issue - at least one other church father believed the Antichrist would be from Syria - but many believed similarly that the Antichrist would be a Jew), it does show that the saints he has in mind must be the church, as he indeed makes explicit at several points. He quotes at length many Old Testament passages, taking a position that most Pre-Tribulationists adhere to, that the four empires prophesied in Daniel's visions are the Babylonians, the Persians, the Greeks, and the Romans (I too take this view, although I sometimes wonder about the identification of the last empire with Rome for reasons not relevant here). He also quotes at length Revelation about the 'Mystery Babylon', including that John saw a *'woman drunken with the blood of the saints, and with the blood of the martyrs of Jesus'.* Again, there is not a hint that the saints for Hippolytus were anything other than the church, thereby severely undermining another key Pre-Tribulation interpretation. Similarly, he ends the quote from Revelation with *'And in her was found the blood of prophets and of saints, and of all that were slain upon the earth'* without any suggestion of some mythical separate 'Tribulation saints'.

Similarly in chapter 47, he quotes both Daniel and Revelation, chiefly about the 'two witnesses' of Revelation who are killed *'because they will not give glory to Antichrist '. For this is meant by the little horn that grows up. He, being now elated in heart, begins to exalt himself, and to glorify himself as God, persecuting the saints and blaspheming Christ, even as Daniel says, 'I considered the horn, and, behold, in the horn were eyes like the eyes of man, and a mouth speaking great things; and he opened his mouth to blaspheme God. And that born made war against the saints, and prevailed against them until the beast was slain, and perished, and his body was given to be burned'.'* Again, passages that Pre-Tribulationists believe are about Israel and the Jews are interpreted as meaning Christians - the saints of Daniel are the church to Hippolytus, not some separate group.

In chapters 49-50, the Post-Tribulational nature of Hippolytus' teaching is made even clearer. He cites Revelation about the mark of the beast (666) and says of the Antichrist that:

> 'being full of guile, and exalting himself against the servants of God, with the wish to afflict them and persecute them out of the world, because they give not glory to him, he will order incense-pans to be set up by all everywhere, that no man among the saints may be able to buy or sell without first sacrificing; for this is what is meant by the mark received upon the right hand. And the word– in their forehead– indicates that all are crowned, and put on a crown of fire, and not of life, but of death. For in this wise, too, did Antiochus Epiphanes the king of Syria, the descendant of Alexander of Macedon, devise measures against the Jews. He, too, in the exaltation of his heart, issued a decree in those times, that all should set up shrines before their doors, and sacrifice, and that they should march in procession to the honour of Dionysus, waving chaplets of ivy; and that those who refused obedience should be put to death by strangulation and torture. But he also met his due recompense at the hand of the Lord, the righteous Judge and all-searching God....
>
> 'But now we shall speak of what is before us. For such measures will he, too, devise, seeking to **afflict the saints in every way**......
>
> But having the mystery of God in our heart, we ought in fear to keep faithfully what has been told us by the blessed prophets, in order that

> when those things come to pass, **we may be prepared for them**, and not deceived. For when the times advance, he too, of whom these things are said, will be manifested.'

Again, there is not a hint that these details are for some separate group of saints, but rather these details about suffering under the Antichrist are applied to the church. Hippolytus emphasizes the need to keep faithfully what we have been told, so that **we** may be prepared for them, and not deceived.

It is also instructive to read chapters 54-6:

> 'For he will call together all the people to himself, out of every country of the dispersion, making them his own, as though they were his own children, and promising to restore their country, and establish again their kingdom and nation, in order that he may be worshipped by them as God, as the prophet says: He will collect his whole kingdom, from the rising of the sun even to its setting: they whom he summons and they whom he does not summon shall march with him. And Jeremiah speaks of him thus in a parable: The partridge cried, (and) gathered what he did not hatch, making himself riches without judgment: in the midst of his days they shall leave him, and at his end he shall be a fool.
>
> It will not be detrimental, therefore, to the course of our present argument, if we explain the art of that creature, and show that the prophet has not spoken without a purpose in using the parable (or similitude) of the creature. For as the partridge is a vainglorious creature, when it sees near at hand the nest of another partridge with young in it, and with the parent-bird away on the wing in quest of food, it imitates the cry of the other bird, and calls the young to itself; and they, taking it to be their own parent, run to it. And it delights itself proudly in the alien pullets as in its own. But when the real parent-bird returns, and calls them with its own familiar cry, the young recognise it, and forsake the deceiver, and betake themselves to the real parent. This thing, then, the prophet has adopted as a simile, applying it in a similar manner to Antichrist. For he will allure mankind to himself, wishing to gain possession of those who are not his own, and promising deliverance to all, while he is unable to save himself.
>
> He then, having gathered to himself the unbelieving everywhere throughout the world, comes at their call to persecute the saints, their enemies and antagonists.....

Once more, this shows Hippolytus' view that the Antichrist is a Jew. (You need to remember that at this point, although many Jews had become Christian and their descendants were part of the church, and some were still coming to Christ, most of the Jewish people were actively against the church, and persecuted the church wherever they could. This was long before the days of Christian persecution of Jews, which didn't start really until at least a century later). Thus again, the saints can't be Jews, but rather the church. Now, Hippolytus isn't explicit about this, but it is possible that in this section there is a hint of the teaching we have found in other church fathers – that the church would be caught up in worldliness and be suddenly snatched up out of it at the time of the Antichrist. In his interpretation of the parable from Jeremiah here, Hippolytus describes the partridge as one that seeks to seduce away the chicks of another partridge with false cries, successfully at first, but then when the true parent partridge returns, the chicks return to their real parent. If this is the case, then it is probably alluding to the teaching of Jesus that end times prophets will 'deceive even the elect, if it were possible'. Either way, once again there is not a sign of a Pre-Tribulation rapture concept anywhere, but a sober warning about what the church will endure (even if Hippolytus was wrong about the exact nationality of the prime perpetrator, and in his claims that the Antichrist would restore the nation of Israel).

I will go on to quote bits from chapters 58-62. Again, Hippolytus starts with a belief that the primary persecutors of the Christians in the last days will be the Jews, whom he states will be:

> rousing themselves against the servants of God, they will seek to obtain vengeance by the hand of a mortal man. And he, being puffed up with pride by their subserviency, will begin to dispatch missives against the saints, commanding to cut them all off everywhere, on the ground of their refusal to reverence and worship him as God, according to the word of Isaiah: *Woe to the wings of the vessels of the land, beyond the rivers of Ethiopia: (woe to him) who sends sureties by the sea, and letters of papyrus (upon the water; for nimble messengers will go) to a nation anxious and expectant, and a people strange and bitter against them; a nation hopeless and trodden down.*
>
> But we who hope for the Son of God are persecuted and trodden down by those unbelievers. For the wings of the vessels are the churches;...... And the top-sails aloft upon the yard are the company of prophets, martyrs, and apostles, who have entered into their rest in the kingdom of Christ.
>
> Now, concerning the tribulation of the persecution which is to fall upon the Church from the adversary, John also speaks thus: And I saw a great and wondrous sign in heaven; a woman clothed with the sun, and the moon under her feet, and upon her head a crown of twelve stars..... And the dragon was angry with the woman, and went to make war with the saints of her seed, which keep the commandments of God, and have the testimony of Jesus.
>
> By the woman then clothed with the sun, he meant most manifestly the Church, endued with the Father's word, whose brightness is above the sun. And by the moon under her feet he referred to her being adorned, like the moon, with heavenly glory. And the words, upon her head a crown of twelve stars, refer to the twelve apostles by whom the Church was founded....... And to the woman were given two wings of the great eagle, that she might fly into the wilderness, where she is nourished for a time, and times, and half a time, from the face of the serpent. That refers to the one thousand two hundred and threescore days (the half of the week) during which the tyrant is to reign and persecute the Church, which flees from city to city, and seeks concealment in the wilderness among the

> mountains, possessed of no other defence than the two wings of the great eagle, that is to say, the faith of Jesus Christ, who, in stretching forth His holy hands on the holy tree, unfolded two wings, the right and the left, and called to Him all who believed upon Him, and covered them as a hen her chickens....
>
> The Lord also says, '*When you shall see the abomination of desolation stand in the holy place (whoso reads, let him understand), then let them which be in Judea flee into the mountains, and let him which is on the housetop not come down to take his clothes; neither let him which is in the field return back to take anything out of his house. And woe unto them that are with child, and to them that give suck, in those days! For then shall be great tribulation, such as was not since the beginning of the world. And except those days should be shortened, there should no flesh be saved*'. And Daniel says, '*And they shall place the abomination of desolation a thousand two hundred and ninety days. Blessed is he that waits, and comes to the thousand two hundred and ninety-five days.*'

Again Hippolytus effectively refutes every notion or possibility of a Pre-Tribulation rapture. The very passages that the Pre-Tribulationists teach must refer to the Jews or the 'Tribulation Saints' are the ones that Hippolytus explicitly says are the church. It is the church that is persecuted in the Tribulation, and the events of the time of the Antichrist, including the desecration of the Jewish temple, is something that the church needs to watch out for. It is immediately after this that Hippolytus quotes 2 Thessalonians in the passage we started out with. We saw from just what was quoted that Hippolytus was teaching Post-Tribulationism, and the preceding context makes it even more clear.

I am going to quote the final chapters in full, from chapter 64, which follows from the 2 Thessalonians 2 quote:

> These things, then, being to come to pass, beloved, and the one week being divided into two parts, and the abomination of desolation being manifested then, and the two prophets and forerunners of the Lord having finished their course, and the whole world finally approaching the consummation, what remains but the coming of our Lord and Saviour Jesus Christ from heaven, for whom we have looked in hope? Who shall bring the conflagration and just judgment upon all who have refused to believe in Him. For the Lord says, And when these things begin to come to pass, then look up, and lift up your heads; for your redemption draws near. And there shall not a hair of your head perish. For as the lightning comes out of the east, and shines even unto the west, so shall also the coming of the Son of man be. For wheresoever the carcass is, there will the eagles be gathered together. Now the fall took place in paradise; for Adam fell there. And He says again, Then shall the Son of man send His angels, and they shall gather together His elect from the four winds of heaven. And David also, in announcing prophetically the judgment and coming of the Lord, says, His going forth is from the end of the heaven, and His circuit unto the end of the heaven: and there is no one hid from the heat

thereof. By the heat he means the conflagration. And Isaiah speaks thus: Come, my people, enter into your chamber, (and) shut your door: hide yourself as it were for a little moment, until the indignation of the Lord be overpast. And Paul in like manner: For the wrath of God is revealed from heaven against all ungodliness and unrighteousness of men, who hold the truth of God in unrighteousness.

Moreover, concerning the resurrection and the kingdom of the saints, Daniel says, And many of them that sleep in the dust of the earth shall arise, some to everlasting life, (and some to shame and everlasting contempt). Isaiah says, The dead men shall arise, and they that are in their tombs shall awake; for the dew from you is healing to them. The Lord says, Many in that day shall hear the voice of the Son of God, and they that hear shall live. And the prophet says, Awake, you that sleep, and arise from the dead, and Christ shall give you light. And John says, Blessed and holy is he that has part in the first resurrection: on such the second death has no power. For the second death is the lake of fire that burns. And again the Lord says, Then shall the righteous shine forth as the sun shines in his glory. And to the saints He will say, Come, you blessed of my Father, inherit the kingdom prepared for you from the foundation of the world. But what says He to the wicked? Depart from me, you cursed, into everlasting fire, prepared for the devil and his angels, which my Father has prepared. And John says, Without are dogs, and sorcerers, and whoremongers, and murderers, and idolaters, and whosoever makes and loves a lie; for your part is in the hell of fire. And in like manner also Isaiah: And they shall go forth and look upon the carcasses of the men that have transgressed against me. And their worm shall not die, neither shall their fire be quenched; and they shall be for a spectacle to all flesh.

Concerning the resurrection of the righteous, Paul also speaks thus in writing to the Thessalonians: We would not have you to be ignorant concerning them which are asleep, that you sorrow not even as others which have no hope. For if we believe that Jesus died and rose again, even so them also which sleep in Jesus will God bring with Him. For this we say unto you by the word of the Lord, that we which are alive (and) remain unto the coming of the Lord, shall not prevent them which are asleep. For the Lord Himself shall descend from heaven with a shout, with the voice and trump of God, and the dead in Christ shall rise first. Then we which are alive (and) remain shall be caught up together with them in the clouds to meet the Lord in the air; and so shall we ever be with the Lord.

These things, then, I have set shortly before you, O Theophilus, drawing them from Scripture itself, in order that, maintaining in faith what is written, and anticipating the things that are to be, you may keep yourself void of offense both toward God and toward men, looking for that blessed hope and appearing of our God and Saviour, when, having raised the saints among us, He will rejoice with them, glorifying the Father. To Him be the glory unto the endless ages of the ages. Amen.

Hippolytus quite explicitly teaches something which I established in my previous book was also the teaching of the New Testament, namely that the resurrection of the saints (aka the 'rapture) happens at the visible return of Jesus, after the Tribulation and the reign of the Antichrist. Notice that Hippolytus quite correctly interprets references to the wrath of God not as the Tribulation, but rather to the judgement at the moment of Christ's return. This is how he applies Paul's teaching in Romans 1.18 about the wrath of God, as well as the prophecy about Israel needing to hide in their houses until the wrath of God is past. This is completely contrary to the Pre-Tribulation position which always holds that the wrath of God means the Tribulation, from which they claim church believers are absent. Hippolytus places the resurrection of the righteous at the Matthew 25 judgement seat of Christ, again, something totally contrary to Pre-Tribulationist teaching. After talking about the destruction at Armageddon, he then goes on to quote the most famous rapture passage of all, 1 Thessalonians 4. He places it after 2 Thessalonians 2 and the reign of the Antichrist, and at the point of earthly judgement of Jesus and the return of Jesus to reign, again, utterly contrary to the false Pre-Tribulation teaching on this passage. His final exhortation to Theophilus also makes clear that these things were not an esoteric, theoretical teaching that had no relevance, but rather practically urge that he would continue '*maintaining in faith what is written, and anticipating the things that are to be, you may keep yourself void of offense both toward God and toward men, looking for that blessed hope and appearing of our God and Saviour, when, having raised the saints among us, He will rejoice with them, glorifying the Father. To Him be the glory unto the endless ages of the ages. Amen.'* Even here, having just ploughed straight through Pre-tribulationist position after position, he also shows how false is the Pre-Tribulationist claim that the passage in Titus 2 '*looking for that blessed hope and appearing of our God and Saviour*' must refer to a separate rapture event as well as the visible return of Jesus. He who lived in an age of great suffering and persecution didn't see it as in any way teaching an escape from the Tribulation via some event separate from the visible coming of Jesus.

Hippolytus also wrote a commentary on the book of Daniel, part of which can be read here : http://www.ccel.org/ccel/schaff/anf05.iii.iv.i.x.iii.html . This bit is known as the Scholia. It is fragmentary, and although there is a rare full version originally translated into Old Slavonic in the 900's, and that has now been translated into English, I haven't been able to get hold of it. We have other fragments of it, some from what are known as 'catenas'. These are the ancient versions of a phenomena we see now often on the internet - of taking a bible verse and then citing lots of different authors commentaries on the verse. (As an interesting aside, Hippolytus also in this work states that Jesus was born on Wednesday the 25th December - although this is only found in some versions.) We will start with the Scholia. Due to the nature of the document, it is a lot less explicit than the one we have just been examining, but even here it is quite clear that he holds that the church will be there to be persecuted by the Antichrist. In his commentary on Chapter 7, a passage that dispensationalists / Pre-Tribulationists believe is talking about Israel, he is quite clear that it is talking about believers of any kind - the saints - at the time of Jesus' visible return, when he comments on verse 17:

'that the indissoluble and everlasting kingdom of the saints may be brought to view, and the heavenly King manifested to all, no longer in figure, like one seen in vision, or revealed in a pillar of cloud upon the top of a mountain, but amid the powers and armies of angels, as God incarnate and man, Son of God and Son of man–coming from heaven as the world's Judge.'

(In addition, in commenting on 7.7 he also talks of the antichrist, although not in a way that sheds any direct light on our topic: *'...and the little horn, which is Antichrist, shall appear suddenly in their midst, and righteousness shall be banished from the earth, and the whole world shall reach its consummation. So that we ought not to anticipate the counsel of God, but exercise patience and prayer, that we fall not on such times. We should not, however, refuse to believe that these things will come to pass.'*)

Commenting on 7.19 and the fourth beast in Daniel's vision, he says:

> And amid these another little horn shall rise, which is that of Antichrist. And it shall pluck by the roots the three others before it; that is to say, he shall subvert the three kings of Egypt, Libya, and Ethiopia, with the view of acquiring for himself universal dominion. And after conquering the remaining seven horns, he will at last begin, inflated by a strange and wicked spirit, to stir up war against the saints, and to persecute all everywhere, with the aim of being glorified by all, and being worshipped as God.

If there is any doubt that these saints are the Christians, the church, then look at his comments on 10.7:

> For it is to His saints that fear Him, and to them alone, that He reveals Himself. For if any one seems to be living now in the Church, and yet has not the fear of God, his companionship with the saints will avail him nothing.

This fits with the consistent teaching of the New Testament and the other early church fathers that only those living righteously and faithfully at the time of Jesus' return (as he asked in one of his parables, 'Will the Son of Man find the faith(fulness) on the earth when he comes?' - OK, so I am taking it slightly out of context, but it is consistent with his teaching on enduring to the end to be saved). His commentary on 12.9 also show Hippolytus meant the church, since he applies 1 Corinthians 2 to these saints of Daniel 12:

> "The words are closed up and sealed." For as a man cannot tell what God has prepared for the saints; for neither has eye seen nor ear heard, nor has it entered into the heart of man (to conceive) these things, into which even the saints, too, shall then eagerly desire to look; so He said to him, "For the words are sealed until the time of the end; until many shall be chosen and tried with fire." And who are they who are chosen, but those who believe the word of truth, so as to be made white thereby, and to cast off the filth of sin, and put on the heavenly, pure, and glorious Holy Spirit, in

> order that, when the Bridegroom comes, they may go in straightway with Him?

Finally, it is instructive to read his comments on 12.1, where he is also explicit that these saints (i.e., the church, us) go through the Tribulation under the Antichrist:

> "There shall be a time of trouble." For at that time there shall be great trouble, such as has not been from the foundation of the world, when some in one way, and others in another, shall be sent through every city and country to destroy the faithful; and the saints shall travel from the west to the east, and shall be driven in persecution from the east to the south, while others shall conceal themselves in the mountains and caves; and the abomination shall war against them everywhere, and shall cut them off by sea and by land by his decree, and shall endeavour by every means to destroy them out of the world; and they shall not be able any longer to sell their own property, nor to buy from strangers, unless one keeps and carries with him the name of the beast, or bears its mark upon his forehead. For then they shall all be driven out from every place, and dragged from their own homes and haled into prison, and punished with all manner of punishment, and cast out from the whole world.

There is also another section where Hippolytus deals with the visions of Daniel and Nebuchadnezzar together, which you can read here http://www.ccel.org/ccel/schaff/anf05.iii.iv.i.x.ii.html . I will simply quote the relevant bits in full, since they are much the same as the last section, and pretty self-explanatory for our purposes:

> Chapter 2: *As Daniel says, "I considered the beast; and, lo, (there were) ten horns behind, among which shall come up another little horn springing from them;" by which none other is meant than the antichrist that is to rise; and he shall set up the kingdom of Judah. And in saying that "three horns" were "plucked up by the roots" by this one, he indicates the three kings of Egypt, Libya, and Ethiopia, whom this one will slay in the array of war. And when he has conquered all, he will prove himself a terrible and savage tyrant, and will cause tribulation and persecution to the saints, exalting himself against them. And after him, it remains that "the stone" shall come from heaven which "smote the image" and shivered it, and subverted all the kingdoms, and gave the kingdom to the saints of the Most High. This "became a great mountain, and filled the whole earth."*
>
> Chapter 7: *'When the times are fulfilled, and the ten horns spring from the beast in the last (times), then Antichrist will appear among them. When he makes war against the saints, and persecutes them, then may we expect the manifestation of the Lord from heaven.'*
>
> Chapter 39: *'The two witnesses, then, shall preach three years and a half; and Antichrist shall make war upon the saints during the rest of the week, and desolate the world, that what is written may be fulfilled: "And they shall make the abomination of desolation for a thousand two hundred and ninety days."*

> Chapter 40: *"'Blessed is he that waits, and comes to the thousand three hundred and five and thirty days;" for when the abomination comes and makes war upon the saints, whosoever shall survive his days, and reach the forty-five days, while the other period of fifty days advances, to him the kingdom of heaven comes. Antichrist, indeed, enters even into part of the fifty days, but the saints shall inherit the kingdom along with Christ.'*

Additionally, there is a work entitled 'On the End of the World' which is purported to be by Hippolytus, but scholars believe had to have been from much later (you can read it here http://www.newadvent.org/fathers/0504.htm), but since it follows much the same lines as Hippolytus, I will cover it here. After an introductory chapter about the message of the prophets about the end times, we read in chapter 2:

> Hence, too, they indicated the day of the consummation to us, and signified beforehand the day of the apostate that is to appear and deceive men at the last times, and the beginning and end of his kingdom, and the advent of the Judge, and the life of the righteous, and the punishment of the sinners, in order **that we all**, bearing these things in mind day by day and hour by hour, as children of the Church, might know that not one jot nor one tittle of these things shall fail, (Matt 5:18) as the Saviour's own word announced. Let **all of you**, then, of necessity open the eyes of your hearts and the ears of your soul, and receive the word which we are about to speak. For I shall unfold to you today a narration full of horror and fear, to wit, the account of the consummation, and in particular, of the seduction of the whole world by the enemy and devil; and after these things, the second coming of our Lord Jesus Christ.

No sign of a separate group of Tribulation Saints - the matters of the antichrist and the end times deception are for 'we all' and 'all of you'. After several chapters citing Old and New Testament passages, in chapter 5 he cites Hosea '.... *'Therefore the prudent shall keep silence in that time, for it is an evil time.'* ***Learn, beloved, the wickedness of the men of that time,*** *how they spoil houses and fields, and take even justice from the just; for when these things come to pass,* ***you*** *may know that it is the end. For this reason are* ***you*** *instructed in the wisdom of the prophet, and the revelation that is to be in those days.'* In chapters 6 and 7, the work goes on to cite Micah 3.5-7, warning of false prophets who prophecy for food or money, going on to comment *'These things we have recounted* ***beforehand, in order that you may know*** *the pain that is to be in the last times, and the perturbation, and the manner of life on the part of all men toward each other, and their envy, and hate, and strife, and the negligence of the shepherds toward the sheep, and the unruly disposition of the people toward the priests.'* Following Jesus' teaching, he warns of strife and family members betraying each other and goes on to comment *'The temples of God will be like houses, and there will be overturnings of the churches everywhere. The Scriptures will be despised, and everywhere they will sing the songs of the adversary. Fornications, and adulteries, and perjuries will fill the land; sorceries, and incantations, and divinations will follow after these with all force and zeal. And, on the whole, from among those who profess to be Christians will rise up then false prophets, false apostles, impostors, mischief-makers, evil-doers, liars* *against each other, adulterers, fornicators, robbers, grasping, perjured, mendacious, hating each other. The shepherds will be like wolves; the priests will embrace falsehood; the monks will lust after the things of the world; the rich will assume hardness of heart; the rulers will not help the poor; the powerful will cast off all pity; the judges will remove justice from the just, and, blinded with bribes, they will call in unrighteousness.'* We see much of this today - apostasy, Scriptures being despised, and a rise of wickedness in the church and its leaders, including judgements in the courts that '*call in unrighteousness*' in many ways. Chapter 9 could also fit our times: '*And multitudes of men will run from the east even to the west, and from the north even to the sea, saying, Where is Christ here? Where is Christ there? But being possessed of a vain conceit, and* ***failing to read the Scriptures carefully****, and not being of an upright mind, they will seek for a name which they shall be unable to find.* ***For these things must first be; and thus the son of perdition****– that is to say, the devil– must be seen.'* So many wrong doctrines and immoral practices are today being justified by people who fail to read the Scriptures carefully, something that - like so many of the other church fathers - this work says will lead to the Antichrist being seen - here with the title 'son of perdition'. Now all of this could theoretically be worked around a Pre-Trib position, with a lot of mental gymnastics, but it far more naturally reads as Post-Tribulational - especially since it is necessary for the saints to know these details, not just the general disasters, but the doings of the anti-Christ in the last 7 years, as we shall see.

Chapter 10 and 11 cover what the apostles said about mockers and false teachers in the end times, and bring a practical conclusion in the need for care for the soul and godly living : '*....what man shall have any excuse who hears these things in the Church from prophets and apostles, and from the Lord Himself, and yet will give no heed to the care of his soul, and to the time of the consummation, and to that approaching hour when we shall have to stand at the judgment-seat of Christ?*' For the next few chapters, the work cites the prophecies and visions of Daniel about empires and the final rule of the Antichrist, concluding in chapter 16 with: '*And by this offshoot horn none other is signified than the Antichrist that is to restore the kingdom of the Jews. And the three horns which are to be rooted out by it signify three kings, namely those of Egypt, Libya, and Ethiopia, whom he will destroy in the array of war; and when he has vanquished them all, being a savage tyrant, he will raise* ***tribulation and persecution against the saints,*** *exalting himself against them.'* There are a number of mentions of saints throughout the work, and no sense that these were some separate group from the church, but rather that they are the church. The next few chapters follow the real Hippolytus in arguing that the Antichrist will be a Jew. Chapter 21 interprets the two halves of Daniels final 'week' as follows; the first half is when Enoch and Elijah come back to preach repentance with signs and wonders, as prophesied in Revelation 11 (it was standard, indeed, pretty much universal, to see the two witnesses in that passage as Enoch and Elijah in the ancient church, not, as is customary among modern day Dispensationalists, as Moses and Elijah). The second half is when the Antichrist and his kingdom will kill them, and then '*he, being lifted up in heart, begins in the end to, exalt himself and glorify himself as God, persecuting the* ***saints*** *and blaspheming Christ.*' In chapters 23-5, the work predicts the Antichrist will seem holy, kind, ascetic, not greedy for money, humble, will work great miracles of healing, and that men will press him to become king, and then he turns violent, proud, hating righteousness and will become an oppressor.

Chapter 25 brings further evidence against any kind of Pre-Tribulation interpretation, when it says: '*Behold,* **you** *who love God, what manner of tribulation there shall rise in those days, such as has not been from the foundation of the world, no, nor ever shall be, except in those days alone. Then the lawless one, being lifted up in heart, will gather together his demons in man's form, and will abominate those who call him to the kingdom, and will pollute many souls.*' Chapter 26 is even more explicit: '*For if, while as yet he does not exhibit himself as the son of perdition, he raises and excites* **against us** *open war even to battles and slaughters, at that time when he shall come in his own proper person, and men shall see him as he is in reality, what machinations and deceits and delusions will he not bring into play, with the purpose of seducing all men, and leading them off from the way of truth, and from the gate of the kingdom?*' No room for 'Tribulation saints' as a separate group here then - it is 'against us', the church - that the Antichrist rages. He enforces his will and power in economic transactions. In chapters 29-30 we read that he will '*send the cohorts of the demons among mountains and caves and dens of the earth, to track out those who have been concealed from his eyes, and to bring them forward to worship him. And those who yield to him he will seal with his seal; but those who refuse to submit to him he will consume with incomparable pains and bitterest torments and machinations, such as never have been, nor have reached the ear of man, nor have been seen by the eye of mortals. Blessed shall they be who overcome the tyrant then. For they shall be set forth as more illustrious and loftier than the first witnesses; for the former witnesses overcame his minions only, but these overthrow and conquer the accuser himself, the son of perdition. With what eulogies and crowns, therefore, will they not be adorned by our King, Jesus Christ!* That these who flee to caves and mountains are primarily Christians comes out in the next few chapters. Chapter 31 describes how those who have taken the 'mark of the beast' will - according to the writer - find themselves deceived and without provision from the Antichrist, whilst he mocks them as they '*perceive that this is the wicked accuser, and will mourn in anguish, and weep vehemently, and beat their face with their hands, and tear their hair, and lacerate their cheeks with their nails, while they say to each other: Woe for the calamity! Woe for the bitter contract! Woe for the deceitful covenant! Woe for the mighty mischance! How have we been beguiled by the deceiver! How have we been joined to him! How have we been caught in his toils! How have we been taken in his abominable net! How have we heard the Scriptures, and understood them not! For truly those who are engrossed with the affairs of life, and with the lust of this world, will be easily brought over to the accuser then, and sealed by him.*' Notice again, that just like the New Testament teaches - as I showed in my last book - here the deciding factor in whether people fall for the lies of the Antichrist is the living of an unholy and worldly-engrossed life. But chapter 32 shows a separate group who are different:

> But many who are hearers of the divine Scriptures, and have them in their hand, and keep them in mind with understanding, will escape his imposture. For they will see clearly through his insidious appearance and

> his deceitful imposture, and will flee from his hands, and betake themselves to the mountains, and hide themselves in the caves of the earth; and they will seek after the Friend of man with tears and a contrite heart; and He will deliver them out of his toils, and with His right hand He will save those from his snares who in a worthy and righteous manner make their supplication to Him.

These are the ones who flee to caves and mountains. Chapter 33 and 34 goes on to say of them and the time in which they live:

> You see in what manner of fasting and prayer the saints will exercise themselves at that time. Observe, also, how hard the season and the times will be that are to come upon those in city and country alike. At that time they will be brought from the east even unto the west; and they will come up from the west even unto the east, and will weep greatly and wail vehemently. And when the day begins to dawn they will long for the night, in order that they may find rest from their labours; and when the night descends upon them, by reason of the continuous earthquakes and the tempests in the air, they will desire even to behold the light of the day, and will seek how they may hereafter meet a bitter death. At that time the whole earth will bewail the life of anguish, and the sea and air in like manner will bewail it; and the sun, too, will wail; and the wild beasts, together with the fowls, will wail; mountains and hills, and the trees of the plain, will wail on account of the race of man, because all have turned aside from the holy God, and obeyed the deceiver, and received the mark of that abominable one, the enemy of God, instead of the quickening cross of the Saviour.
>
> And the churches, too, will wail with a mighty lamentation, because neither oblation nor incense is attended to, nor a service acceptable to God; but the sanctuaries of the churches will become like a garden-watcher's hut, and the holy body and blood of Christ will not be shown in those days. The public service of God shall be extinguished, psalmody shall cease, the reading of the Scriptures shall not be heard; but for men there shall be darkness, and lamentation on lamentation, and woe on woe. At that time silver and gold shall be cast out in the streets, and none shall gather them; but all things shall be held an offense. For all shall be eager to escape and to hide themselves, and they shall not be able anywhere to find concealment from the woes of the adversary; but as they carry his mark about them, they shall be readily recognised and declared to be his. Without there shall be fear, and within trembling, both by night and by day. In the street and in the houses there shall be the dead; in the streets and in the houses there shall be hunger and thirst; in the streets there shall be tumults, and in the houses lamentations. And beauty of countenance shall be withered, for their forms shall be like those of the dead; and the beauty of women shall fade, and the desire of all men shall vanish.

Following the teaching of Jesus in the Gospels, chapter 35 gives a ray of comfort in this anguish:

> Notwithstanding, not even then will the merciful and benignant God leave the race of men without all comfort; but He will shorten even those days and the period of three years and a half, and He will curtail those times on account of the remnant of those who hide themselves in the mountains and caves, that the phalanx of all those saints fail not utterly. But these days shall run their course rapidly; and the kingdom of the deceiver and Antichrist shall be speedily removed. And then, in fine, in the glance of an eye shall the fashion of this world pass away, and the power of men shall be brought to nought, and all these visible things shall be destroyed.

Then in the following sections we find the return of Jesus, the resurrection, or rapture, and the judgement seat of Christ. The major difference between this work and the others we have looked at so far is that it takes a position called Amillenialism, something that became increasingly popular in church history - this is the belief that the Millenium - the 1000 year reign of Jesus on earth at the end of the age - is not real, it is symbolic, and that the return of Jesus is also the point when eternity and the new heavens and earth come in, plus that there is just one judgement and one general resurrection of the dead together, not an earlier separate resurrection of the righteous. However, in terms of this general judgement, in accord with those earlier church fathers, there is a warning in chapter 38 for those who think they are Christians, but live immoral and unjust lives, because at that judgement as well: *'Then shall rise up those who have not kept the love of the Lord, mute and gloomy, because they condemned the light commandment of the Saviour, which says, You shall love thy neighbour as yourself. Then they, too, shall weep who have possessed the unjust balance, and unjust weights and measures, and dry measures, as they wait for the righteous Judge.'*

The later chapters expand on these events, with the eternal destruction of the Antichrist, and with Matthew 25 interpreted and expanded about judgement day. There is no separation of Old Testament and New Testament saints, but they are treated as one (chapter 41 on), when the Lord welcomes them into the heavenly kingdom:

> 'Come, you prophets, who were cast out for my name's sake. Come, you patriarchs, who before my advent were obedient to me, and longed for my kingdom. Come, you apostles, who were my fellows in my sufferings in my incarnation, and suffered with me in the Gospel. Come, you martyrs, who confessed me before despots, and endured many torments and pains. Come, you hierarchs, who did me sacred service blamelessly day and night, and made the oblation of my honourable body and blood daily. Come, you saints, who disciplined yourselves in mountains and caves and dens of the earth, who honoured my name by continence and prayer and virginity. Come, you maidens, who desired my bride-chamber, and loved no other bridegroom than me, who by your testimony and habit of life were wedded to me, the immortal and incorruptible Bridegroom. Come, you friends of the poor and the stranger. Come, you who kept my love, as I am love. Come, you who possess peace, for I own that peace. Come, you blessed of my Father, inherit the kingdom prepared for you, you who esteemed not riches, you who had compassion on the poor, who aided the orphans, who

> helped the widows, who gave drink to the thirsty, who fed the hungry, who received strangers, who clothed the naked, who visited the sick, who comforted those in prison, who helped the blind, who kept the seal of the faith inviolate, who assembled yourselves together in the churches, who listened to my Scriptures, who longed for my words, who observed my law day and night, who endured hardness with me like good soldiers, seeking to please me, your heavenly King. Come, inherit the kingdom prepared for you from the foundation of the world. Behold, my kingdom is made ready; behold, paradise is opened; behold, my immortality is shown in its beauty. Come all, inherit the kingdom prepared for you from the foundation of the world.'

This eternal reward is – like the New Testament strongly implies in Matthew 25 – also for those who cared for the Christian poor, especially in the last days, those who *'clothed them, and fed them, and gave them to drink, I mean the poor who are my members, you have done it unto me.'* (chapter 44). The next chapters go on to expand on the judgement of the wicked in Matthew 25, and at the end again provides sober warning for we who say we are Christians in chapter 48 and 49, as well as practical application, things that we in the West fail to do all too often these days:

> Then shall they also make answer to the dread Judge, who accepts no man's person: 'Lord, when saw we You an hungered, or thirsty, or a stranger, or naked, or sick, or in prison, and ministered not unto You? Lord, do You know us not? You formed us, You fashioned us, You made us of four elements, You gave us spirit and soul. On You we believed; Your seal we received, Your baptism we obtained; we acknowledged You to be God, we knew You to be Creator; in You we wrought sights, through You we cast out demons, for You we mortified the flesh, for You we preserved virginity, for You we practised chastity, for You we became strangers on the earth; and You say, I know you not, depart from me!' Then shall He make answer to them, and say, 'You acknowledged me as Lord, but you kept not my words. You were marked with the seal of my cross, but you deleted it by your hardness of heart. You obtained my baptism, but you observed not my commandments. You subdued your body to virginity, but you kept not mercy, but you did not cast the hatred of your brother out of your souls. For not every one that says to me, Lord, Lord, shall be saved, but he that does my will. And these shall go away into everlasting punishment, but the righteous into life eternal.
>
> You have heard, beloved, the answer of the Lord; you have learned the sentence of the Judge; you have been given to understand what kind of awful scrutiny awaits us, and what day and what hour are before us. Let us therefore ponder this every day; let us meditate on this both day and night, both in the house, and by the way, and in the churches, that we may not stand forth at that dread and impartial judgment condemned, abased, and sad, but with purity of action, life, conversation, and confession; so that to us also the merciful and benignant God may say, 'Your faith has saved you, go in peace;' and again, 'Well done, good and faithful servant; you have

> been faithful over a few things, I will make you ruler over many, things: enter into the joy of your Lord.' Which joy may it be ours to reach, by the grace and kindness of our Lord Jesus Christ, to whom pertain glory, honour, and adoration, with His Father, who is without beginning, and His holy, and good, and quickening Spirit, now and ever, and to the ages of the ages. Amen.

Doctrinal correctness is not the primary point at judgement day, nor even the ability to do supernatural miracles, or some semblance of purity, but rather obedience and mercy and love, and conformity to the merciful heart of God.

So, again, if anyone tells you that Hippolytus (or those writing in his name) taught the Pre-Tribulation rapture, they are most assuredly lying to you, no matter how sincerely they may believe it.

Origen and Clement of Alexandria

Origen was from Alexandria, a large city in Northern Egypt that in his time was *the* major centre of intellectual and philosophical thought in the ancient world, with a world-class library, and which also quickly became a major centre of Christianity. However, Alexandria was perhaps the major entry point for Greek philosophical thought to enter the church, and gave rise to a school of thought known as Alexandrian theology which was noted for interpreting the bible primarily allegorically rather than literally (although at least the early proponents also understood the bible 'literally', but didn't make much of it, being more interested in the 'secret' meanings they divined). They did this primarily by introducing Platonic philosophy into Christian doctrine and understanding. Origen was a brilliant scholar and the disciple of an early church father called Clement of Alexandria, and like his mentor was an early and major proponent of this approach. His work on the nature of Jesus Christ was a major milestone in the development in Christian doctrine on the subject, but he also held to views such as re-incarnation, or something very similar, and he shared the Greek philosophical distaste for the physical, and so rejected ideas of an earthly kingdom. It is for these reasons that he has earned himself both the titles 'Father of Orthodoxy' and 'Father of Heresy' even in the early church. His role in the Alexandrian school of theology is probably why he isn't quoted very much, if at all, in support of the Pre-Tribulation rapture. For instance, he is mentioned repeatedly by the Pre-Tribulation Research Centre, but virtually always in the context of his allegorizing and the way it was foundational to later rejections of belief in a literal Millenial rule of Jesus after his Second Coming.

Apart from a few videos where Origen is named as teaching the rapture, but no evidence given, and the odd reference to Pre-Tribulationist Hal Lindsey apparently believing Origen taught the rapture, I have been unable to find any passage from Origin cited as proof, so I shall say no more, other than to note that there is one passage mentioned by the Pre-Trib Research Centre from Origen's work 'Against Celsus' in which he quotes 2 Thessalonians 2 and links it to the prophecies in Daniel about the Antichrist's desecration of the Temple, but says nothing about the church in this regard. This means it could be interpreted just as easily as either Pre-Tribulation or Post-Tribulation and thus has no real bearing on the issue.

Similarly I could not find any citation from Clement of Alexandria being used to say he taught a Pre-Tribulation rapture. The Pre-Trib Research Centre notes he thought Daniels prophecy of 70 weeks was fulfilled by AD70, (but also cites him as saying that the bible taught that at the time of Jesus' return, it would somehow both be a time of business as usual *and* great distress, which is also how I understand the New Testament teaching).

So if anyone tells you either Origen or Clement of Alexandria taught the Pre-Tribulation rapture, ask them for actual evidence, and then see if they are telling the truth or not.

Lactantius

Lactantius lived to see the persecution of Christians by the Romans end and Constantine become the first Christian emperor, and he actually became a spiritual advisor to the emperor. He occasionally appears on videos as an alleged teacher of the Pre-Tribulation rapture, but more commonly on lists of church fathers who believed in the future Millennial kingdom and taught that wonderfully elastic concept of 'imminency'. The Pre-Trib Research Centre cites him for such reasons, and in other essays combating 'replacement theology.' His writing is quite philosophically oriented, and he often quoted the oracles of pagan prophets and soothsayers as speaking of Christ. However, he does talk about the end times in two of his works - or at least that was all I could find, apart from a brief mention of a false belief that the brutal emperor Nero from the New Testament times would return as the Antichrist in his work 'On the Manner in which the persecutors died'. The two works in question are the final book of his 'Treatises, Book 7 - On a Happy Life', and 'Epitome of the Divine Institutes'.

We will start with the former. After several chapters talking about virtue, vice and how eternal souls will rise again, with vindication for the oppressed righteous in this life, Lactantius turns specifically to issues of the end of time in chapter 14 (see http://www.newadvent.org/fathers/07017.htm if you want to read the work for yourself). Like many of the church fathers he believed that there would be 6000 years of this age to match the 6 days of creation, with the Millennium occupying the last 7000 years to match the Sabbath of creation week. In chapter 15 he details how wickedness would increase greatly before the end, invoking ancient Roman pagan prophecies to the same effect. Chapter 16 talks of the unrest and violence and natural disasters that will ensue, in the midst of which the antichrist will appear, from the far north, he believes. The heavenly bodies will be darkened and shaken, and 90% of the earth's population will perish, cursing God, and as well *'Of the worshippers of God also, two parts will perish; and the third part, which shall have been proved, will remain.'* He doesn't state per se that these are Christians, the church, but we can assume that, particularly as he mentions nothing about the church not being there when the antichrist arises. The same applies to chapter 17, which I will quote in full (he seems to confuse the roles of the false prophet and the antichrist somewhat if we look at how Revelation describes them):

> 'But I will more plainly set forth the manner in which this happens. When the close of the times draws near, a great prophet shall be sent from God to turn men to the knowledge of God, and he shall receive the power of doing wonderful things. Wherever men shall not hear him, he will shut up the heaven, and cause it to withhold its rains; he will turn their water into blood, and torment them with thirst and hunger; and if any one shall endeavour to injure him, fire shall come forth out of his mouth, and shall burn that man. By these prodigies and powers he shall turn many to the worship of God; and when his works shall be accomplished, another king shall arise out of Syria, born from an evil spirit, the overthrower and destroyer of the human race, who shall destroy that which is left by the former evil, together with himself. He shall fight against the prophet of God, and shall overcome, and slay him, and shall suffer him to lie unburied; but after the third day he shall come to life again; and while all look on and wonder, he shall be caught up into heaven. But that king will not only be most disgraceful in himself, but he will also be a prophet of lies; and he will constitute and call himself God, and will order himself to be worshipped as the Son of God; and power will be given him to do signs and wonders, by the sight of which he may entice men to adore him. He will command fire to come down from heaven, and the sun to stand and leave his course, and an image to speak; and these things shall be done at his word–by which miracles many even of the wise shall be enticed by him. Then he will attempt to destroy the temple of God, and persecute the righteous people; and there will be distress and tribulation, such as there never has been from the beginning of the world.
>
> As many as shall believe him and unite themselves to him, shall be marked by him as sheep; but they who shall refuse his mark will either flee to the mountains, or, being seized, will be slain with studied tortures. He will also enwrap righteous men with the books of the prophets, and thus burn them; and power will be given him to desolate the whole earth for forty-two months. That will be the time in which righteousness shall be cast out, and innocence be hated; in which the wicked shall prey upon the good as enemies; neither law, nor order, nor military discipline shall be preserved; no one shall reverence hoary locks, nor recognise the duty of piety, nor pity sex or infancy; all things shall be confounded and mixed together against right, and against the laws of nature. Thus the earth shall be laid waste, as though by one common robbery. When these things shall so happen, then the righteous and the followers of truth shall separate themselves from the wicked, and flee into solitudes. And when he hears of this, the impious king, inflamed with anger, will come with a great army, and bringing up all his forces, will surround all the mountain in which the righteous shall be situated, that he may seize them. But they, when they shall see themselves to be shut in on all sides and besieged, will call upon God with a loud voice, and implore the aid of heaven; and God shall hear

> them, and send from heaven a great king to rescue and free them, and destroy all the wicked with fire and sword.'

Again, no sign of a rapture anywhere there. Chapter 18 quotes pagan prophecies to similar effect. Chapter 19 and the first half of chapter 20 read:

> The world therefore being oppressed, since the resources of men shall be insufficient for the overthrow of a tyranny of immense strength, inasmuch as it will press upon the captive world with great armies of robbers, that calamity so great will stand in need of divine assistance. Therefore God, being aroused both by the doubtful danger and by the wretched lamentation of the righteous, will immediately send a deliverer. Then the middle of the heaven shall be laid open in the dead and darkness of the night, that the light of the descending God may be manifest in all the world as lightning: of which the Sibyl spoke in these words:–
>
> When He shall come, there will be fire and darkness in the midst of the black night.
>
> This is the night which is celebrated by us in watchfulness on account of the coming of our King and God: of which night there is a twofold meaning; because in it He then received life when He suffered, and hereafter He is about to receive the kingdom of the world. For He is the Deliverer, and Judge, and Avenger, and King, and God, whom we call Christ, who before He descends will give this sign: There shall suddenly fall from heaven a sword, that the righteous may know that the leader of the sacred warfare is about to descend; and He shall descend with a company of angels to the middle of the earth, and there shall go before Him an unquenchable fire, and the power of the angels shall deliver into the hands of the just that multitude which has surrounded the mountain, and they shall be slain from the third hour until the evening, and blood shall flow like a torrent; and all his forces being destroyed, the wicked one shall alone escape, and his power shall perish from him.
>
> Now this is he who is called Antichrist; but he shall falsely call himself Christ, and shall fight against the truth, and being overcome shall flee; and shall often renew the war, and often be conquered, until in the fourth battle, all the wicked being slain, subdued, and captured, he shall at length pay the penalty of his crimes. But other princes also and tyrants who have harassed the world, together with him, shall be led in chains to the king; and he shall rebuke them, and reprove them, and upbraid them with their crimes, and condemn them, and consign them to deserved tortures. Thus, wickedness being extinguished and impiety suppressed, the world will be at rest, which having been subject to error and wickedness for so many ages, endured dreadful slavery. No longer shall gods made by the hands be worshipped; but the images being thrust out from their temples and couches, shall be given to the fire, and shall be burnt, together with their wonderful gifts: which also the Sibyl, in accordance with the prophets, announced as about to take place:–

> But mortals shall break in pieces the images and all the wealth.
>
> The Erythræan Sibyl also made the same promise:–
>
> > And the works made by the hand of the gods shall be burnt up.
>
> After these things the lower regions shall be opened, and the dead shall rise again, on whom the same King and God shall pass judgment, to whom the supreme Father shall give the great power both of judging and of reigning. And respecting this judgment and reign, it is thus found in the Erythræan Sibyl:–
>
> > When this shall receive its fated accomplishment, and the judgment of the immortal God shall now come to mortals, the great judgment shall come upon men, and the beginning.
>
> Then in another:–
>
> > And then the gaping earth shall show a Tartarean chaos; and all kings shall come to the judgment-seat of God.
>
> And in another place in the same:–
>
> > Rolling along the heavens, I will open the caverns of the earth; and then I will raise the dead, loosing fate and the sting of death; and afterwards I will call them into judgment, judging the life of pious and impious men.
>
> Not all men, however, shall then be judged by God, but those only who have been exercised in the religion of God. For they who have not known God, since sentence cannot be passed upon them for their acquittal, are already judged and condemned, since the Holy Scriptures testify that the wicked shall not arise to judgment. Therefore they who have known God shall be judged, and their deeds, that is, their evil works, shall be compared and weighed against their good ones: so that if those which are good and just are more and weighty, they may be given to a life of blessedness; but if the evil exceed, they may be condemned to punishment.....

Here Lactantius goes back to a philosophical discussion of the eternal nature of souls, going on for several chapters before picking up the theme again in chapter 24:

> Now I will subjoin the rest. Therefore the Son of the most high and mighty God shall come to judge the quick and the dead, as the Sibyl testifies and says:–
>
> > For then there shall be confusion of mortals throughout the whole earth, when the Almighty Himself shall come on His judgment-seat to judge the souls of the quick and dead, and all the world.
>
> But He, when He shall have destroyed unrighteousness, and executed His great judgment, and shall have recalled to life the righteous, who have lived from the beginning, will be engaged among men a thousand years, and will

> rule them with most just command. Which the Sibyl proclaims in another place, as she utters her inspired predictions:–
>
> > Hear me, you mortals; an everlasting King reigns.
>
> Then they who shall be alive in their bodies shall not die, but during those thousand years shall produce an infinite multitude, and their offspring shall be holy, and beloved by God; but they who shall be raised from the dead shall preside over the living as judges. But the nations shall not be entirely extinguished, but some shall be left as a victory for God, that they may be the occasion of triumph to the righteous, and may be subjected to perpetual slavery. About the same time also the prince of the devils, who is the contriver of all evils, shall be bound with chains, and shall be imprisoned during the thousand years of the heavenly rule in which righteousness shall reign in the world, so that he may contrive no evil against the people of God. After His coming the righteous shall be collected from all the earth, and the judgment being completed, the sacred city shall be planted in the middle of the earth, in which God Himself the builder may dwell together with the righteous, bearing rule in it. And the Sibyl marks out this city when she says:–
>
> > And the city which God made, this He made more brilliant than the stars, and sun, and moon."

In goes on to describe in detail the blessing and abundance of the Millennium, and then in chapter 25, he talks of the issue of when this will happen and then what happens during and after the Millennium in chapter 26:

> Perhaps some one may now ask when these things of which we have spoken are about to come to pass? I have already shown above, that when six thousand years shall be completed this change must take place, and that the last day of the extreme conclusion is now drawing near. It is permitted us to know respecting the signs, which are spoken by the prophets, for they foretold signs by which the consummation of the times is to be expected by us from day to day, and to be feared. When, however, this amount will be completed, those teach, who have written respecting the times, collecting them from the sacred writings and from various histories, how great is the number of years from the beginning of the world. And although they vary, and the amount of the number as reckoned by them differs considerably, yet all expectation does not exceed the limit of two hundred years. The subject itself declares that the fall and ruin of the world will shortly take place; except that while the city of Rome remains it appears that nothing of this kind is to be feared. But when that capital of the world shall have fallen, and shall have begun to be a street, which the Sibyls say shall come to pass, who can doubt that the end has now arrived to the affairs of men and the whole world? It is that city, that only, which still sustains all things; and the God of heaven is to be entreated by us and implored– if, indeed, His arrangements and decrees can be delayed– lest, sooner than we think for, that detestable tyrant should come who will undertake so great a deed, and dig out that eye, by

the destruction of which the world itself is about to fall. Now let us return, to set forth the other things which are then about to follow.

We have said, a little before, that it will come to pass at the commencement of the sacred reign, that the prince of the devils will be bound by God. But he also, when the thousand years of the kingdom, that is, seven thousand of the world, shall begin to be ended, will be loosed afresh, and being sent forth from prison, will go forth and assemble all the nations, which shall then be under the dominion of the righteous, that they may make war against the holy city; and there shall be collected together from all the world an innumerable company of the nations, and shall besiege and surround the city. Then the last anger of God shall come upon the nations, and shall utterly destroy them; and first He shall shake the earth most violently, and by its motion the mountains of Syria shall be rent, and the hills shall sink down precipitously, and the walls of all cities shall fall, and God shall cause the sun to stand, so that he set not for three days, and shall set it on fire; and excessive heat and great burning shall descend upon the hostile and impious people, and showers of brimstone, and hailstones, and drops of fire; and their spirits shall melt through the heat, and their bodies shall be bruised by the hail, and they shall smite one another with the sword. The mountains shall be filled with carcasses, and the plains shall be covered with bones; but the people of God during those three days shall be concealed under caves of the earth, until the anger of God against the nations and the last judgment shall be ended.

Then the righteous shall go forth from their hiding-places, and shall find all things covered with carcasses and bones. But the whole race of the wicked shall utterly perish; and there shall no longer be any nation in this world, but the nation of God alone. Then for seven continuous years the woods shall be untouched, nor shall timber be cut from the mountains, but the arms of the nations shall be burnt; and now there shall be no war, but peace and everlasting rest. But when the thousand years shall be completed, the world shall be renewed by God, and the heavens shall be folded together, and the earth shall be changed, and God shall transform men into the similitude of angels, and they shall be white as snow; and they shall always be employed in the sight of the Almighty, and shall make offerings to their Lord, and serve Him for ever. At the same time shall take place that second and public resurrection of all, in which the unrighteous shall be raised to everlasting punishments. These are they who have worshipped the works of their own hands, who have either been ignorant of, or have denied the Lord and Parent of the world. But their lord with his servants shall be seized and condemned to punishment, together with whom all the band of the wicked, in accordance with their deeds, shall be burnt for ever with perpetual fire in the sight of angels and the righteous.

This is the doctrine of the holy prophets which we Christians follow; this is our wisdom, which they who worship frail objects, or maintain an empty philosophy, deride as folly and vanity, because we are not accustomed to defend and assert it in public, since God orders us in

> quietness and silence to hide His secret, and to keep it within our own conscience; and not to strive with obstinate contention against those who are ignorant of the truth, and who rigorously assail God and His religion not for the sake of learning, but of censuring and jeering. For a mystery ought to be most faithfully concealed and covered, especially by us, who bear the name of faith. But they accuse this silence of ours, as though it were the result of an evil conscience; whence also they invent some detestable things respecting those who are holy and blameless, and willingly believe their own inventions.

The other work, as its name suggests is just a summary of the Divine Institutes, and the passages on the end times in chapters 71-2 contain no relevant material not already in the quotes above, but you can read it, if you want at http://www.newadvent.org/fathers/0702.htm .

Now, if we consider what we have read, then past all the complexities and the use of pagan sources for support, three things jump out. Firstly, as we noted, there is not a hint of a rapture before the Tribulation anywhere. The antichrist oppresses the righteous, a generic term that could mean the church, but could also fit the 'Tribulation saints' context; however, since we have seen no sign of a rapture before the Tribulation, the most natural reading is that the righteous are the church, especially as this was the unanimous position of all the other church fathers on the topic. Secondly, the 'resurrection of the righteous' is explicitly placed after the return of Jesus visibly from heaven at the start of the Millennium, an overtly Post-Tribulation position. Finally, even though very few other than youtube videos claim Lactantius taught an actual Pre-Tribulation rapture, many claim him in support because he allegedly taught 'imminence'. Yet when we looked through, there was not a hint of the return of Jesus being something that could happen at any moment. Instead, it was crystal clear that a number of things had to happen including the reign of the antichrist and the false prophet, their slaying of the two witnesses of God, not to mention the destruction of Rome, and the fact that Jesus' return is to be placed around 6000 years after creation. If that's Dispensationalist 'imminence', then call me a fit, slim young hunk, someone, please!

So if anyone tells you that Lactantius taught a Pre-tribulation rapture, or even the doctrine of 'imminence', they are lying to you, no matter how sincerely they may believe it.

Commodianus

We know little about Commodianus, not even for sure when he lived. Most scholars seem to think about 250AD, but we only find his material in much later authors, so some believe him to be from several centuries later. He was apparently a pagan who converted to Christianity in his old age, and there are two surviving works in poetic form – in one he wrote 80 poems as a means of instruction (see http://www.newadvent.org/fathers/0411.htm) and in that his work on the end times is chiefly in a set of five poems in the middle of the collection, and in the other he wrote extensively of the Antichrist and the end-times, including a belief (apparently widespread in some quarters) that the wicked Nero would return to persecute the believes once more. That work is known as 'Carmen Apologeticum' or 'Carmen de Deobus Populis', and you can find the relevant section translated at http://christianlatin.blogspot.co.uk/2008/08/excerpt-from-commodianus-carmen.html . We need to remember that in writing these poems he was tied to particular forms, which may explain some apparent oddities. His basic pattern of thought is just like the other early fathers, so mostly I have just highlighted those bits where he depicts, or appears to depict (this is poetry, after all) the people of God undergoing the Tribulation or being preserved through the end times judgement, or resurrection of the just specifically at the start of the Millennium. I also find it interesting that he appears to predict Jesus' return specifically for Israel in the form of the lost tribes who have been 'hidden from our sight' in Poem 42 and in the 'Carmen Apologeticum', and indeed, in the latter work it culminates in a passage that says the purpose of it all has been to unite the two peoples of God (Israel and the church) into one people for eternity, again something that very much cuts across the core tenet of dispensational preaching. That work is broadly similar to the poems we will quote below, but with much more detail, but since it is quite lengthy, I have put it in an Appendix of its' own. On to poems of Commodianus, then (and by the way, Elias is another old spelling of Elijah):

41. Of the Time of Antichrist.

Isaiah said: This is the man who moves the world and so many kings, and under whom the land shall become desert. Hear how the prophet foretold concerning him. I have said nothing elaborately, but negligently. Then, doubtless, the world shall be finished when he shall appear. He himself shall divide the globe into three ruling powers, when, moreover, Nero shall be raised up from hell, Elias shall first come to seal the beloved ones; at which things the region of Africa and the northern nation, the whole earth on all sides, for seven years shall tremble. But Elias shall occupy the half of the time, Nero shall occupy half. Then the whore Babylon, being reduced to ashes, its embers shall thence advance to Jerusalem; and the Latin conqueror shall then say, I am Christ, whom you always pray to; and, indeed, the original ones who were deceived combine to praise him. He does many wonders, since his is the false prophet. Especially that they may believe him, his image shall speak. The Almighty has given it power to appear such. The Jews, recapitulating Scriptures from him, exclaim at the same time to the Highest that they have been deceived.

42. Of the Hidden and Holy People of the Almighty Christ, the Living God.

Let the hidden, the final, the holy people be longed for; and, indeed, let it be unknown by us where it abides, acting by nine of the tribes and a half...; and he has bidden to live by the former law. Now let us all live: the tradition of the law is new, as the law itself teaches, I point out to you more plainly. Two of the tribes and a half are left: wherefore is the half of the tribes separated from them? **That they might be martyrs, when He**

should bring war on His elected ones into the world; or certainly the choir of the holy prophets would rise together upon the people who should impose a check upon them whom the obscene horses have slaughtered with kicking heel; nor would the band hurry rashly at any time to the gift of peace. Those of the tribes are withdrawn, and all the mysteries of Christ are fulfilled by them throughout the whole age. Moreover, they have arisen from the crime of two brothers, by whose auspices they have followed crime. Not undeservedly are these bloody ones thus scattered: they shall again assemble on behalf of the mysteries of Christ. But then the things told of in the law are hastening to their completion. **The Almighty Christ descends to His elect,** who have been darkened from our view for so long a time– they have become so many thousands– that is the true heavenly people. The son does not die before his father, then; nor do they feel pains in their bodies, nor polypus in their nostrils. They who cease depart in ripe years in their bed, fulfilling all the things of the law, and therefore they are protected. They are bidden to pass on the right side of their Lord; and when they have passed over as before, He dries up the river. Nor less does the Lord Himself also proceed with them. He has passed over to our side, they come with the King of heaven; and in their journey, what shall I speak of which God will bring to pass? Mountains subside before them, and fountains break forth. The creation rejoices to see the heavenly people. Here, however, they hasten to defend the captive matron. But the wicked king who possesses her, when he hears, flies into the parts of the north, and collects all his followers. Moreover, when the tyrant shall dash himself against the army of God, his soldiery are overthrown by the celestial terror; the false prophet himself is seized with the wicked one, by the decree of the Lord; they are handed over alive to Gehenna. From him chiefs and leaders are bidden to obey; then will the holy ones enter into the breasts of their ancient mother, that, moreover, they also may be refreshed whom he has evil persuaded. With various punishments he will torment those who trust in him; they come to the end, whereby offenses are taken away from the world. The Lord will begin to give judgment by fire.

43. Of the End of This Age.

The trumpet gives the sign in heaven, the lion being taken away, and suddenly there is darkness with the din of heaven. The Lord casts down His eyes, so that the earth trembles. He cries out, so that all may hear throughout the world: Behold, long have I been silent while I bore your doings in such a time. They cry out together, complaining and groaning too late. They howl, they bewail; nor is there room found for the wicked. What shall the mother do for the sucking child, when she herself is burnt up? **In the flame of fire the Lord will judge the wicked. But the fire shall not touch the just,** but shall by all means lick them up. In one place they delay, but a part has wept at the judgment. Such will be the heat, that the stones themselves shall melt. The winds assemble into lightnings, the heavenly wrath rages; and wherever the wicked man flees, he is seized upon by this fire. There will be no succour nor ship of the sea. Amen flames on the nations, and the Medes and Parthians burn for a thousand years, as the hidden words of John declare. For then after a thousand years they are delivered over to Gehenna; and he whose work they were, with them are burnt up.

44. Of the First Resurrection.

From heaven will descend the city in the first resurrection; this is what we may tell of such a celestial fabric. We shall arise again to Him, who have been devoted to Him. And they shall be incorruptible, even already living without death. And neither will there be any grief nor any groaning in that city. **They shall come also who overcame cruel martyrdom under Antichrist, and they themselves live for the whole time, and receive blessings because they have suffered evil things; and they themselves marrying, beget for a thousand years.** There are prepared all the revenues of the earth, because the earth renewed without end pours forth abundantly. Therein are no rains; no cold comes into the golden camp. No sieges as now, nor rapines, nor does that city crave the light of a lamp. It shines from its Founder. Moreover, Him it obeys; in breadth 12,000 furlongs and length and depth. It levels its foundation in the earth, but it raises its head to heaven. In the city before the doors, moreover, sun and moon shall shine; he who is evil is hedged up in torment, for the sake of the nourishment of the righteous. But from the thousand years God will destroy all those evils.

45. Of the Day of Judgment.

I add something, on account of unbelievers, of the day of judgment. Again, the fire of the Lord sent forth shall be appointed. The earth gives a true groan; then those who are making their journey in the last end, and then all unbelievers, groan. **The whole of nature is converted in flame, which yet avoids the camp of His saints.** The earth is burned up from its foundations, and the mountains melt. Of the sea nothing remains: it is overcome by the powerful fire. This sky perishes, and the stars and these things are changed. Another newness of sky and of everlasting earth is arranged. Thence they who deserve it are sent away in a second death, but the righteous are placed in inner dwelling-places.

A few further comments are in order. Due to the poetic nature of the work, it is difficult to discern exactly what is meant, but towards the end of Poem 42, describing the returning saints with Jesus we find '*then will the holy ones enter into the breasts of their ancient mother, that, moreover, they also may be refreshed whom he has evil persuaded.*' Given that the poem appears in part to be about restoration of the Jews, the ancient mother might well be Jerusalem / Israel, and Israel may be the 'captive matron' that the heavenly armies rescue. Now I suppose it is just about possible to see a dispensational Pre-Tribulation rapture here if you really stretch. For instance, near the start of Poem 42, when it starts to talk about the lost tribes of Israel, it asks why they have been separated, and answers *'That they might be martyrs, when He should bring war on His elected ones into the world'.*

Now, I am not sure if the capitals here are those of the original, or those of the translators, but if they are correct, this is actually saying that God himself brings war on his saints (or 'elected ones'), very different to the notions of the Pre-Tribbers who continually cry that God loves his bride too much to let her suffer the Tribulation.

My response to that is simple and twofold - firstly we worship the same God who specifically afflicted rebellious Israel to win back her affection and allegiance, and this seems to be implied at the end of the poem where 'the holy ones' seem to be those who have been persuaded by evil (the deception of the antichrist?). The poem goes on to say that *'With various punishments he will torment those who trust in him; they come to the end, whereby offenses are taken away from the world.'* It is unclear who the 'he' is. It could be that here the topic has switched to the punishment of the wicked who trusted the antichrist, but at least some of the context suggests to me otherwise - that there is torment for those who trust in God, but in the end sin is removed. In other words, God uses the torment to purify his church and win her back to himself. This is consistent with the teaching of the bible, specifically Daniel, who repeatedly tells of the final ruler who will be given power to crush the people of God and break their power (see Daniel 12.7 for just one example), and also that some of the wise will 'stumble' (a term interestingly often used specifically of sexual sin, at least in later Jewish thought), specifically so that they might be purified and made spotless at the end of the age (Daniel 11.*35 'Some of the wise will stumble, so that they may be refined, purified and made spotless until the time of the end, for it will still come at the appointed time.'*). These verses and the principles they contain, I suggest, apply to the whole people of God in the last days, whether Jew or Christian. In general, we should interpret Commodianus to teach the same thing as all the other church fathers, unless we have exceptionally good reason to think otherwise.

But secondly, these verses can't be describing some separate 'Tribulation saints' or such after a rapture, because, of Poem 44, where Commodianus places the 'first resurrection'. He puts it at the time of the visible return of Jesus with the saints, specifically when the city, meaning the heavenly Jerusalem, descends to earth. He first explicitly says that at that point '***we** rise to meet him'* meaning the church, but if the rapture was before the Tribulation, then this would be the second resurrection. However, even more to the point he quickly includes in this first resurrection those who '*overcame cruel martyrdom under Antichrist*' leaving absolutely no room to doubt - there is no teaching of a Pre-Tribulation rapture in Commodianus. In taking this line, he is, as we saw in my book 'Rapture Rupture!', taking exactly the same line and approach as the book of Revelation.

Finally, can you see a hint of any sense of 'imminence' here? I can't, as it teaches specific things that must happen before the return of Jesus, even in this poetic form.

There is one brief mention about the Antichrist in the final poem, 80, which also strongly suggests the same - that the church suffers under the Antichrist; it says: *'This has pleased Christ, that the dead should rise again, yea, with their bodies; and those, too, whom in this world the fire has burned, when six thousand years are completed, and the world has come to an end. The heaven in the meantime is changed with an altered course, for then the wicked are burnt up with divine fire. The creature with groaning burns with the anger of the highest God.* ***Those who are more worthy, and who are begotten of an illustrious stem, and the men of nobility under the conquered Antichrist, according to God's command living again in the world for a thousand years,...'***

Oh, one more minor point. The Pre-Trib Research Centre only mention Commodianus a couple of times, but even with so few mentions they certainly seem to give a false impression on how close he is to their own teaching. They state in the article 'Some Key Issues in the History of Premillennialism' that like Ireneaus he 'spoke of the procreation of children during the millennium'. This is true enough, but most Dispensationalist thinking on the issue holds that the survivors of the Antichrist, the alleged 'Tribulation saints' plus perhaps surviving Jews, are those who procreate. It is just possible to claim that Commodianus taught this by forcing his terms, but very difficult, since when he talks of procreation it is in the context of the first resurrection, specifically of those who *'overcame cruel martyrdom under Antichrist'* which most naturally reads as if it is those who have been martyred, not those who escaped being martyred and survived to the return of Jesus. And given that he is probably even more explicit in his other work (see the appendix) that it is the church that suffers under the Antichrist, along with the Jews, we can very safely say that......

If anyone tells you that Commodianus taught a Pre-Tribulation Rapture, they are lying to you, no matter how sincerely they may believe it.

Methodius

Methodius is someone you occasionally see cited in lists of church fathers who allegedly taught the Pre-Tribulation rapture, but I have never seen any actual quotes, and little more than a reference to his alleged 'clear but crude' dispensationalism on the Pre-Trib research centre, but without actual supporting evidence. He was an opponent of Origen, writing a work 'On the Resurrection' to refute Origen's followers, arguing strongly for a bodily resurrection of the dead. He is believed to have been martyred in about 311 AD. I could find only one reference to the antichrist in his works, and although quite brief, it too supports what we would call a Post-Tribulation position. It comes from his work called 'The Banquet of the Ten Virgins' or 'On Chastity' Discourse 6, chapter 4, which you can read at http://www.newadvent.org/fathers/062306.htm . The passage reads:

> Let us then supply now the oil of good works abundantly, and of prudence, being purged from all corruption which would weigh us down; lest, while the Bridegroom tarries, our lamps may also in like manner be extinguished. For the delay is the interval which precedes the appearing of Christ. Now the slumbering and sleeping of the virgins signifies the departure from life; and the midnight is the kingdom of Antichrist, during which the destroying angel passes over the houses. But the cry which was made when it was said, Behold the bridegroom comes, go out to meet him,

> is the voice which shall be heard from heaven, and the trumpet, when the saints, all their bodies being raised, shall be caught up, and shall go on the clouds to meet the Lord. (1 Thessalonians 4:16-17)
>
> For it is to be observed that the word of God says, that after the cry all the virgins arose, that is, that the dead shall be raised after the voice which comes from heaven, as also Paul intimates, (1 Thessalonians 4:16) that the Lord Himself shall descend from heaven with a shout, with the voice of the archangel, and with the trump of God: and the dead in Christ shall rise first; that is the tabernacles, for they died, being put off by their souls. Then we which are alive shall be caught up together with them, meaning our souls. For we truly who are alive are the souls which, with the bodies, having put them on again, shall go to meet Him in the clouds, bearing our lamps trimmed, not with anything alien and worldly, but like stars radiating the light of prudence and continence, full of ethereal splendour.

Firstly, we can see here the continuation of a theme in the New Testament teaching, namely the need to be living pure lives before the coming of Jesus. Methodius is interpreting the parable of the 10 virgins in Matthew 25, which is indeed about the return of Jesus. The reason why this passage is explicitly 'Post-Trib' is because Methodius says that midnight in the parable is the kingdom of the Antichrist, which is then followed by a cry greeting the Bridegroom - and this cry he identifies with the rapture as described in 1 Thessalonians 4 in the bible.

So, if anyone tells you Methodius taught the Pre-Tribulation rapture, they are lying to you, no matter how sincerely they may believe it.

(By the way, there is a later work falsely attributed to Methodius which talks a lot about the Antichrist, and which sometimes people mistakenly believe was written by the genuine Methodius; we will deal with that later on.)

Victorinus

Victorinus was an early church father born in Greece, who quite possibly was a bishop, and was martyred in a town now in Slovenia, near the border with Austria. Only a couple of his writings survive, namely 'On the Creation of the World' (http://www.newadvent.org/fathers/0711.htm) and 'Commentary on the Apocalypse' (http://www.newadvent.org/fathers/0712.htm). The former has very little relevant to us, except that it preserves the common teaching that there would be about 7000 years of the world, matching the seven days of creation, and that the last thousand would be the rule of Christ, the 'Sabbath' period. However, in the second, Victorinus has a totally different interpretation of the Millennium - either he had totally changed his views, or someone has tampered with one of his works; personally I suspect the former (or we have misunderstood completely what he meant in the first work - his comments aren't particularly lengthy). He was one of the first church fathers to abandon belief in the 1000 year reign and adopted a position that we today call 'Post-Millenial'. He believed it was symbolic and covered the age between Jesus' death and resurrection, and his return, the 'church age'. Many

- perhaps most - more recent Post-millenialists taught that the age would get better and better and the church more triumphant, until the world was ready for Jesus' return in triumph. Victorinus, however, maintained the classic interpretation of the time before Jesus' return - that it would be a time of persecution under the antichrist. Victorinus appears too, to have been one of the first to realize that the accounts in the book of Revelation do not run consecutively, but concurrently, an approach I have come to hold to as well. (Revelation is an Apocalyptic work, and it was quite common in Apocalyptic writings to look at the same events several times from different perspectives. In Revelation there are three sets of seven - seven seals, seven trumpets and seven bowls, and at the end of each sequence there is language that fits the situation at the return of Jesus - for instance at the 6th and 7th seals people rush to hide from the wrath of the Lamb, at the 7th trumpet the kingdoms of the world become the kingdoms of our God and of His Christ, and at the 7th bowl, a voice from heaven cries out 'It is finished' - plus in each case the same set of events happen after the 7th instance - hail, thunder, lightning and a huge earthquake. This is a sign that the same point has been reached, and the material after that is going back to cover similar ground again.) Anyway, for our purposes, Victorinus did not teach a Pre-Trib rapture, despite claims to the contrary. There is one passage from his work that is routinely cited as 'proof' he taught a Pre-Tribulation rapture, and it comes from his commentary on Revelation 15.1, where he says:

> *'And I saw another great and wonderful sign, seven angels having the seven last plagues; for in them is completed the indignation of God.'* For the wrath of God always strikes the obstinate people with seven plagues, that is, perfectly, as it is said in Leviticus; and these shall be in the last time, when the Church shall have gone out of the midst.

That last phrase is jumped upon by Pretribulationists as proof that he believed in the rapture. But that only works firstly, if he can have had no other meaning here, which is doubtful to say the least, especially when, as we have seen and will go on to see, a number of church fathers taught that the church would separate itself from society or civilization at the very end - and secondly it can only be 'proof' of a Pre-tribulation rapture if the church being 'gone out of the midst' happened much earlier in Revelation. If we just accept for the moment that this really is a reference to some kind of 'rapture' event, it is just as compatible with a belief in a 'Mid-Tribulation' or 'Pre-Wrath' position. It is even compatible with at least one form of Post-Tribulation rapture understanding. You see, even if all of the seven seals, trumpets and bowls are sequential, one after the other instead of parallel or somehow overlapping (the latter is what I believe - probably they cover shorter and shorter periods of time, but all finish at the same point in time), then these bowls are explicitly the 'last' and there is no indication of any length of time between each of the bowls being poured out - they could happen within the space of a minute, and the 6th bowl has the nations being gathered together at Armageddon for the final battle against Jesus. Thus this could be the rapture, happening as Jesus descends to earth for the final battle, with at most a day or two between the 'rapture' and Jesus touching down on earth.

So, as ever, to gain understanding, we will have to look at what else Victorinus says on the subject. The first passage I want to cite is not a direct proof or disproof over the timing of the rapture, but it does not fit the Pre-Tribulation notion of God sparing his church suffering. Commenting on Revelation 1.15, Victorinus says: *'His feet were like yellow brass, as if burned in a furnace.* ***He calls the apostles His feet, who, being wrought by suffering, preached His word in the whole world;*** *for He rightly named those by whose means the preaching went forth, feet. Whence also the prophet anticipated this, and said: We will worship in the place where His feet have stood. Because where they first of all stood and confirmed the Church, that is, in Judea, all the saints shall assemble together, and will worship their Lord.'* Similarly his commentary on the third of the letters to the seven churches in chapter 2.11: *'The third order of the saints shows that they are men who are strong in faith, and who are* ***not afraid of persecution****;...'*

In his commentary on chapter 6 (which covers the first six of the seven seals that Jesus opens), Victorinus makes various symbolic interpretations of some passages that we probably would not make, but they make quite clear his understanding that the church, or saints, will undergo great persecution at this time in the account of the book of Revelation. Since the Pre-Tribulation position holds that the church is absent from earth from chapter 4 on, this is a direct indication that he cannot have held to anything like a 'Pre-Tribulation' position. Here is what he has to say on the last few verses of chapter 6:

> Verse 12. *And I saw, when he had opened the sixth seal, there was a great earthquake.* In the sixth seal, then, was a great earthquake: **this is that very last persecution**.
>
> *And the sun became black as sackcloth of hair.* The sun becomes as sackcloth; that is, **the brightness of doctrine will be obscured by unbelievers.**
>
> *And the entire moon became as blood.* By the moon of blood is set forth **the Church of the saints as pouring out her blood for Christ.**
>
> Verse 13. *And the stars fell to the earth.* The falling of the stars are the **faithful who are troubled for Christ's sake.**
>
> *Even as a fig-tree casts her untimely figs.* The fig-tree, when shaken, loses its untimely figs– **when men are separated from the Church by persecution**.
>
> Verse 14. *And the heaven withdrew as a scroll that is rolled up.* For the heaven to be rolled away, that is, **that the Church shall be taken away**.
>
> *And every mountain and the islands were moved from their places.* Mountains and islands removed from their places intimate that **in the last persecution all men departed from their places; that is, that the good will be removed, seeking to avoid the persecution**.

Whatever precisely is meant by this, it is quite clear that in Victorinus' understanding, the church goes through the last persecution, that the church, or the saints, suffer greatly, their blood being poured out. He sees this persecution as driving many from the church (a part of the last days apostasy indicated in the New Testament - as is the darkening of 'the brightness of doctrine'). Whatever is meant in verse 14 by the church being taken away or good men being removed, the context strongly suggests not a spiritual rapture event, but people physically moving to escape persecution, a theme we have found in other church fathers' teaching on the issue.

The next passage is Victorinus' quite lengthy comments on Revelation 7.2 (which comes between the 6th and 7th seals in the first pattern of '7' in Revelation). In it, he expresses what came to be a standard view of the last seven year period - that the first half is the preaching of Elijah and Enoch returned to earth (in Revelation this occurs in chapter 11), and the second half is the rule of the Antichrist from Jerusalem once they are slain. I think that Victorinus may be confused, because by applying that concept here, at the end of a pattern of seven, he seems to be making difficulties for himself, because he claims Elijah (pictured as an angel - since the term just means messenger) comes to restore the churches from 'the great persecution'. He later on refers to Jesus' teaching on the great suffering at the time of the end, and how it will be cut short for the sake of the 'elect', which strongly suggests when he talks of '*the great and intolerable persecution'* he means the same as we do by the term 'the Tribulation'. However, it may be that Victorinus is not confused, but believes that even before the coming of the Antichrist there will be a great persecution of the churches. Anyway, here is what he says:

> *And I saw another angel ascending from the east, having the seal of the living God.* He speaks of Elias the prophet, who is the precursor of the times of Antichrist, for the **restoration and establishment of the churches from the great and intolerable persecution.** We read that these things are predicted in the opening of the Old and New Testament; for He says by Malachi: Lo, I will send to you Elias the Tishbite, to turn the hearts of the fathers to the children, according to the time of calling, to recall the Jews to the faith of the people that succeed them. And to that end He shows, as we have said, that the number of those that shall believe, of the Jews and of the nations, is a great multitude which no man was able to number. Moreover, we read in the Gospel that the prayers of the Church are sent from heaven by an angel, and that they are received against wrath, and that the kingdom of Antichrist is cast out and extinguished by holy angels; for He says: 'Pray that you enter not into temptation: for there shall be a great affliction, such as has not been from the beginning of the world; and except the Lord had shortened those days, no flesh should be saved'. (Mark 13:18-20). Therefore He shall send **these seven great archangels to smite the kingdom of Antichrist; for He Himself also thus said: *'Then the Son of man shall send His messengers; and they shall gather together His elect from the four corners of the wind, from the one end of heaven even to the other end thereof.'* (Mark 13:27)** For, moreover, He previously says by the prophet: Then shall there be peace for our land, when there shall arise in it seven shepherds and eight attacks of men; **and they shall encircle Assur, that is, Antichrist, in the trench of Nimrod, (Micah 5:5-6) that is, in the**

> **nation of the devil, by the spirit of the Church.** Similarly when the keepers of the house shall be moved. Moreover, the Lord Himself, in the parable to the apostles, when the labourers had come to Him and said, 'Lord, did not we sow good seed in Your field? Whence, then, has it tares?' Answered them, 'An enemy has done this'. And they said to Him, 'Lord, will You, then, that we go and root them up?' And He said, 'Nay, but let both grow together until the harvest; and in the time of the harvest I will say to the reapers, that they gather the tares and make bundles of them, and burn them with fire everlasting, but that they gather the wheat into my barns.' (Matthew 13:27-30). The Apocalypse here shows, therefore, that these reapers, and shepherds, and labourers, are the angels. And the trumpet is the word of power. And although the same thing recurs in the phials, still it is not said as if it occurred twice, but because what is decreed by the Lord to happen shall be once for all; for this cause it is said twice. What, therefore, He said too little in the trumpets, is here found in the phials. We must not regard the order of what is said, because frequently the Holy Spirit, when He has traversed even to the end of the last times, returns again to the same times, and fills up what He had before failed to say. Nor must we look for order in the Apocalypse; but we must follow the meaning of those things which are prophesied. Therefore in the trumpets and phials is signified either the desolation of the plagues that are sent upon the earth, or **the madness of Antichrist himself, or the cutting off of the peoples, or the diversity of the plagues, or the hope in the kingdom of the saints,** or the ruin of states, or the great overthrow of Babylon, that is, the Roman state.

I have included this quite lengthy passage to show something of how Victorinus linked in various passages. What is quite clear from the bits that I have put in bold is that he sees the church, or the saints, as being around at the same time as the Antichrist. He uses both terms - church and saints - in the same way - so there is no room for a separate church age and then 'Tribulation saints' under the Antichrist.

He goes on to comment on verse 9:

> *After this I beheld, and, lo, a great multitude, which no man was able to number, of every nation, tribe, and people, and tongue, clothed with white robes.* What the great multitude out of every tribe implies, is to show the number of the elect out of all believers, who, being cleansed by baptism in the blood of the Lamb, have made their robes white, keeping the grace which they have received.

Victorinus doesn't comment on every verse. These two paragraphs are his entire commentary on chapter 7. But given his understanding that we have seen in chapter 6, of a great final persecution in which many are shaken from the church (and salvation, it would seem), and given that Revelation 7 a few verses later describes this great multitude in white as *'These are they who have come out of the great tribulation; they have washed their robes and made them white in the blood of the Lamb.'* then Victorinus seems to be saying, when he says that this is '*the number of the elect out of all believers'* that he means those who have not abandoned the faith during the Tribulation, since in doing so they have been '*keeping the grace which they have received*'. When he says 'cleansed by baptism in the blood of the Lamb' it is likely that he is not referring to baptism, but those who have identified with the slain Lamb by themselves being slain, or being faithful under the threat of being slain, and so have been purified and '*made their robes white*', which again is consistent with what the New Testament and many of the church fathers taught about the nature and divine purpose of the last days Tribulation.

I will quote in full his very brief and partial commentary on chapters 8 and 9.

> 8.1. *And when He had opened the seventh seal, there was silence in heaven for about half an hour.* Whereby is signified the beginning of everlasting rest; but it is described as partial, because the silence being interrupted, he repeats it in order. For if the silence had continued, here would be an end of his narrative.
>
> 8.13. *And I saw an angel flying through the midst of heaven.* By the angel flying through the midst of heaven is signified the Holy Spirit bearing witness in two of the prophets that a great wrath of plagues was imminent. If by any means, even in the last times, any one should be willing to be converted, any one might even still be saved.
>
> 9.13-14. *And I heard a voice from the four horns of the golden altar which is in the presence of God, saying to the sixth angel which had the trumpet, Loose the four angels.* That is, the four corners of the earth which hold the four winds.
>
> *Which are bound in the great river Euphrates.* By the corners of the earth, or the four winds across the river Euphrates, are meant four nations, because to every nation is sent an angel; as said the law, '*He determined them by the number of the angels of God*', until the number of the saints should be filled up. They do not overpass their bounds, because at the last they shall come with Antichrist.

(The reference to the passage of '*the number of the angels of God*' refers to a common view in both Judaism and early Christianity that holds that each nation is linked to particular angels in God's scheme of things, and the bounds and numbers of nations are determined by this relationship). In a dispensationalist or Pre-Tribulationist view, the number of the 'saints' being filled up and not 'overpassing their bounds' could mean that the final church age saints come into the church just before the rapture and the Antichrist, but Victorinus specifically says that '*at the last they shall come* ***with*** *Antichrist*'. Alternatively, they could argue that this is specifically a reference to the alleged special 'Tribulation saints'. However, as we have already seen, Victorinus uses church and saints interchangeably, and taught that they would undergo the Tribulation and the wrath of the Antichrist. Thus the most natural explanation, especially in the light of his comments on 8.13 about people being converted and saved right up to the end, is that the last of the elect or the saints come in to the church by conversion under the reign of the Antichrist, directly contradicting the definite distinctions of dispensationalist teaching on the end times.

His comments on chapter 12.7-9 are also instructive:

> *There was a battle in heaven: Michael and his angels fought with the dragon; and the dragon warred, and his angels, and they prevailed not; nor was their place found any more in heaven. And that great dragon was cast forth, that old serpent: he was cast forth into the earth.* This is the beginning of Antichrist; yet previously Elijah must prophesy, and there must be times of peace. And afterwards, when the three years and six months are completed in the preaching of Elijah, he also must be cast down from heaven, where up till that time he had had the power of ascending; and all the apostate angels, as well as Antichrist, must be roused up from hell. Paul the apostle says: *'Except there come a falling away first, and the man of sin shall appear, the son of perdition; and the adversary who exalted himself above all which is called God, or is worshipped'.* (2 Thessalonians 2:3-4)

Although he doesn't make explicit how he integrates his understanding of Revelation and the last seven years of this age with the passage he quotes from Paul, it effectively rules out any notion of a 'Pre-Tribulation rapture' in the sense of a rapture seven years before the return of Jesus, since Victorinus saw Elijah's preaching as lasting half that period, and, as we saw earlier, with the specific purpose of restoring a battered church. It suggests he understood 2 Thessalonians to be teaching what we could call a Post-Tribulation position, and at the very most, could mean a Mid-Tribulation position, but that is rather ruled out by what Victorinus says elsewhere, as we have seen.

The next passage we look at, completely and utterly scotches any claim of a Pre-Trib position, when Victorinus comments on Revelation 13.13 about the Antichrist's false prophet:

> *And he shall make fire come down from heaven in the sight of men.* Yes (as I also have said), in the sight of men. Magicians do these things, by the aid of the apostate angels, even to this day. He shall cause also that a golden image of Antichrist shall be placed in the temple at Jerusalem, and that the apostate angel should enter, and thence utter voices and oracles. Moreover, he himself shall contrive that his servants and children should receive as a mark on their foreheads, or on their right hands, the number of his name, lest any one should buy or sell them. Daniel had previously predicted his contempt and provocation of God. And he shall place, says he, his temple within Samaria, upon the illustrious and holy mountain that is at Jerusalem, an image such as Nebuchadnezzar had made. (Daniel 11:45) Thence here he places, and by and by here he renews, that of which the Lord, **admonishing His churches concerning the last times and their dangers,** says: *But when you shall see the contempt which is spoken of by Daniel the prophet standing in the holy place, let him who reads understand.* (Matthew 24:15; Daniel 9:27) It is called a contempt when God is provoked, because idols are worshipped instead of God, or **when**

> **the dogma of heretics is introduced in the churches. But it is a turning away because steadfast men, seduced by false signs and portents, are turned away from their salvation.**

Now, despite Victorinus' obvious confusion on some issues (he seems to think Samaria is in Jerusalem), it is crystal clear from the passages I have put in bold that it is specifically the church that the false prophet deceives, and the church that undergoes a falling away, not in some lead up to the Tribulation, but specifically at the point of the Antichrist's desecration of the Jerusalem Temple. Pre-Tribulationists will tell you until they are blue in the face that Matthew 24.15 cannot be a warning to the church, but that it is meant for 'Tribulation Saints', or Jews who come to faith during the Tribulation, but this is clearly not the way that Victorinus takes it.

Thus, when we come to that quote we started with on Revelation 15.1, Victorinus absolutely could not have been teaching any kind of 'secret rapture' before the Tribualation. His comments on 15.2, which talks of those who have triumphed over the 'beast', its image in the Temple, and the mark, make this all the clearer: *'Standing upon the sea of glass, having harps.' That is, that they stood steadfastly in the faith upon their baptism, and having their confession in their mouth, that they shall exult in the kingdom before God. But let us return to what is set before us.'* The saints who retain their salvation, in other words, are those who have not given in and taken the mark of the beast, or fallen away from the faith they were baptized into.

In his comments on Revelation 17.16, Victorinus believes that the Antichrist will be Jewish and will be taken by his fellow Jews as an acceptable king or leader. Whether he is right or wrong about that, it means that when Victorinus goes on to say of the Antichrist: '*Finally, also, he will recall the saints, not to the worship of idols, but to undertake circumcision, and, if he is able, to seduce any;*' we can best understand it in a Post-Tribulation understanding. These saints aren't some new, special group, but the church of Jesus.

We have already noted that Victorinus was one of the first to take a Postmillenial position, and his teaching on this is found in his comments on Revelation 20. I will quote his comments on 20.1-3 in full, so you can see how he tries to do this. The important point is that, even though he has to make several fairly forced exegetical manoeuvres to do it, he combines his position on the Millennium with a fidelity to the apostolic teaching that the church would undergo the rule and terror of the Antichrist:

> *And I saw an angel come down from heaven, having the key of the abyss, and a chain in his hand. And he held the dragon, that old serpent, which is called the Devil and Satan, and bound him for a thousand years, and cast him into the abyss, and shut him up, and set a seal upon him, that he should deceive the nations no more, till the thousand years should be finished: after this he must be loosed a little season.* Those years wherein Satan is bound are in the first advent of Christ, even to the end of the age; and they are called a thousand, according to that mode of speaking, wherein a part is signified by the whole, just as is that passage, the word which He commanded for a thousand generations, although they are not a

> thousand. Moreover that he says, and he cast him into the abyss, he says this, because the devil, excluded from the hearts of believers, began to take possession of the wicked, in whose hearts, blinded day by day, he is shut up as if in a profound abyss. And he shut him up, says he, and put a seal upon him, that he should not deceive the nations until the thousand years should be finished. He shut the door upon him, it is said, that is, he forbade and restrained his seducing those who belong to Christ. Moreover, he put a seal upon him, because it is hidden who belong to the side of the devil, and who to that of Christ. For we know not of those who seem to stand whether they shall not fall, and of those who are down it is uncertain whether they may rise. Moreover, that he says that he is bound and shut up, that he may not seduce the nations, **the nations signify the Church**, seeing that of them it itself is formed, and which being seduced, he previously held until, he says, the thousand years should be completed, that is, what is left of the sixth day, to wit, of the sixth age, which subsists for a thousand years; after this he must be loosed for a little season. The little season signifies three years and six months, in which **with all his power the devil will avenge himself under Antichrist against the Church**. Finally, he says, after that the devil shall be loosed, and will seduce the nations in the whole world, and **will entice war against the Church,** the number of whose foes shall be as the sand of the sea.

Finally, Victorinus comments on chapters 21 and 22 together by commenting solely on chapter 21.16. Like our opening passage in chapter 1, his comments wouldn't in themselves absolutely preclude a Pre-Tribulation interpretation (since Pre-Tribbers often will say they accept the church goes through tribulation, just not *the* Tribulation), but it does blow away a central argument by showing what purpose tribulation has for the church, and given, as we have seen, that Victorinus clearly talked of the way the church would go through and be shaken or purified by the Great Tribulation, we can understand it as particularly referring to the church in that last Tribulation under the Antichrist:

> *And the city is placed in a square.* The city which he says is squared, he says also is resplendent with gold and precious stones, and has a sacred street, and a river through the midst of it, and the tree of life on either side, bearing twelve manner of fruits throughout the twelve months; and that the light of the sun is not there, because the Lamb is the light of it; and that its gates were of single pearls; and that there were three gates on each of the four sides, and that they could not be shut. I say, in respect of the square city, he shows forth the **united multitude of the saints, in whom the faith could by no means waver**. As Noah is commanded to make the ark of squared beams, that it might **resist the force of the deluge**, by the precious stones he sets forth the **holy men who cannot waver in persecution, who could not be moved either by the tempest of persecutors, or be dissolved from the true faith by the force of the rain**, because they are associated of pure gold, of whom the city of the great King is adorned. Moreover, the streets set forth **their**

> **hearts purified from all uncleanness**, transparent with glowing light, that the Lord may justly walk up and down in them

Like the New Testament, and like so many of the other church Fathers, Victorinus teaches that the purpose of the church going through the Tribulation under the Antichrist is specifically to weed out the tares from the church, from the kingdom of Jesus, and to purify the church to be a fit bride for Jesus to return to.

So, if anyone tells you that Victorinus taught the Pre-Tribulation rapture, they are most assuredly lying to you, no matter how sincerely they may believe it.

Macarius, and a change of situation

I came across a work by one Macarius whilst doing my research that mentioned the Antichrist. As far as I know, it hasn't been claimed in support of a Pre-Tribulation rapture, but I will cover it briefly here. The work is called Apocritis, by someone called Macarius, possibly Macarius the Magnesian, but very little is known about him, and there is much speculation as to who wrote it (be careful, as there were a number of prominent bishops and monks in the 4th Century called Macarius. I found a link to the article on a page that took it to be the work of St Macarius the Great who was a very influential hermit monk in Egypt, to whom many works have been ascribed). The work (what remains of it) is replies to a philosophical opponent of Christianity, and it has one brief reference to the Antichrist in Book 2, chapter 21, (see http://www.intratext.com/IXT/ENG1052/_PS.HTM). The relevant section reads: *'In fact, their relation may be compared with that of the divine Son and Father. As those who believe the Son are brought to the Father as His heirs, so those who believe the Slanderer are dragged from their true Father by that Antichrist, and brought to his father who is the opposite of God.'* The context is a discussion of John 8.43-4 where Jesus talks of Satan being 'the Father of lies'. It is not conclusive, but it does suggest a position more in line with Post-Tribulation positions, in that the writer obviously believes that the Antichrist persuades people from 'their true Father', meaning church members or saints who are persuaded away from the true faith. Since it is specifically the Antichrist that does this, the church must be around at the time of the Antichrist. In a Pre-Tribulation scenario, at the time of the Antichrist there may be people coming out of deception into the light and becoming those alleged 'Tribulation saints', but not the other way round. The church has already gone in that scenario.

So, if anyone tells you that Macarius taught the pre-tribulation rapture, they are lying to you, no matter how sincerely they may believe it.

Thus far, our survey of early church fathers has brought us to roughly the period when the Roman Emperor became a Christian, and persecutions against Christians per se ceased, at least in the Roman Empire. From now on, the church fathers – apart from a few on the fringes – lived in situations where the church had significant power and influence. The first few examples lived most of their lives, or had most of their ministries during a time when the memory of persecution was fresh, but the current reality was one of freedom from fear of persecution - unless you happened to be on the currently wrong side of the doctrine wars that engulfed Christianity in the Roman empire, with each side aiming to gain imperial support.

Athanasius

Athanasius was very much involved in these doctrine wars on the side of Orthodoxy, so much so that one of the major creeds of the church that endures to this day is named after him. His main opponents were Arius (whom he called the forerunner or Harbinger of the Antichrist, as did several of the church leaders at this time) and his followers, who harassed him greatly, so we have a great deal in his writings about them. He wrote a good deal, and nothing directly relevant to our subject to see, except that there is no indication at all that he thought that the church would escape the attentions of the Antichrist. He was writing primarily to oppose the Arians (who believed Jesus was not fully divine). He saw them as paving the way for the Antichrist to move against the church, which is inconsistent with any idea that the church will escape the Antichrist by means of a Pre-Tribulation rapture. You can look it up for yourself as this line of thinking is particularly strong in the last part of his work 'The History of the Arians', which you can read for yourself at the following webpage: http://www.newadvent.org/fathers/28158.htm . It is from this section that the only mention of Athanasius and the Antichrist occurs on the Pre-Tribulation Research Centre website, and even then they only are using it to argue against another approach to the end-times, not as proof of the Pre-Tribulation rapture. I have been unable to find anything online other than the occasional use of Athanasius in lists of names said to support a Pre-Tribulation rapture.

So, if anyone tells you that Athanasius taught the pre-tribulation rapture, they are lying to you, no matter how sincerely they may believe it.

(The Real) Ephrem the Syrian

(sometimes also pronounced Ephraem)

Ephraem was from a town called Nsibis, in Mesopotamia (roughly now Iraq), and ended up in Edessa (now in Turkey) which back then was a major centre of Christianity. You will frequently find him cited online as teaching a Pre-Tribulation rapture in the 4th Century. However, if you actually read what he wrote, there is no such reference. This is because, as most (not all) of these articles acknowledge, the relevant quote is from a much later work written in his name, and so is known as 'Pseudo-Ephraem'. I will deal with it in the time that it most likely comes from, long after the fall of the Western Roman Empire, probably at about the time of the rise of Islam against the church. If anyone tells you that Ephrem the Syrian / Ephrem of Nsibis teaches a Pre-Tribulation rapture, you can put them right in more than one way! (Some online videos do explicitly list the real Ephrem as teaching the rapture, as does at least one article on the Pre-Tribulation Research Centre site.)

Basil 'the Great' and the two Gregory's

('The Cappadocian Fathers')

Basil was a bishop in what is now Turkey, and is given the title 'the Great' by the Eastern Orthodox churches. He too, like Athanasius, was a powerful opponent of the Arian heresy, using both his powerful mind and his political connections to great effect, although originally he held a kind of compromise position. He was also one of the founders of Eastern monasticism. Even the Pre-Trib Research centre's chief mention of him acknowledges he was not a 'Pre-Tribulationist', so we will not spend much time on him at all. I searched much of his work online and could find no reference to end times, the antichrist and so on (but I did not look at his letters, 360 plus was a few too many for even me!). However, ironically enough, the single quote from the Pre-Trib Research centre contains a passage from one of his letters that it clearly demonstrates a Post-Tribulation position. It comes from his letter to the Alexandrians - http://www.newadvent.org/fathers/3202139.htm , Alexandria being a major centre of conflict between the Arian heretics and their opponents. The letter was written in response to major persecution of orthodox Christians by the Arians. It is worth quoting at length because it illustrates well an attitude to suffering that is more biblical than many modern Pre-Tribulation teachings, as well as demonstrating what can happen when Christians turn on each other, something Jesus predicted would happen in the last days before his return.

> I have already heard of the persecution in Alexandria and the rest of Egypt, and, as might be expected, I am deeply affected. I have observed the ingenuity of the devil's mode of warfare. When he saw that the Church increased under the persecution of enemies and flourished all the more, he changed his plan. He no longer carries on an open warfare, but lays secret snares against us, hiding his hostility under the name which they bear, in order that we may both suffer like our fathers, and, at the same time, seem not to suffer for Christ's sake, because our persecutors too bear the name of Christians. With these thoughts for a long time we sat still, dazed at the news of what had happened, for, in sober earnest, both our ears tingled on hearing of the shameless and inhuman heresy of your persecutors. They have reverenced neither age, nor services to society, nor people's affection. They inflicted torture, ignominy, and exile; they plundered all the property they could find; they were careless alike of human condemnation and of the awful retribution to come at the hands of the righteous Judge. All this has amazed me and all but driven me out of my senses. To my reflections has been added this thought too; can the Lord have wholly abandoned His Churches? Has the last hour come, and is 'the falling away' thus coming upon us, that now *the lawless one may be revealed, the son of perdition who opposes and exalts himself above all that is called God and is worshipped?* (2 Thessalonians 2:4) **But if the temptation is for a**

> **season, bear it, you noble athletes of Christ. If the world is being delivered to complete and final destruction, let us not lose heart for the present, but let us await the revelation from heaven, and the manifestation of our great God and Saviour Jesus Christ. If all creation is to be dissolved, and the fashion of this world transformed, why should we be surprised that we, who are apart of creation, should feel the general woe, and be delivered to afflictions which our just God inflicts on us according to the measure of our strength,** not letting us *be tempted above that we are able, but with the temptation giving us a way to escape that we may be able to bear it?* (1 Corinthians 10:13) Brothers, martyrs' crowns await you. The companies of the confessors are ready to reach out their hands to you and to welcome you into their own ranks. Remember how none of the saints of old won their crowns of patient endurance by living luxuriously and being courted; but all were tested by being put through the fire of great afflictions. For some had trial of cruel mockings and scourgings, and others were sawn asunder and were slain with the sword. These are the glories of saints. Blessed is he who is deemed worthy to suffer for Christ; more blessed is he whose sufferings are greater, since *the sufferings of this present time are not worthy to be compared with the glory that shall be revealed in us.* (Romans 8:18)

It is quite clear that, shaken by what had happened, Basil considered the possibility that they were near the time of the end that Paul talked of in 2 Thessalonians 2, yet he evidently had not even the slightest notion that the church would escape, but urged his readers to stand ready to suffer if it was indeed the last days. He is quite clear that what the saints were to wait for in such circumstances was not a secret rapture before the rise of the Antichrist, but the visible return of Jesus when the world would be transformed.

Basil was one of a set of three church fathers known as the 'Cappadocian fathers', named after the area they all came from. One was Gregory of Nanzianus, whom Basil met abroad and far from home, and journeyed with for several years, and the other was Basil's brother, Gregory of Nyssa, who was also a bishop and theologian. There is a brief reference to the Antichrist in one of Gregory of Nyssa's works, at the end of Book 11 of his 'Against Eunomius', a heretic whom he was refuting. You can read it at http://www.newadvent.org/fathers/290111.htm . The exact nature of the controversy is not important for our purposes, but how Gregory uses the concept of the Antichrist is. The relevant quote reads as follows:

> Do ye not perceive that he stirs himself up against the Name at which all must bow, so that in time the Name of the Lord shall be heard no more, and instead of Christ Eunomius shall be brought into the Churches? Do ye not yet consider that this preaching of godlessness has been set on foot by the devil as a rehearsal, preparation, and prelude of the coming of Antichrist? For he who is ambitious of showing that his own words are more authoritative than those of Christ, and of transforming the faith from the Divine Names and the sacramental customs and tokens to his

> own deceit,– what else, I say, could he properly be called, but only Antichrist?

His concern is about false teaching in the church, which he sees as a demonic rehearsal for the coming of Antichrist. He obviously had no conception of some separate group of Tribulation saints who should face the Antichrist. Rather, he believed that the Antichrist would not only deceive the world generally, but introduce heresy and false teaching into the Church, meaning that he assumed completely what we would call a 'Post-Tribulation' position.

So, if anyone tells you that any of the Cappadocian Fathers - Basil 'the Great', his brother Gregory of Nyssa or their friend Gregory Nanzianus believed or taught the pre-tribulation rapture, they are lying to you, no matter how sincerely they may believe it.

Cyril of Jerusalem

Cyril was roughly contemporary with the Cappadocian fathers we covered above. His major surviving work is his 'Catechetical lectures'. These were lectures designed for teaching new converts as they prepared for, or had just undergone, baptism. Interestingly, in this intensely practical work, there are numerous references to the Antichrist when it deals with the return of Jesus. The first mention is in the fourth lecture - http://www.newadvent.org/fathers/310104.htm - in the section on the judgement to come. The passage reads:

> 'This Jesus Christ who is gone up shall come again, not from earth but from heaven: and I say, not from earth, because there are many Antichrists to come at this time from earth. For already, as you have seen, many have begun to say, I am the Christ (Matthew 24:5): and **the abomination of desolation is yet to come,** assuming to himself the false title of Christ. But **look thou for the true Christ,** the Only-begotten Son of God, coming henceforth no more from earth, but from heaven, appearing to all more bright than any lightning and brilliancy of light, with angel guards attended, that He may judge both quick and dead, and reign in a heavenly, eternal kingdom, which shall have no end. For on this point also, I pray you, make yourself sure, since there are many who say that Christ's Kingdom has an end.

Just from this one fragment, we can notice that a Post-Tribulation position is at least implicit, since Cyril is teaching the new converts practical points to distinguish the true return of Jesus from that of an imposter, meaning that he thought that the church would face the Antichrist. There is no hint of the church escaping the Tribulation of that time. What is perhaps implicit here, is made absolutely explicit in his Fifteenth Catechetical lecture, which is devoted entirely to end time issues. It is too lengthy to quote in full, but you can read it here - http://www.newadvent.org/fathers/310115.htm .

Cyril starts out by focusing on the differences between the two comings of Jesus, saying of his two descents *'one, the unobserved, like rain on a fleece ; and a second His open coming, which is to be.'* Taken out of context that could almost be a description of the Pre-Tribulation rapture. I am almost surprised it isn't used by Pre-Tribulationists to claim Cyril as one of their own. However, the unobserved coming is not a 'secret rapture' but his first coming; the second will be an 'open coming'. No trace of a Pre-Trib rapture there, then!

Paragraph four is more explicit:

> But since it was needful for us to know the signs of the end, and **since we are looking for Christ,** therefore, **that we may not die deceived and be led astray by that false Antichrist**, the Apostles, moved by the divine will, address themselves by a providential arrangement to the True Teacher, and say, *Tell us, when shall these things be, and what shall be the sign of Your coming, and of the end of the world ?* We look for You to come again, but Satan transforms himself into an Angel of light; put us therefore on our guard, that we may not worship another instead of You. And He, opening His divine and blessed mouth, says, Take heed that no man mislead you. Do you also, my hearers, as seeing Him now with the eyes of your mind, hear Him saying the same things to you; Take heed that no man mislead you. And this word exhorts you all to give heed to what is spoken; for it is not a history of things gone by, but a prophecy of things future, and which will surely come. Not that we prophesy, for we are unworthy; but that the things which are written will be set before you, and the signs declared. Observe thou, which of them have already come to pass, and **which yet remain; and make yourself safe.**

There is practical need for his hearers to know the signs. Just like end-times preachers today, he cites the wars and unrests, famines and the like of his time as possible evidence. But he goes further in paragraph 7, noting something I rarely see in accounts of the end times now:

> But we seek our own sign of His coming; **we Churchmen seek a sign proper to the Church.** And the Saviour says, *And then shall many be offended, and shall betray one another, and shall hate one another.* (Matthew 24:10) If you hear that bishops advance against bishops, and clergy against clergy, and laity against laity even unto blood, be not troubled ; for it has been written before.... But the sign concerns not only rulers, but the people also; for He says, *And because iniquity shall abound, the love of the many shall wax cold.* (Matthew 24:12)

What comes next in paragraph 9 completely scotches any possibility of a Pre-Tribulationist position:

> And what comes to pass after this? He says next, *When therefore you see the abomination of desolation, which was spoken of by Daniel the Prophet, standing in the Holy Place, let him that reads understand.* And again, Then if any man shall say unto you, Lo, here is the Christ, or, Lo, there; believe it not. **Hatred of the brethren makes room next for**

> **Antichrist; for the devil prepares beforehand the divisions among the people, that he who is to come may be acceptable to them.** But God forbid that any of Christ's servants here, or elsewhere, should run over to the enemy! Writing concerning this matter, the Apostle Paul gave a manifest sign, saying, *For that day shall not come, except there came first the falling away, and the man of sin be revealed, the son of perdition, who opposes and exalts himself against all that is called God, or that is worshipped; so that he sits in the temple of God, showing himself that he is God. Do you not remember that when I was yet with you, I told you these things? And now you know that which restrains, to the end that he may be revealed in his own season. For the mystery of iniquity does already work, only there is one that restrains now, until he be taken out of the way. And then shall the lawless one be revealed, whom the Lord Jesus shall slay with the breath of His mouth, and shall destroy with the brightness of His coming. Even him, whose coming is after the working of Satan, with all power and signs and lying wonders, and with all deceit of unrighteousness for them that are perishing.* (2 Thessalonians 2:3-10) ...... This therefore is the falling away, and the enemy is soon to be looked for: and meanwhile he has in part begun to send forth his own forerunners , that he may then come prepared upon the prey. **Look therefore to yourself, O man, and make safe your soul. The Church now charges you before the Living God; she declares to you the things concerning Antichrist before they arrive**. Whether they will happen in your time we know not, or whether they will happen after you we know not; but it is well that, knowing these things, you should make yourself secure beforehand.

It is quite possible some of the new converts he was preaching to were Jews, since he was in Jerusalem, and Jews were still coming to the faith, although not in great numbers. However, Cyril made it clear in paragraph 11, contrary to what modern dispensationalists would have us believe, that the Antichrist would deceive both Jews and Gentiles. He said that the devil had prepared for the first coming by planting false fables about god's begetting among the pagans to try and discredit Jesus' divine conception, and goes on to say that similarly '*so now, since the true Christ is to come a second time, the adversary, taking occasion by the expectation of the simple, and especially of them of the circumcision, brings in a certain man who is a magician , and most expert in sorceries and enchantments of beguiling craftiness; who shall seize for himself the power of the Roman empire, and shall falsely style himself Christ; by this name of Christ deceiving the Jews, who are looking for the Anointed , and seducing those of the Gentiles by his magical illusions.*' In paragraph 12 he warns that the Antichrist will '*At first indeed ... put on a show of mildness (as though he were a learned and discreet person), and of soberness and benevolence:..... he shall afterwards be characterized by all kinds of crimes of inhumanity and lawlessness, so as to outdo all unrighteous and ungodly men who have gone before him; displaying against all men,* ***but especially against us Christians****, a spirit murderous and most cruel, merciless and crafty. And after perpetrating such things for three years and six months only, he shall be destroyed by the glorious second advent from heaven of the only-begotten Son of God, our*

Lord and Saviour Jesus, the true Christ, who shall slay Antichrist with the breath of His mouth , and shall deliver him over to the fire of hell.'

He calls this understanding the tradition of the church that had been handed down, including that the four beasts in Daniel's vision were the Babylonians, the Persians, the Greeks and the Romans. Like many early church fathers, he believed that the Antichrist would rebuild the Jerusalem temple for the Jews, going on in Chapter 15 to say that again that he would be *'at first indeed making a pretence of benevolence, but afterwards displaying his relentless temper, and that chiefly against the Saints of God.'*

In Chapter 16 he again makes it clear that the reign of the Antichrist and the teaching of Jesus about the need to flee refer to the church, not just Jewish believers:

> For this cause the Lord knowing the greatness of the adversary grants indulgence to the godly, saying, *Then let them which be in Judæa flee to the mountains.* (Matthew 24:16) But if any man is conscious that he is very stout-hearted, to encounter Satan, let him stand (**for I do not despair of the Church's nerves**), ... But, let **those of us** who are fearful provide for **our own safety**; and those who are of a good courage, stand fast: *for then shall be great tribulation, such as has not been from the beginning of the world until now, no, nor ever shall be.* (Matthew 24:21) But thanks be to God who has confined the greatness of that tribulation to a few days; for He says, *But for the elect's sake those days shall be shortened* ; and Antichrist shall reign for three years and a half only. We speak not from apocryphal books, but from Daniel; for he says, *And they shall be given into his hand until a time and times and half a time.* A time is the one year in which his coming shall for a while have increase; and the times are the remaining two years of iniquity, making up the sum of the three years; and the half a time is the six months. And again in another place Daniel says the same thing, *And he swore by Him that lives for ever that it shall be for a time, and times, and half a time.* (Daniel 12:7) And some perhaps have referred what follows also to this; namely, a thousand two hundred and ninety days ; and this, *Blessed is he that endures and comes to the thousand three hundred and five and thirty days.* **For this cause we must hide ourselves and flee;** for perhaps we shall not have gone over the cities of Israel, till the Son of Man be come Matthew 10:23 .

He says in paragraph 17 that the martyrs of that time will 'excel all martyrs':

> Who then is the blessed man, that shall at that time devoutly witness for Christ? For I say that the Martyrs of that time excel all martyrs. For the Martyrs hitherto have wrestled with men only; but in the time of Antichrist they shall do battle with Satan in his own person. And former persecuting kings only put to death; they did not pretend to raise the dead, nor did they make false shows of signs and wonders. But in his time there shall be the evil inducement both of fear and of deceit, so that if it be possible the very elect shall be deceived. (Matthew 24:24) Let it never enter into the heart of any then alive to ask, 'What more did Christ do? For by what power does this man work these things? Were it not God's will, He

> would not have allowed them.' The Apostle warns you, and says beforehand, '*And for this cause God shall send them a working of error*;' (send, that is, shall allow to happen;) not that they might make excuse, but that they might be condemned. Wherefore? They, he says, who believed not the truth, that is, the true Christ, but had pleasure in unrighteousness, that is, in Antichrist. But as in the persecutions which happen from time to time, so also then God will permit these things, not because He wants power to hinder them, but because according to His wont He will through patience crown His own champions like as He did His Prophets and Apostles; to the end that having toiled for a little while they may inherit the eternal kingdom of heaven....

In paragraph 18, he exhorts his new converts to:

> Guard yourself then, O man; you have the signs of Antichrist; and remember them not only yourself, but impart them also freely to all. If you have a child according to the flesh, admonish him of this now; if you have begotten one through catechizing , put him also on his guard, lest he receive the false one as the True. For the mystery of iniquity does already work. 2 Thessalonians 2:7 I fear these wars of the nations ; I fear the schisms of the Churches; I fear the mutual hatred of the brethren. But enough on this subject; only God forbid that it should be fulfilled in our days; nevertheless, let us be on our guard. And thus much concerning Antichrist.

He obviously did not teach, as the false teachers of the Pre-Tribulation rapture do today, that we should look for escape from the Tribulation, but warned his hearers to prepare for it. What they should look for was the visible return of Jesus, and for this he points in paragraph 19 to the very passage that the Pre-Tribulationists falsely claim support their position:

> But let us wait and look for the Lord's coming upon the clouds from heaven. Then shall Angelic trumpets sound; *the dead in Christ shall rise first* (1 Thessalonians 4:16)–the godly persons who are alive shall be caught up in the clouds, receiving as the reward of their labours more than human honour, inasmuch as theirs was a more than human strife; according as the Apostle Paul writes, saying, *For the Lord Himself shall descend from heaven with a shout, with the voice of the Archangel, and with the trump of God: and the dead in Christ shall rise first. Then we which are alive and remain shall be caught up together with them in the clouds, to meet the Lord in the air; and so shall we ever be with the Lord.*

He evidently had no problem in understanding this passage as referring to the visible return of Jesus. He then spends a number of paragraphs on the theme, placing this rapture passage at the time of the judgement of God on all men (paragraphs 20-21). Like many of the early church fathers, he believed that the visible return of Jesus would be preceded by a bright cross in the sky, the 'sign of the Son of Man in heaven' that would proclaim the identity of the returning King, the one crucified, a sign of joy to his own, but mourning and terror for those who did not. Paragraph 22 talks about this and concludes :

> For that His Elect may not be confused with His foes, *He shall send forth His Angels with a great trumpet, and they shall gather together His elect from the four winds.* (Matthew 24:31) He despised not Lot, who was but one; how then shall He despise many righteous? *Come, you blessed of My Father,* will He say to them who shall then ride on chariots of clouds, and be assembled by Angels.

In paragraph 23 he deals with the classic 'one shall be taken, one shall be left' passages as follows:

> But someone present will say, 'I am a poor man', or again, 'I shall perhaps be found at that time sick in bed'; or, 'I am but a woman, and I shall be taken at the mill: shall we then be despised?' Be of good courage, O man; the Judge is no respecter of persons; He will not judge according to a man's appearance, nor reprove according to his speech. He honours not the learned before the simple, nor the rich before the needy. Though you are in the field, the Angels shall take you; think not that He will take the landowners, and leave you the husbandman. Though you are a slave, though you are poor, be not any whit distressed; He who *took the form of a servant* despises not servants. Though you are lying sick in bed, yet it is written, *Then shall two be in one bed; the one shall be taken, and the other left.* (Luke 17:34)......He who brought forth Joseph out of slavery and prison to a kingdom, shall redeem you also from your afflictions into the kingdom of heaven. Only be of good cheer, only work, only strive earnestly; for nothing shall be lost. Every prayer of yours, every Psalm you sing is recorded; every alms-deed, every fast is recorded; every marriage duly observed is recorded; continence kept for God's sake is recorded; but the first crowns in the records are those of virginity and purity; and you shall shine as an Angel. But as you have gladly listened to the good things, so listen again without shrinking to the contrary. Every covetous deed of yours is recorded; your every act of fornication is recorded, your every false oath is recorded, every blasphemy, and sorcery, and theft, and murder. All these things are henceforth to be recorded, if you do the same now after having been baptized; for your former deeds are blotted out.

He then goes on to describe the Matthew 25 judgement seat of Christ for all the nations - in his view, the dead and the living (Paragraph 24) '*from Adam to this day*'. (Just as an aside, this passage goes on to refute the common notion today that the ancient church writers were not aware of just how small the earth was compared to the universe. He majors on this very point: *The whole earth is but as a point in the midst of the one heaven, and yet contains so great a multitude; what a multitude must the heaven which encircles it contain? And must not the heaven of heavens contain unimaginable numbers?*) This and paragraph 25 go on to warn of the judgement day and the need for holy living, for:

> '*you shall rise clothed with your own sins, or else with your righteous deeds.....*
>
> He shall separate them one from another, as the shepherd divides his sheep from the goats. How does the shepherd make the separation? Does he

> examine out of a book which is a sheep and which a goat? Or does he distinguish by their evident marks? Does not the wool show the sheep, and the hairy and rough skin the goat? In like manner, if you have been just now cleansed from your sins, your deeds shall be henceforth as pure wool; and your robe shall remain unstained, and you shall ever say, I have put off my coat, how shall I put it on ? By your vesture shall you be known for a sheep. But if you be found hairy, like Esau, who was rough with hair, and wicked in mind, who for food lost his birthright and sold his privilege, you shall be one of those on the left hand. But God forbid that any here present should be cast out from grace, or for evil deeds be found among the ranks of the sinners on the left hand!

The primary criteria, he notes in paragraph 26, is doing good and continuing to do good to the poor and suffering Christians whilst using your gifts and talents wisely and living faithfully and purely.

The next few paragraphs refute particular false views, mainly that Jesus will cease to reign after his enemies are put under his feet, before ending in paragraph 33 as follows:

> ..... But you, O hearer, worship only Him as your King, and flee all heretical error...... And may the God of the whole world keep you all in safety, bearing in mind the signs of the end, **and remaining unsubdued by Antichrist. You have received the tokens of the Deceiver who is to come; you have received the proofs of the true Christ, who shall openly come down from heaven. Flee therefore the one, the False one; and look for the other, the True**. You have learned the way, how in the judgment you may be found among those on the right hand; *guard that which is committed to you* (1 Timothy 6:20) concerning Christ, and be conspicuous in good works, that you may stand with a good confidence before the Judge, and inherit the kingdom of heaven:– Through whom, and with whom, be glory to God with the Holy Ghost, for ever and ever. Amen.

He leaves absolutely no room for anything even remotely resembling a Pre-Tribulation rapture, and makes clear he is speaking with the tradition of the church's interpreters. He was not proposing anything novel, but sticking with the old, the tried and tested. He warned against new false teachings, different to ours today, to be sure, but the Pre-Tribulation rapture is proving emphatically to be just such a new and false teaching.

So, if anyone tells you that Cyril taught a rapture before the Tribulation, by which the church escapes the Tribulation and the Antichrist, they are lying to you, no matter how sincerely they may believe it.

Jerome

One thing you may have noticed about Cyril of Jerusalem's teaching was that there was no mention of the Millennium, and that he held to just one judgement of all at the return of Jesus. He was almost certainly 'A-millennial' in his beliefs, and in the church at this time, this became more and more the prominent view, accompanied by, unfortunately, an increasingly vicious anti-semitism.

Such was the case with our next church father Jerome. He too held to an Amillennial position. He spent time in Rome, having to leave after some considerable controversies (accused of improper relations with a widow and of having caused the death of a popular young lady by so rebuking her for her lifestyle that she went to extreme asceticism and died months later) but ended up his days near Bethlehem in Judea, where he learned Hebrew from local Jewish Christians.

You will most often find Jerome used in the rapture debate by Pre-Tribulationists when they counter the charge that 'the word rapture isn't in the bible'. They will correctly say that neither is the word Trinity, but the bible teaches the Trinity nonetheless. You will very often find Jerome mentioned because he translated the bible into the Latin, in what is now known as the Vulgate translation, and he used the Latin word for 'seize' or 'snatch away' when translating the classic rapture passage in 1 Thessalonians 4. This Latin word is the one we get the word 'rapture' from.

However, Jerome himself provides some evidence on the issue of the church and the end times. We have at least a couple of references in his letters to the Antichrist, but mostly in contexts such as rebuking a deacon who had committed adultery and also tried to seduce a nun within the actual cave of Jesus' birth (*'like a new apostle of the Antichrist, when you are found out in one city you pass to another'*). The other reference is in his letter to Ageruchia, a noble widow in Gaul (now France) which can be read here - http://newadvent.org/fathers/3001123.htm . It is only a passing reference at the start of paragraph 16, since his main reason for writing was to persuade her not to marry again. It runs *'He that lets is taken out of the way, and yet we do not realize that Antichrist is near. Yes, Antichrist is near whom the Lord Jesus Christ shall consume with the spirit of his mouth. (2 Thessalonians 2:7-8) Woe unto them, he cries, that are with child, and to them that give suck in those days. (Matthew 24:19).* He follows this with a long list of woes about how the barbarians are overrunning both Gaul and Rome. He held to a view common among some church fathers, even before the time of Constantine, that when Paul in the 2 Thessalonians 2 passage quoted spoke of the one who hinders being taken out of the way to make way for the Antichrist he was referring to the Roman empire as that which restrained the coming of the Antichrist (as against modern dispensationalists who usually believe that the restrainer is the Holy Spirit or the Spirit in the church). We will cover his views in his commentary on Daniel below, but writing of Daniel 7.8 he says '*We should therefore concur with the traditional interpretation of all the commentators of the Christian Church, that at the end of the world, when the Roman Empire is to be destroyed, there shall be ten kings who will partition the Roman world amongst themselves.'* This is followed by a description of the rise of the Antichrist. Coming back to this letter, he asks the noble lady whether she should marry and have children again in disastrous times like the ones she was living in. For our purposes, what is clear is that passages that dispensationalists think should be kept separate, Jerome links together. Matthew 24.19 is one that Pre-Tribulatonists insist must refer only to Jews, and not to the church, which they believe will be absent, but Jerome applies it to a Christian woman, and makes it clear that he believes it has immense practical bearing on her present decisions because he believed that the time of the Antichrist was near. If he believed in any way that the church was to evade the Tribulation by means of a rapture event, his reasoning and argument would be totally pointless.

However, most of Jerome's references to the Antichrist occur - unsurprisingly - in his commentary on the book of Daniel (http://www.tertullian.org/fathers/jerome_daniel_02_text.htm). This was written in particular to refute the charges of a pagan opponent of Christianity called Porphry, who took a line followed in the last couple of centuries by modernist scholars. He said that the prophecies in Daniel were only accurate up to the time of the Maccabees (a Jewish priestly family who rebelled against pagan oppression about 150 years before Jesus) and that therefore the book had to be written about that time and was only pretending to be the prophet Daniel from an earlier age. Unlike the earlier commentary on Revelation we looked at, Jerome wrote a very detailed commentary. He actually wrote the commentary on the book of Daniel and the apocryphal additions as found in Roman Catholic bibles, although from a comment right at the end of his commentary, it seems he regarded the original Hebrew/Aramaic (the 12 chapters of Daniel as we know it) as canonical, but the rest as not fully canonical (properly belonging to the bible as the holy word of God). In it he repeatedly refers to the Antichrist as crushing the saints, particularly when commenting on Daniel 7, which states exactly that. Since pre-tribulationists believe this refers to the Jews and / or a special group of 'Tribulation saints', before looking in detail about what Jerome said about the saints and the antichrist, we should find out how Jerome used the term 'saints' in this work.

I found that Jerome used the term quite indiscriminately of both righteous Jews (those of the Old Testament such as Daniel and his friends, and those of the times after the Old Testament, such as the Maccabees) and of Christians (for instance, in his comments on Daniel 3.19 where he talks of 'Christ and His saints'). He quite often also refers to Jesus as the 'Saint of Saints'. However, when he is interpreting the crucial Daniel 7 verses, it is clear that he cannot be referring just to Jews, because he describes the saints who rule as ruling a heavenly, not an earthly kingdom. Since almost all dispensationalists believe that in the Millennium, the Jews and perhaps Tribulation Saints who have survived the Antichrist will rule an earthly kingdom, whilst Christian saints from the church age reign from a heavenly Jerusalem, this understanding of Jerome's cuts across most dispensationalist teaching. (Incidentally, he had no truck with any concept of a Millennium at all. He says in his comments on Daniel 7.17-8 *'But the saints shall never possess an earthly kingdom, but only a heavenly. Away, then, with the fable about a millennium!'*) He also in commenting on Daniel 7.25 clearly has the Jews and the saints existing at the same time, when he says *'During this period the saints are to be given over to the power of the Antichrist, in order that those Jews might be condemned who did not believe the truth but supported a lie.'* In fact, in discussing how Jerome used the term saints, we have pretty much answered the question of how he viewed the church in relation to the Antichrist - it is there when he is around, not somehow taken out of the way.

I will quote a few more passages that are relevant. For instance, when commenting on Daniel 11.32, Jerome says: *'But in my opinion this will take place in the time of the Antichrist, when the love of many shall wax cold. It is concerning these people that our Lord says in the Gospel, "Dost thou think that the Son of man, when He comes, will find faith upon the earth?" (Luke 18:8).* He quotes Jesus about the state of men's hearts during the Tribulation, and a parable which ends asking if Jesus will find faith on the earth when he returns. He comments on v33: '*But let no one doubt that these things are going to happen under the Antichrist, when many shall resist his authority and flee away in various directions.*' He mentions the purpose of the persecution when he deals with v34-5: *'Our writers, however, would have it understood that the small help shall arise under the reign of the Antichrist, for the saints shall gather together to resist him, and afterwards a great number of the learned shall fall. And this shall take place in order that they may be refined as by fire in the furnace, and that they may be made white and may be chosen out, until the time before determined arrives — for the true victory shall be won at the coming of Christ.'*

Modern dispensationalists will often make much of their belief that believing Jews in the Tribulation will flee to Petra, now in Jordan. In commenting on 11.40-1, Jerome says this is for the saints in general: '*The Antichrist also is going to leave Idumaea, Moab, and the children of Ammon (i.e., Arabia) untouched, for the saints are to flee thither to the deserts.*' Given the flexible way he used the words saints, he could mean primarily Jewish believers, but also given the way he uses the terms for the church under the Antichrist, it could just as easily refer to any believers in the area. Again, his comments on 12.11 indicate that he believed in both a restoration of the Jewish Temple and a simultaneous persecution of the saints (the church) under the rule of the Antichrist: *'... it is apparent that the three and a half years are spoken of in connection with the time of the Antichrist, for he is going to persecute the saints for three and a half years, or one thousand two hundred and ninety days, and then he shall meet his fall on the famous, holy mountain. And so from the time of the removal of the endelekhismos, which we have translated as "continual sacrifice," i.e., the time when the Antichrist shall obtain possession of the world (variant: the city) and forbid the worship of God, unto the day of his death the three and a half years, or one thousand two hundred and ninety days, shall be fulfilled.'*

One thing that is particularly useful in Jerome's commentary, is his dealing with the famous 'Seventy weeks' prophecy in Daniel 9, which is so central to dispensational and Pre-Tribulation doctrine. He notes that the passage had been much debated by others, so he was simply going to quote the different views he was aware of (including that of Jews) and let the reader decide. There was a quite wide range of interpretation, and lots of detailed examination of the best histories of the period they could find, as well as astronomical and calendrical calculations, much like today's debate on this subject. Most of the people quoted did not have anything directly relevant to say to the issue we are looking at, but there is one, Apollinarius of Laodicea (whom Jerome rightly thinks ventures into very unsafe waters because he predicted a particular future date for the events of the last of Daniel's weeks), who is of great interest, because he, like Jerome, seems to combine a belief in a literal rebuilt Temple with a belief that the saints of God (the church) will be around at the same time. The relevant quote from Apollinarius is as follows:

> '.....Jerusalem and the Temple shall be rebuilt during three and a half years within the final week, beginning with the advent of Elias, who according to the dictum of our Lord and Savior is going to come and turn back the hearts of the fathers towards their children. And then the Antichrist shall come, and according to the Apostle he is going to sit in the temple of God (II Thess. 2) and be slain by the breath of our Lord and Savior after he has **waged war against the saints**. And thus it shall come to pass that the middle of the week shall mark the confirmation of God's covenant with the saints, and the middle of the week in turn shall mark the issuing of the decree under the authority of Antichrist that no more sacrifices be offered. For the Antichrist shall set up the abomination of desolation, that is, an idol or statue of his own god, within the Temple. Then shall ensue the final devastation and the condemnation of the Jewish people, who after their rejection of Christ's truth shall embrace the lie of the Antichrist.

One more thing to note, as a sober warning; Jerome, in his letter to Nepotian, which you can read at http://www.newadvent.org/fathers/3001052.htm , makes one passing reference to the time of the end, indicating that many church leaders will become foolish and depart from wisdom: *...when our Lord in the gospel declares that in the end of the world– when the shepherd shall grow foolish, according to the prophecy of Zechariah (11.15) – the love of many shall wax cold, (Matthew 24:12).*

So, if anyone tells you that Jerome taught the pre-tribulation rapture, they are lying to you, no matter how sincerely they may believe it.

Rufinus

Rufinus was a particular object of Jerome's ire - and Jerome could get exceedingly iresome indeed! - since Jerome thought him a heretic, and it seems there was no love lost between them. However, in one of his surviving works, 'Commentary on the Apostles Creed' which you can read here -
http://www.newadvent.org/fathers/2711.htm , in paragraph 34, Rufinus talks of the Antichrist, and he does so by quoting several bible passages in such a way as to show he cannot have believed in a Pre-Tribulation rapture, but rather sought to warn his readers against being deceived by the Antichrist in very practical terms. The relevant passage reads as follows:

> Yet it behooves us to know that the enemy is wont to counterfeit this salutary advent of Christ with cunning fraud in order to deceive the faithful, and in the place of the Son of Man, Who is looked for as coming in the majesty of His Father, to prepare the Son of Perdition with prodigies and lying signs, that instead of Christ he may introduce Antichrist into the world; of whom the Lord Himself warned the Jews beforehand in the Gospels, *Because I have come in My Father's Name, and you received Me not, another will come in his own name, and him you will receive.* And again, *When you shall see the abomination of desolation, spoken of by Daniel the Prophet, standing in the holy place, let him that reads understand.* Daniel, therefore, in his visions speaks very fully and amply of the coming of that delusion: but it is not worthwhile to cite instances, for we have enlarged enough already; we therefore refer anyone who may wish to know more concerning these matters to the visions themselves. The Apostle also himself says, *Let no than deceive you by any means, for that day shall not come except there come a falling away first, and that man of sin be revealed, the Son of Perdition, who opposes and exalts himself above everything that is called God, or that is worshipped, so that he sits in the temple of God, showing himself as though himself were God.* And soon afterwards, *Then shall that wicked one be revealed, whom the Lord Jesus shall slay with the breath of His mouth, and shall destroy with the brightness of His coming: whose coming is after the working of Satan with all power and signs and lying wonders.* And again, shortly afterwards, *And therefore the Lord shall send unto them strong delusion, that they may believe a lie, that all may be judged who have not believed the truth.* For this reason, therefore, is this delusion foretold unto us by the words of Prophets, Evangelists, and Apostles, lest anyone should mistake the coming of Antichrist for the coming of Christ. But as the Lord Himself says, *When they shall say unto you, lo, here is Christ, or lo, He is there, believe it not. For many false Christs and false prophets shall come and shall seduce many.* But let us see how He has pointed out the judgment of the true Christ: *As the lightning shines from the east unto the west, so shall the coming of the Son of Man be.* When, therefore, the true Lord Jesus Christ shall come, He will sit and set up his throne of judgment. As also He says in the Gospel, *He shall separate the sheep from the goats, that is, the righteous from the unrighteous*; as the Apostle writes, *We must all stand before the judgment-seat of Christ, that every man may receive the awards due to the body, according as he has done, whether they be good or evil.* Moreover, the judgment will be not only for deeds, but for thoughts also, as the same Apostle says, *Their thoughts mutually accusing or else excusing one another, in the day when God shall judge the secrets of men.* But on these points let this suffice.

Having read this, simply ask yourself, is there any hint that Rufinus believed the church would escape the Tribulation. What's more, like his opponent Jerome, he has no problem in linking together passages that modern day 'Pre-Tribulation' proponents claim must refer to the rapture as a separate event to the visible return of Jesus. The prophecy of the abomination in the Temple has direct relevance for

Christians, because it is evidence that the delusion of the Antichrist is occurring. The sign of the true Christ is a very visible coming, says Rufinus, following the teaching of Jesus, something very different from the alleged 'secret' Pre-Tribulation rapture. If the church was to be raptured before the time of the Antichrist, all of this would be totally unnecessary.

Thus, if anyone tells you that Rufinus taught the pre-tribulation rapture, they are lying to you, no matter how sincerely they may believe it.

Ambrose

Ambrose was born into a wealthy family in Trier (on the border of modern day France and Germany), was educated in Rome and ended up a governor and then bishop (by popular acclaim when he hadn't even been baptized, thought a devout Christian) in Milan in northern Italy. We find several references to the Antichrist in his works. The first is passing, but rather telling, and occurs in Book 2, chapter 15 (para 135) of his work 'Exposition of the Christian Faith, which you can read here: http://www.newadvent.org/fathers/34042.htm . The context is a refutation of the powerful and influential Arian heresy, something that Ambrose had to deal with, like all the church fathers of his time. Ambrose says:

> John, likewise, says that heretics are Antichrists, plainly marking out the Arians. For this heresy began to be after all other heresies, and has gathered the poisons of all. As it is written of the Antichrist, that he *opened his mouth to blasphemy against God, to blaspheme His Name, and to make war with His saints*, (Revelation 13:6) so do they also dishonour the Son of God, and His martyrs have they not spared.

He calls his opponents Antichrists, and he compares them to *the* Antichrist as described in the book of Revelation who makes war with the saints, noting that the Arians similarly persecuted the true church. It would be very difficult for him to make such a linkage had he believed that the saints referred to in Revelation 13 were a very different group of Tribulation saints, as is held in the modern Pre-Tribulation position.

The other two references occur in his work 'On the Holy Spirit', one that attracted the fearsome ire of Jerome who spoke very disparagingly and unfairly of it. One has no bearing on our debate, but the other does, although by an indirect route. It occurs in book 3, chapter 7 (paragraph 44) of that work, which you can read at http://www.newadvent.org/fathers/34023.htm , during a detailed discussion of the relationship between and unity of Christ and the Holy Spirit and how they work together and not apart. Dispensationalists mostly believe that the Holy Spirit is somehow removed with the church at the Pre-Tribulation rapture, enabling the Antichrist to come to power. However, Ambrose here uses the very same passage (2 Thessalonians 2) in a way that strongly implies that the Holy Spirit must be present to weigh up the just judgement for the Antichrist. Here is the passage:

> But what should we say of the other points? We have heard that the Lord Jesus not only judges in the Spirit but punishes also. For neither would He punish Antichrist, whom, as we read, *the Lord Jesus shall slay with the Spirit of His mouth*, (2 Thessalonians 2:8) unless He had before judged of his deserts. Yet here is not a grace received, but the unity remains undivided, since neither can Christ be without the Spirit, nor the Spirit without Christ. For the unity of the divine nature cannot be divided.

Since Jesus is in heaven during the reign of the Antichrist, and yet there is undivided unity between Christ and the Spirit, then it is the Spirit who remains to guide Jesus Christ in his just punishment of the Antichrist, according to this view.

Hence, if anyone tells you that Ambrose taught the pre-tribulation rapture, they are lying to you, no matter how sincerely they may believe it.

Sulpitius Severus

No, not the name of a character from the darkside in Harry Potter; Severus was a priest who wrote chiefly in praise of his local bishop in what is now southern France, Martin of Tours (who originally was from Hungary). Martin had a reputation as a holy man, a defender of the poor and oppressed, and a worker of miracles, including raising the dead, healing those bitten by poisonous snakes and other similar healings. He was actually made bishop of Tours after being lured there by the ruse of asking him to come and pray for a sick person; instead, he was proclaimed bishop, a role he accepted only reluctantly.

There is a reference to the Antichrist in Sulpitius Severus' work 'On the Life of St. Martin', chapter 24, which you can read in full at http://www.newadvent.org/fathers/3501.htm . The passage goes:

> It was found, again, that about the same time there was a young man in Spain, who, having by many signs obtained for himself authority among the people, was puffed up to such a pitch that he gave himself out as being Elias. And when multitudes had too readily believed this, he went on to say that he was actually Christ; and he succeeded so well even in this delusion that a certain bishop named Rufus worshipped him as being the Lord. For so doing, we have seen this bishop at a later date deprived of his office. Many of the brethren have also informed me that at the same time one arose in the East, who boasted that he was John. We may infer from this, since false prophets of such a kind have appeared, that the coming of Antichrist is at hand; for he is already practicing in these persons the mystery of iniquity.

The passage then goes on to tell of a vision Martin had in which Satan tried to deceive him by portraying himself as Jesus, about to return. Back then, as now, all sorts of false teachers and prophets arose, who led people astray, and some of them declared themselves to be Christ himself. Severus' assessment is that these showed that the coming of the Antichrist was near. What is relevant to us is that it was the deception of people *within the church* that is taken as evidence that Satan is practicing for the coming of the Antichrist, which strongly suggests that the church will be there at the time of the Antichrist. Conclusive? No. But likely? Yes.

In another work, Dialogue 2 : Concerning the virtues of St Martin, after recounting several stories about St Martin, Severus goes on to quote the accounts and views of a 'Gallic friend' who spoke about St Martin's experiences and views (see http://www.newadvent.org/fathers/35032.htm). In the final chapter, this Gallic friend goes on to recount what Martin taught about the end times and the Antichrist, as follows:

> But when we questioned him concerning the end of the world, he said to us that Nero and Antichrist have first to come; that Nero will rule in the Western portion of the world, after having subdued ten kings; and that a persecution will be carried on by him, with the view of compelling men to worship the idols of the Gentiles. He also said that Antichrist, on the other hand, would first seize upon the empire of the East, having his seat and the capital of his kingdom at Jerusalem; while both the city and the temple would be restored by him. He added that **his persecution would have for its object to compel men to deny Christ as God**, while he maintained rather that he himself was Christ, and ordered all men to be circumcised, according to the law. He further said that Nero was to be destroyed by Antichrist, and that the whole world, and all nations, were to be reduced under the power of Antichrist, until that impious one should be overthrown by the coming of Christ. He told us, too, that there was no doubt but that Antichrist, having been conceived by an evil spirit, was already born, and had, by this time, reached the years of boyhood, while he would assume power as soon as he reached the proper age. Now, this is the eighth year since we heard these words from his lips: you may conjecture, then, how nearly about to happen are those things which are feared in the future.

Now putting aside notions that the Antichrist was alive at that time (and I have heard the same claims 1600 years later - who knows, this time it could be true), what is interesting, apart from the belief in the old Emperor Nero somehow being alive and having a rival kingdom to the Antichrist, is that the persecution of the Antichrist is specifically '*to compel men to deny Christ as God*'. This is hard to explain in a Pre-Tribulation position, where the church has been vanished and all that are left are those who haven't believed. Yes, some of them are supposed to come to believe, but why would the Antichrist start a persecution to make people deny Christ as God if most people left did not believe that. It makes much more sense that behind this understanding is a belief that the church will go through the Tribulation under the Antichrist.

There are also several references to the Antichrist in book 2 of Severus' work 'Sacred History' which can be read here - http://www.newadvent.org/fathers/35052.htm . One is just a brief mention in relation to the prophecies of Daniel, but the other two are more relevant and occur in chapters 28 and 33, as part of a long train of linked history. It starts out with reference to the quite bizarre, but as we have seen, rather common view that the emperor Nero, who was the first ruler to launch major persecution against Christians, would return at the time of the Antichrist.

> Luke made known the doings of the apostles up to the time when Paul was brought to Rome under the emperor Nero. As to Nero, I shall not say that he was the worst of kings, but that he was worthily held the basest of all men, and even of wild beasts. It was he who first began a persecution; and I am not sure but he will be the last also to carry it on, if, indeed, we admit, as many are inclined to believe, that he will yet appear immediately before the coming of Antichrist...... He first attempted to **abolish the name of Christian**, in accordance with the fact that vices are always inimical to virtues, and that all good men are ever regarded by the wicked as casting reproach upon them. For, at that time, our divine religion had obtained a wide prevalence in the city. Peter was there executing the office of bishop, and Paul, too.....

Chapter 29 recounts how Nero, blamed by the Roman populous for the great fire which devastated Rome, fastened upon Christians as a scapegoat to blame: *'In this way, cruelty first began to be manifested against the* ***Christians****. Afterwards, too,* ***their religion was prohibited*** *by laws which were enacted; and by edicts openly set forth it was* ***proclaimed unlawful to be a Christian****.'I*

There follows a long history of the persecution of Christians (and initially the Jews too):

> But on the opposite side, others and Titus himself thought that the temple ought specially to be overthrown, in order that the religion of the Jews and of the Christians might more thoroughly be subverted; for that these religions, although contrary to each other, had nevertheless proceeded from the same authors; that the Christians had sprung up from among the Jews; and that, if the root were extirpated, the offshoot would speedily perish. Thus, according to the divine will, the minds of all being inflamed, the temple was destroyed, three hundred and thirty-one years ago.

Chapters 32 and 33 detail the long series of nine persecutions under Roman emperors, from Nero through to the exceptionally severe persecutions just before the Roman Emperor Constantine converted to Christianity. Chapter 33 continues:

> Well, the end of the persecutions was reached eighty-eight years ago, at which date the emperors began to be Christians. For Constantine then obtained the sovereignty, and he was the first Christian of all the Roman rulers. At that time, it is true, Licinius, who was a rival of Constantine for the empire, had commanded his soldiers to sacrifice, and was expelling from the service those who refused to do so. But that is not reckoned among the persecutions; it was an affair of too little moment to be able to inflict any wound **upon the churches**. From that time, we have continued to enjoy tranquillity; nor do I believe that there will be any further persecutions, **except that which Antichrist will carry on just before the end of the world.** For it has been proclaimed in divine words, that the world was to be visited by ten afflictions; and since nine of these have

> already been endured, the one which remains must be the last. During this period of time, it is marvellous how the Christian religion has prevailed.....

It is quite clear from this, that he expected the attentions of the Antichrist would be upon Christians, just like all the preceding persecutions had been. Again, there was no notion of some separate group of 'Tribulation saints' who would endure his reign. Like all the other fathers, the position assumed here is one that we would call 'Post-Tribulational'.

Now, I don't remember seeing any claims that Martin of Tours or Sulpitius Severus taught the Pre-Tribulation rapture, but if anyone tells you that taught it, they are lying to you, no matter how sincerely they may believe it.

Hilary of Poitiers

Hilary was for a long time bishop of Poitiers in Western France, where he was born. I bring him up here to illustrate one more general point. In many of the church fathers about this time, battling, as did Hilary, against the Arian and other related heresies, we find references to their opponents as 'pre-cursors' or 'emissaries' of the antichrist, or indeed 'servants of their king, the Antichrist.' There are several instances of this type of accusation or styling in Hilary's major work 'On the Trinity', including this one in Book 2 : *'Let the preachers whose apostleship is of the newest fashion– an apostleship of Antichrist– come forward and pour their mockery and insult upon the Son of God.'* My simple point is this - if there was any expectation that the church would be snatched from the antichrist's afflictions by anything like a Pre-Tribulation rapture, such accusations would lose much of their rhetorical force, because they depend on a level of continuity between the current heretics and the final antichrist - in that both either do, or will, afflict and oppose the same one universal true church.

If anyone tells you that Hilary of Poitiers taught the pre-tribulation rapture, they are lying to you, no matter how sincerely they may believe it.

The Apostolic Constitutions

This was a work setting out the responsibilities of bishops especially, but also a number of aspects of church order, from probably about AD 400. It actually utilizes a lot of the Didache, the document with which we began, something that wasn't realized in modern times until separate copies of Didache were found. In book 7, chapter 32 (http://www.newadvent.org/fathers/07157.htm) we find a section lifted from Didache's final chapter and adapted. It reads as follows:

> For in the last days false prophets shall be multiplied, and such as corrupt the word; and the sheep shall be changed into wolves, and love into hatred: for through the abounding of iniquity the love of many shall wax cold. For men shall hate, and persecute, and betray one another. And then shall

> appear the deceiver of the world, the enemy of the truth, the prince of lies, (2 Thessalonians 2) *whom the Lord Jesus shall destroy with the spirit of His mouth,* who takes away the wicked with His lips; *and many shall be offended at Him. But they that endure to the end, the same shall be saved. And then shall appear the sign of the Son of man in heaven;* (Isaiah 11:4; Matthew 24) and afterwards shall be the voice of a trumpet by the archangel; and in that interval shall be the revival of those that were asleep. *And then shall the Lord come, and all His saints with Him, with a great concussion above the clouds, with the angels of His power,* (Matthew 24:27) in the throne of His kingdom, to condemn the devil, the deceiver of the world, and to render to everyone according to his deeds. Then shall *the wicked go away into everlasting punishment, but the righteous shall go into life eternal,* (Matthew 25:46) to inherit those things *which eye has not seen, nor ear heard, nor have entered into the heart of man, such things as God has prepared for them that love Him*; (1 Corinthians 2:9) and they shall rejoice in the kingdom of God, which is in Christ Jesus.

Whilst the original Didache has been adapted in several ways - probably chiefly to conform to the by now standard A-millennial understanding; hence the removal of specific reference to a resurrection of the righteous only - it emphatically retains an absolutely explicit Post-Tribulation position, placing the rapture after the Antichrist and at the time of Jesus' visible return.

So, again, although I don't believe I've seen anyone claim this, if anyone tells you that the Apostolic Constitutions teach the pre-tribulation rapture, they are lying to you, no matter how sincerely they may believe it.

Revelation of Esdras

No-one is sure when this work was written, but it is in the form of a vision about heaven and hell, which you can read here - http://www.newadvent.org/fathers/0829.htm . We find this passage in the description of hell:

> And they took me away to the north, and I saw there a man bound with iron chains. And I asked: 'Who is this?' And he said to me: 'This is he who said, I am the Son of God, that made stones bread, and water wine'. And the prophet said: 'My lord, let me know what is his form, and I shall tell the race of men, that they may not believe in him'. And he said to me: 'The form of his countenance is like that of a wild beast; his right eye like the star that rises in the morning, and the other without motion; his mouth one cubit; his teeth span long; his fingers like scythes; the track of his feet of two spans; and in **his face an inscription, Antichrist.** *He has been exalted to heaven; he shall go down to Hades.* (Matthew 11:23) At one time he shall become a child; at another, an old man'. And the prophet said: 'Lord, and how do You permit him, and he deceives the race of men?' And God said: 'Listen, my prophet. He becomes both child and

> old man, and no one believes him that he is my beloved Son'. **And after this a trumpet, and the tombs shall be opened, and the dead shall be raised incorruptible**. (1 Corinthians 15:52) Then the adversary, hearing the dreadful threatening, shall be hidden in outer darkness. Then the heaven, and the earth, and the sea shall be destroyed.

Ignoring all the bizarre stuff, very different to earlier claims (in other works the Antichrist is known by his deeds, but here he is known by his hideous form and apparently has 'Antichrist' stamped on his face, literally), the simple point is that the resurrection / rapture is explicitly described as being *after* the Antichrist.

The (Second) Revelation of St John

Again, no-one is sure exactly when this work was written, but the 5th Century is generally thought to be a good bet. It pretends to be a Revelation given to St John, but it has blatant parallels with the previous work we have just covered, as we shall see - you can read it here http://www.newadvent.org/fathers/0831.htm .

When I first scanned the work for the term 'Antichrist' I saw a passage that I was very surprised hadn't been used by Pre-Tribulationists, since it mentions the Antichrist after describing the rapture. But as usual, when looking at the context, this work, although bizarre in many ways, also maintains a Post-Tribulation position. In this work, firstly there will be great natural and agricultural abundance, followed by great famine. When God is asked what happens next, he says:

> Then shall appear the denier, and he who is set apart in the darkness, who is called Antichrist. And again I said: Lord, reveal to me what he is like. And I heard a voice saying to me: The appearance of his face is dusky; the hairs of his head are sharp, like darts; his eyebrows like a wild beast's; his right eye like the star which rises in the morning, and the other like a lion's; his mouth about one cubit; his teeth span long; his fingers like scythes; the print of his feet of two spans; and on his face an inscription, Antichrist; he shall be exalted even to heaven, and shall be cast down even to Hades, making false displays. And then will I make the heaven brazen, so that it shall not give moisture upon the earth; and I will hide the clouds in secret places, so that they shall not bring moisture upon the earth; and I will command the horns of the wind, so that the wind shall not blow upon the earth.

Like the previous work we looked at, the focus is on the alleged bizarre physical appearance of the Antichrist, not his deeds. The additional detail is that he rules at a time of famine and drought, something one or two other works also have taught. The work conforms to normal church thought by then describing the appearance of Enoch and Elijah. Then, contrary to all other documents, it claims that every single human on earth will die, but then they will all be resurrected at the sound of an angelic trumpet. Apparently there will be no more racial difference, all will be about the age 30 at the resurrection, and the unrighteous will not be able to recognize each other. It also teaches - in what other church fathers would call heresy - that the resurrection is not with actual physical bodies. God is then asked what happens next, and replies:

> **Then will I send forth mine angels over the face of all the earth, and they shall lift off the earth everything honourable**, and everything precious, and the venerable and holy images, and the glorious and precious crosses, and the sacred vessels of the churches, and the divine and sacred books; and **all the precious and holy things shall be lifted up by clouds into the air**. And then will I order to be lifted up the great and venerable sceptre, on which I stretched forth my hands, and all the orders of my angels shall do reverence to it. **And then shall be lifted up all the race of men upon clouds, as the Apostle Paul foretold. (1 Thessalonians 4:17) Along with them we shall be snatched up in clouds to meet the Lord in the air.** And then shall come forth every evil spirit, both in the earth and in the abyss, wherever they are on the face of all the earth, from the rising of the sun even to the setting, and they shall be united to him that is served by the devil, that is, Antichrist, and they shall be lifted up upon the clouds.

I am somewhat amazed, given the propensity of the Pre-Tribulation crowd for taking snippets out of context, that the bits in bold haven't been used to proclaim a belief in the rapture, but as far as I can find they haven't. From the context, it seems that the writer believes that there will be a kind of raising up to the heavens of all the dead, righteous and unrighteous, whilst the earth is destroyed, as the work goes on to say:

> Hear, righteous John. Then shall I send forth mine angels over the face of all the earth, and they shall burn up the earth eight thousand five hundred cubits, and the great mountains shall be burnt up, and all the rocks shall be melted and shall become as dust, and every tree shall be burnt up, and every beast, and every creeping thing creeping upon the earth, and every thing moving upon the face of the earth, and every flying thing flying in the air; and there shall no longer be upon the face of all the earth anything moving, and the earth shall be without motion.

This shows an obvious relationship of some sort with the previous work we looked at, since both are using similar language, although this work is more wordy. It goes on to say that God will send four winds that will sweep sin from the earth and flatten it completely, and then make it smell sweet ready for the descent of Jesus to earth with his angels, preceded by his heavenly sign, which the 'worker of iniquity with his servants' will see and be distressed (it doesn't explain how these have survived when earlier the whole of humanity died, unless these are the wicked resurrected).

Then Jesus and the angels do descend and punish the Antichrist and his servants. It then goes on to describe seven seals which when opened destroy the heavens and all in them (although this may be understood to be earlier on – this is revealed in response to a question from the visionary about what happens to the heavens).

God then answers questions about judgement, with the order being, the Antichrist and evil spirits, then pagans, then unbelieving Jews, and then Christians, those who have received baptism. Of these, the wicked are sent to hell, but the righteous to paradise, and then he will also bring his 'other sheep' - those who have not been baptised but have lived righteously - to paradise.

For our purposes, despite the bizarre language, and contradictions, the key point is that in this work too, the rapture / resurrection event comes after the Antichrist, and so is effectively Post-Tribulation in viewpoint.

Apocalypse of Elijah

This work is, somewhat unusually for this type of work, not written as if it were by the Old Testament figure, but is known by this title simply because Elijah is mentioned in it. It came from Egypt, and was probably written in its current form about 50 years either side of AD300 (some scholars believe there was an earlier Jewish original, heavily adapted). I have placed it here because it is an apocalyptic work like the two we have just covered. It features in just one quite recent article from the Pre-Tribulation Research Centre - http://www.pre-trib.org/articles/view/history-of-the-rapture-update . Interestingly, this article by leading Pre-Tribulation propagandist Thomas Ice, takes time to explain that Ice had previously come across the work and concluded it did not teach such a position, and thought it taught the rapture was after the Tribulation, but he goes on to cite a 2013 scholarly work by a lecturer and Bible Scholar called Francis X Gumerlock, Professor of Historical Theology at Providence Theological Seminary in Colorado Springs (I mention this because I checked, he is real, unlike the guy supposed to be saying the rapture was in the Dead Sea Scrolls!). I'd come across his name before because the Pre-Trib Research Centre has mentioned him several times in other contexts as someone who was not a Pre-Tribulationist, and so was a 'hostile witness' and therefore all the more credible when he writes about belief in a Pre-Tribulation rapture in church history. From his website, he certainly does appear to be a Post-Tribulationist, and he is cited most often in connection with 'Brother Dolcino' (see below) from a 1000 years later, which is the only text I have found that arguably *does* teach something like the Pre-Tribulation rapture. The article in question by Gumerlock is http://francisgumerlock.com/wp-content/uploads/Rapture-in-the-Apocalypse-of-Elijah-Gumerlock2.pdf . You can find the full text of the original in translation in several locations, none of them in the easiest to read formats - if you want to read it, pick your favourite format from these (the first two are the same translation) http://www.3-in-1.net/Pseudepigrapha/Apocalypse%20of%20Elijah/The%20Apocalypse%20of%20Elijah.htm ,
http://www.coptica.ch/apocalypse-of-elijah_alcock_2013.pdf
or an alternative translation at
https://archive.org/stream/pdfy-8kXMoCqhZarIc0pj/The%20Apocalypse%20Of%20Elijah_djvu.txt .

However, when I studied both Gumerlock's article and the original text, I have concluded that Thomas Ice's original assessment was correct, and that Gumerlock is in error here. Gumerlock labels the work 'a teaching similar to Pre-Tribulationism'. The work is reconstructed from several fragments from different languages (Greek, and ancient Egyptian dialects of what has now called the Coptic language). Chapter 1 starts out about how Jesus by his first coming 'had mercy upon you so that He might save us from the captivity of this age'. He talks of the importance of fasting in the process of overcoming and the end times reward:

> Remember that He has prepared thrones and crowns for you in heaven, saying, "Everyone who will obey Me will receive thrones and crowns among those who are Mine." The Lord said, "I will write My name upon their forehead and I will seal their right hand, and they will not hunger or thirst. Neither will the son of lawlessness prevail over them, nor will the thrones hinder them, but they will walk with the angels up to My city." .....
>
> Hear, O wise men of the land, concerning the deceivers who will multiply in the last times so that they will set down for themselves doctrines which do not belong to God, setting aside the Law of God, those who have made their belly their God, saying, "The fast does not exist, nor did God create it," making themselves strangers to the covenant of God and robbing themselves of the glorious promises. Now these are not ever correctly established in the firm faith. Therefore don't let those people lead you astray.
>
> Remember that from the time when He created the heavens, the Lord created the fast for a benefit to men on account of the passions and desires which fight against you so that the evil will not inflame you. ....The one who fasts continually will not sin although jealousy and strife are within him.....
>
> But a pure fast is what I created, with a pure heart and pure hands. It releases sin. It heals diseases. It casts out demons. It is effective up to the throne of God for an ointment and for a release from sin by means of a pure prayer. .... no one is able to enter the holy place if he is double minded. .....Therefore be single-minded in the Lord at all times so that you might know every moment.

Chapters two and three are prophecies about battles between Egyptian and Persian and Assyrian kings, who will invade Egypt and fight each other, the text says, reminding readers from the start that "now therefore <those who are Mine> will not be overcome" says the Lord, "nor will they fear in the battle." It describes the conflict and oppression in Egypt at that time in terms that make it quite clear this is the Great Tribulation, and it goes on to describe the actions of the Antichrist who arises in the middle of this conflict, and interestingly it describes before his time kings urging inter-religious union, saying 'The name of God is one' (there is lots in brackets because we have fragments and because in some cases the words were left just understood – these words in brackets are the translators / editors additions to help make it flow in English):

> And a king who will be called "the king of peace" will rise up in the west. 7.He will run upon the sea like a roaring lion. He will kill the king of injustice, and he will take vengeance on Egypt with battles and much bloodshed.
>
> It will come to pass in those days that he will command a p[eace] and a [vain] gift in Egypt. He will give] peace to these who are holy, [saying], "The name of [God] is one." [He will] give honours to the s[aints and] an exalting to the places of the saints. He will give vain gifts to the house of God. He will wander around in the cities of Egypt with guile, without their knowing. He will take count of the holy places. He will weigh the idols of the heathen. He will take count of their wealth. He will establish priests for them. ...
>
> Now I will tell you his signs so that you might know him .For he has two sons: one on his right and one on his left. .The one on his right will receive a demonic face, (and) he will fight against the name of God. Now four kings will descend from that king. In his thirtieth year he will come up to Memphis, (and) he will build a temple in Memphis. On that day his own son will rise up against him and kill him. The whole land will be disturbed. On that day he will issue an order over the whole land so that the priests of the land and all of the saints will be seized, saying, "You will repay doubly every gift and all of the good things which my father gave to you." He will shut up the holy places. He will take their houses. He will take their sons prisoner. He will order and sacrifices and abominations and bitter evils will be done in the land. He will appear before the sun and the moon. On that day the priests of the land will tear their clothes.

Conditions will be so bad that all economic transactions will cease and people will try and commit suicide.

> In those days, three kings will arise among the Persians, and they will take captive the Jews who are in Egypt. They will bring them to Jerusalem, and the will inhabit it and dwell there. Then when you hear that there is security in Jerusalem, tear you garments, O priests of the land, because the son of perdition will soon come. In those days, the lawless one will appear in the holy places –

At this time, the Persians assassinate the Assyrian King in Memphis:

> The Persians will take vengeance on the land, and they will command to kill all the heathen and the lawless ones. They will command to build the temples of the saints. They will give double gifts to the house of God. They will say, "The name of God is one." The whole land will hail the Persians. Even the remnant, who did not die under the afflictions, will say, "The Lord has sent us a righteous king so that the land will not become a desert..... In the fourth year of that king, the son of lawlessness will appear, saying, "I am the Christ," although he is not. Don't believe him! When the Christ comes, He will come in the manner of a covey of doves with the crown of doves surrounding Him. He will walk upon the heaven's vaults

> with the sign of the cross leading Him. The whole world will behold Him like the sun which shines from the eastern horizon to the western. This is how He will come, with all his angels surrounding Him. But the son of lawlessness will begin to stand again in the holy places.....

The passage goes on to describe all the deceptive miracles the Antichrist will do, concluding:

> He will multiply his signs and his wonders in the presence of everyone. He will do the works which the Christ did, except for raising the dead alone. In this you will know that he is the son of lawlessness, because he is unable to give life. For behold I will tell you his signs so that you might know him.

It then goes on to describe his bizarre physical appearance, and the fact that apparently he will be able to transform his appearance except for the bizarre hair on his head, by which we can know him. The reason I quote all of this is to show the context. If the writer really believes that the church will be raptured out of the way, why all the emphasis on the signs identifying the Antichrist?

Chapter 4 is a detailed and complex account of the end days. A New Testament female figure, Tabitha, is risen from the dead to confront the Antichrist before being slain by him, and then comes Enoch and Elijah to oppose the Antichrist who before they are slain by him, say:

> Are you indeed not ashamed? When you attach yourself to the saints,... you are always estranged. You have been hostile to those who belong to heaven. You have acted against those belonging to the earth.

After they are raised from the dead again, they say to him:

> "O shameless one, O son of lawlessness. Are you indeed not ashamed of yourself since you are leading astray the people of God for whom you did not suffer? Do you not know that we live in the Lord?...... we will kill you since you are unable to speak on that day because we are always strong in the Lord.

The Antichrist (the son of lawlessness) is angry and fights against them in Jerusalem, but:

> The son of lawlessness will not prevail over them. He will be angry at the land, and he will seek to sin against the people. He will pursue all of the saints. They and the priests of the land will be brought back bound. He will kill them and destroy them...

The passage goes on to describe the brutal tortures he inflicts on God's people and continues:

> Now those who are unable to bear up under the tortures of that king will take gold and flee over the fords to the desert places. They will lie down as one who sleeps. The Lord will receive their spirits and their souls to Himself. Their flesh will petrify. No wild animals will eat them until the last day of the great judgment. And they will rise up and find a place of

> rest, but they will not be in the kingdom of the Christ as those who have endured because the Lord said, "I will grant to them that they sit on my right hand."

Those who have endured are rewarded appropriately:

> They will receive favour over others, and they will triumph over the son of lawlessness. And they will witness the dissolution of heaven and earth. They will receive the thrones of glory and the crowns.

Then a further '60 righteous ones' prepared for this hour will run to Jerusalem to fight against the Antichrist, and he will burn them alive in sacrifice. I give this all for context, because it is only in the final fifth chapter that we have the alleged 'rapture passage'. Since it comes after a description of the Antichrist in Jerusalem and fighting against and slaying Enoch and Elijah as per the teaching of Revelation, with the torture and persecution of the saints, this can hardly be a Pre-Tribulation rapture can it?

The alleged 'Rapture passage' comes in 5.2-6 and reads as follows:

> On that day the Christ will pity those who are His own. And He will send from heaven his sixty-four thousand angels, each of whom has six wings. The sound will move heaven and earth when they give praise and glorify. Now those upon whose forehead the name of Christ is written and upon whose hand is the seal both the small and the great, will be taken up upon their wings and lifted up before his wrath. Then Gabriel and Uriel will become a pillar of light leading them into the holy land. It will be granted to them to eat from the tree of life. They will wear white garments...and angels will watch over them. They will not thirst, nor will the son of lawlessness be able to prevail over them.

I will quote chapter 5 in full later, but I will note that Gumerlock thinks this must be a separate rapture to the second coming because afterwards '*Eventually wildlife will die out and the sea will evaporate. Sinners will roam to and fro about the earth, searching for water but finding none. These sinners will regret that they followed the lawless one and will realize that they are experiencing the wrath of God.*' The Antichrist recognizes his time is short, turns into a dragon to try and pursue the saints in the air, but angels will rescue them. Then Enoch and Elijah return and slay the Antichrist, and Jesus and the saints descend to earth with Jesus. Even if the surmise is true that there is some period of time before the saints return with Jesus, this is clearly not a Pre-Tribulation position, but at best a 'Pre-Wrath' position (a position that states that the church goes through most of the Tribulation under the Antichrist, but is raptured before God's wrath is poured out at the very end).

However, Gumerlock believes in spite of this (he thinks that the clear allusions in chapter 5 to Revelation 12 means that likely this 'rapture' was believed to be 3 ½ years before the return of Jesus, what we would call a mid-tribulation position) this is analogous to modern Pre-Tribulation teaching. This is primarily because of the reason for the rapture given here. He says:

> In this text the rapture is portrayed as an act of compassion on the part of Christ (5.2). The author specifically stated the reason for the transport: so that the small and great who are sealed by Christ might be 'removed from the wrath' (5.4). After the saints are brought by the angels to safety, the text states that there in paradise, the lawless one will no longer 'have power over them' (5.6).

Apparently, one version of the text has those left behind talking about how they will die 'in famine and Tribulation'. For this reason, Gumerlock concludes we can call this a form of Pre-Tribulation rapture teaching, despite the detailed description earlier of the saints being tortured by the Antichrist. He goes on to deny other interpretations are possible:

> The rapture in the *Apocalypse of Elijah* is not for the purpose of standing before God for the last judgement, the view of most Catholics and mainline Protestants. Nor is it for the purpose of going out to meet the King as He is coming, as explained by some representatives of Eastern orthodoxy. Also this rapture is not for the purpose of escaping the grand conflagration of the heavens and the earth, as advocated by some early medieval Christians and some Puritan theologians like Cotton Mather and John Gill. Rather, like modern pretribulationism, its purpose is specifically related to removal from the wrath of the Antichrist and escape from the tribulation sent on the world by God in the last days..... With respect to its purpose, the rapture in the Apocalypse of Elijah shows closer affinity with the pretribulational view than with the posttribulational view.

I would first observe that it is quite possible for several of these views to be simultaneously true - the purpose could be both escape from God's wrath in the last day on the world and the Antichrist, whilst going to meet the King as he comes in wrath, and thus escaping the associated grand conflagration of the heavens and the earth. Indeed, I will go on to show that the most rational explanation of the chapter, despite its allusions to Revelation 12. I will also note that Gumerlock assumes that the 'holy land' the angels lead the saints to is paradise - heaven. This is presumably in part because v6 talks of these saints that *'it will be granted to them to eat from the tree of life. They will wear white garments... and angels will watch over them. They will not thirst, nor will the son of lawlessness be able to prevail over them.'* However, I suggest there are at least two valid alternative interpretations. Firstly, the context is just after the Antichrist has slain Enoch and Elijah, then been unable to defeat them when they were raised from the dead, and so turned his attention to persecution the saints and burning alive the 60 righteous ones. If he is about to enter into an even more vicious persecution of the church, then this is what Jesus will be rescuing them from. After all, he did say that he will *'cut short those days for the sake of the elect'* in the gospels. Secondly, as we shall see, when the Antichrist tries to pursue these saints, he does not pursue them to heaven, but into the desert, sending his followers when they complain that the land is barren because the righteous have left it, to '*run forth to the desert. Seize the robbers and kill them. Bring up the saints*'. When they appeal for his help, he '*will take his fiery wings and fly out after the saints. He will fight with them again. The angels will hear and come down. They will fight with him a battle of many swords.*' Why would the angels have to 'come down' and fight if the saints are already with the angels in heaven, even if we ignore the fact that the Antichrist pursues them into the desert, specifically. Pre-tribulationists say that the 'Tribulation saints' go into the desert in Jordan to escape the Antichrist - surely this is just something similar, especially when you see that the Archangels are described as leading the saints as '*a pillar of light leading them into the holy land*'. This is a reminder of how God rescued his people in the Exodus, and he led them initially *through the desert* and eventually to the holy land once they were purified, which is significant as we shall see.

In short, there is every reason to doubt Gumerlock and others' claims that here the saints are being raptured to heaven. This is especially when we consider the context, because then even the reference to them eating from the tree of life and the antichrist not prevailing over them and so on makes sense. Remember, in chapter 4, the text has noted that some who flee the antichrist into the desert and die there will find rest, but will not reign with Jesus. The text has now turned to those who have remained faithful, but are facing the Antichrist's wrath and have thus far not been slain. These are the ones that are given angelic protection and guidance to go out into safety in the desert places. In the language of Revelation they have overcome and so they *will* - notice the text describes their reward in the future tense - gain their reward. True, the whole passage as prophetic is in the future tense, but the simplest way to explain these references to paradise and the tree of life, against the rest of the text which clearly has an earthly destination for their rescue is that 5.6 is describing their future reward for faithful overcoming. They are moved to an area of physical safety whilst the wrath of God is poured out on the Antichrist, much as Lot and his family were so moved before the destruction of Sodom and Gomorrah, and Noah and his family were given physical safety in the Ark. In this way, the alleged long length of time is no problem for a Post-tribulation point of view, because this is not the rapture event.

But let us assume for the moment that this is indeed a supernatural rapture event where the saints go to meet Jesus in the air (elements conspicuously absent from the narrative, as even Gumerlock noted in his article), is it true to say that there *must* be a long length of time between this 'rapture' and the return of Jesus? I suggest probably not, and at this point we should perhaps quote the chapter in full, coming after the Antichrist's destruction of the righteous who opposed him in chapter 4, interspersed with my observations:

> And on that day the heart of many will harden and they will flee from him, saying, "This is not the Christ. The Christ does not kill the righteous. He does not pursue men so that he might seek them, but He persuades them with signs and wonders."

These could be deceived Christians or Jews, or even others who have started to realize that the Antichrist is not the promised Messiah, but I suggest that given the religious rational, these are either deceived Jews or Christians. Notice the '*on that day*'. It is true that the phrase can sometimes be used to mean a general period of time, but I suggest that as it repeatedly pops up with the most frequency in this final chapter because it is meaning this all happens within a day. It is actually quite possible, as we shall see.

> On that day the Christ will pity those who are His own. And He will send from heaven his sixty-four thousand angels, each of whom has six wings. The sound will move heaven and earth when they give praise and glorify. Now those upon whose forehead the name of Christ is written and upon whose hand is the seal both the small and the great, will be taken up upon their wings and lifted up before his wrath. Then Gabriel and Uriel will become a pillar of light leading them into the holy land. It will be granted to them to eat from the tree of life. They will wear white garments...and angels will watch over them. They will not thirst, nor will the son of lawlessness be able to prevail over them.

We have, of course, already discussed this in detail, but the passage goes on to describe what happens in that day:

> And on that day the earth will be disturbed, and the sun will darken, and peace will be removed from the earth. The birds will fall on the earth, dead. The earth will be dry. The waters of the sea will dry up. The sinners will groan upon the earth saying, "What have you done to us, O son of lawlessness, saying I am the Christ, when you are the devil? You are unable to save yourself so that you might save us. You produced signs in our presence until you alienated us from the Christ who created us. Woe to us because we listened to you. Lo now we will die in a famine. Where indeed is now the trace of a righteous one and we will worship him, or where indeed is the one who will teach us and we will appeal to him. Now indeed we will be wrathfully destroyed because we disobeyed YHWH. We went to the deep places of the sea, and we did not find water. We dug in the rivers and papyrus reeds, and we did not find water."

I think Gumerlock has allowed the prevailing mood of naturalism to colour his interpretation here. Firstly, there is no reason to think that the writers would have assumed naturalistic processes for the sea drying up and so on. The judgements of God displayed on the day of the Lord will be to display his awesome power and show that he is the Lord, not the Antichrist. More to the point, this looks like a culmination of processes – when the sinners complain to the Antichrist describing the previous activities to try and find water, which indeed may have taken some time, but they are only describing it now.

> Then on that day, the shameless one will speak, saying, "Woe to me because my time has passed by for me while I was saying that my time would not pass by for me. My years became months and my days have passed away as dust passes away. Now therefore I will perish together with you. Now therefore run forth to the desert. Seize the robbers and kill them. Bring up the saints. For because of them, the earth yields fruit. for because of them the sun shines upon the earth. For because of them the dew will come upon the earth." The sinners will weep saying, "You made us hostile to YHWH. If you are able, rise up and pursue them." Then he will take his fiery wings and fly out after the saints. He will fight with them again. The

> angels will hear and come down. They will fight with him a battle of many swords. It will come to pass on that day that the Lord will hear and command the heaven and the earth with great wrath. And they will send for fire. And the fire will prevail over the earth seventy-two cubits. It will consume the sinners and the devils like stubble. A true judgment will occur. On that day, the mountains and the earth will utter speech. The byways will speak with one another, saying, "Have you heard today the voice of a man who walks who has not come to the judgment of the Son of YHWH." The sins of each one will stand against him in the place where they were committed, whether those of the day or of the night. Those who belong to the righteous and ... will see the sinners and those who persecuted them and those who handed them over to death in their torments. Then the sinners [in torment] will see the place of the righteous. And thus grace will occur. In those days, that which the righteous will ask for many times will be given to them. On that day, YHWH will judge the heaven and the earth. He will judge those who transgressed in heaven, and those who did so on earth.

This is the apocalyptic final judgement, at the time Jesus returns, where the wrongs are avenged - the wicked are tormented and seen by the righteous they themselves had tormented, a classic reversal prophesied in both Old and New Testaments. Additionally, it is interesting to note that the Antichrist does just what Pharaoh did at the Exodus - he orders an army to go out and bring back the people of God who are fleeing under divine guidance - in the Exodus a pillar of fire and smoke, here two angels who are a pillar of light.

> He will judge the shepherds of the people. He will ask about the flock of sheep, and they will be given to Him, without any deadly guile existing in them.

If, as seems likely, this is a reference to judgement of the church, it is significant that it happens at the same time as the rest of the world, contrary to Pre-Tribulationist positions which say the church has already been judged in heaven.

> After these things, Elijah and Enoch will come down. They will lay down the flesh of the world, and they will receive their spiritual flesh.

This is a reference to the resurrection, the 'rapture' transformation. It is unclear how the writer squares this with the fact that these two have already died and been resurrected, although it is possible that he saw that resurrection as being back to the physical mortal body, as was the case with Lazarus.

> They will pursue the son of lawlessness and kill him since he is not able to speak. On that day, he will dissolve in their presence like ice which was dissolved by a fire. He will perish like a serpent which has no breath in it. They will say to him, "Your time has passed by for you. Now therefore you wand those who believe you will perish." They will be cast into the bottom of the abyss and it will be closed for them. On that day, the Christ, the King and all His saints will come forth from heaven. He will burn the earth. He will spend a thousand years upon it. Because the sinners

> prevailed over it, He will create a new heaven and a new earth. No deadly devil will exist in them. He will rule with His saints, ascending and descending, while they are always with the angels and they are with the Christ for a thousand years.

In short, everything in this passage is a description of the visible return of Jesus in triumph, and all the events could easily happen within a day through the supernatural power of God, but also some of the descriptions could describe the culmination of processes that had been ongoing for some time. Thus, if anyone tells you that the Apocalypse of Elijah teaches a Pre-Tribulation rapture, they are almost certainly lying to you, no matter how sincerely they may believe it.

John Chrysostum

John Chrysostum (the latter name was his nick-name 'Golden-mouth' for his preaching which frequently got applause from the congregation) was born originally in Antioch, a major centre of Christianity, and became bishop of Constantinople, the 'New Rome' of the East, before eventually being exiled and dying in rough circumstances (basically a forced march). We have a huge amount of written material from him, including hundreds of sermons. Aside from a couple of passing references, unsurprisingly, all of his teaching on the Antichrist is found in his commentaries or sermons on Matthew 24 and 1 and 2 Thessalonians.

The relevant comments on Matthew 24 are here
http://www.newadvent.org/fathers/200176.htm and here
http://www.newadvent.org/fathers/200177.htm.
John Chrysostum's approach to interpreting Matthew 24 is firstly to say that all references to the destruction and desecration of Jerusalem and the Temple are prophecies already fulfilled in the Roman invasion of AD70, several centuries before (v15-22). He interprets the verses beforehand as applying to that time too. This is a view that dispensationalists dislike greatly, called preterism. They believe these verses apply to a future set of events under the Antichrist, and they believe it applies solely to the Jews. Chrysostum also thought it solely applied to the Jews too, but for different reasons. He may have been nicknamed 'Goldenmouth', but unfortunately he was anything but goldenmouthed about the Jews, like most of the church fathers of his time. He interpreted the war against them in AD70 and the resulting exile as punishment for crucifying Jesus, one that would never end. He then interprets everything from v23 on as referring to the future, to the time of the Antichrist, noting:

> But mark how here He says nothing of war (for He is interpreting the doctrine concerning His advent), but of them that attempt to deceive. For some in the days of the apostles deceived the multitude, for they shall come, says He, *and shall deceive many*; (Matthew 24:11) and others shall do so before His second coming, who shall also be more grievous than the former. For they shall show, He says, *signs and wonders, so as to deceive if possible the very elect*: (Matthew 24:24) here He is speaking of Antichrist,

> and indicates that some also shall minister to him. Of him Paul too speaks on this wise. Having called him man of sin, and son of perdition, He added, *Whose coming is after the working of Satan, with all power and signs and lying wonders; and with all deceivableness of unrighteousness in them that perish.* (2 Thessalonians 2:9-10)
>
> And see how He secures them; Go not forth into the deserts, enter not into the secret chambers. He did not say, Go, and do not believe; but, Go not forth, neither depart there. For great then will be the deceiving, because that even deceiving miracles are wrought.

In other words, Jesus' command not to pay heed to alleged 'secret comings' of Jesus is what protects from deceptions, particularly at the time of the Antichrist, which is not an interpretation we would expect if Chrysostum believed that the church would escape by means of a 'secret rapture'. He then goes on to compare the coming of the Antichrist with the coming of Jesus:

> Having told them how Antichrist comes, as, for instance, that it will be in a place; He says how Himself also comes. How then does He Himself come? As the lightning comes out of the east, and shines even unto the west, so shall also the coming of the Son of Man be.... (Matthew 24:27-28)

He goes on to say that Jesus' return does not need a herald but is seen in the whole world. There is great tribulation for the believers, he says, because there are so many deceivers, before the final signs of the darkened sun in Matthew 24.49, but:

> ...it is not protracted to a length of time. For if the Jewish war was shortened for the elect's sake, much more shall this temptation be limited for these same's sake. Therefore, He said not, after the tribulation, but immediately after the tribulation of those days shall the sun be darkened, for almost at the same time all things come to pass. For the false prophets and false Christs shall come and cause confusion, and immediately He Himself will be here. Because no small turmoil is then to prevail over the world.....
>
> Do you see how fearfully He has pictured His coming? How He has stirred up the spirits of His disciples? For this reason, let me add, He puts the mournful things first, and then the good things, that in this way also He may comfort and refresh them. And of His passion He suggests to them the remembrance, and of His resurrection, and with a display of glory, He mentions His cross, so that they may not be ashamed nor grieve, whereas indeed He comes then setting it forth for His sign. And another says, They shall look on Him whom they pierced. Therefore it is that they shall mourn, when they see that this is He.
>
> And then again, He will send His angels with a great trumpet, and they shall gather the elect from the four winds, from one end of Heaven to the other. (Matthew 24:31)

So once again, the order is -Tribulation, then rapture. Chrysostum says the order is for the edification and comfort of believers, that good things will come; as well,

Chrysostum believes that the wars and conflicts are partly a warning to unbelievers of what awaits them, but also:

> by this again rousing the disciples, and indicating from how many evils they should be delivered, and how many good things they shall enjoy.
>
> And why now does He call them by angels, if He comes thus openly? To honor them in this way also. But Paul says, that they shall be caught up in clouds. And He said this also, when He was speaking concerning a resurrection. For 1 Thessalonians 4:16: *the Lord Himself,* it is said, *shall descend from Heaven with a shout, with the voice of an archangel.* So that when risen again, the angels shall gather them together, when gathered together the clouds shall catch them up; and **all these things are done in a moment, in an instant**. For it is not that He abiding above calls them, but He Himself comes with the sound of a trumpet. And what mean the trumpets and the sound? They are for arousing, for gladness, to set forth the amazing nature of the things then doing, for grief to them that are left.

This is Chrysostum's version of 'left behind'. He clearly ties in rapture passages about transformation in an instant with the return of Jesus with angels, and specifically says it is done that way to publicly honour the saints. Those who are left are the ones who face God's judgement, not in the Tribulation, but at the throne of judgement. Contrary to rapture-believers, he preached the importance of suffering for Christ's sake:

> And apart from these things, we should consider another point also, that even if we do not choose to suffer any of the things that are painful for Christ's sake, we must in other ways most assuredly endure them. For neither, though you should not have died for Christ, will you be immortal

Since Pre-Tribulationists make much of the issue of 'imminence', it is instructive to see how John Chrysostum interprets the classic passage that are, according to Pre-Tribbers, evidence of the doctrine of imminence.

> 'And that you may learn by another thing also, that the silence is not a mark of ignorance on His part, see, together with what we have mentioned, how He sets forth another sign also. But as in the days of Noe (Noah) they were eating and drinking, marrying and giving in marriage, until the day that the flood came, and took all away; so shall also the coming of the Son of Man be. And these things He spoke, showing that He should come on a sudden, and unexpectedly, and when the more part were living luxuriously. For Paul too says this, writing on this wise, *When they shall speak of peace and safety, then sudden destruction comes upon them; and to show how unexpected, He said, as travail upon a woman with child.* (1 Thessalonians 5:3) How then does He say, after the tribulation of those days? For if there be luxury then, and peace, and safety, as Paul says, how does He say, after the tribulation of those days? If there be luxury, how is there tribulation? Luxury for them that are in a state of insensibility and peace. Therefore He said not, when there is peace, but when they speak of peace and safety,

> indicating their insensibility to be such as of those in Noah's time, for that amid such evils they lived in luxury.

In other words, just as I explained in my previous book, 'Rapture Rupture' when I discussed the 'thief in the night' passages, the issue is not one of imminence, in the sense modern Pre-Tribbers believe, but immoral versus moral living. He goes on to say:

> But not so the righteous, but they were passing their time in tribulation and dejection. Whereby He shows, that when Antichrist has come, the pursuit of unlawful pleasures shall be more eager among the transgressors, and those that have learned to despair of their own salvation. Then shall be gluttony, then revellings, and drunkenness. Wherefore also most of all He puts forth an example corresponding to the thing. For like as when the ark was making, they believed not, says He; but while it was set in the midst of them, proclaiming beforehand the evils that are to come, they, when they saw it, lived in pleasure, just as though nothing dreadful were about to take place; so also now, Antichrist indeed shall appear, after whom is the end, and the punishments at the end, and vengeance intolerable; but they that are held by the intoxication of wickedness shall not so much as perceive the dreadful nature of the things that are on the point of being done. Wherefore also Paul says, as travail upon a woman with child, even so shall those fearful and incurable evils come upon them.

The flood of Noah's day should not have been unexpected, because Noah preached it was coming, but those who chose to disbelieve and continue in evil were taken by surprise, taken in their luxury and ease. He interprets Jesus' command to 'Watch, for you do not know the hour', not as the basis of a doctrine that Jesus could come at any moment, but as a practical guard against complacency:

> ....again He deters them from the inquiry, from a desire that they should be striving always. Therefore He says, *Watch,* showing that for the sake of this, He did not tell it......For this intent He tells them not, in order that they may watch, that they may be always ready; therefore He says, *When ye look not for it, then He will come,* desiring that they should be anxiously waiting, and continually in virtuous action. But His meaning is like this: if the common sort of men knew when they were to die, they would surely strive earnestly at that hour. In order therefore that they may strive, not at that hour only, therefore He tells them not either the common hour, or the hour of each, desiring them to be ever looking for this, that they may be always striving. Wherefore He made the end of each man's life also uncertain. After this, He openly calls Himself Lord, having nowhere spoken so distinctly. But here He seems to me also to put to shame the careless, that not even as much care as they that expect a thief have taken for their money, not even this much do these take for their own soul. For they indeed, when they expect it, watch, and suffer none of the things in their house to be carried off; but you, although knowing that He will come, and come assuredly, continue not watching, says He, and ready so as not to be carried away hence unprepared. **So that the day comes unto**

> **destruction for them that sleep.** For as that man, if he had known, would have escaped, so also ye, if you be ready, escape free.

This warning of Jesus is especially given for those who are teachers in the church, who should work to be found doing what Jesus wants when he returns, discharging their duties faithfully, and not stealing or embezzling; this return of Jesus is, as we have seen, according to Chrysostum 'after the Tribulation'. Similarly, the rich should be sharing their wealth with the poor, gaining reward on the day of judgement, when Jesus returns. Those who abuse their flock and live a life of dissolution will be the ones taken unawares and condemned. The issue of a bad servant (church minister) is not one of lack of knowledge, but evil intent: *it was not because the day is not known, but because the servant is evil.* The bad minister says that the Lord is delaying, and so finds justification for doing evil, but the faithful minister does not think like that. Chrysostum then goes on to cite passages that are supposed to teach 'imminence' (that Jesus can return at any time without warning). The purpose of the lack of knowledge of the timing is motivation to righteous living :

> What then is the purport of that which follows? *For He shall come in a day when he looks not for Him, and in an hour that he is not aware of*; (Matthew 24:50) and shall inflict upon him extreme punishment. Do you see how even everywhere He puts this, ... and by this making them always earnest minded? For this is the point at which He labors, that we should be always on the watch; and since it is always in luxury that we are supine, but in afflictions we are braced up, therefore everywhere He says this, that when there is relaxation, then come the terrors. And as further back He showed this by the example of Noah, even so here He says it is, when that servant is drunken, when he is beating, and that his punishment shall be intolerable.

God desires, Chrysostum goes on to say, giving to the poor, not living in luxury and '*pleasing the belly*'. He then spends a long time on the theme of living righteously and generously and with self-control in this life, especially in giving to the poor and using the gift we are given, concluding that he is:

> ...persuaded that it is not possible for one to be saved, who has not looked to the common good, and seeing this man that was cut asunder, and him that buried his talent, let us choose this way, that we may also attain unto eternal life, unto which God grant we may all attain, by the grace and love towards man of our Lord Jesus Christ, to whom be glory, world without end. Amen.

In short, Chrysostum's approach to the 'imminence' passages was much more in accord with the teaching of the New Testament than the modern-day dispensationalist approach. We may sum it up as follows: *The day and hour not being known is not to teach us that there are no signs before the end, but to motivate us to live the holy, obedient and vigilant life that will enable us to not miss the significance of the signs that God has ordained and warned us about.*

We know turn to John Chrysostum's interpretation of 1 Thessalonians 4 (the classic 'rapture' passage) and 5. You can read the relevant bits in his commentary for chapter 4 here - http://www.newadvent.org/fathers/230408.htm, and for the first parts of chapter 5 here - http://www.newadvent.org/fathers/230409.htm .

> Let us then see what he now also says. For this we say unto you by the word of the Lord, that we that are alive, that are left unto the coming of the Lord, shall in nowise precede them that are fallen asleep. For the Lord Himself shall descend from heaven, with a shout, with the voice of the Archangel, and with the last trump. For then, he says, *The powers of the heavens shall be shaken.* (Matthew 24:29) ..... This also Christ says in another place: *He shall send forth his Angels with a great trumpet, and they shall gather together his Elect from the four winds, from one end of heaven to the other.* (Matthew 24:31) And everywhere you see the Angels running to and fro. The Archangel therefore I think is he, who is set over those who are sent forth, and who shouts thus: 'Make **all men ready**, for the Judge is at hand'. And what is at the last trumpet? Here he implies that there are many trumpets, and **that at the last the Judge descends**. *And the dead,* he says, *in Christ shall rise first. Then we that are alive, that are left, shall together with them be caught up in the clouds, to meet the Lord in the air: and so shall we ever be with the Lord.....* If He is about to descend, on what account shall we be caught up? For the sake of honor. For when a king drives into a city, those who are in honor go out to meet him; but the condemned await the judge within. And upon the coming of an affectionate father, his children indeed, and those who are worthy to be his children, are taken out in a chariot, that they may see and kiss him; but those of the domestics who have offended remain within. We are carried upon the chariot of our Father. For He received Him up in the clouds, and we shall be caught up in the clouds. (Acts 1:9) Do you see how great is the honor? And as He descends, we go forth to meet Him, and, what is more blessed than all, so we shall be with Him.

From these comments alone, it is clear that Chrysostum takes a definitely Post-Tribulational position. He links in 1 Thessalonians 4 with Matthew 24.29 and 24.31, clearly identifying - contrary to the Pre-Tribulationists who insist these must be two separate events - the rapture of 1 Thessalonians 4 with the 'gathering of the elect' in Matthew 24 at Jesus' visible return after the Tribulation, as well as with the universal judgement (presumably because John follows most fathers of his time in denying a literal millennium and its associated two-stage resurrection). He goes on:

> 'Those who are dead are raised first, and thus the meeting takes place together. Abel who died before all shall then meet Him together with those who are alive. So that they in this respect will have no advantage, but he who is corrupted, and has been so many years in the earth, shall meet Him with them, and so all the others. For if they awaited us, that we might be crowned, as elsewhere he says in an Epistle, God having provided some better thing concerning us, that apart from us they should not be made perfect (Hebrews 11:40), much more shall we also await them; or rather, they indeed awaited, but we not at all. For the Resurrection takes place in a

moment, in the twinkling of an eye..... They are caught up **after the descent, after that they are gathered together**.

For this is also done without any one being aware. For when they see the earth agitated, the dust mingling, the bodies rising perchance on every side, no one ministering to this, but the shout being sufficient, the whole earth filled (for consider how great a thing it is that all the men from Adam unto His coming shall then stand with wives and children)–when they see so great a tumult upon the earth–then they shall know. As therefore in the Dispensation that was in the Flesh, they had foreseen nothing of it, so also will it then be.

When these things then are done, then also will be the voice of the Archangel shouting and commanding the Angels, and the trumpets, or rather the sound of the trumpet. What trembling then, what fear will possess those that remain upon the earth. For one woman is caught up and another is left behind, and one man is taken, and another is passed over. (Matthew 24:40-41; Luke 17:34-35) What will be the state of their souls, when they see some indeed taken up, but themselves left behind? Will not these things be able to shake their souls more terribly than any hell? Let us represent then in word that this is now present. For if sudden death, or earthquakes in cities, and threatenings thus terrify our souls; when we see the earth breaking up, and crowded with all these, when we hear the trumpets, and the voice of the Archangel louder than any trumpet, when we perceive the heaven shriveled up, and God the King of all himself coming near– what then will be our souls? Let us shudder, I beseech you, and be frightened as if these things were now taking place. Let us not comfort ourselves by the delay. For when it must certainly happen, the delay profits us nothing.

Here Chrysostum takes more classic 'rapture passages', about 'one shall be taken' and 'one shall be left', and actually uses the term 'left behind' at least once, but all explicitly at the Matthew 24 return of Jesus. Clearly, there was no concept of 'implications of imminence' in these verses for this Greek-speaking church father who lived so much closer in time of the apostles than we do, strongly suggesting he is closer than the Dispensationalists in understanding of the apostles teaching too. He then spends some time dealing with people who don't believe that the accounts of the return of Jesus or damnation and judgement are true, going on to explain that:

'On this account it is that He compares His coming with the days of Noah, because as some disbelieved in that deluge, so will they in the deluge of hell. Were these things a threat? Were they not a fact? Then will not He, who then brought punishment upon them so suddenly, much more inflict it now also? For the things that are committed now are not less than the offenses of that time. How?– because then, it says, the sons of God went in unto the daughters of men Genesis 6:4, and those mixtures were the great offense. But now there is no form of wickedness, which is unattempted. Do you then believe that the deluge took place? Or does it seem to you a

> fable? And yet even the mountains where the ark rested, bear witness; I speak of those in Armenia.
>
> But, even superabundantly, I will turn my discourse to another thing more evident than that. Has any one of you ever traveled in Palestine? For I will no longer mention report, but facts, and yet the other were clearer than facts. For whatever things the Scripture says, are more to be trusted than things we see. Has any one of you then ever traveled in Palestine? I suppose so. What then? Bear witness then for me, you who have seen the places, to those who have not been there. For above Ascalon and Gaza up to the very end of the river Jordan there is a country wide and fruitful– or rather there was– for it is not now. This then is that which was as a garden.

He goes on to describe the barren state of the Holy Land further, noting that just as the warnings and judgements against Sodom and Gomorrah were fulfilled, and the evidence is still there, so it is with the warnings about the last days - and he explicitly mentions those who 'love boys' especially citing in one breath both homosexuality and paedophilia, both of which are greatly increasing in our day. He goes on to warn that believers who continue in sin won't escape:

> Would you see those also punished, who were of the number of believers, and who held fast to God, but were not of upright life? Hear Paul saying, *Neither let us commit fornication, as some of them committed, and fell in one day three and twenty thousand. Neither let us murmur, as some of them murmured, and perished by the destroyer. Neither let us tempt Christ, as some of them tempted, and perished by the serpents.* (1 Corinthians 10:8-10) And if fornication, and if murmuring had such power, what will not be the effect of our sins?

If the Jews suffered for their rampant sins, how much more we who have Christ's salvation if we do the same, he says, listing many punishments for those who disobeyed God in the bible, including Ananias and Saphira, and yet many who do the same things have not yet been similarly punished, so surely their punishment must be coming at the end, concluding:

> I say not these things as wishing to frighten you, nor to lay a burden on your souls, but to make them wise, and render them easier. I could wish also myself that there were no punishment– yes, myself most of all men. And why so? Because while each of you fears for his own soul, I have to answer for this office also in which I preside over you. So that most of all it is impossible for me to escape. But it cannot be that there is not punishment and a hell. What can I do? Where then, they say, is the kindness of God to men? In many places. But on this subject I will rather discourse at some other season, that we may not confuse the discourses concerning hell. In the meantime let not that slip, which we have gained. For it is no small advantage to be persuaded concerning hell. For the recollection of such discourses, like some bitter medicine, will be able to clear off every vice, if it be constantly settled in your mind. Let us therefore use it, that having a pure heart, we may so be thought worthy to see those things, which eye has not seen, nor ear heard, nor have entered into the

> heart of man. Which may we all obtain by the grace and mercy of our Lord Jesus Christ, with whom, etc.

Chrysostum then turns to 1 Thessalonians 5.1-2 and one of the 'thief in the night' passages that Pre-tribbers insist 'prove' their particular doctrine about the rapture. In this sermon, he says God deliberately does not give the time of his return, just as he does not tell people the time of their own death, and for the same reason; so that people will work on righteousness because they do not know the time, otherwise people might live wickedly, planning to repent at the end:

> And if you would know on what account it is concealed, and why it so comes as a thief in the night, I will tell you how I think I can well account for it. No one would have ever cultivated virtue during his whole life; but knowing his last day, and, after having committed numberless sins, then having come to the Laver, he would so have departed. For if now, when the fear arising from its uncertainty shakes the souls of all, still all, having spent their whole former life in wickedness, at their last breath give themselves up to Baptism,– if they had fully persuaded themselves concerning this matter, who would ever have cultivated virtue? If many have departed without Illumination, and not even this fear has taught them, while living, to cultivate the things that are pleasing to God; if this fear also had been removed, who would ever have been sober, or who gentle? There is not one! And another thing again. The fear of death and the love of life restrain many. But if each one knew that tomorrow he would certainly die, there is nothing he would refuse to attempt before that day, but he would murder whomsoever he wished, and would retrieve himself by taking vengeance on his enemies, and would perpetrate ten thousand crimes.

He works to dissuade people from speculating about dates and times and to live in righteousness, but he combines this with a clear understanding that the rapture is at the end of the Tribulation, when wickedness will be great on the earth, saying:

> You see how many advantages there are, and yet there are more than these that arise from not knowing the time of our end. Meanwhile it is sufficient to learn these. On this account He so comes as a thief in the night; that we may not abandon ourselves to wickedness, nor to sloth; that He may not take from us our reward. *For yourselves know perfectly*, he says. Why then are you curious, if you are persuaded? But that the future is uncertain, learn from what Christ has said. For that on this account He said it, hear what he says, *Watch therefore: for you know not at what hour the thief comes.* (Matthew 24:42) On this account also Paul said,

He then goes on to verse 3 of chapter 5, and we see how he deftly unties what for Pre-Tribulationists is an alleged Gordian knot that proves this passage can't mean the return of Jesus at the very end. How does the day come as a thief in the night on those living in peace and safety if it is the public second coming of Jesus? He says, and he is worth quoting quite fully here:

Ver. 3. *When they are saying peace and safety, then sudden destruction comes upon them, as travail upon a woman with child; and they shall in nowise escape.*

Here he has glanced at something which he has also said in his second Epistle. For since they indeed were in affliction, but they that warred on them at ease and in luxury, and then while he comforted them in their present sufferings by this mention of the Resurrection, the others insulted them with arguments taken from their forefathers, and said, When will it happen?– which the Prophets also said, *Woe unto them that say, Let him make speed, let God hasten his work, that we may see it: and let the counsel of the Holy One of Israel come, that we may know it!* (Isaiah 5:19); and again *Woe unto them that desire the day of the Lord.* (Amos 5:18) He means this day; for he does not speak simply of persons who desire it, but of those who desire it because they disbelieve it: *and the day of the Lord,* he says, *is darkness, and not light*– see then how Paul consoles them, as if he had said, Let them not account their being in a prosperous state, a proof that the Judgment is not coming. For so it is that it will come.

But it may be worthwhile to ask, 'If Antichrist comes, and Elijah comes, how is it when they say *Peace and safety,* that then a *sudden destruction comes upon them*?' For these things do not permit the day to come upon them unawares, being signs of its coming. But he does not mean this to be the time of Antichrist, and the whole day, because that will be a sign of the coming of Christ, but Himself will not have a sign, but will come suddenly and unexpectedly. For travail, indeed, you say, does not come upon the pregnant woman unexpectedly: for she knows that after nine months the birth will take place. And yet it is very uncertain. For some bring forth at the seventh month, and others at the ninth. And at any rate the day and the hour is uncertain. With respect to this therefore, Paul speaks thus. And the image is exact. For there are not many sure signs of travail; many indeed have brought forth in the high roads, or when out of their houses and abroad, not foreseeing it. And he has not only glanced here at the uncertainty, but also at the bitterness of the pain. For as she while sporting, laughing, not looking for anything at all, being suddenly seized with unspeakable pains, is pierced through with the pangs of labor– so will it be with those souls, when the Day comes upon them.

Ver. 4. *But you, brethren, are not in darkness, that that day should overtake you as a thief.*

Here he speaks of a life that is dark and impure. For it is just as corrupt and wicked men do all things as in the night, escaping the notice of all, and inclosing themselves in darkness. For tell me, does not the adulterer watch for the evening, and the thief for the night? Does not the violator of the tombs carry on all his trade in the night? What then? Does it not overtake them as a thief? Does it not come upon them also uncertainly, but do they know it beforehand? How then does he say, 'You have no need that anything be written unto you?' **He speaks here not with respect to**

the uncertainty, but with respect to the calamity, that is, it will not come as an evil to them. For it will come uncertainly indeed even to them, but it will involve them in no trouble. That that Day, he says, may not overtake you as a thief. For in the case of those who are watching and who are in the light, if there should be any entry of a robber, it can do them no harm: so also it is with those who live well. **But those who are sleeping he will strip of everything, and go off; that is, those who are trusting in the things of this life.**

Ver. 5. *For you are all, he says, sons of light, and sons of the day.*

And how is it possible to be sons of the day? Just as it is said, 'sons of destruction' and ssons of hell'. Wherefore Christ also said to the Pharisees, *Woe unto you– for you compass sea and land to make one proselyte, and when he has become so, you make him a son of hell.* (Matthew 23:15) And again Paul said, *For which things' sake comes the wrath of God upon the sons of disobedience.* (Colossians 3:6) That is, those who do the works of hell and the works of disobedience. So also sons of God are those who do things pleasing to God; so also sons of day and sons of light, those who do the works of light. And we are not of the night nor of darkness.

Ver. 6, 7, 8. *So then let us not sleep, as do also the rest, but let us watch and be sober. For they that sleep sleep in the night; and they that be drunken are drunken in the night. But let us, since we are of the day, be sober.*

Here he shows, that to be in the day depends on ourselves. .... it is in our power always to have it day, it is in our power always to watch. For to shut the eyes of the soul, and to bring on the sleep of wickedness, is not of nature, but of our own choice. *But let us watch*, he says, *and be sober.* For it is possible to sleep while awake, by doing nothing good. ..... The drunkenness he here speaks of is not that from wine only, but that also which comes of all vices. For riches and the desire of wealth is a drunkenness of the soul, and so carnal lust; and every sin you can name is a drunkenness of the soul. On what account then has he called vice sleep? Because in the first place the vicious man is inactive with respect to virtue: again, because he sees everything as a vision, he views nothing in its true light, but is full of dreams, and oftentimes of unreasonable actions: and if he sees anything good, he has no firmness, no fixedness. Such is the present life. It is full of dreams, and of phantasy. Riches are a dream, and glory, and everything of that sort. He who sleeps sees not things that are and have a real subsistence, but things that are not he fancies as things that are. Such is vice, and the life that is passed in vice. It sees not things that are, that is, spiritual, heavenly, abiding things, but things that are fleeting and fly away, and that soon recede from us.

But it is not sufficient to watch and be sober, we must also be armed. For if a man watch and is sober, but has not arms, the robbers soon dispatch him. When therefore we ought both to watch, and to be sober, and to be armed, and we are unarmed and naked and asleep, who will hinder him from thrusting home his sword? Wherefore showing this also, that we have need of arms, he has added:

Ver. 8. *Putting on the breastplate of faith and love: and for a helmet the hope of salvation.*

Of faith and love, he says. Here he glances at life and doctrine. He has shown what it is to watch and be sober, to have the breastplate of faith and love. Not a common faith, he says, but as nothing can soon pierce through a breastplate, but it is a safe wall to the breast–so do thou also, he says, surround your soul with faith and love, and none of the fiery darts of the devil can ever be fixed in it. For where the power of the soul is preoccupied with the armor of love, all the devices of those who plot against it are vain and ineffectual. For neither wickedness, nor hatred, nor envy, nor flattery, nor hypocrisy, nor any other thing will be able to penetrate such a soul. He has not simply said love, but he has bid them put it on as a strong breastplate. And for a helmet the hope of salvation. For as the helmet guards the vital part in us, surrounding the head and covering it on every side, so also this hope does not suffer the reason to falter, but sets it upright as the head, not permitting anything from without to fall upon it. And while nothing falls on it, neither does it slip of itself. For it is not possible that one who is fortified with such arms as these, should ever fall. *For now abides faith, hope, love.* (1 Corinthians 13:13) Then having said, Put on, and array yourselves, he himself provides the armor, whence faith, hope, and love may be produced, and may become strong.

Ver. 9. *For God appointed us not unto wrath, but unto the obtaining of salvation through our Lord Jesus Christ, who died for us.*

Thus God has not inclined to this, that He might destroy us, but that He might save us. And whence is it manifest that this is His will? He has given His own Son for us. So does He desire that we should be saved, that He has given His Son, and not merely given, but given Him to death. From these considerations hope is produced. For do not despair of yourself, O man, in going to God, who has not spared even His Son for you. Faint not at present evils. He who gave His Only-Begotten, that He might save you and deliver you from hell, what will He spare henceforth for your salvation? So that you ought to hope for all things kind. For neither should we fear, if we were going to a judge who was about to judge us, and who had shown so much love for us, as to have sacrificed his son. Let us hope therefore for kind and great things, for we have received the principal thing; let us believe, for we have seen an example; let us love, for it is the extreme of madness for one not to love who has been so treated.

Ver. 10, 11. *That, whether we wake or sleep, he says, we should live together with Him. Wherefore exhort one another, and build each other up, even as also ye do.*

And again, whether we wake or sleep; by sleep there he means one thing, and here another. For here, whether we sleep signifies the death of the body; that is, **fear not dangers; though we should die, we shall live**. Do not despair because you are in danger. You have a strong security. He would not have given His Son if He had not been inflamed by vehement love for us. So that, though you should die, you will live; for He Himself also died. Therefore whether we die, or whether we live, we shall live with Him. This is a matter of indifference: it is no concern of mine, whether I live or die; for we shall live with Him. Let us therefore do everything for that life: looking to that, let us do all our works. Vice, O beloved, is darkness, it is death, it is night; we see nothing that we ought, we do nothing that becomes us. As the dead are unsightly and of evil odor, so also the souls of those who are vicious are full of much impurity. Their eyes are closed, their mouth is stopped, they remain without motion in the bed of vice; or rather more wretched than those who are naturally dead. For they truly are dead to both, but these are insensible indeed to virtue, but alive to vice..... Let us not be mad for external things, and we shall continue in sobriety. Let us discipline ourselves on every side. And as men who walk upon a tight rope cannot be off their guard ever so little, for that little causes great mischief: for the man losing his balance is at once precipitated down and perishes; so neither is it possible for us to be off our guard. We walk upon a narrow road intercepted by precipices on either side, not admitting of two feet at the same time. Do you see not how much carefulness is necessary? Do you see not how those who travel on such roads guard not only their feet, but their eyes also? For if he should choose to gaze on one side, though his foot stand firm, his eye becoming dizzy from the depth, plunges the whole body down. ..... Let us take heed to the narrow way, let us walk with fear and trembling. No one, who is traveling such a road, is dissolved in laughter nor heavy with drunkenness, but travels such a road with sobriety and fasting. No one traveling such a road carries with him any superfluities; for he would be contented even lightly equipped to be able to escape. No one entangles his own feet, but leaves them disengaged, and free to move.

But we, chaining ourselves down with numberless cares, and carrying with us the numberless burdens of this life, staring about, and loosely rambling, how do we expect to travel in that narrow road? He has not merely said that *narrow is the way* (Matthew 7:14), but with wonder, *how narrow is the way*, that is, exceedingly narrow. And this we also do in things that are quite objects of wonder. And straitened, he says, is the way which leads unto life. And he has well said it. For when we are bound to give an account of our thoughts, and words, and actions, and all things, truly it is narrow. But we ourselves make it more narrow, spreading out and widening ourselves, and shuffling out our feet. For the narrow way is difficult to every one, but especially to him who is incumbered with fat, as he who makes himself lean will not perceive its narrowness. So that he who has practiced himself in being pinched, will not be discouraged at its pressure.

> Let not any one therefore expect that he shall see heaven with ease. For it cannot be. Let no one hope to travel the narrow road with luxury, for it is impossible. Let no one traveling in the broad way hope for life. When therefore you see such and such an one luxuriating ... think not yourself unhappy, as not partaking of these things, but lament for him, that he is traveling the way to destruction. For what is the advantage of this way, when it ends in tribulation? And what is the injury of that straitness, when it leads to rest? Tell me, if any one invited to a palace should walk through narrow ways painful and precipitous, and another led to death should be dragged through the midst of the market-place, which shall we call happy? Which shall we commiserate? Him, shall we not, who walks through the broad road? So also now, let us think happy, not those who are luxurious, but those who are not luxurious. These are hastening to heaven, those to hell.

I have quoted him in full, partly because the sermon was so full and relevant to our days generally, but also to show how completely different he was in approach to the 'Pre-Tribulationists'. He has no notion of 'imminence' passages meaning a separate coming, but follows the New Testament pattern of teaching that it is immoral living that makes the day of Jesus' return come as a 'thief in the night'. He also leaves no place for the 'a loving Saviour won't let his church suffer' line of too many Pre-Tribulationists, but warns of the necessity of facing danger and death and narrow and hard places for the sake of Jesus. He also quite clearly interprets 'not appointed to wrath' as meaning eternal judgement, not the Tribulation, contrary to Pre-Tribulationists insistence that this 'proves' their theory about the church escaping the Tribulation. Once again this is, as I showed in 'Rapture Rupture', the teaching of the New Testament, and unlike the Dispensationalists, Chrysostum interprets the New Testament correctly in this regard.

We now turn to Chrysostum's treatment of 2 Thessalonians, another source of alleged 'proofs' of the Pre-Tribulation rapture. Like many preachers or commentators today, sometimes Chrysostum started with a general introduction to the book he is about to comment on, and so he does with 2 Thessalonians. You can read it in its entirety here: http://www.newadvent.org/fathers/23051.htm . He believed that the particular false belief that now faced the Thessalonians was the same as one that Timothy faced in Ephesus: 'as in his Epistle to Timothy he says, *They subvert the faith of some, saying that the Resurrection is already past* (from 2 Timothy 2:18); that the faithful henceforth hoping for nothing great or splendid, might faint under their sufferings.' These false teachers who had said that the resurrection had already happened, also said that '*the Judgment and the coming of Christ were at hand, that they might involve even Christ in a falsehood, and having pointed out to them that there is hereafter no retribution, nor judgment-seat, nor punishment and vengeance for those who had done them evil, they might both render these more bold, and those more dispirited.'* In other words, the rapture had already happened, and that the final judgement was happening ora bout to happen. They forged a letter or message from Paul to try and back up their false teaching. In response, in 2 Thessalonians, Paul '*comforts them, ... both praising them from their present state, and encouraging them from a prospect of the futurity, and from the punishment, and from the recompense of good things prepared for them; and* ***he more clearly enlarges upon the topic, not indeed revealing the time itself, but showing the sign of the time, namely, Antichrist.*** ' Chrysostum notes that Jesus himself gave '*many signs, one indeed, and that the most important, saying, when the Gospel shall be preached to all nations (from Matthew 24:14), and another also, that they should not be deceived with respect to His coming. 'As the lightning' (Matthew 24:27), He says, shall He come; not concealed in any corner, but shining everywhere. It requires no one to point it out, so splendid will it be, even as the lightning needs no one to point it out.*'

Once again, so much for 'imminence'. Chrysostum warns against deception over the Antichrist, or fascination with fables about his name (a timely warning for some in our own time, too), and notes : '*Paul therefore, in speaking of Antichrist, would not have passed over these things if they had been profitable. Let us not therefore enquire into these things. For he will ...come ... exalting himself against all that is called God, or that is worshipped; so that he sits in the temple of God, setting himself forth as God. (2 Thessalonians 2:4)* and saying that for this reason he begs his hearers to flee from the same sin of pride, a theme he goes on for the rest of the sermon with.

In the next sermon, http://www.newadvent.org/fathers/23052.htm , he talks about the righteous judgement of God in relation to persecuted Christians - showing that in chapter 1 Paul:

> 'comforts them, showing that from their own labors and toils they are crowned, and according to the proportion of righteousness. But he puts their part first. For although a person even vehemently desires revenge, yet he first longs for reward. For this reason he says,' *That ye may be counted worthy of the kingdom of God, for which you also suffer.*'
>
> This then does not come to pass from the circumstance that those who injure them are more powerful than they, but because it is so that they must enter into the kingdom. *For through many tribulations, he says, we must enter into the kingdom of God.* (Acts 14:22)

I include this, just to remind again of how different an interpretation the early church fathers had to the 'the church won't have to suffer in the Tribulation' mindset so much of the evangelical church has today.

Chrysostum goes on to exhort faithfulness and purity in the light of the coming judgement, which is coming on those who do not obey God, urging them to the fear of God by thinking on the judgement to come, and the nature of that judgement:

> If we always think of hell, we shall not soon fall into it. For this reason God has threatened punishment; if it was not attended with great advantage to think of it, God would not have threatened it. .... Let us not then overlook the great advantage arising from it, but let us continually advert to it, at our dinners, at our suppers. For conversation about pleasant things profits the soul nothing, but renders it more languid, while that about things painful and melancholy cuts off all that is relaxed and

dissolute in it, and converts it, and braces it when unnerved. He who converses of theatres and actors does not benefit the soul, but inflames it more, and renders it more careless. ... But he who converses about hell incurs no dangers, and renders it more sober.

But do you fear the offensiveness of such words? Have you then, if you are silent, extinguished hell? Or if you speak of it, have you kindled it? Whether you speak of it or not, the fire boils forth. Let it be continually spoken of, that you may never fall into it. It is not possible that a soul anxious about hell should readily sin. ...... A soul that is fearful of giving account cannot but be slow to transgression. Let us not remember the kingdom so much as hell. For fear has more power than the promise. ......No one of those who have hell before their eyes will fall into hell. No one of those who despise hell will escape hell. For as among us those who fear the judgment-seats will not be apprehended by them, but those who despise them are chiefly those who fall under them, so it is also in this case. If the Ninevites had not feared destruction, they would have been overthrown, but because they feared, they were not overthrown. If in the time of Noah they had feared the deluge, they would not have been drowned. And if the Sodomites had feared they would not have been consumed by fire. It is a great evil to despise a threat. He who despises threatening will soon experience its reality in the execution of it..... For the soul is a sort of wax. For if you apply cold discourses, you harden and make it callous; but if fiery ones, you melt it; and having melted it, you form it to what you will, and engrave the royal image upon it. Let us therefore stop up our ears to discourses that are vain. It is no little evil; for from it arise all evils.....For words are the road to works. First we think, then we speak, then we act. ..... For our soul is neither good nor evil by nature, but becomes both the one and the other from choice. As therefore the sail carries the ship wherever the wind may blow, or rather as the rudder moves the ship, if the wind be favorable, so also thought will sail without danger, if good words from a favorable quarter waft it. But if the contrary, often they will even overwhelm the reason. For what winds are to ships, that discourses are to souls. Wherever you will, you may move and turn it. For this reason one exhorting says, Let your whole discourse be in the law of the Most High. ......Let us not avoid discourses concerning hell, that we may avoid hell. Let us not banish the remembrance of punishment, that we may escape punishment. If the rich man had reflected upon that fire, he would not have sinned; but because he never was mindful of it, therefore he fell into it. .... When we are about to stand before a human tribunal concerning matters of this life, we move everything, we solicit all men, we are constantly anxious about it, we do everything for the sake of it: but when we are about, after no long time, to come before the Judgment-seat of Christ, we do nothing either by ourselves, or by others; we do not entreat the Judge. And yet He grants to us a long season of forbearance, and does not snatch us away in the midst of our sins, but permits us to put them off, and that Goodness and Lovingkindness leaves nothing undone of all that belongs to Himself. But

> all is of no avail; on this account the punishment will be the heavier. But God forbid it should be so! Wherefore, I beseech you, let us even if but now become watchful. Let us keep hell before our eyes. Let us consider that inexorable Account, that, thinking of those things, we may both avoid vice, and choose virtue, and may be able to obtain the blessings promised to those who love Him...

I have quoted this part quite fully, even though it isn't directly pertinent to our topic, partly because I think this is something that the church today often lacks, and partly to give context to what follows.

He carries on the theme in his next sermon http://www.newadvent.org/fathers/23053.htm , but also turns to the rewards of the righteous when Jesus returns. God is glorified in all the saints because when those who persecute the saints now see those they persecuted: '*it is His glory, or rather it is their glory, both theirs and His; His indeed, because He did not forsake them; theirs, because they* ***were thought worthy of so great honor****. For as it is His riches, that there are faithful men, so also it is His glory that there are those who are to enjoy His blessings... For through them He is shown to be admirable, when He brings to so much splendor those who were pitiable and wretched, and who had suffered unnumbered ills, and had believed. His power is shown then; because although they seem to be deserted here, yet nevertheless they there enjoy great glory;.... when those are brought into public view, who have suffered unnumbered ills, deigned to make them apostatize from the faith, and yet have not yielded, but have believed, God is glorified.....For tribulation for the sake of Christ is glory, and that thing he everywhere calls glory. And by how much the more we suffer anything dishonorable, so much the more illustrious we become. Then again showing that this also itself is of God, he says, according to the grace of our God and the Lord Jesus Christ; that is, this grace He Himself has given us, that He may be glorified in us, and that He may glorify us in Him. How is He glorified in us? Because we prefer nothing before Him. How are we glorified in Him? Because we have received power from Him, so that we do not at all yield to the evils that are brought upon us. For when temptation happens, at the same time God is glorified, and we too. For they glorify Him, because He has so nerved us; they admire us, because we have rendered ourselves worthy. And all these things are done by the grace of God.*'

Again, consider how different this approach is to many current day preachers of the Pre-Tribulation rapture, who boast about how the church will escape suffering, and how much closer this is to the teaching of Jesus and the apostles about suffering in the New Testament.

Chrysostum then turns to Chapter 2:

> 2:1, 2. *Now we beseech you, brethren, touching the coming of our Lord Jesus Christ, and our gathering together unto Him; to the end that you be not quickly shaken from your mind.*
>
> When the Resurrection will be, he has not said, but that it will not be now, he has said. And our gathering together unto Him. This also is no little matter. See how the exhortation also is again accompanied with

> commendation and encouragement, in that He and all the Saints will certainly appear with us. Here he is discoursing concerning the resurrection and our gathering together. For these things will happen at the same time.
>
> Here he seems to me to intimate that certain persons went about having forged an Epistle, as if from Paul, and showing this, said that **the Day of the Lord is at hand,** that thence they might lead many into error. Therefore that they might not be deceived, Paul gives security by the things he writes....

Notice that bit that I have put it in bold. Another legitimate translation would be that the false teachers were saying that 'the Day of the Lord is imminent', for 'at hand' essentially means 'imminence', exactly what Pre-Tribulationists preach and major on. Chrysostum describes the effects of such a belief system - it leads many into error. He goes on:

> Having therefore secured them on every side, he thus sets forth his own doctrine, and says:
>
> Ver. 3, 4. *Let no man beguile you in any wise: for it will not be, except the falling away come first, and the man of sin be revealed, the son of perdition, he that opposes and exalts himself against all that is called God or that is worshipped; so that he sits in the temple of God, setting himself forth as God.*
>
> Here he discourses concerning the Antichrist, and reveals great mysteries. What is the falling away? He calls him Apostasy, as being about to destroy many, and make them fall away. *So that if it were possible, He says, the very Elect should be offended.* (From Matthew 24:24)

This Antichrist:

> exalts himself against all that is called God or is worshipped. For he will not introduce idolatry, but will be a kind of opponent to God; he will abolish all the gods, and will order men to worship him instead of God, and he will be seated in the temple of God, not that in Jerusalem only, but also in every Church. Setting himself forth, he says; he does not say, saying it, but endeavoring to show it. For he will perform great works, and will show wonderful signs.

Paul, Chrysostum says, has to remind the Thessalonians of these things, just like in his first letter to them he had to remind them that when he was them in person he had warned them that we need to suffer tribulation and affliction (1 Thess 3.4), so he now needed to remind them of what he had already taught them.

He goes on to preach against the love of money and position and appearance, and against pride, but he takes our subject matter up in his next sermon (http://www.newadvent.org/fathers/23054.htm). He turns, first of all, to an obscure topic that is much discussed by Pre-Tribulationists today - the subject of 'the restrainer' in 2 Thessalonians 2:6-9 (which reads*: And now ye know that which restrains, to the end that he may be revealed in his own season. For the mystery of lawlessness does already work: only there is one that restrains now, until he be taken* *out of the way. And then shall be revealed the lawless one, whom the Lord Jesus shall slay with the breath of His mouth, and bring to nought by the manifestation of His coming: even he whose coming is according to the working of Satan*). Modern day dispensationalists usually say that this one who restrains is the Holy Spirit, which is theologically problematic, since the Holy Spirit sustains the universe, so His withdrawal would constitute the dissolution of the entire earth. Chrysostum actually finesses that suggestion so that it could work, by saying specifically that some in his day taught that it was the 'grace of the Spirit' that is removed (and this is almost certainly people who believed that the church would go through the Tribulation, since the early church taught nothing else, so it still leaves a potential problem for Pre-Tribulationists in that the Holy Spirit indwells believers by grace), but he still dismisses it:

> One may naturally enquire, what is that which withholds, and after that would know, why Paul expresses it so obscurely. What then is it that withholds, that is, hinders him from being revealed? Some indeed say, the grace of the Spirit, but others the Roman empire, to whom I most of all accede. Wherefore? Because if he meant to say the Spirit, he would not have spoken obscurely, but plainly, that even now the grace of the Spirit, that is the gifts, withhold him. And otherwise he ought now to have come, if he was about to come when the gifts ceased; for they have long since ceased. But because he said this of the Roman empire, he naturally glanced at it, and speaks covertly and darkly. For he did not wish to bring upon himself superfluous enmities, and useless dangers. For if he had said that after a little while the Roman empire would be dissolved, they would immediately have even overwhelmed him, as a pestilent person, and all the faithful, as living and warring to this end. And he did not say that it will be quickly, although he is always saying it– but what? that he may be revealed in his own season, he says,
>
> *For the mystery of lawlessness does already work.* He speaks here of Nero, as if he were the type of Antichrist. For he too wished to be thought a god. And he has well said, the mystery; that is, it works not openly, as the other, nor without shame. For if there was found a man before that time, he means, who was not much behind Antichrist in wickedness, what wonder, if there shall now be one? But he did not also wish to point him out plainly: and this not from cowardice, but instructing us not to bring upon ourselves unnecessary enmities, when there is nothing to call for it. So indeed he also says here. Only there is one that restrains now, until he be taken out of the way, that is, when the Roman empire is taken out of the way, then he shall come. And naturally. For as long as the fear of this empire lasts, no one will willingly exalt himself, but when that is dissolved, he will attack the anarchy, and endeavor to seize upon the government both of man and of God. For as the kingdoms before this were destroyed, for example, that of the Medes by the Babylonians, that of the Babylonians by the Persians, that of the Persians by the Macedonians, that of the Macedonians by the Romans: so will this also be by the Antichrist, and he

> by Christ, and it will no longer withhold. And these things Daniel delivered to us with great clearness.
>
> And then, he says, *shall be revealed the lawless one*. And what after this? The consolation is at hand. *Whom the Lord Jesus shall slay with the breath of His mouth, and bring to nought by the manifestation of His coming, even he whose coming is according to the working of Satan.*
>
> ...... (Christ) will put a stop to the deceit, by only appearing.

One thing to notice here, is that although Pre-Tribulationists are adamant that only a Pre-Tribulation rapture position offers consolation, in the last paragraph, Chrysostum explicitly says that when the Antichrist is revealed, then the consolation comes *'after this'* and applies it only to Jesus visible second coming, where he slays the Antichrist with the 'breath of his mouth'.

It is interesting that when Chrysostum talks about the deceit that stops people in the last times from believing in Jesus, it involves the very arguments that Islam uses against Christ and Christianity:

> Ver. 10. *And with all deceit of unrighteousness for them that are perishing.*
>
> Why then, you say, did God permit this to be? And what dispensation is this? And what is the advantage of his coming, if it takes place for the ruin of our race? Fear not, beloved.... What then is the advantage? That these very men who are perishing will be put to silence. How? Because both if he had come, and if he had not come, they would not have believed in Christ; He comes therefore to convict them. For that they may not have occasion to say, that since Christ said that He was God–**although He nowhere said this openly–but since those who came after proclaimed it, we have not believed. Because we have heard that there is One God from whom are all things, therefore we have not believed**. This their pretext then Antichrist will take away. For when he comes, and comes commanding nothing good, but all things unlawful, and is yet believed from false signs alone, he will stop their mouths. For if you believe not in Christ, much more ought you not to believe in Antichrist. For the former said that He was sent from the Father, but the latter the contrary. For this reason Christ said, I have come in My Father's name, and you receive Me not: if another shall come in his own name. him you will receive. (John 5:43) But we have seen signs, you say. But many and great signs were also wrought in the case of Christ; much more therefore ought ye to have believed in Him. And yet many things were predicted concerning this one, that he is the lawless one, that he is the son of perdition, that his coming is after the working of Satan. But the contrary concerning the other, that He is the Saviour, that He brings with Him unnumbered blessings.

Chrysostum goes on to make it quite clear that the faithful will be there in this hour, during the reign of the Antichrist, saying :

> But fear not. In those that perish he will have his strength. For Elijah too will then come to **give confidence to the faithful**, and this Christ says;

> *Elijah comes, and shall restore all things.* (Matthew 17:11) *Therefore it is said, In the spirit and power of Elijah.* (Luke 1:17) For he neither wrought signs nor wonders, as Elijah did. For John, it is said, did no miracle, but all things which John spoke of this Man were true. How then was it in the spirit and power of Elijah? That is, he will take upon him the same ministry. As the one was the forerunner of His first Coming, so will the other be of His second and glorious Coming, and for this he is reserved. Let us not therefore fear. He has calmed the minds of the hearers. **He causes them no longer to think present things dreadful but worthy of thankfulness.**

He talks of the need for great faith to be established and not shaken when commenting on v13-14:

> This too is no little thing, if Christ considers our salvation His glory. For it is the glory of the Friend of man that they that are saved should be many. Great then is our Lord, if the Holy Spirit so desires our salvation. Why did he not say faith first? Because even after sanctification we have yet need of much faith, that we may not be shaken. Do you see how He shows that nothing is of themselves, but all of God?

He uses the words of verse 15, which refers to whatever the Thessalonians had been taught by Paul, whether written or by spoken word to argue the need to heed church tradition, to avoid being one of those that are shaken in their faith, which I suggest we should start doing in regard to the end times, where the church tradition was completely unified in this issue of the church and the Antichrist and the Tribulation, as we have seen. Finally, he comments on v 16-17

> Now our Lord Jesus Christ Himself, and God our Father, which loved us, and gave us eternal comfort and good hope through grace, comfort your hearts, and establish them in every good work and word.
>
> Again a prayer after an admonition. For this is truly to benefit. Which loved us, he says, and gave us eternal comfort and good hope through grace. Where now are those who lessen the Son, because He is named in the grace of the Laver after the Father? For, lo, here it is the contrary. Which loved us, he says, and gave us eternal comfort. Of what sort then is this? Even the hope of things future. Do you see how by the method of prayer he stirs up their mind, giving them the unspeakable care of God for pledges and signs. Comfort your heart, he says, in every good work and word, that is, through every good work and word. For this is the comfort of Christians, to do something good and pleasing to God. See how he brings down their spirit. Which gave us comfort, he says, and good hope through grace. **At the same time he makes them also full of good hopes with respect to future things. For if He has given so many things by grace, much more things future.** I indeed, he says, have spoken, but the whole is of God. *Stablish;* confirm you, that you be not shaken, nor turned aside. **For this is both His work and ours, so that it is in the way both of doctrines, and of actions.** For this is comfort, to be established. **For when any one is not turned aside, he bears all**

things, whatever may happen to him, with much longsuffering; whereas if his mind be shaken, he will no longer perform any good or noble action, but like one whose hands are paralyzed, so also his soul is shaken, when it is not fully persuaded that it is advancing to some good end.

I include this last comment in full, because it shows - contrary to Pre-Tribulationists - who preach that anyone denying their dispensationalist doctrine on this matter is robbing people of the 'Blessed Hope' and fear-mongering - how one can preach about the Tribulation and what the church will endure whilst still maintaining hope. The church should stand firm in its tradition and doctrines, he says, and doing good and pleasing God, for there is great grace and hope to come. People should stand firm and not be turned aside in evil days either from true doctrine, or true actions. Amen.

So, there is not a hint of a rapture in Chrysostum; if anyone tells you that Chrysostum taught the pre-tribulation rapture, they are lying to you, no matter how sincerely they may believe it.

Augustine

Augustine was a contemporary of John Chrysostum from North Africa, and like him wrote an immense amount that has survived (in fact, we have numerous letters they wrote to each other). John Chrysostum was in a way one of the founding fathers of Eastern Orthodox churches, and similarly Augustine's teaching and doctrine became foundational for and instrumental in the formation of what we now call the Roman Catholic church and Western Christian civilization. His father was pagan until he converted on his deathbed, his mother Christian. Augustine was raised a Christian, but his education led to him turning to the pagan Manichean religious belief system; however in his very early 30's he returned to faith in Christ whilst in Italy and became a priest and then bishop in Hippo, in North Africa, with hundreds of his sermons preserved. Soon after his death, the city was burned by pagan tribes who had converted to the heretical Arian form of Christianity, but they spared Augustine's cathedral and library, thus letting much of his work survive to this day. He combated slavery, and also violence against Jews, but is most well known for his formulation of the concept of 'Original sin'. As I said, like Chrysostum, a huge amount of his writings have been preserved, probably reflecting how immensely influential and foundational he was to Western theological thought. And he wrote a lot - just one of his most famous works, Confessions, had 13 books, totalling 276 chapters!

Augustine is mentioned numerous times on the Pre-Tribulation Research Centre site, but never as teaching the rapture. Instead, they focus on his role as 'the father of amillennialism'. Originally, Augustine believed in the Millennium as an actual thousand year of Jesus (pre-millienialism) but later changed to an amillennial view. (One of the reasons was apparently the perception that the proponents of 'Chilialism' which we today would call pre-millennialism' where focusing on the earthly delights of feasting and drinking involved.) Augustine wasn't the originator of the a (or post) millennial position, but some have dubbed him 'the father of amillennialism' because he was so influential in shaping the views of the Western church in particular. After his time, the church teaching was absolutely dominated by amillennialism up until at least the Reformation.

We will first look at his seminal work, 'City of God'. The very first reference we come to is clearly post-tribulational; a passing reference in book 16 (http://www.newadvent.org/fathers/120116.htm) chapter 24, where Augustine is discussing the 'binding of Isaac' in Genesis 22. He says:

> When it is added, *And when the sun was now setting there was a flame, and lo, a smoking furnace, and lamps of fire, which passed through between those pieces*, this signifies that at the end of the world the carnal shall be judged by fire. **For just as the affliction of the city of God, such as never was before, which is expected to take place under Antichrist**, was signified by Abraham's horror of great darkness about the going down of the sun, that is, when the end of the world draws near–so at the going down of the sun, that is, at the very end of the world, there is signified by that fire the day of judgment, which separates the carnal who are to be saved by fire from those who are to be condemned in the fire.

For Augustine, the city of God in these days means primarily the church, Christians, so he clearly expects them to be afflicted terribly under the Antichrist. Augustine says similar things in book 18 (http://www.newadvent.org/fathers/120118.htm) chapters 52 and 53, where he starts by discussing the idea some had that there would be no more persecution until the antichrist. Again, he is quite explicitly post-tribulation in understanding:

> I do not think, indeed, that what some have thought or may think is rashly said or believed, that **until the time of Antichrist the Church of Christ** is not to suffer any persecutions besides those she has already suffered–that is, ten–**and that the eleventh and last shall be inflicted by Antichrist.** They reckon as the first that made by Nero, the second by Domitian, the third by Trajan, the fourth by Antoninus, the fifth by Severus, the sixth by Maximin, the seventh by Decius, the eighth by Valerian, the ninth by Aurelian, the tenth by Diocletian and Maximian. For as there were ten plagues in Egypt before the people of God could begin to go out, they think this is to be referred to as showing **that the last persecution by Antichrist** must be like the eleventh plague, in which the Egyptians, while following the Hebrews with hostility, perished in the Red Sea when the people of God passed through on dry land.

After discussing why this belief about the 11 persecutions is incorrect, he goes on to say:

> **Truly Jesus Himself shall extinguish by His presence that last persecution which is to be made by Antichrist**. For so it is written, that *He shall slay him with the breath of His mouth,* and empty him with the brightness of His presence. It is customary to ask, 'When shall that be?'

> But this is quite unreasonable. For had it been profitable for us to know this, by whom could it better have been told than by God Himself, the Master, when the disciples questioned Him? For they were not silent when with Him, but inquired of Him, saying, *Lord, will You at this time present the kingdom to Israel, or when?* (Acts 1:6-7) But He said, *It is not for you to know the times, which the Father has put in His own power.*

Here he quotes 2 Thessalonians 2, and since he states that the Antichrist will be behind the last persecution of the church, he is therefore again teaching an explicitly post-Tribulation position.

Book 20 has numerous references to the Antichrist, starting with this in chapters 12 and 13:

> In this place *fire out of heaven* is well understood of the firmness of the saints, wherewith they refuse to yield obedience to those who rage against them. For the firmament is heaven, by whose firmness these assailants shall be pained with blazing zeal, **for they shall be impotent to draw away the saints to the party of Antichrist.** This is the fire which shall devour them, and this is from God; **for it is by God's grace the saints become unconquerable,** and so torment their enemies. .....by this fire coming down out of heaven and consuming them, John meant that blow wherewith Christ in His coming is to strike those **persecutors of the Church whom He shall then find alive upon earth, when He shall kill Antichrist with the breath of His mouth,** (2 Thessalonians 2:8) then even this is not the last judgment of the wicked; but the last judgment is that which they shall suffer when the bodily resurrection has taken place.
>
> This last persecution by Antichrist shall last for three years and six months, as we have already said, and as is affirmed both in the book of Revelation and by Daniel the prophet.

Augustine here is talking about Revelation 20 and the Millennium, which he believes is the church age before Jesus' return. He debates whether the final 3 ½ years should be reckoned within the thousand years, along the way saying:

> And therefore during these three years and a half the souls of those who were slain for His testimony, both those which formerly passed from the body and those which shall pass in that last persecution, shall reign with Him till the mortal world come to an end, and pass into that kingdom in which there shall be no death. **And thus the reign of the saints with Christ** shall last longer than the bonds and imprisonment of the devil, because **they shall reign with their King the Son of God for these three years and a half during which the devil is no longer bound.**

Chapter 19 is devoted to a discussion of the interpretation of 2 Thessalonians 2 and the Antichrist, so it is worth quoting fully because it mentions the various views in his day of the 'restrainer' that his contemporary Chrysostum also briefly discussed, as we saw above:

No one can doubt that [Paul] wrote this of Antichrist and of the day of judgment, which he here calls the day of the Lord, nor that he declared that this day should not come unless he first came who is called the apostate – apostate, to wit, from the Lord God. And if this may justly be said of all the ungodly, how much more of him? But it is uncertain in what temple he shall sit, whether in that ruin of the temple which was built by Solomon, **or in the Church**; for the apostle would not call the temple of any idol or demon the temple of God. And on this account some think that in this passage Antichrist means not the prince himself alone, but his whole body, that is, the mass of men who adhere to him, along with him their prince; and they also think that we should render the Greek more exactly were we to read, not *in the temple of God*, but *for or as the temple of God*, as if he himself were the temple of God, the Church. Then as for the words, *And now ye know what withholds*, i.e., you know what hindrance or cause of delay there is, that he might be revealed in his own time; they show that he was unwilling to make an explicit statement, because he said that they knew. And thus we who have not their knowledge wish and are not able even with pains to understand what the apostle referred to, especially as his meaning is made still more obscure by what he adds. For what does he mean by *For the mystery of iniquity does already work: only he who now holds, let him hold until he be taken out of the way: and then shall the wicked be revealed*? I frankly confess I do not know what he means. I will nevertheless mention such conjectures as I have heard or read.

Some think that the Apostle Paul referred to the Roman empire, and that he was unwilling to use language more explicit, lest he should incur the calumnious charge of wishing ill to the empire which it was hoped would be eternal; so that in saying, *For the mystery of iniquity does already work*, he alluded to Nero, whose deeds already seemed to be as the deeds of Antichrist. And hence some suppose that he shall rise again and be Antichrist. Others, again, suppose that he is not even dead, but that he was concealed that he might be supposed to have been killed, and that he now lives in concealment in the vigor of that same age which he had reached when he was believed to have perished, and will live until he is revealed in his own time and restored to his kingdom. But I wonder that men can be so audacious in their conjectures. However, it is not absurd to believe that these words of the apostle, *Only he who now holds, let him hold until he be taken out of the way*, refer to the Roman empire, as if it were said, *Only he who now reigns, let him reign until he be taken out of the way*. And then shall the wicked be revealed: no one doubts that this means Antichrist. But others think that the words, *You know what withholds*, and *The mystery of iniquity works*, refer only to the wicked and the hypocrites **who are in the Church, until they reach a number so great as to furnish Antichrist with a great people**, and that this is the mystery of iniquity, because it seems hidden; also that the apostle is exhorting the faithful tenaciously to hold the faith they hold when he says, *Only he who now holds, let him hold until he be taken out of the way*, that is, until the

> mystery of iniquity which now is hidden **departs from the Church**. For they suppose that it is to this same mystery John alludes when in his epistle he says, *Little children, it is the last time: and as you have heard that Antichrist shall come, even now are there many antichrists; whereby we know that it is the last time. They went out from us, but they were not of us; for if they had been of us, they would no doubt have continued with us.* (1 John 2:18-19) As therefore there went out from the Church many heretics, whom John calls many antichrists, **at that time prior to the end, and which John calls the last time, so in the end they shall go out who do not belong to Christ, but to that last Antichrist, and then he shall be revealed.**
>
> Thus various, then, are the conjectural explanations of the obscure words of the apostle. **That which there is no doubt he said is this, that Christ will not come to judge quick and dead unless Antichrist, His adversary, first come to seduce those who are dead in soul; although their seduction is a result of God's secret judgment already passed**. For, as it is said his presence shall *be after the working of Satan, with all power, and signs, and lying wonders, and with all seduction of unrighteousness in them that perish.* For then shall Satan be loosed, and by means of that Antichrist shall work with all power in a lying though a wonderful manner....... Why they are called signs and lying wonders, we shall then be more likely to know when the time itself arrives. But whatever be the reason of the name, they shall be such signs and wonders as shall seduce those who shall deserve to be seduced, because they received not the love of the truth that they might be saved. Neither did the apostle scruple to go on to say, *For this cause God shall send upon them the working of error that they should believe a lie.* For God shall send, because God shall permit the devil to do these things, the permission being by His own just judgment, though the doing of them is in pursuance of the devil's unrighteous and malignant purpose, that they all might be judged who *believed not the truth, but had pleasure in unrighteousness.* Therefore, being judged, they shall be seduced, and, being seduced, they shall be judged. But, being judged, they shall be seduced by those secretly just and justly secret judgments of God, with which He has never ceased to judge since the first sin of the rational creatures; and, being seduced, they shall be judged in that last and manifest judgment administered by Jesus Christ, who was Himself most unjustly judged and shall most justly judge.

Augustine took a different line to Chrysostum, and one that I suspect is closer to the truth. He believes that it is only when apostasy, hypocrisy and wickedness in the church reaches a particular level and overwhelms the power of the righteous that the way for the Antichrist is paved. However, it is again quite clear from the start of the passage that he believed that the church would still be around when the Antichrist reigned, as he debated whether he would reign in the church, or in the ruins of the Jewish Temple in Jerusalem. (Augustine clearly didn't believe here in the restoration of the Temple, unlike many of his predecessors). He also could not be more explicit when he raises the issue again in chapter 23:

> **But he who reads this passage, even half asleep, cannot fail to see that the kingdom of Antichrist shall fiercely, though for a short time, assail the Church before the last judgment of God shall introduce the eternal reign of the saints**. For it is patent from the context that the time, times, and half a time, means a year, and two years, and half a year, that is to say, three years and a half. Sometimes in Scripture the same thing is indicated by months. For though the word times seems to be used here in the Latin indefinitely, that is only because the Latins have no dual, as the Greeks have, and as the Hebrews also are said to have. Times, therefore, is used for two times. As for the ten kings, whom, as it seems, Antichrist is to find in the person of ten individuals when he comes, I own I am afraid we may be deceived in this, and that he may come unexpectedly while there are not ten kings living in the Roman world. For what if this number ten signifies the whole number of kings who are to precede his coming.

Unfortunately, dispensationalists have been so seduced and put to sleep by a false doctrine that they do fail to see what is obvious to anyone not indoctrinated by them. In the final chapter 30 of this book, he says:

> That the last judgment, then, shall be administered by Jesus Christ in the manner predicted in the sacred writings is denied or doubted by no one, unless by those who, through some incredible animosity or blindness, decline to believe these writings, though already their truth is demonstrated to all the world. **And at or in connection with that judgment the following events shall come to pass, as we have learned: Elias the Tishbite shall come; the Jews shall believe; Antichrist shall persecute; Christ shall judge; the dead shall rise; the good and the wicked shall be separated; the world shall be burned and renewed**. All these things, we believe, shall come to pass; but how, or in what order, human understanding cannot perfectly teach us, but only the experience of the events themselves. My opinion, however, is, that they will happen in the order in which I have related them.

That middle section in bold might as well summarize the teaching of the entire church fathers on the end times. The persecution of the church by the Antichrist is fundamental to all of them (except perhaps Origen who said little on the topic, and unclearly for our purposes). There is a brief mention of the Antichrist in book 21 (http://www.newadvent.org/fathers/120121.htm) chapter 26 which again makes it clear there is no distinction between the saints or church of former times and that under the Antichrist:

> The persecutions, too, which have crowned the martyrs, and **which Christians of all kinds suffer,** try both buildings like a fire, consuming some, along with the builders themselves, if Christ is not found in them as their foundation, while others they consume without the builders, because Christ is found in them, and they are saved, though with loss; and other buildings still they do not consume, because such materials as abide for ever are found in them. **In the end of the world there shall be in the**

> **time of Antichrist tribulation such as has never before been.** How many edifices there shall then be, of gold or of hay, built on the best foundation, Christ Jesus, which that fire shall prove, bringing joy to some, loss to others, but without destroying either sort, because of this stable foundation!

Also in Augustine's 3rd Homily on 1st John (http://www.newadvent.org/fathers/170203.htm) we find another statement in support:

> But lest any be sluggish to go forward, let him hear: Children, it is the last hour. Go forward, run, grow; it is the last hour. This same last hour is long; yet it is the last. For he has put hour for the last time; because it is in the last times that our Lord Jesus Christ is to come. But some will say, How the last times? How the last hour? Certainly antichrist will first come, and then will come the day of judgment. John perceived these thoughts: lest people should in a manner become secure, and think it was not the last hour because antichrist was to come, he said to them, And as you have heard that antichrist is to come, now are there come many antichrists. Could it have many antichrists, except it were the last hour?

In this sermon, Augustine shows no distinction between a church afflicted with antichrists, and the church afflicted with the final Antichrist. He teaches John didn't want his hearers sluggish by saying, since the Antichrist is not here, we can rest easy, but rather warned of many antichrists before the last one. Unlike rapture teachers today, Augustine doesn't claim that 'imminence' means the church will escape, but says quite clearly 'Certainly antichrist will first come, and then will come the day of judgment.' There is not a hint of any pre-tribulation rapture escape here, despite his concern for people who were correctly saying it isn't the last time because the Antichrist has not come forth.

He goes on to warn that anyone who denies Christ by living wickedly whilst professing faith in Christ is just as much an antichrist as those heretics who deny true doctrine about Jesus by speaking contrary to what is taught in the bible.

In his 7th sermon on 1 John (http://www.newadvent.org/fathers/170207.htm) we find one more fragment that may well indicate the same teaching:

> 'Now, says he, *are you of God little children, and have overcome him*: (1 John 4:4) whom but Antichrist?

Now the context is mainly about antichrists - the many false teachers, but in each case Augustine either uses the plural or says 'an Antichrist', suggesting that here he might specifically mean the final Antichrist. This would not be a firm evidence if it were on its own, but given the rest of Augustine's teaching on the subject matter, this is likely an implicit teaching that the church will face *the* Antichrist, just as it faces many antichrists now.

Aside from general references to heretics as 'antichrists' or 'children of the antichrist', plus a reference to the Jews seeking the Antichrist (in other words, having denied the true Messiah, they are still looking, and so will be open to the false Messiah), there is only one other relevant reference I could find in Augustine (although I admit I didn't go through his commentaries on the Psalms) - namely in his tractate on John 7.14-18 (http://www.newadvent.org/fathers/1701029.htm).

> *He that speaks of himself seeks his own glory*: **'This will be he who is called Antichrist,'** *exalting himself*, as the apostle says, *above all that is called God, and that is worshipped.* (2 Thessalonians 2:4) The Lord, declaring that this same it is that will seek his own glory, not the glory of the Father, says to the Jews: *I have come in my Father's name, and you have not received me; another will come in his own name, him you will receive.* (John 5:45) He intimated that they would receive Antichrist, who will seek the glory of his own name, puffed up, not solid; and therefore not stable, but assuredly ruinous. .... But He that seeks His glory that sent Him, the same is true, and no unrighteousness is in Him. In Antichrist, however, there is unrighteousness, and he is not true; because he will seek his own glory, not His by whom he was sent: for, indeed, he was not sent, but only permitted to come. **Let us all**, therefore, **that belong to the body of Christ**, seek not our own glory, **that we be not led into the snares of Antichrist**. But if Christ sought His glory that sent Him, how much more ought we to seek the glory of Him who made us?

Although the main focus is on the Jews receiving the Antichrist, the end of the paragraph makes it quite clear that Augustine must also be thinking that the church, the body of Christ, would be around at the time, or else he would not be urging his hearers to make sure that they truly belong to the body of Christ so that they may not be trapped by the snares of Antichrist.

I don't recall seeing anyone claim that Augustine taught the Pre-Tribulation rapture, but if anyone does, they are lying to you, no matter how sincerely they may believe it.

John Cassian

John Cassian was an early monk in the East of the Mediterranean, and there is one relevant quote in chapter four of his fourth 'Conference' (http://www.newadvent.org/fathers/350808.htm) where he is arguing that often prophetic passages of scripture are fulfilled twice, to do with both Jesus' first and second comings. He says:

> ...where Elijah came in the person of John, (Matthew 11:14) and is again to be the precursor of the Lord's Advent: and in the matter of the *Abomination of desolation which stood in the holy place*, by means of that idol of Jupiter which, as we read, was placed in the temple in Jerusalem, and **which is again to stand in the Church through the coming of Antichrist**, and all those things which follow in the gospel, which we take as having been fulfilled before the captivity of Jerusalem and still to be fulfilled at the end of this world.

He did not believe that the antichrist would desecrate a literal temple, but the Church, and so therefore must have believed that the church would still be around at the time of the Antichrist. Thus, if anyone tells you that John Cassian taught the pre-tribulation rapture, they are lying to you, no matter how sincerely they may believe it.

John of Damascus

John was an Arab (Arabic name probably Yana), born in Damascus, and thought to have served as a main administrator to the Muslim Caliph of Damascus before becoming a monk at about the time that the Caliph intensified the Islamicization of his administration; he died near Jerusalem, and was a brilliant theologian, lawyer, philosopher and musician, whose hymns are still sung today, and who harshly criticized the Quran. He talks quite a bit about the Antichrist in the 4th book of his work 'An Exposition of the Orthodox Faith'
(http://www.newadvent.org/fathers/33044.htm) chapters 26 and 27:

> It should be known that the Antichrist is bound to come. Every one, therefore, who confesses not that the Son of God came in the flesh and is perfect God and became perfect man, after being God, is Antichrist. (1 John 2:22) But in a peculiar and special sense he who comes at the consummation of the age is called Antichrist. First, then, it is requisite that the Gospel should be preached among all nations, as the Lord said (Matthew 24:14), and then he will come to refute the impious Jews. For the Lord said to them: *I have come in My Father's name and you receive Me not: if another shall come in his own name, him you will receive.* (John 5:43) And the apostle says, *Because they received not the love of the truth that they might be saved, for this cause God shall send them a strong delusion that they should believe a lie: that they all might be damned who believed not the truth, but had pleasure in unrighteousness.* The Jews accordingly did not receive the Lord Jesus Christ who was the Son of God and God, but receive the impostor who calls himself God. For that he will assume the name of God, the angel teaches Daniel, saying these words, *Neither shall he regard the God of his fathers.* (Daniel 11:37) And the apostle says: *Let no man deceive you by any means: for that day shall not come except there come a falling away first, and that man of sin be revealed, the son of perdition: who opposes and exalts himself above all that is called God or that is worshipped, so that he sits in the temple of God* (2 Thessalonians 2:3-4) , showing himself that he is God; in the temple of God he said; not our temple, but the old Jewish temple. For he will come not to us but to the Jews: not for Christ or the things of Christ: wherefore he is called Antichrist.
>
> First, therefore, it is necessary that the Gospel should be preached among all nations (Matthew 24:14*): And then shall that wicked one be revealed, even him whose coming is after the working of Satan with all power and signs and lying wonders , with all deceivableness of unrighteousness in*

> *them that perish, whom the Lord shall consume with the word of His mouth and shall destroy with the brightness of His coming.* The devil himself , therefore does not become man in the way that the Lord was made man. God forbid! But he becomes man as the offspring of fornication and receives all the energy of Satan. For God, foreknowing the strangeness of the choice that he would make, allows the devil to take up his abode in him.
>
> He is, therefore, as we said, the offspring of fornication and is nurtured in secret, and on a sudden he rises up and rebels and assumes rule. And in the beginning of his rule, or rather tyranny, he assumes the role of sanctity. **But when he becomes master he persecutes the Church of God and displays all his wickedness**. But he will come with signs and lying wonders (2 Thessalonians 2:9), fictitious and not real, and he will deceive **and lead away from the living God those whose mind rests on an unsound and unstable foundation, so that even the elect shall, if it be possible, be made to stumble** (Matthew 24:24) .
>
> But Enoch and Elijah the Tishbite shall be sent and shall turn the hearts of the fathers to the children , that is, the synagogue to our Lord Jesus Christ and the preaching of the apostles: and they will be destroyed by him. And the Lord shall come out of heaven, just as the holy apostles beheld Him going into heaven, perfect God and perfect man, with glory and power, and will destroy the man of lawlessness, the son of destruction, with the breath of His mouth. (Acts 1:11) **Let no one, therefore, look for the Lord to come from earth, but out of Heaven, as He himself has made sure** (2 Thessalonians 2:8).......

After going on to discuss the resurrection of the body at the end of the age, with multiple quotes from Old and New Testaments, John concludes in chapter 27:

> We shall therefore rise again, our souls being once more united with our bodies, now made incorruptible and having put off corruption, **and we shall stand beside the awful judgment-seat of Christ: and the devil and his demons and the man that is his, that is the Antichrist and the impious and the sinful**, will be given over to everlasting fire: not material fire like our fire, but such fire as God would know. But those who have done good will shine forth as the sun with the angels into life eternal, with our Lord Jesus Christ, ever seeing Him and being in His sight and deriving unceasing joy from Him, praising Him with the Father and the Holy Spirit throughout the limitless ages of ages. Amen.

The quotes I have put in bold make it absolutely clear that John of Damascus believed that the church would undergo the brutal attentions of the Antichrist, even if only by implication in some cases (for instance - the context in which Jesus returns, seen by the church in the same way as he was seen by the apostles when he ascended, which is linked to his slaying of the Antichrist - in other words he comes for the church at the very end, not before). Therefore, if anyone tells you that John of Damascus taught a Pre-Tribulation rapture, they are lying to you, no matter how sincerely they may believe it.

Abbot Ceolfrid's Latin Codex Amiatinus and the Venerable Bede

These - especially Bede - were contemporaries of John of Damascus, but on the other side of the Christian world of that time. I am especially interested in this claim because these two were abbots of an ancient monastery just a few miles from where I live, work and worship, in the North East of England. You will generally see these claimed as evidence in quotes like this:

> But, some Medieval writers such as Ephraem of Nisibis (306-373), Abbot Ceolfrid's Latin Codex Amiatinus (ca. 690-716), and Brother Dolcino wrote statements that distinguish the Rapture from the Second Coming.

Whoever originally wrote this, this sentence appears all over the internet on forums by people trying to claim that the early church fathers taught the rapture and that the rapture wasn't invented in the 19th Century. We will deal with the others in a moment, but I smelt a rat as soon as I saw this since the Codex Amiatinus is simply a Latin translation of the bible. A little digging soon revealed a more specific source for this claim, a paper entitled 'The Rapture in Twenty Centuries of Biblical Interpretation' which you can view here http://www.tms.edu/m/tmsj13e.pdf . The relevant quote is as follows:

> **Codex Amiatinus (ca. 690-716)**
>
> This significant Latin manuscript from England was commissioned by Abbot Ceolfrid of the monastaries of Jarrow and Wearmouth in Northumberland. Ceolfrid intended to give it to the Pope as a gift but died on his way to see him. It was produced during the era of the commentaries of Venerable Bede, who was also a monk at Jarrow and whose works were heavily influenced by Jerome's Vulgate. In the title to Psalm 22 (Psalm 23 in the Vulgate), the following appears: "*Psalm of David, the voice of the Church after being raptured.*" The Latin phrase *post raptismum* contains a verb from the root *rapio* which can mean either "*to snatch, hurry away*" or "*to plunder, take by assault.*" This title is not carried over from Jerome's Vulgate and thus is likely the product of the Jarrow monastary. A history of the period of Ceolfrid's life presents no evidence of invasion or suffering as if the title was inserted for comfort in light of a difficult condition in the church. In contrast, Ceolfrid writes of the Christ's future sudden return and the resurrection of the believer, "[W]e show that we rejoice in the most certain hope of our own resurrection, which we believe will take place on the Lord's Day." Though not conclusive and still in need of further study, it appears that Codex Amiatinus presents another example of pretribulational thought in the Middle Ages.

However, this is yet another example of a Pre-Tribulationist, however scholarly, desperately searching for straws with which to try and prop up their position. In this case, as with all the other claims we have seen, the adage applies - they are using the evidence like a drunk uses a lamppost - for support, not illumination. Let's follow the alleged logic here. Firstly, the passage that supposedly supports the idea of a specifically 'Pre-Tribulation' rapture is from a heading of a Psalm that has never otherwise - as far as I am aware - been used to teach about the end times. Far from it. In fact, it was and is most often used in the church to describe Jesus' death and resurrection, and it is the Psalm that Jesus quoted from the cross at least once - where he quoted it's opening lines '*My God, my God, why have you forsaken me?*' and quite possibly quoted it in arguably his last dying words on the cross '*It is finished!*'. It is considered to be a prophecy about Jesus' crucifixion, not just because of these quotes, but also because it goes on to talk of a great deal of suffering, in a way very consistent with what a crucified person would suffer, but later vindication by God. The first question to ask is, if the title phrase was indeed added by the monks to refer to the church at the end times and referred to a 'rapture' event, which timing of the rapture would be more consistent with such a Psalm about suffering - a Pre-Tribulation rapture where the church escaped intense suffering, or a Post-Tribulation rapture in which the church suffered immensely? The question answers itself, and yet this writer is desperate to believe and for us to believe that a use of the Latin 'raptismum' must mean a belief in a Pre-Tribulation rapture, despite the context in no way indicating it.

He tries to shore up his 'argument' by noting that though the meanings of the word means 'snatch / hurry away' or 'plunder, take by assault', '*A history of the period of Ceolfrid's life presents no evidence of invasion or suffering as if the title was inserted for comfort in light of a difficult condition in the church.*' That might be true, but given that I know well the general history of my home area at that time, I doubt it - there was always violence and war of some sort or another, and even if it was true that this particular locality had peace at that time, they would have known about violence and suffering in other areas, as monasteries kept in close contact with their equivalents over a very wide geographical area. After all, this copy of the Bible was intended for the pope in Rome. This was not some letter to a particular circumstance, but a bible that was meant to be used in the future and in distant lands, and it was a heading for a Psalm of suffering. So, just because the monks may have lived in a time and place of relative peace, that is no reason to assume that putting that heading to interpret the Psalm as being a complaint or cry of the church undergoing violent assault is at all impossible. Thus the basis for claiming that the use of the 'rapture' word in Latin must mean the modern teaching of a 'rapture' of the church before the Tribulation is simply not there.

There is another devious slight of hand. The way the writer puts it, even though he is not explicit, it looks like in the same passage Coelfrid goes on to say what he does about the resurrection. In fact, the footnotes indicate the latter quote comes from a letter of Coelfrid to Nechtan in Bede's 'A History of the English Church and People'. A quick google search revealed that Nechtan was a king of the Picts (in what is now Scotland) who later gave up the throne to become a monk, and that the letter was about the bitter controversy that was dividing the British church then about the proper date for the celebration of Easter - the traditional Celtic Christian date, or the Roman Catholic date (see for instance https://en.wikipedia.org/wiki/Nechtan_mac_Der-Ilei). However, even without that knowledge, there are several things that should make you smell a rat, apart from the extraordinary shortness of the quotation. Firstly, notice how the writer, one 'James F. Stitzinger Associate Professor of Historical Theology' (who quite frankly should know better than to mishandle historical and theological sources so badly, if he is a professor of Historical Theology), smoothes over the gap by spinning the quote thus:

> 'Ceolfrid writes of the Christ's future sudden return and the resurrection of the believer'

priming his already indoctrinated dispensationalist readers to read the actual quote in a dispensational way, as teaching 'imminence' and therefore a pre-tribulation rapture. But if we look at the quote even as it is cited, without context, it says nothing about the suddenness or otherwise of Jesus' return, only the day of the week (a Sunday) on which they believe he will return :

> 'We show that we rejoice in the most certain hope of our own resurrection, which we believe will take place on the Lord's Day'

However, the problem is even worse when you read the passage in context, which you can do online here - http://www.sacred-texts.com/chr/bede/hist138.htm (Naitan is just a different spelling of Nechtan). According to Bede, Nechtan had decided to abandon the Celtic date for Easter and conform to the Roman Catholic church, and he wrote to Coelfrid asking for a letter to help him persuade those who wanted to continue the Celtic customs and dates. It is a long letter full of detailed biblical and astronomical calculations and arguments, but I will quote it in its immediate context:

> Thus, after the rising of the sun at the equinox, and after the full moon of the first month following in her order, that is, after the end of the fourteenth day of the same month, all which we have received by the Law to be observed, we still, as we are taught in the Gospel, wait in the third week for the Lord's day; and so, at length, we celebrate the offering of our Easter solemnity, to show that we are not, with the ancients, doing honour to the casting off of the yoke of Egyptian bondage; but that, with devout faith and love, we worship the Redemption of the whole world, which having been prefigured in the deliverance of the ancient people of God, was fulfilled in Christ's Resurrection, and that we may signify that we rejoice in the sure and certain hope of our own resurrection, which we believe will likewise happen on the Lord's day.
>
> Now this computation of Easter, which we set forth to you to be followed, is contained in a cycle of nineteen years, which began long since to be observed in the Church, to wit, even in the time of the Apostles, especially at Rome and in Egypt, as has been said above. But by the industry of Eusebius, who took his surname from the blessed martyr Pamphilus, it was reduced to a plainer system; insomuch that what till then used to be enjoined every year throughout all the Churches by the Bishop of Alexandria...... etc, etc

As you can see, there is not a hint of any kind of Pre-Tribulational or dispensationalist thought. It is a passing reference to a belief that the final resurrection will be on a Sunday, just like Jesus' own resurrection.

The writer ends with a veneer of scholarly caution:

> Though not conclusive and still in need of further study, it appears that Codex Amiatinus presents another example of pretribulational thought in the Middle Ages.

As we have seen, it appears nothing of the sort, but this is the basis of the bald claims we started out with that Coelfrid taught a separate rapture. He did no such thing!

Finally, since we have touched on Bede, we can look at his immensely popular and lasting 'Commentary on Revelation', which, unsurprisingly, has many references to the Antichrist. The first reference is to Revelation 3.10, ironically a favourite of Pre-Tribulationists who claim it teaches their position (see http://www.apocalyptic-theories.com/theories/bede/bedei3.html). Bede says:

> *Because thou hast kept My example in suffering adversity, I also will keep thee from the impending afflictions*, not, indeed, that you may not be tempted, but that you may not be overcome by adversity. And although the Church is always tried by adversity, yet, in this place, the hour of temptation, and the humiliation of the Jews **in the time of antichrist**, may be signified; that, as frequently happens in the course of this book at the sixth in order, so here also at the sixth angel, the last persecution may be designated. But as to this, **it is well believed that the wicked Jews will be deceived as well as deceive, but that others will understand the law spiritually through the instruction of the great prophet Elijah, and will be incorporated among the members of the Church, and bravely overcome the enemy**.

That passage alone scotches any notion of both a dispensationalist divide between the Church and Israel / the Jews, but also the Pre-Tribulation rapture, since those Jews who turn to Jesus through the preaching of Elijah will join the Church, even under the reign of the Antichrist.

He interprets the sun being darkened and the moon turning to blood in Revelation 6.12 as follows
(see http://www.apocalyptic-theories.com/theories/bede/bedei6.html):

> sun. This is, as if the power of Christ were hidden, or His doctrine temporarily obscured, or covered by a veil, when **the servants of Antichrist are brought to attack the servants of Christ.**
>
> moon. **The Church, more than is wont, will shed her blood for Christ**. And he said "the whole," because the last earthquake will be in the whole world. But before that, as it is written, "there will be earthquakes through divers places."

Any notion that the 'servants of Christ' in the first paragraph could be taken as some special 'Tribulation saints' is scotched by the interpretation of the blood-red moon in the second - it is the church that is suffering under the Antichrist.

So, we come to chapter 7 (http://www.apocalyptic-theories.com/theories/bede/bedei7.html) where there are also several mentions of the Antichrist, none at all decisive for our purposes, but I will quote them here starting with the four angels in v1:

> four angels. That is, four principal kingdoms, namely, of the Assyrians, and Persians, and Greeks, and Romans. And as in the former seals, after the manifold conflicts of the Church, he saw the joys of triumphant souls, so now, also, he is to prove by examples the victory over the preceding kingdoms of the world, who have now submitted to the Church of Christ, which is to follow the reign of Antichrist. For greater matters must of necessity be confirmed by greater proofs.

This is not quite explicit, but if we follow the logic, it strongly suggests - and especially given the rest of Bede's teaching - that the church goes through the Tribulation, because out of the four empires, the people of God, whether Israel or the church, had to endure persecution by at least three of them (the probable exception being the Persians), and Bede notes a pattern of the 'conflicts of the church' followed by seeing 'the joys of triumphant souls'; all the preceding kingdoms, he says, have now submitted to the Church, and so in talking of the Antichrist, he implies that the people of God will also endure greater persecution but then triumph, as suggested by the final sentence 'For greater matters must of necessity be confirmed by greater proofs'.

The second reference in v5 is simply stating a belief that the tribe of Dan is not mentioned in Revelation because the Antichrist will come from that tribe, which, as we have seen, was a fairly common belief in the early church. However, Bede's comments on v14 are more clearly post-Tribulation in import and worth quoting in full:

> tribulation. "Through many tribulations we must enter into the kingdom of God," but who knows not that the tribulation of Antichrist will be greater than all the rest?
>
> washed. He speaks not of martyrs alone. They are washed in their own blood. But the blood of Jesus, the Son of God, cleanses the **whole Church** from all sin, therefore are they before the throne of God. **For they are accounted worthy to stand there together in the service of God, who in the midst of adverse things are faithful confessors of His Name**.

There is not a hint of the church escaping this 'greater tribulation' that 7.14 mentions, but rather that the church that faithfully endures, whether its members are martyred or not, will be worthy of special honour.

Bede's commentary on 8.v1 (www.apocalyptic-theories.com/theories/bede/bedi81.html) and the opening of the seventh seal is worth quoting in full:

> seal. **It is believed that after the death of Antichrist, there will be some little rest in the Church,** which Daniel thus foretold: "*Blessed is he who waiteth and cometh to the one thousand three hundred and thirty-five days.*" And it is thus interpreted by the blessed Jerome: "Blessed," he says, "is he, who when Antichrist is slain, beyond the one thousand two hundred and ninety days, that is, three years and a half, waits for the forty-five days, in which the Lord and Saviour is to come in His own Majesty. Now for what reason, after the destruction of Antichrist, there is silence for forty-five days, is a subject of divine knowledge, unless perhaps we say, the deferring of the kingdom of the saints is the trial of patience." **Observe that at the sixth seal, he sees the greatest afflictions of the Church, at the seventh, rest.** For the Lord was crucified on the sixth day of the week, and rested on the Sabbath, awaiting the time of resurrection. Thus far concerning the opening of the closed book. and the six seals. But now he recapitulates from the beginning, as he is about to say the same things in another manner.

Now, whether or not we accept this particular interpretation, given that the bible in 2 Thessalonians talks of Jesus slaying the Antichrist at his coming, not before, what is quite clear again is that Bede accepted and believed without doubt that the church would endure the reign of the Antichrist. If there was some commentary or widespread alternative view, we would expect him (or at least someone among the early fathers) to interact with it, or to spend time justifying why they believed the church would be there, but he, like the other church fathers doesn't, he just states it baldly as a universally accepted fact. (I also find it interesting that, quite correctly, in my view, Bede interprets Revelation not as consecutive, but as recapitulating - going over the same period several times.)

We move on to 8.2-13 (http://www.apocalyptic-theories.com/theories/bede/bedeii82.html) starting with his comments on v2 and the '7 trumpets' of Revelation:

> trumpets. The Church, which is often presented under the number seven, is commended to the office of preaching. And here the first trumpet denotes the common destruction of the ungodly in the fire and hail; the second, the expulsion of the devil from the Church for the fiercer burning of the sea of the world; the third, the falling away of heretics from the Church, and their corruption of the streams of Holy Scripture; the fourth, the defection of false brethren in the darkening of the stars; the fifth, the greater hostility of heretics, the precursors of the time of Antichrist; **the sixth, the open war of Antichrist and his own against the Church**, and the destruction of the same enemy interposed by a recapitulation from the advent of the Lord; the seventh, the day of judgement, in which the Lord is to render to His own their reward, and to examinate those who have corrupted the earth.

Now, I don't quite know what 'interposed by a recapitulation from the advent of the Lord' means, but it is again clear that Bede taught that the church suffered under the Antichrist. Not only that, but he is teaching that the seventh trumpet announces the day of judgement, the day of Jesus' return, an interpretation I totally agree with. Similarly instructive for us are his comments on v13:

> eagle. The voice of this eagle daily flies through the mouths of eminent doctors in the Church, when they announce that the cruelty of Antichrist and the day of judgment will come with all the severity to those who are lovers of the earth; while they say, "In the last days perilous times will be at hand, and men will be lovers of themselves" and below, "men corrupt in mind, reprobate concerning the faith;" and in another place, "Then will the wicked one be revealed, who opposes and exalts himself above all that is called God, or is worshipped;" and again, "The day of the Lord will so come, as a thief in the night; for when they shall say, peace and security, then sudden destruction comes upon them"

What is of interest here is that Bede links passages together that dispensationalists maintain are evidence of separate comings of Jesus - specifically he has no problem with the alleged 'imminence' in the final quote from 1 Thessalonians 5, which dispensationalists take to require a belief in a Pre-Tribulation rapture. He applies it specifically to the wicked, which, as I showed in my earlier book, is the exact way the New Testament consistently uses 'thief in the night' imagery such as this.

So, on to chapter 9 (http://www.apocalyptic-theories.com/theories/bede/bedeii9.html) where we find three references to the Antichrist, starting with v12 and v13:

> past. Since he had foretold that three woes were to come, he now mentions that one hath already come, in the deceit of heresy, and that two remain, which will happen to the perverse in the time of Antichrist, and at the day of judgement.
>
> sixth. The sixth angel denotes the preachers of the last conflict, who, as the Gospel forwarns, detect the frauds of Antichrist. For the horns of the golden altar are the Gospels, which rise above the Church.

Followed by v20:

> repented not. To an ungodly religion they add also an unholy manner of life. After he has described the cruelty of Antichrist, in order to shew his fall, he recapitulates in the usual way the commencement from the birth of Christ, and the glory of the Church.

There is not much directly relevant to our purposes, but I include these for completeness. Moving on to chapter 11 (http://www.apocalyptic-theories.com/theories/bede/bedeii11.html) starting with v2, where Bede is again quite explicit on the matter of the Antichrist and the church:

> tread. **Not only are they driven from the Church, but they also fight against the Church itself**, with the heathen as their allies, for three years and a-half. It is **not that they only trample upon it then in the time of the Antichrist**; but that in that time all the body of the wicked, "in

> whom the ministry of iniquity already works" is joined as it were, to its own head.

Moving on to v11-13, which talks of the resurrection of the two witnesses God sends to preach to the earth, Bede has an interesting interpretation which is worth quoting in full, because even if it is not correct, it shows again how passages and concepts that dispensationalists believe must refer to separate events are in fact taken easily by other interpreters to refer to the single return of Jesus:

> V11: days. Thus far the angel has spoken of the future, and now he brings in, as accomplished, that which he hears is to come to pass, namely that, after the reign of Antichrist has been destroyed, the saints have risen to glory.
>
> fear. He has spoken of all the living, because even the righteous who shall remain alive will greatly fear at the resurrection of those who sleep.
>
> v12: cloud. This is the same that the Apostle said, "We shall be caught up in the clouds into the air, to meet the Lord."
>
> enemies. Here he has distinguished the unrighteous from those of whom he had said, that they feared in common with them.
>
> V13: earthquake. When the terror of the judgement comes upon them, all the city of the devil, which is built upon the sand, with all its builders, will fall to the ground. For, both ten and seven are perfect numbers. But if it were not so, the whole would be to be understood from a part.
>
> affrighted. Who of all men will boast that he has a pure heart, when "the powers of heaven shall be shaken."
>
> gave glory. They are built upon a rock, who, from their own stability, glorify the Lord when others fall at the earthquake. For "the righteous will rejoice when he seeth the punishment of the wicked." Some understand the two prophets to be Enoch and Elijah, and that they are to preach for three years and a-half, and confirm the hearts of the faithful against the perfidy of Antichrist, which is presently to follow; and that, after their death, his cruelty is to rage for the same period of time, and then, when the conflict is at length renewed by the saints, who in the protection of their hiding-places were supposed to be dead, is to be overcome. And these, because of their fellowship in one body, are said to rise as prophets themselves; and when the persecution is intensified at the sight of those who were already thought to be dead, many of those who were supposed to be worthy of the number seven, or ten, will fall. For Daniel says, "*He will confirm the covenant with many for one week, and in the half of the week the oblation and sacrifice will cease, and the abomination of desolation shall be in the temple*," and the following, "*and when the abomination which makes desolate shall be set up, there will be a thousand two hundred and ninety days*" which number is close upon the course of three years and a-half. Finally, Elijah of old destroyed his adversaries by fire, and was hidden for three years and a-half, and withheld the rain; and at length, when the false

> prophets were put to death, by means of the sacrifice which had been consumed, he turned Israel unto the Lord.

He interprets the two witnesses as being, according to church tradition, Enoch and Elijah, but he doesn't believe that they are resurrected literally after 3 and a half days, but believes this is a symbolic reference to a three and a half year period of the persecution of the church under the Antichrist. Bede believes that the resurrection is the resurrection of the righteous, and he says the cloud in v12 is the same cloud referred to in the rapture passage in 1 Thessalonians 4. He believes that the preaching of Elijah and Enoch will have so strengthened the true church that, though in hiding, they will come out and boldly proclaim the truth that the two witnesses had preached. He notes that in the Bible Elijah preached, and then was hidden for 3 ½ years in the wilderness, and after that period turned Israel back to the true God, implying that this is what Elijah and the rejuvenated saints do between them in the last days.

Chapter 12 (http://www.apocalyptic-theories.com/theories/bede/bedeii12.html) has one mention, on verse 7:

> heaven. **The heaven signifies the Church**, in which he says that Michael, with his angels, fights against the devil, for that, according to the will of God, he contends for the Church in her sojourning, by praying and ministering help; of whom Daniel also said, that he would come to the aid of the Church in the last and most grievous affliction; from which they suppose that Antichrist is to be slain by him.

Again, we don't need to agree with Bede's specific interpretation to see that he sees the church as enduring persecution in the last days under the Antichrist.

Chapter 13 (http://www.apocalyptic-theories.com/theories/bede/bedeii13.html if you wish to read it) has several references to the Antichrist, but none relevant to our purposes.

Moving on to chapter 15 (http://www.apocalyptic-theories.com/theories/bede/bedeiii15.html) we find an interesting, if somewhat difficult to interpret, comment by Bede (although it is clear enough that he teaches the church's faith is proved under the Antichrist's persecutions):

> V7: seven vials. These are the bowls which are carried with their odours by the living creatures and the elders, who are the Church, and who are also the seven angels. The same bowls are said to contain both the sweetness of supplications, and the wrath of punishments. For they are poured forth by the saints before the advent of the kingdom of God, when the judgements of God, which are now no longer secret as the abyss, but open as the bowls, are announced as being salvation to the righteous, but destruction to the ungodly. As the Apostle says, "*Because we are unto God a sweet savour of Christ in those who are saved, and in those who perish.*"

> V8: smoke. The Church, when it is to preach to the nations, is first influenced itself with the fire of love, and sends forth the smoke of pious confession, while it "gives thanks to God for His unspeakable gift."
>
> enter. No one is able to be incorporated among the members of the Church, but he who hears the mysteries of faith from the preachers, and learns that Jesus is constituted by God the Judge both of the living and the dead. **But if thou shalt interpret the smoke to be the secret judgement of God,** these remain impenetrable, and closed to mortal men "until" after the plagues of the present age are ended, *"the Lord come, Who is both to bring to light even the hidden things of darkness, and make manifest*" **how much the coming of Antichrist confers which is either of utility in proving the faith of the Church**, or of judgement in blinding the eyes of the Jews, "Who received not the love of the truth, that they might be saved"

Clearly, even if we disagree with several aspects of Bede's various interpretations, he does not see the Jews being deceived by the Antichrist as happening in a way that means they are separate from the church, chronologically, as a dispensationalist position would requir, but rather that this happens *at the same time* as the church is suffering persecution.

So we come to chapter 16 (http://www.apocalyptic-theories.com/theories/bede/bedeiii16.html) where Bede's comments on v3 again show he believes that Christians will suffer persecution under the Antichrist and his followers:

> sea. They who not only are stamped with the mark of Antichrist, **but who also assail the steadfastness of the servants of Christ with the waves of bitter persecution**, will be punished with a spiritual retribution which he calls blood; and they who boasted that they were alive, will be proved to have served the author of death.

Chapter 17 (http://www.apocalyptic-theories.com/theories/bede/bedeiii17.html) has several references to the Antichrist, but none relevant to our purposes.

Chapter 19 (http://www.apocalyptic-theories.com/theories/bede/bedeiii19.html) is interesting because of the way Bede covers the return of Jesus and how it relates to the church. There is no hint that the wedding of the Lamb has already happened here when Jesus returns. For instance, his comments on v7 are revealing:

> marriage. It is the marriage of the Lamb, when the Church is to be united unto the Lord in the marriage-chamber of the heavenly kingdom.
>
> ready. By always insisting on works of righteousness, she has shewn herself worthy of the spiritual feast and the everlasting kingdom. It may also be taken in accordance with the parable of the Gospel, which relates, that on the bridegroom's coming, "the virgins arise and trim their lamps," that is, reckon with themselves their works, for which they expect to receive eternal blessedness.

In the Dispensationalist scenario, the judgement of the acts of the saints will already have happened seven years before this moment. On v14, Bede's comments far better fit a scenario where the church has gone through the Tribulation:

> armies. That is to say, the Church in white bodies imitated Him. For because of the intensity of its conflict, it rightly receives the name of an army.

They have imitated him who is the Lamb who was slain, and suffered greatly. Bede makes a somewhat allegorical interpretation of v17, but again, we don't have to agree with it to see the significance of his comments for our purposes:

> sun. That is, preaching in **the Church, which shines more brightly, and thunders forth the more freely, the more it is oppressed.**

Not decisive in itself, but given the rest of Bede's teaching, it fits very well a Post-Tribulation scenario, but not so much a Pre-Tribulation viewpoint.

The bottom line? If anyone tells you that either Coelfrid or Bede taught a Pre-Tribulation rapture, they are lying to you, no matter how sincerely they may believe it.

Pseudo-Ephraem

You will find a great deal made of this 'proof' on many 'Rapture' websites, including the Pre-Tribulation Research Centre site. The snippet that keeps getting quoted as irrefutable proof that the early church (or at least someone in it) taught the Pre-Tribulation rapture is this:

> "For all the saints and Elect of God are gathered, prior to the tribulation that is to come, and are taken to the Lord lest they see the confusion that is to overwhelm the world because of our sins."

On the face of it, that might seem quite reasonable - it talks of a gathering and taking to the Lord before the tribulation - but it is an exceedingly small quote, without context, which is always a big red flag, as we have seen. The 'discoverer' of this rapture passage was one Grant Jeffrey, who stated that he only found it after a decade of scouring the church fathers. The reason for such dedication? Well, he believed that the New Testament teaching on the Pre-Tribulation was so strong that it was impossible that there be no trace of it in the early church writings. In fact, it was of his claims about Pseudo-Ephraem that I first came across that wonderful quote about using evidence like a drunk uses a lamp-post - for support rather than illumination, which as we have seen, aptly sums up the entire dispensationalist approach to the church fathers. Now, in one sense the logic that motivated Jeffrey was sound - given that the early church fathers placed such a great store on continuity with the apostolic teaching and tradition, both that found in the writings of what we now call the New Testament, and the oral teachings passed down from the apostles to the church elders, we would expect them to have adhered closely to what the apostles taught, and this, as I have shown in this and my previous book, is indeed the case. However, the fact that there is no sign of any teaching about the Pre-Tribulation rapture should have given people like Jeffrey pause, to consider if their interpretation was wrong, but they are so bound up in the dispensationalist indoctrination that they can't seen the great evidential elephant staring them in the face, and so any straw, however flimsy, seems to do as 'proof' for them.

So, back to the text at hand. Many sites just state this is from AD 373 and Ephraem the Syrian, which in fact nearly all scholars would say is wrong. It is a much later text that was written in the name of Ephraem (also sometimes spelt Ephraim), and so is more usually known as 'Pseudo-Ephraem'. It is a quite short sermon about the Antichrist and the end of the World. You will see a lot of sites which quote that one passage and also says that it comes just after a passage that talks about the rapture being 'imminent' or 'overhanging', and they say 'See, he taught imminence, so it must be a Pre-Tribulation rapture', but very many will only state that and not quote the context at all. There are some sites that will put more context, sometimes even most of the sermon (just one word of warning - we have a number of different versions of this sermon, as it was translated into at least two languages from the original - probably Syriac was original, and we also have Greek and Latin versions, with the Latin version also containing passages from another similar sermon known as Pseudo-Methodius; also the sermon is sometimes attributed to another writer, St Isidore), but usually with commentary that works to claim that the sermon is teaching imminence, or that only unbelievers will see the Day of the Lord. I don't have time to interact with every line taken on the details of this sermon, but the fact that there are so many different interpretations by people who are so convinced he is teaching just what modern dispensationalists / pre-tribulation teachers teach should raise a flag - if it is so clear, why is there so much variation in interpretation?

To read both versions, see http://www.bible.ca/rapture-pseudo-ephraem-latin-syraic-texts.htm . The relevant passage only appears in the Latin version, it seems (this caveat is there, just in case some obscure version in Syriac has it, but I've only ever seen it in translations of the Latin, and that seems to be the universal understanding from other websites too). Thus I will focus mainly on the Latin version, but before I do that, I will note two things - first of all the main reason scholars believe this must be from much later than the real Ephraim is the detailed account near the start of the sermon of two invasions, that of the Huns, which happened around 450 AD, and that of the Ishmaelites (meaning Muslims - and as a human rights worker as well as theologian, it is interesting to observe that what was done to the Christians in the first invasion is exactly what Islamic State is doing to Christians in Iraq and Syria now - splitting up families, slaying them, putting them in slavery, and demanding tribute, spreading terror). Secondly, even though the word 'church' is not mentioned, it is pretty clear that the church is there under the Antichrist - the saints, or the elect, oppose him, and the text gives absolutely no sign that these are some special group that only exist in the Tribulation (from the Syriac version):

> The elect will flee from his presence to the peaks of mountains and hills, and there will be calamity on earth unlike any that came before. Fear will fall upon all people and they will be overcome with terror. Children will

> renounce their father and follow after the Evil One; priests will abandon their altars to serve as his heralds. People will flee to cemeteries and hide themselves among the dead, pronouncing the good fortune of the deceased who had avoided the calamity: 'Blessed are you for you were borne away (to the grave) and hence you escaped from the afflictions! But as for us, woe is us! For when we die, vultures will serve as escort for us!' And if the days of that time were not shortened, the elect would never survive the calamities and afflictions. For Our Lord revealed (and) disclosed to us in his Gospel when He said: 'Those days will be shortened for the sake of the elect and the saints.' And when he has harassed the whole of creation, (when) the Son of Destruction (has bent it) to his will, Enoch and Elijah will be sent that they might persuade the Evil One. With a gentle question the saints will come before him, in order to expose the Son of Destruction before the assemblies surrounding him: 'If you are indeed God, tell us what we ask of you: Where is the place that you have hidden the elders Elijah and Enoch?' The Evil One will respond and say to the saints at that time: 'When I wish (it), they are in the height(s), rr again should I choose, they are within the sea; for I have authority over habitations, since there is no other god apart from me and I can make anything on earth (and) also in heaven!' They will answer the Son of Destruction as follows: 'If you are truly God, call out to the deceased so that they will rise! For it is written within the books ff the prophets and the apostles that when the Messiah reveals Himself, He will resurrect the dead from the graves. If you cannot show us this (sign), then the One who was crucified is greater than you! For he roused and resurrected those who were dead, and was exalted in great splendor.' Then the Evil One will become enraged with the saints at that time; He will draw his terrible sword and sever the necks of the righteous ones.

Interestingly, in the light of what Bede taught about the Antichrist being slain a while before Jesus returns, the sermon has the archangels slaying the Antichrist before Jesus' visible return, although unlike Bede, it doesn't say how long a period there was between the two - it may have envisioned Jesus returning immediately after the archangels do the slaying.

But let us return to the Latin version, which is somewhat different. Since this is quoted as evidence so widely, I will quote it in full (the two sections usually quoted by rapture advocates - <u>underlined</u> - are in the second section of the sermon, and I have put in **bold** bits that show evidence explicitly contrary to the pre-tribulation position, approach or attitude):

> Section 1 Dearly beloved brothers, believe the Holy Spirit who speaks in us. We have already told you that the end of the world is near, the consummation remains. Has not faith withered away among mankind? How many foolish things are seen among youths, how many crimes among prelates, how many lies among priests, how many perjuries among deacons! There are evil deeds among the ministers, adulteries in the aged, wantonness in the youths–in mature women false faces, in virgins dangerous traces! In the midst of all this there are the wars with the

Persians, and we see struggles with diverse nations threatening and "kingdom rising against kingdom." When the Roman empire begins to be consumed by the sword, the coming of the Evil One is at hand. It is necessary that the world come to an end at the completion of the Roman empire. In those days two brothers will come to the Roman empire who will rule with one mind; but because one will surpass the other, there will be a schism between them. And so the Adversary will be loosed and will stir up hatred between the Persian and Roman empires. In those days many will rise up against Rome; the Jewish people will be her adversaries. There will be stirrings of nations and evil reports, pestilences, famines, and earth quakes in various places. All nations will receive captives; there will be wars and rumours of wars. From the rising to the setting of the sun the sword will devour much. The times will be so dangerous that in fear and trembling they will not permit thought of better things, because many will be the oppressions and desolations of regions that are to come.

Section 2 We ought to understand thoroughly therefore, my brothers, what is imminent or overhanging. Already there have been hunger and plagues, violent movements of nations and signs, which have been predicted by the Lord, they have already been fulfilled (consummated), and there is not other which remains, except the advent of the wicked one in the completion of the Roman kingdom. Why therefore are we occupied with worldly business, and why is our mind held fixed on the lusts of the world or on the anxieties of the ages? Why therefore do we not reject every care of worldly business, and why is our mind held fixed on the lusts of the world or on the anxieties of the ages? **Why therefore do we not reject every care of earthly actions and prepare ourselves for the meeting of the Lord Christ, so that he may draw us from the confusion, which overwhelms all the world?** Believe you me, dearest brother, because the coming (advent) of the Lord is nigh, believe you me, because the end of the world is at hand, believe me, because it is the very last time. Or do you not believe unless you see with your eyes? See to it that this sentence be not fulfilled among you of the prophet who declares: "Woe to those who desire to see the day of the Lord!" For all the saints and elect of God are gathered, prior to the tribulation that is to come, and are taken to the Lord lest they see the confusion that is to overwhelm the world because of our sins. And so, brothers most dear to me, it is the eleventh hour, and the end of the world comes to the harvest, and angels, armed and prepared, hold sickles in their hands, awaiting the empire of the Lord. And we think that the earth exists with blind infidelity, arriving at its downfall early. Commotions are brought forth, wars of diverse peoples and battles and incursions of the barbarians threaten, and our regions shall be desolated, and we neither become very much afraid of the report nor of the appearance, in order that we may at least do penance; because they hurl fear at us, and we do not wish to be changed, although we at least stand in need of penance for our actions!

Section 3 When therefore the end of the world comes, there arise diverse wars, commotions on all sides, horrible earthquakes, perturbations of nations, tempests throughout the lands, plagues, famine, drought throughout the thoroughfares, great danger throughout the sea and dry land, constant persecutions, slaughters and massacres everywhere, fear in the homes, panic in the cities, quaking in the thoroughfares, suspicions in the male, anxiety in the streets. In the desert people become senseless, spirits melt in the cities. A friend will not be grieved over a friend, neither a brother for a brother, nor parents for their children, nor a faithful servant for his master, but one inevitability shall overwhelm them all; neither is anyone able to be recovered in that time, who has not been made completely aware of the coming danger, but all people, who have been constricted by fear, are consumed **because of the overhanging evils**.

Section 4 Whenever therefore the earth is agitated by the nations, people will hide themselves from the wars in the mountains and rocks, by caves and caverns of the earth, by graves and memorials of the dead, and there, as they waste away gradually by fear, they draw breath, because there is not any place at all to flee, but there will be concession and intolerable pressure. And those who are in the east will flee to the west, and moreover, those who are in the west shall flee to the east, and there is not a safer place anywhere, because the world shall be overwhelmed by worthless nations, whose aspect appears to be of wild animals more than that of men. Because those very much horrible nations, most profane and most defiled, who do not spare lives, and shall destroy the living from the dead, shall consume the dead, they eat dead flesh, they drink the blood of beasts, they pollute the world, contaminate all things, and the one who is able to resist them is not there. **In those days people shall not be buried, neither Christian, nor heretic, neither Jew, nor pagan, because of fear and dread there is not one who buries them; because all people, while they are fleeing, ignore them.**

Section 5 Whenever the days of the times of those nations have been fulfilled, after they have destroyed the earth, it shall rest; and now the kingdom of the Romans is removed from everyday life, **and the empire of the Christians is handed down by God and Peter; and then the consummation comes, when the kingdom of the Romans begins to be fulfilled, and all dominions and powers have been fulfilled. Then that worthless and abominable dragon shall appear**, he, whom Moses named in Deuteronomy, saying:-Dan is a young lion, reclining and leaping from Basan. Because he reclines in order that he may seize and destroy and slay. Indeed (he is) a young whelp of a lion not as the lion of the tribe of Judah, but roaring because of his wrath, that he may devour. "And he leaps out from Basan." "Basan" certainly is interpreted "confusion." He shall rise up from the confusion of his iniquity. The one who gathers together to himself a partridge the children of confusion, also shall call them, whom he has not brought forth, just as Jeremiah the prophet says. Also in the last day they shall relinquish him just as confused.

Section 6 When therefore the end of the world comes, that abominable, lying and murderous one is born from the tribe of Dan. He is conceived from the seed of a man and from an unclean or most vile virgin, mixed with an evil or worthless spirit. But that abominable corrupter, more of spirits than of bodies, while a youth, the crafty dragon appears under the appearance of righteousness, before he takes the kingdom. Because he will be craftily gentle to all people, not receiving gifts, not placed before another person, loving to all people, quiet to everyone, not desiring gifts, appearing friendly among close friends, so that men may bless him, saying;-he is a just man, not knowing that a wolf lies concealed under the appearance of a lamb, and that a greedy man is inside under the skin of a sheep.

Section 7 But when the time of the abomination of his desolation begins to approach, having been made legal, he takes the empire, and, just as it is said in the Psalm:-They have been made for the undertaking for the sons of Loth, the Moabites and the Ammanites shall meet him first as their king. Therefore, when he receives the kingdom, he orders the temple of God to be rebuilt for himself, which is in Jerusalem; who, after coming into it, he shall sit as God and order that he be adored by all nations, since he is carnal and filthy and mixed with worthless spirit and flesh. Then that eloquence shall be fulfilled of Daniel the prophet:-*And he shall not know the God of their fathers, and he shall not know the desires of women.* Because the very wicked serpent shall direct every worship to himself. Because he shall put forth an edict so that people may be circumcised according to the rite of the old law. Then the Jews shall congratulate him, because he gave them again the practice of the first covenant; then all people from everywhere shall flock together to him at the city of Jerusalem, and the holy city shall be trampled on by the nations for forty-two months, just as the holy apostle says in the Apocalypse, which become three and a half years, 1,260 days.

Section 8 In these three years and a half the heaven shall suspend its dew; because there will be no rain upon the earth, and the clouds shall cease to pass through the air, and the stars shall be seen with difficulty in the sky because of the excessive dryness, which happens in the time of the very fierce dragon. Because all great rivers and very powerful fountains that overflow with themselves shall be dried up, torrents shall dry up their water-courses because of the intolerable age, **and there will be a great tribulation**, as there has not been, since people began to be upon the earth, and there will be famine and an insufferable thirst. And children shall waste away in the bosom of their mothers, and wives upon the knees of their husbands, by not having victuals to eat. Because there will be in those days lack of bread and water, and no one is able to sell or to buy of the grain of the fall harvest, unless he is one who has the serpentine sign on the forehead or on the hand. Then gold and silver and precious clothing or precious stones shall lie along the streets, and also even every type of pearls along the thoroughfares and streets of the cities, but there is not one who may extend the hand and take or desire them, but they consider all things as good as nothing because of the extreme lack and famine of bread, because the earth is not protected by the rains of heaven, and there will be neither dew nor moisture of the air upon the earth. **But those who wander through the deserts, fleeing from the face of the serpent**, bend their knees to God, just as lambs to the udders of their mothers, being **sustained by the salvation of the Lord**, and while wandering in states of desertion, they eat herbs.

Section 9 **Then, when this inevitability has overwhelmed all people, just and unjust, the just, so that they may be found good by their Lord; and indeed the unjust, so that they may be damned forever with their author the Devil**, and, as God beholds the human race in danger and being tossed about by the breath of the horrible dragon, he sends to them consolatory proclamation by his attendants, the prophets Enoch and Elijah, who, while not yet tasting death, are the servants for the heralding of the second coming of Christ, and in order to accuse the enemy. And when those just ones have appeared, they confuse indeed the antagonistic serpent with his cleverness **and they call back the faithful witnesses to God, in order to (free them) from his seduction** ...

Section 10 **And when the three and a half years have been completed, the time of the Antichrist, through which he will have seduced the world, after the resurrection of the two prophets, in the hour which the world does not know, and on the day which the enemy of son of perdition does not know, will come the sign of the Son of Man, and coming forward the Lord shall appear with great power and much majesty, with the sign of the wood of salvation going before him, and also even with all the powers of the heavens with the whole chorus of the saints, with those who bear the sign of the holy cross upon their shoulders, as the angelic trumpet precedes him, which shall sound and declare: Arise, O sleeping ones, arise, meet Christ, because his hour of judgment has come! Then Christ shall come and the enemy shall be thrown into confusion,** and the Lord shall destroy him by the spirit of his mouth. And he shall be bound and shall be plunged into the abyss of everlasting fire alive with his father Satan; and all people, who do his wishes, shall perish with him forever; but the righteous ones shall inherit everlasting life with the Lord forever and ever.

My first observation is that it is still just possible to interpret this in a Pre-Tribulation sense, but only if you *assume* Pre-Tribulation doctrine in the first place. For instance, when opponents of the Pre-Tribulation rapture say, quite correctly, I believe, that the rapture / resurrection is placed in section 10 (in bold, just above), I have seen Pre-Tribulation rapture supporters claim that a) no resurrection is explicitly mentioned - which is false, because sleeping was and is a well-known euphemism for death in Christian circles, and the context is quite clear that this is what is being talked about here, especially when you consider that the elements of the rapture as taught in 1 Thessalonians 4 are taught here - trumpet by angel, resurrection of the righteous / saints before the coming of Jesus, and b) they claim that this is not a problem for Pre-Tribulation scenarios, because they believe that there will be saints saved in the Tribulation after the church has been raptured. This is a case where they have to *assume* a Pre-Tribulation position to 'prove' it, which I showed in my last book was always the case when it came to forcing the Pre-Tribulation position onto the New Testament scriptures too. For an example of this, see http://without-excuses.blogspot.co.uk/2015/04/pseudo-ephraem-does-teach-rapture.html which uses these arguments.

On that second point, this violates the rules of context, because we are supposed to understand what the author / preacher had in mind, not import notions of 'Tribulation saints' from modern dispensationalist doctrine back into the text. For instance, if you look at the sermon above, there are only two mentions explicitly of the term 'saints'. The first is in the underlined passage in section 2 which is claimed to be about a Pre-Tribulation rapture. The second is in the bit in bold in section 10, and what completely undermines the Pre-Tribulation position here is not only that the language used is that of the rapture as taught in 1 Thessalonians 4, but also the way the text links this resurrection to the second coming. Let's look at the quote again

> And when the three and a half years have been completed, the time of the Antichrist, through which he will have seduced the world, after the resurrection of the two prophets**, in the hour which the world does not know, and on the day which the enemy of son of perdition does not know**, will come the sign of the Son of Man, and coming forward the Lord shall appear with great power and much majesty, with the sign of the wood of salvation going before him, and also even **with all the powers of the heavens with the whole chorus of the saints, with those who bear the sign of the holy cross upon their shoulders**, as **the angelic trumpet precedes him, which shall sound and declare**: Arise, O sleeping ones, arise, meet Christ, because his hour of judgment has come! Then Christ shall come and the enemy shall be thrown into confusion

Firstly, even words that explicitly contain the concept of 'imminence' (first bold section) which Pre-Tribulationists claim must be evidence of a Pre-Tribulation rapture in the New Testament, are here placed explicitly in a *post-tribulation* context. Clearly Pseudo-Ephraem did not, contrary to the claims of dispensationalists, see any 'contradiction' between a belief in the seven year period of Tribulation and no-one knowing the precise hour or day on which Jesus will return. Secondly, it is true that here the saints are said to be coming to earth with Jesus (second bold section), but let's look at the order. The New Testament teaches that first will appear 'the sign of the Son of Man', which, like many of the church fathers, Pseudo-Ephraem interprets as the sign of the wooden cross on which Jesus was crucified, and then comes all the powers of the heavens which includes the 'whole chorus of the saints'. But the third bold section immediately explains how this could be - not, as with Pre-Tribulational teaching, because the church has been in heaven all this preceding Tribulation time with Jesus - but because as well as the sign of the cross goes before him, also an angelic trumpet precedes him, and those who are 'dead in Christ' are raised, just as 1 Thessalonians 4 teaches. It is true that it doesn't explicitly mention the transformation of the living saints, but his hearers would know the passages from 1 Thessalonians 4 and Matthew 24 which are alluded to, and they would know what was included in the concept.

Notice also how deceptively many Pre-Tribulation claims are handled. They say that the term or concept of 'imminence' is used just before the claimed reference to the Rapture. But even if for the sake of argument we accepted for a moment that the passage in section two was describing a Pre-Tribulation rapture, the context shows quite clearly that it is not the return of Jesus or the rapture that is 'imminent' or 'overhanging'. The preacher has spent the first section detailing all the moral failings in the church and the troubles in the world that were happening in his day (as in ours) and were general signs Jesus predicted about the end times. He then says:

> We ought to understand thoroughly therefore, my brothers, what is imminent or overhanging. Already there have been hunger and plagues, violent movements of nations and signs, which have been predicted by the Lord, they have already been fulfilled (consummated), and there is not other which remains, except the advent of the wicked one in the completion of the Roman kingdom. Why therefore are we occupied with worldly business, and why is our mind held fixed on the lusts of the world or on the anxieties of the ages? Why therefore do we not reject every care of worldly business, and why is our mind held fixed on the lusts of the world or on the anxieties of the ages? Why therefore do we not reject every care of earthly actions and prepare ourselves for the meeting of the Lord Christ, so that he may draw us from the confusion, which overwhelms all the world?

Firstly, he explicitly says that what is imminent is not the return of Jesus, but the only thing that remains, in Pseudo-Ephraem's view, which is the ending of the Roman empire and the associated advent of the Antichrist (here called 'the wicked one'). This is what is imminent or overhanging. Now, if he were teaching a Pre-Tribulation rapture, there would be no need to mention this, because the church - his hearers - would be raptured out of the way before the Antichrist comes to power, but he urges them not to be caught up in world affairs precisely so that we should 'prepare ourselves for the meeting of the Lord Christ, so that he may draw us from the confusion, which overwhelms all the world'. In other words, because his hearers will have to face all the terrible trials of the Tribulation that will so confuse the world, they should prepare now, mentally and spiritually for what is to come, what Jesus and the apostles taught would occur before his return, and not be caught up in the apostasy of the end of the age (see 2 Thessalonians 2), because, as Jesus said '*only those who endure to the end will be saved*'. The only other reference to 'overhanging' (i.e. - something that is imminent) is in section 3, and it backs this interpretation up:

> neither is anyone able to be recovered in that time, who has not been made completely aware of the coming danger, but all people, who have been constricted by fear, are consumed because of the overhanging evils.

The matter which is 'overhanging' and urgent, is the evils that are to come. This is a practical sermon, with practical implications, not an esoteric discussion of things that the hearers will never experience because they will be 'raptured out of here', as in so many end times sermons today. There is an explicit rebuke for the teaching of the Pre-Tribulationists here, and a showing of the great evil that is in that false teaching. It says that no-one will be able to be recovered (saved - or recovered from the apostasy?) in that time of Tribulation who has not been made *completely* aware of the coming danger, but the Pre-Tribulation position actively teaches that there is no such coming danger for the church, and mocks as unbiblical those who do warn of the coming danger.

Sections 3 and 4 tell of what this danger is, at the time of the coming of the Antichrist - that there is turmoil and unrest so bad that there will not be a safe place to be found, and no-one - true Christian or heretic, Jew or pagan - will have time to bury the dead (I am reminded hear of the Armenian Holocaust a century ago where this fate befell at least a million Christians, for instance).

So that leaves us with the question. What is Pseudo-Ephraem talking about in the section that is claimed to be a reference to the Pre-Tribulation rapture? Well, firstly, we find that there is another gathering going on. In section 5, like many early church fathers, this writer taught that the Antichrist would come from the Israeli tribe of Dan, and he interprets a passage from the Old Testament about Dan which describes him as a lion leaping from Bashan thus:

> "Basan" certainly is interpreted "confusion." He shall rise up from the confusion of his iniquity. The one who gathers together to himself a partridge the children of confusion, also shall call them, whom he has not brought forth, just as Jeremiah the prophet says. Also in the last day they shall relinquish him just as confused.

So, Jesus gathers his own to save them from the confusion of the world that is coming, but the antichrist gathers to himself the 'children of confusion' who remain just as confused at the end of his reign as at the start. We have seen that the sermon warns its hearers not to be so caught up in worldly affairs and concerns that they are not prepared for the meeting with Jesus that will be preceded by such confusion. This 'gathering of his own' by Jesus would fit another possible interpretation, which holds that Pseudo-Ephraem was imitating the language of the genuine Ephraem, who used the term 'gathering' of evangelism and conversion of people to the kingdom of Christ. In this view, Pseudo-Ephraem is predicting a huge influx of converts to Jesus in the time just before the rise of the Antichrist. This would fit some modern views which believe that there will be a huge harvest of souls before the end, by a great revival. People who hold this view point out that revivals have almost always either followed, or preceded, a time of great persecution and tribulation.

Another possible interpretation I have seen which may have merit is that this is a reference to Revelation 12 where the 'child born to the woman' is 'snatched up' to God and his throne. In Latin one word for 'snatch up' is the word from which we get the term 'rapture'. The passage in Revelation goes on to talk of the woman - who many interpreters took as the church or the elect people of God - fleeing into hiding for 3 ½ years in the Tribulation period. Thus this gathering to the Lord could be the fleeing of the church into the wilderness to escape the persecution under the Antichrist. This matches up with what a lot of the early church fathers taught, and indeed, later on in this sermon there is reference to those who in the Tribulation:

> wander through the deserts, fleeing from the face of the serpent, bend their knees to God, just as lambs to the udders of their mothers, being sustained by the salvation of the Lord, and while wandering in states of desertion, they eat herbs.

In fact, there is more to be said about this passage, particularly in the light of the theme we have seen in many church fathers of God rescuing much of the church from the last days apostasy that precedes the Antichrist. We have seen how this teaching, which is implicit in Paul in 2 Thessalonians 2, was made more explicit by many church fathers, and I suggest that the context indicates this is exactly the line Pseudo-Ephraem is taking here. The Syriac version, for instance, notes that many priests will abandon their altars (churches) and go and be heralds for the Antichrist. But sticking to just the Latin version, let's go back to the context:

> We ought to understand thoroughly therefore, my brothers, what is imminent or overhanging. Already there have been hunger and plagues, violent movements of nations and signs, which have been predicted by the Lord, they have already been fulfilled (consummated), and there is not other which remains, except the advent of the wicked one in the completion of the Roman kingdom. Why therefore are we occupied with worldly business, and why is our mind held fixed on the lusts of the world or on the anxieties of the ages? Why therefore do we not reject every care of worldly business, and why is our mind held fixed on the lusts of the world or on the anxieties of the ages? Why therefore do we not reject every care of earthly actions and prepare ourselves for the meeting of the Lord Christ, so that he may draw us from the confusion, which overwhelms all the world? Believe you me, dearest brother, because the coming (advent) of the Lord is nigh, believe you me, because the end of the world is at hand, believe me, because it is the very last time. Or do you not believe unless you see with your eyes? See to it that this sentence be not fulfilled among you of the prophet who declares: "Woe to those who desire to see the day of the Lord!" For all the saints and elect of God are gathered, prior to the tribulation that is to come, and are taken to the Lord lest they see the confusion that is to overwhelm the world because of our sins. And so, brothers most dear to me, it is the eleventh hour, and the end of the world comes to the harvest, and angels, armed and prepared, hold sickles in their hands, awaiting the empire of the Lord. And we think that the earth exists with blind infidelity, arriving at its downfall early. Commotions are brought forth, wars of diverse peoples and battles and incursions of the barbarians threaten, and our regions shall be desolated, and we neither become very much afraid of the report nor of the appearance, in order that we may at least do penance; because they hurl fear at us, and we do not wish to be changed, although we at least stand in need of penance for our actions!

The preacher starts out by noting that most of the signs mentioned by Jesus as signs of his coming had already been fulfilled, and there was only the terrible time of the Antichrist to come, he believed, when the Roman empire would fall (this was after Rome itself had fallen, but the Eastern half of the empire, the Byzantine empire, was still standing, although increasingly beleaguered by Islam - it would take a number of centuries more to fall). His question then was one that is very apt for us today - why, then is the church caught up in worldly affairs, affections and anxieties, rather than preparing themselves for 'the meeting of the Lord Christ'. This spiritual preparation is necessary 'so that he may draw us from the confusion, which overwhelms all the world'. We have seen how that confusion is the hallmark of the Antichrist in a later section. The primary confusion that overwhelms the world is a result of lawlessness - rejecting the guidance of God. The preacher urges his hearers to 'See to it that this sentence be not fulfilled among you of the prophet who declares *Woe to those who desire to see the day of the Lord!*' This is almost certainly a reference to a passage in Amos 5. The context of Amos 5 is a call to Israel, the people of God, to repentance, and to abandon idolatry and injustice and unrighteousness, in order to escape death. He calls on them to hate evil and love what is good, and then perhaps God will have mercy on the remnant of his people. It is in this context that the prophet Amos says:

> What sorrow awaits you who say 'If only the day of the Lord were here!' You have no idea what you are wishing for. That day will bring darkness and not light. In that day you will be like a man who runs from a lion, only to meet a bear. Escaping from the bear, he leans his hand against a wall in his house - and he's bitten by a snake. Yes, the day of the Lord will be dark and hopeless, without a ray of joy or hope.

After going on to say how much God hated their hypocritical practice of religion, God warns in chapter 6 of the sorrow coming on those called by his name who 'lounge in luxury' and 'feel secure', with words that are very apt for those who believe in the false doctrine of the Pre-Tribulation and desperately try to find any excuse to cling to this dangerous doctrine:

> You push away every thought of coming disaster, but your actions only bring the day of judgement closer.... Therefore you will be the first to be led away as captives. Suddenly, all your parties will end.

So this is the context of the Scripture that Pseudo-Ephraem cites, and it exactly matches what he says in his sermon. For instance, the passage talks of someone who desired the day of the Lord, yet lived in wickedness, reeling from one disaster to another, one danger to another, and this is exactly the kind of situation Pseudo-Ephraem describes in the sections immediately following - people fleeing from east to west, from one disaster after another. He asks whether people will not believe unless they 'see with their own eyes' - in other words, if they experience it for themselves. He has called on them to spiritually prepare themselves for what is to come.

> Or do you not believe unless you see with your eyes? See to it that this sentence be not fulfilled among you of the prophet who declares: "Woe to those who desire to see the day of the Lord!" For all the saints and elect of

> God are gathered, prior to the tribulation that is to come, and are taken to the Lord lest they see the confusion that is to overwhelm the world because of our sins.

In the first instance, they are urged to prepare and so escape the confusion that is overwhelming or will overwhelm the world. Notice in this second section about being rescued from the confusion (that will lead people to be seduced by the Antichrist, as we see later in the sermon) that the saints and elect are 'taken to the Lord' so they won't see (experience) the confusion that overwhelms the world **because of *our* sins.** Not the sins of the world, but because of the church's sins. This fits with the theme that the way is opened for the Antichrist because of apostasy in the church. Those who are true saints and chosen by God, even if they may be enmeshed in some of this apostasy, will be gathered back to a true relation with the Lord - taken to the Lord, so that they will not be part of the confusion and deception. (Remember that Jesus said that in the last days, false prophets will 'deceive even the elect, if it were possible). The preacher goes on to give the practical application, and it is not to be 'rapture ready':

> And so, brothers most dear to me, it is the eleventh hour, and the end of the world comes to the harvest, and angels, armed and prepared, hold sickles in their hands, awaiting the empire of the Lord. And we think that the earth exists with blind infidelity, arriving at its downfall early. Commotions are brought forth, wars of diverse peoples and battles and incursions of the barbarians threaten, and our regions shall be desolated, and we neither become very much afraid of the report nor of the appearance, in order that we may at least do penance; because they hurl fear at us, and we do not wish to be changed, although we at least stand in need of penance for our actions!

His hearers, he believes, like so many of us are today, see the confusions, the wars - in our case the rise of radical Islam and other powers of destruction within and without our societies - and yet we are so spiritually dull and unaware that indeed we 'neither become very much afraid of the report nor of the appearance', nor do we repent and come back close to Jesus, even in spite of the fear facing us: we indeed 'do not wish to be changed, although we at least stand in need of penance for our actions'. This is the true message of this passage from Pseudo-Ephraem for our day, not the soothing, seducing fantasy of a Pre-Tribulation rapture. This is the context that the dispensationalists ignore when they try and claim Pseudo-Ephraem as one of their own. They think they see, but they are blind, and they lead their followers to stand unafraid, unprepared. What we face now is forewarnings of the far worse time that is to come, and we should be getting prepared.

If we consider the penultimate paragraph of the sermon, this too sheds light on the issue. In a Pre-Tribulation scenario, the righteous escape the tribulation, but this is not what Pseudo-Ephraem teaches - quite the opposite:

> Then, when this inevitability has overwhelmed all people, just and unjust, the just, so that they may be found good by their Lord; and indeed the unjust, so that they may be damned forever with their author the Devil, and, as God beholds the human race in danger and being tossed about by

> the breath of the horrible dragon, he sends to them consolatory proclamation by his attendants, the prophets Enoch and Elijah, who, while not yet tasting death, are the servants for the heralding of the second coming of Christ, and in order to accuse the enemy. And when those just ones have appeared, they confuse indeed the antagonistic serpent with his cleverness and they call back the faithful witnesses to God, in order to (free them) from his seduction...

The tribulation proves an instrument of judgement and revelation, as well as purification. The righteous are purified by it (again, a teaching consistent with that of the teaching of the bible about the end times - such as Daniel talking about the purification of the wise who stumble and fall for a time). The unrighteous are damned because they persist in unrighteousness and do not heed the call to repentance. God sends Enoch and Elijah to confound the enemy, and they 'call back the faithful witnesses to God, in order to free them from his seduction....'. They are part of the purification and the calling of the elect to be taken to be with the Lord, not in a rapture, but in a spiritual movement of repentance and calling out.

So, if anyone tells you that Pseudo-Ephraem teaches the Pre-Tribulation rapture, they are lying to you, no matter how sincerely they may believe it, and you need to tell them so, and bring them the true message and teaching of this powerful sermon which is that we desperately need to get ready for the Great Tribulation that is about to come upon us - we have even more signs than Pseudo-Ephraim that it is close, namely the restoration of Israel in 1948, and the fact that within two years at most, every language will have some message of the gospel preached to its speakers in their own tongue, something Jesus said would need to happen before his return (Matthew 24).

Pseudo-Methodius

We are coming towards the end of our survey of the early church fathers. I include this text, not because it has anything to say for our purposes, but because it was such a hugely important and popular document as the church moved into the Middle Ages, and because some of what it deals with are relevant to us today. It pretends to be written by Methodius; there were two church leaders of this name in the fourth century. However, it is from the seventh century, written just after the new religion of Islam had seized control of the largely Christian Middle East and the Holy Lands. The Syriac version of Pseudo-Ephraem appears to have lifted some of its content from this sermon. You can read the text here - http://http-server.carleton.ca/~jopp/3850/3-3.htm and I will summarize it. It starts out with mythical descriptions of Alexander the Great supernaturally locking up the kings of the North behind mountains for the end times. It then talks of the Persian and Roman empires, with the Persian Empire being wiped out. (It is written pretending to be a prophecy of the future. The Persian and the Roman (Byzantine) Empires had fought conflicts battles that weakened them both, and eventually let the new Muslim / Arab armies take them both out). The key quote is:

> In the final seventh millennium the Persian empire will be wiped out. In this seventh millennium the seed of Ishmael will begin to go forth from the desert of Ethribus. ......And so the Lord God will give them (i.e., the sons of Ishmael) the **power to conquer the land of the Christians, not because he loves them, but because of the sin and iniquity committed by the Christians. Such sins have not nor shall be committed for all generations. Men will get themselves up as false women wearing prostitutes clothes. Standing in the streets and squares of the cities openly before all they will be adorned like women; they will exchange natural sex for that which is against nature. As the blessed and holy Apostle says, "men have acted like women" (Rom. 1:26–7))" A father, his son, his brothers, and all the relatives will be seen to unite with one woman.**

God, as he does in the Old Testament, uses these enemies to punish his people for their sins. The Muslims are allowed to conquer Christian lands because of sins, particularly three that are increasingly rife in our societies today - homosexuality, cross-dressing, particularly by men dressing in 'sexy' prostitutes clothes, and 'swinging' or family members all having sex with the same women - perhaps meaning sexual depravity generally.

Then there is a brand new teaching, possibly taken from pagan prophecies, which involved a Roman king rising up to attack the enemies of Christendom and subduing them for a while, until the nations of the north, allegedly stopped up by Alexander the Great burst forth and conquer the Holy Lands. The mighty Christian king will defeat them and live in the Holy Land for a number of years, but then the Antichrist will arise. The Roman king will put his crown on the cross of Jesus in Jerusalem, and the cross, crown and king ascend to heaven, making way for the Antichrist to rule. This is all pretty bizarre stuff and a departure from the teaching of the church up until that point. One reason it was so popular was that it gave justification to physically fight back against the Muslim oppressors of Christianity - you would be like the final Christian king who destroys the enemies of God. The text was used for over a thousand years in both the East and the West, and was quoted and used especially when Islam was invading. So, if anyone tells you that Pseudo-Methodius taught the pre-tribulation rapture, they are lying to you, no matter how sincerely they may believe it.

Joachim of Fiore, Brother Dolcino and beyond

We are now out of the early church fathers period, so I will only comment in a general way. You will often find two Italian figures from the 12th and 13th Centuries cited as being believers in a Pre-Tribulation rapture, Joachim of Fiore, and Brother Dolcino. Joachim of Fiore demonstrates a pattern amongst Pre-Tribulation claims for medieval Christian writers and thinkers. You see, from Augustine on, by far the predominant view about the end times was either a- or post-millennialism, along with a belief in Christendom - the confluence of (then) Roman Catholicism and political power. However, there were a few examples of writers who maintained or retained the original apostolic teaching about the end times of pre-millennial belief - or at least, something somewhat resembling it. The typical approach by Pre-Trib authors is to note this and some kind of 'imminence' and then claim that this means they also taught the Pre-Trib rapture, or probably would have done, if only they knew the full truth that had been suppressed, or that the idea was there in 'seed form', as the Pre-Tribulation research centre tries to claim for many of the early church fathers. There are also claims by some such scholars that they have scholarly friends who say they have found untranslated medieval Latin documents that also allegedly teach the Pre-Tribulation rapture, but these never seem to get translated. I smell a rat, and very strongly suspect that these will be more of the same - holdouts or revivals of some form of pre-millennial beliefs, but not a 'Pre-Tribulation rapture'. For a more general assessment of the mysterious Joachim of Fiore, if you are interested, try http://www.nsu.ru/classics/resetclassics/syllabi/Joachim%20of%20Fiore-1.pdf . Also see https://en.wikipedia.org/wiki/Premillennialism#Medieval_and_Reformation_amillennialism for a bit more about his beliefs.

Brother Dolcino is another matter. I have been unable to find actual texts for him, but in this case I have little reason to substantially doubt the Pre-Tribulationist's interpretations. Little is known about him, but see https://en.wikipedia.org/wiki/Fra_Dolcino . He joined a movement that was originally pacifist, but became very savagely violent, possibly under his leadership. This was one of those groups that believed that the end was nigh, and in a coming Millennium. He was said to have opposed the church hierarchy and been what we would call today socialist in outlook. He left no writings, but we do have a couple of writings from the 14th century fairly soon after his execution by local people who were either sympathetic, or his followers, but also one by someone who opposed him called 'The History of Brother Dolcino'. The relevant passage reads:

> Again, [Dolcino believed and preached and taught] that within those three years Dolcino himself and his followers will preach the coming of the Antichrist. And that the Antichrist was coming into this world within the bounds of the said three and a half years; and after he had come, then he [Dolcino] and his followers would be transferred into Paradise, in which are Enoch and Elijah. And in this way they will be preserved unharmed from the persecution of Antichrist. And that then Enoch and Elijah themselves would descend on the earth for the purpose of preaching [against] Antichrist. Then they would be killed by him or by his servants, and thus Antichrist would reign for a long time. But when the Antichrist is dead, Dolcino himself, who then would be the holy pope, and his preserved followers, will descend on the earth, and will preach the right faith of Christ to all, and will convert those who will be living then to the true faith of Jesus Christ."

Whether Dolcino believed he would be the pope is dubious - this could have been a slander put out by the writer to make him seem a megalomaniac. However, we do know he was involved in leading a violent movement that itself was violently suppressed by the local church and secular authorities. So here we genuinely *do* have a teaching that somewhat resembles a Pre-Tribulation rapture, in that we have some 'Christians' being taken into heaven for at least half of the Tribulation. However, this does not appear to be because of any Dispensationalist type teaching, but to associate the movement's leader with Enoch and Elijah who went to heaven directly. In this belief system, the Antichrist is killed, but not by Jesus at his return, and Brother Dolcino and his movement would then be sent back to earth to reform the church and convert everybody, which is more of a Post-Millennial type teaching than anything else. It is a weird amalgam of beliefs, and there are parallels with Islamic beliefs that Christ would return before the end of the age to preach (but in that case, against Christianity and the cross, and for Islam).

So, this is it. We have one possible reference to something like a 'secret rapture' by an obscure, violent and probably megalomaniac socialist cult leader who in modern terms could be more on a par with David Koresh or Jim Jones, and this is the sole actual real evidence the Pre-Tribulationists have for a Pre-Tribulation teaching in the entire first thirteen centuries of the church! That doesn't bode well. If anyone tells you that Brother Dolcino taught the Pre-Tribulation rapture, just say 'Yes, and? Why should we pay attention to the teachings of a violent cult leader?'

Moving on, during the Reformation, there was some move back towards biblical teaching and away from allegory, although many things remained. Many of the Reformers tended to take a 'historicist' view of Revelation and believed that the Antichrist was not one end-times individual but rather the ongoing institution of the Papacy in Rome - this is still the view of many very traditional conservative Protestants and has found an outworking in many modern day Dispensationalists who believe in an end-times individual Antichrist, but believe that the Roman Catholic church and the papacy will have a major role in his rule and power structure. The 'radical Reformation' was somewhat different, and when we get to the 17th and 18th Centuries, where dispensationalists claim a number of writers had views more approaching their own, the Puritan and other movements did preach a more 'literal' interpretation of the bible. There was much interest in the Jews / Israel and their role in bible prophecy, and indeed, many started predicting - correctly - that God would restore the Jews to their ancient homeland in the end times. However, even here, dispensationalists often claim support for a Pre-Tribulation rapture where there is none. I can't say for sure that there is none- one or two may be valid, but the bottom line is that by and large the claim that the Pre-Tribulation rapture only arose in the early to mid 19th Century in England are correct (I am not even going to get into the issue of Jesuits allegedly earlier 'seeding' the concept to break up the Reformation's hostility to the Papacy - even if it is correct, it hardly does any favours to the belief to say it was sparked in deliberate deception at an earlier date). There was not a hint of it in over a thousand years of church history, and the first remotely genuine example of it was from a violent cult leader. In short, time and again, we find that the claims for the teaching in the early church are built on an exegetical - or should that be eisegetical - quick-sand or fairy-fog, mirages which when examined have absolutely nothing of substance to them.

Conclusions and Applications

I can't say with *absolute* certainty that I have covered every single relevant passage in the available texts from the early church fathers, but I have to have come pretty close. There were some commentaries on the Psalms that I didn't cover, and for the later texts, I simply searched for the term 'antichrist' since this seems to have become the standard way to refer to the evil end-times figure. If one or two of them reverted to using some of the earlier terms such as son of perdition, son of destruction, the wicked one, the black one, and so on, then I may have missed a few. But I am confident that I have covered more than enough to be sure of the position of each church fathers, and of the teaching of the early church as a whole, more than enough to utterly falsify and refute the attempts by the Pre-Tribulation Research centres and others to muddy the waters by claiming that there were various and contradictory early traditions about the end times by the early church fathers. Let us remind ourselves of exactly what they said:

> As was typical of every area of the early church's theology, their views of prophecy were undeveloped and sometimes contradictory, containing a seedbed out of which could develop various and diverse theological viewpoints. While it is hard to find clear pretribulationism spelled out in the fathers, there are also found clear pre-trib elements which if systematized with their other prophetic views contradict posttribulationism but support pretribulationism.
>
> Since imminency is considered to be a crucial feature of pretribulationism by scholars such as John Walvoord, it is significant that the Apostolic Fathers, though posttribulational, at the same time just as clearly taught the pretribulational feature of imminence. Since it was common in the early church to hold contradictory positions without even an awareness of inconsistency, it would not be surprising to learn that their era supports both views. Larry Crutchfield notes, "This belief in the imminent return of Christ within the context of ongoing persecution has prompted us to broadly label the views of the earliest fathers, 'imminent intratribulationism.

That term 'imminent intratribulationism' is just a construct of their imagination to try and get round the fact that the early church was utterly consistently and unambiguously 'Post-Trib' in their teaching. Their views of prophecy did seem to evolve somewhat - that may be because some of the earliest texts are short - and there was, naturally, some considerable variation on details, and it is true that there was a major shift in views over the issue of the Millennium, but through all this, there was a clear, consistent and irrefutable common ground that the church *would* go through the Tribulation under the Antichrist, something that many Pre-Tribulationists have tried to disguise by profoundly dishonest tactics such as claiming that Didache taught both a Pre-Trib rapture and the 'Tribulation Saints'. This is simply circular argument based on reading one verse out of context ('it teaches 'imminence' - it must prove the rapture', they cry) and then therefore the reference to saints or the church suffering at a later time must refer to some separate group of saints. As is typical, they assume the very concept they are trying to prove to provide 'proof'.

So let's summarily review each text or author:

The Didache - This taught that the church would suffer under the Antichrist, and that Christians' faith will count for nothing if they fall away in these times - only those who endure to the end will be saved - that end is described as the rapture, happening at the time of Jesus' visible return, and specifically, all the concepts of Matthew 24 about the saints in the last days are applied to Gentile Christians, except those that pertained specifically to the Jews (issues around Temple desecration and Sabbath). Pre-Tribbers claims on this text can only made by them because they take one sentence out of context and ignore or dissemble about the rest of the passage. We should remember that this work was like the official church manual for Gentile churches and came from the apostles of Jesus - it was their official teaching for Gentile churches.

Dead Sea Scrolls - any claim that the Dead Sea Scrolls taught a Pre-Tribulation rapture are completely and utterly false and the main claim is a complete fraud. To claim that a non-Christian document stated that Jesus will rapture the believers to heaven while the others are 'Left Behind' is so ludicrous that even the most unscholarly person should be able to see the fraud, yet there are still some websites that proclaim this tripe.

Justin Martyr - He made it quite clear that believers would go through terrible persecution under the Antichrist, and leaves absolutely no room for any fiction about the separate so-called 'Tribulation saints' by making it clear that the Antichrist acts 'against *us* Christians'.

The Shepherd of Hermas - contrary to the claims made about this work, it emphatically does not teach a Pre-Tribulation rapture - quite the opposite. It taught that those who did not remain faithful to Jesus in the tribulation - whether by denying him outright, or by acts of unrighteousness - would forfeit their salvation, and it explicitly urged church leaders to prepare their flocks by teaching righteous living and faithfulness to Jesus, no matter what.

Epistle attributed to Barnabas - this work taught that Christians in the last days would face many stumbling blocks, and that only those who remained in the faith to the end would be saved. He taught that the only way to gain the Kingdom of God was to go through the suffering and dark times of the last days unstinting in faith, and living righteously. Depending on your interpretation of a couple of key words, it also looks like he taught that unrighteousness and apostasy in the church is what would make room for and enable the Antichrist, and this interpretation is all the more likely since other later church fathers were absolutely explicit in this teaching.

Papias – the fragments of this very early and well-connected writer that we have do not contain any reference or teaching about a Pre-Tribulation rapture. To suggest otherwise is profoundly dishonest. He did teach a literal Millennium, but that is emphatically not the same thing, and proves nothing.

1 and 2 Clement (Clement of Rome) – These taught clearly and practically that the church would go through the end-times Tribulation and only be redeemed or rescued at the visible second coming of Jesus. It urged ongoing repentance, righteousness and faithfulness in the face of end-times suffering. The passage that is usually taken as 'proof' of the Pre-Tribulation rapture can only be such a proof if Clement suddenly uses key terms in completely different ways to that which he does in the rest of his letter and if you conveniently ignore everything else he said on the subject.

Ignatius of Antioch – in his letters he barely mentions the second coming at all. The only reference is a very vague one that, contrary to the claims made, didn't even teach any form of 'imminence', but just the need to wait for the one who is 'outside time'.

Polycarp - only one writer managed to actually cite any part of this text, and he only claimed it as 'proof' by using so much spin it would make a gyroscope dizzy and have to go and lie down. In actual fact, Polycarp's letter urged the need for 'unlimited endurance'.

Cyprian – wrote a considerable amount on this subject to already deeply suffering saints, and he wrote to exhort them to be strong in the even worse suffering they would – as Cyprian believed – have to endure in the Great Tribulation – and it was these sufferings that were 'imminent', not the coming of the Lord which would only come after. He was absolutely explicit in his teaching that the church would suffer under the Antichrist, and wrote at least one letter and his longest treatise exclusively to practical exhortations to endure in the face of such terrible suffering. The passages that Pre-Tribulationists snip out of context as 'proof' he taught otherwise are all in that context, and many are also really about the blessedness of Christians dying of the plague, precisely *because* they no longer need face the prospect of the degredations of the Antichrist. In the process of doing so, he uses many passages of the bible that Pre-Tribulationists say can 'only' be used legitimately of a Pre-Tribulation rapture, or 'imminence', and uses them in a way that is both true to their basic biblical context and directly opposite to the teaching of Pre-Tribulationists.

Irenaeus – wrote extensively on the subject, and the passage of his that is most often claimed as teaching a Pre-Tribulation rapture is doing nothing of the sort, as can be clearly seen from those Pre-Tribbers who are prepared to quote even a tiny bit of the context. In fact, it teaches that the church will be caught up in confusion and worldliness, but just before the Antichrist, the true church will be rescued by God from such worldliness. Irenaeus emphasized both that his teaching came from the hearers of the apostles and that the church would go through the Tribulation under the

Antichrist. He also directly contradicted modern dispensationalist concepts on a number of points, clearly teaching that the last days church would be there on earth when the Temple was rebuilt and the sacrifices restarted, and when the Antichrist desecrated the Temple. Additionally, he taught that the destinies of the church and Israel were not separate, but united, completely contrary to the dispensationalist doctrine that drives much modern day 'secret rapture' teaching. In fact, he could be said to belong to a stream of teaching in the early church that condemned as *heresy* views that at least have significant parallels with dispensationalist and Pre-Trib doctrines as taught today.

Tertullian - the only quote allegedly teaching a 'Pre-Tribulation rapture' turns out to be nothing of the kind, because it refers explicitly to the public and visible return of Jesus to reign. In another place, Tertullian absolutely and explicitly places the church enduring suffering under the Antichrist in such a way as to exclude any concept of separate 'Tribulation saints'.

Hippolytus (and 'Pseudo Hippolytus') - he wrote extensively on the end times, and was also absolutely explicit that the church endured the Great Tribulation under the Antichrist, at a time of great general turmoil. He also seems to have hinted that most of even the true believers would initially be deceived by the Antichrist, although would later return to true faith in Jesus. He did explicitly say that much of the church would escape to live in caves and in the wilderness in great trouble, and even then would be hunted down. He explicitly taught that the resurrection of the righteous (i.e., the 'rapture') would happen at the same time as the Matthew 25 judgement seat of Christ.

Origen and Clement of Alexandria - these were early proponents of allegorical approaches to interpreting the Bible, and I could find no material that would give us any clues where they stood on the issue we are touching on. However, given their basic approach, it is very unlikely, to say the least, that they would have entertained notions as directly antithetical to their allegorical approach as those entailed by a 'Pre-Tribulation' rapture scenario.

Lactantius - wrote of the end times in such a way that showed that he too, believed in a Post-Tribulation position, as we would call it today, with the resurrection of the righteous happening at the visible return of Jesus and the judgement associated with it.

Commodianus - a somewhat obscure poet, but his poems are clearly Post-Tribulational, in our terms (and so is his prose work - see Appendix 5) with the church suffering under the Antichrist, possibly with the intention or effect of purifying the church, something consistent with some of the other church fathers' teaching on the subject.

Methodius (the real one) - has only one surviving relevant passage, and this is clearly Post-Tribulational, applying the classic 'Rapture' passage of 1 Thessalonians 4 to the visible return of Jesus, among other things.

Victorinius - in his commentary on Revelation makes it quite clear that it is the church per se which goes through the Antichrist's malign attentions, and that it is under his reign that the last converts are gathered into the church. In addition, he is *absolutely explicit* that the warnings of Jesus in Matthew 24 about the Antichrist desecrating the temple are there for the *whole* church, not just Jewish believers.

Macarius - his sole small relevant comment is a little ambiguous, but is most easily understood in the light of a 'Post-Trib' position.

Athanasius and the real Ephrem / Ephraem of Syria - I could find no directly relevant material in these writers, although Athanasius repeatedly called his heretical opponents in the church 'heralds of Antichrist' which best fits with a position that holds that the Antichrist afflicts the church, in other words, anything but a Pre-Tribulation position.

Basil the Great and Gregory of Nyssa - wrote very little that was relevant, but what they did write suggests very strongly that they had no concept of a separate group of 'Tribulation saints'. Basil was so shaken by contemporary events that he considered it likely the time of the Antichrist was near, but used this opportunity to exhort the already suffering faithful to endure all the more, and Gregory of Nyssa saw a heretical opponent within the church as a 'herald of the Antichrist', strongly suggesting that the church would likewise be afflicted by the deceptions of the Antichrist.

Cyril of Jerusalem - wrote extensively about the Antichrist in works written especially to give practical instruction to converts and others preparing for baptism, his rationale being neatly summed up in the following quote, that it is: '*needful for us to know the signs of the end, and since we are looking for Christ, therefore, that we may not die deceived and be led astray by that false Antichrist*' which would be pointless if he believed in any kind of 'secret rapture' before the Antichrist, as would the following quotes: '....*the things which are written will be set before you, and the signs declared. Observe thou, which of them have already come to pass, and which yet remain; and make yourself safe* and *Look therefore to yourself, O man, and make safe your soul. The Church now charges you before the Living God; she declares to you the things concerning Antichrist before they arrive. Whether they will happen in your time we know not, or whether they will happen after you we know not; but it is well that, knowing these things, you should make yourself secure beforehand.*' He taught that the Antichrist would deceive both Jews and the church, and taught that division and oppression within the church would pave the way for the Antichrist: *Hatred of the brethren makes room next for Antichrist; for the devil prepares beforehand the divisions among the people, that he who is to come may be acceptable to them.* (It is particularly ironic that Cyril was based in Jerusalem, because intra-

Christian persecution was one of the main reasons that the Christians in Jerusalem and the Holy Land later welcomed the invading Muslims, hoping for better treatment under them.) Amidst the conclusion of his teaching to new converts is this: '...... *And may the God of the whole world keep you all in safety, bearing in mind the signs of the end, and remaining unsubdued by Antichrist. You have received the tokens of the Deceiver who is to come; you have received the proofs of the true Christ, who shall openly come down from heaven. Flee therefore the one, the False one; and look for the other, the True'*, something that also makes absolutely no sense if he held to any form of Pre-Tribulation position. He emphasized that he was teaching the universal teaching of the church on the matter which had been faithfully handed down from the apostles themselves.

Jerome and Rufinus - these two were at loggerheads, with Jerome denouncing Rufinus in no uncertain terms, yet both taught the same thing on this issue. Jerome taught that the saints would undergo persecution under the Antichrist when the Temple was rebuilt in his commentary on Daniel, and also raised the issue of the coming Antichrist in a letter to a Christian noblewoman urging her not to wed for this very reason. Rufinus similarly uses Daniel to teach the same thing, warning that his hearers need to be aware that Satan (the enemy) will counterfeit the return of Christ. In addition, Jerome quotes at least one other church father to the same effect, and also emphasizes that he is following on here in the teaching of the church handed down to him through the generations.

Ambrose - who also attracted the ire of Jerome, linked the heretics of his day with the Antichrist in a way that makes little sense unless he was assuming the continuity of the church in his time with the church in the time of the Antichrist, and he also was quite explicit that, contrary to many modern Dispensationalist views, the Holy Spirit remains on earth during the reign of the Antichrist, to guide and direct the judgements of Christ in the last days.

Martin of Tours and Sulpitius Severus - describe the reign of the Antichrist in terms that make little sense in a Pre-Tribulation rapture scenario, namely the abolishing of the name of Christian and the effort to make men deny their faith in Christ. They saw the persecutions under the Antichrist as simply the last in a long line of persecutions of the church, persecutions which had paused since Emperor Constantine had become a Christian.

Hilary of Potiers and the Apostolic Constitutions - demonstrate the continued faithfulness to the earliest teaching of the apostles as contained in the Didache, and also how much of the earliest church fathers rhetoric against heretics is significantly lessened or nullified if they had any notion of a Pre-Tribulation rapture in which the church escaped the Antichrist.

Revelation of Esdras and (second) Revelation of St John - these works, although bizarre in many ways, maintain a clear Post-Tribulation position

Apocalypse of Elijah - this early Egyptian Coptic work, despite the claims made about it, does not appear to teach the rapture as a separate event at all. It describes the church suffering under the Antichrist in some detail, as well as events involving persecution of the church leading up to the time of the Antichrist, and its reference to the church being taken by angels to save them from the Antichrist and the wrath against him refers to the surviving church being led to safety in the desert, not snatched up to heaven.

John Chrysostum - wrote extensively about the Antichrist in his sermons on Matthew 24 and 1 Thessalonians 4 and 5 and 2 Thessalonians. Even though he held to a view that was 'preterist' to a certain extent (he believed much, although not all, of Matthew 24 had been fulfilled in AD70) he maintained a belief in a future Antichrist who would afflict the church grievously and preached on the need for suffering to be made like Jesus. He also used 'imminence' passages to teach moral living rather than any Pre-Tribulation rapture concept or similar. He repeatedly linked in classic 'rapture' passages like 1 Thessalonians 4 with the visible return of Jesus, as well as 'one shall be taken, one shall be left' teaching. He even uses the very words 'left behind' - not of unbelievers going through the Tribulation, but of unbelievers facing judgement at the visible return of Jesus.

Augustine - also taught the church would undergo the Tribulation, although he was unsure if the abomination that desecrates in 2 Thessalonians 2 happens in the church, or at the ruins of the Jewish Temple. Not only that, but he believed that the 'iniquity' of lawlessness was a secret force working through the church and subverting it from within, and that eventually there would be sufficient wicked hypocrites in the church to make room for the Antichrist to emerge and rule. The practical application was to urge the church to not live for their own glory, to avoid being seduced by the Antichrist, but rather to live for the glory of Christ. Like many of the church fathers, he believed the persecution of the church by the Antichrist would be for 3 ½ years, and that Enoch and Elijah would preach and oppose him, converting many Jews in the process.

John Cassian - taught that the desecrating abomination would be in the church, not the Jewish temple, thus demonstrating a belief that the church would be there during the Antichrist's reign.

Abbot Coelfrid and the Venerable Bede - Coelfrid did not in any way teach a secret rapture, nor indeed 'imminence', despite claims to the contrary, and Bede in his commentary on Revelation repeatedly taught that the church underwent the Antichrist's tribulation, as a form of purification. Not only that but he made it crystal clear that the Jews / Israel and the church will suffer simultaneously, not separately. He thought that Enoch and Elijah's preaching would so raise the courage of the persecuted church that, even though they will hide in caves and mountains, at the very end they will come out to denounce the Antichrist.

Pseudo-Ephraem - despite the many claims to the contrary, this powerful and in many ways quite sophisticated sermon on the Antichrist and the end times does not preach a Pre-Tribulation rapture, but quite the opposite: its main purpose is to prepare and challenge a slumbering church to face the terrible times of the Great Tribulation under the Antichrist, warning that they will end up in the wilderness eating wild plants, and also warning that the terrible times that come upon the earth are specifically because of the church's sins and apostasy which paves the way for the confusion of the Antichrist, an apostasy that God will gather the true saints out of in the time just before the great persecution, in part through the preaching of Enoch and Elijah as described in Revelation.

Pseudo-Methodius - taught that before the Antichrist, Muslims would overrun Christian lands, because of the sinfulness of Christians, particularly in the areas of homosexuality, immorality or 'swinging', and men cross-dressing in female prostitute's clothing.

Joachim of Fiore - taught concepts that have some parallel with Pre-millennialism, but nothing about a Pre-Tribulation rapture.

Hildegard of Bingen - clearly and in great detail taught that the church would suffer under the Antichrist. I have not included her in the main body of the work, but see Appendix 6 for a full quote.

Brother Dolcino - did in fact teach something a little like the Pre-Tribulation rapture, but this was well over a 1000 years after the time of the Apostles, plus he was a violent heretic.

And beyond - a few other medieval writers may have bucked the trend and taught some form of Pre-millennialism, but not a sign of the Pre-Tribulation rapture, and at best there were only a few incoherent expressions of possibly related concepts in the 17th and 18th centuries, but for anything like a full blown Pre-Tribulation rapture teaching the earliest you will get is the 1830's.

So, in conclusion, anyone tells you that anyone in the early church whose writings we have covered taught the pre-tribulation rapture, they are lying to you, no matter how sincerely they may believe it. The only exception is one medieval violent cult leader who was several hundred years closer to our time than to that of Jesus. On this issue, the church fathers were absolutely united; they spoke with one voice, contrary to the devious attempts of false teachers like the Pre-Tribulation Research Centre to claim otherwise and muddy the waters with slanders that the early church fathers were confused and contradictory, even within individual writings. It is the Pre-Trib proponents who are ignorant, confused and contradictory, imagining fictional 'contradictions' that can 'only be explained' by injecting elements of dispensational belief into the early church fathers; they do this precisely because they impose or read into the church fathers modern day dispensationalist themes and fail at the basic exegetical task of understanding the early church fathers on their own terms, because in fact, for all their faults, the early church fathers were broadly far more biblical than modern day dispensationalists. They were part of a church that placed huge emphasis on maintaining the true teaching of the apostles, and despite accretions and even the inroads of Greek philosophy in the 3rd Century, by and large they succeeded in that mission for long after the Roman Empire became Christian. Ignoring relatively small differences such as the nationality of the Antichrist, and the precise interpretations of Revelation, there was complete unanimity over many centuries, even close to two millennia, in the teaching of the church, whether East or West, ancient or medieval or even Reformation and beyond, that the church would go through the Tribulation under the Antichrist. This was taught in sermons to challenge the church (Pseudo-Ephraim, that dispensationalists falsely claim over and over taught their position), and was taught in some practical detail to new converts to the faith, warning them they needed to be on the lookout and to know the signs of the Antichrist to avoid being taken in by him (Cyril of Jerusalem). This unanimity held through the change from a severely persecuted church to a stunningly privileged church when the Roman Empire converted to Christianity officially; it held through the associated shift from belief in a literal Millennium to the somewhat allegorical approach of amillennialism; it held for theologians and church leaders stretching from the deserts of Damascus to the bleak British North Sea shore, from the cities of North Africa to the towns of Slovenia, from Greece and Turkey to Rome, Spain and France; it held whether the native tongues of the teachers were Syriac, Greek, Latin or the languages of ancient Great Britain; it held whether the church fathers in question exchanged friendly letters across the Mediterranean or denounced each other as dangerous heretics and it held regardless of whether the writers believed that the 'abomination of Desolation' referred to in New and Old Testaments was a rebuilt Jewish temple, the current ruins of it, or the church. Each and every single one for about 1200 years after Jesus and the New Testament spoke with one voice, loud, clear, utterly unanimous: THE CHURCH WILL GO THROUGH THE TRIBULATION UNDER THE ANTICHRIST. And we only say about 1200 years because of one violent heretical cult leader. If we ignore him, which we probably should, as not being part of the true church, then this unanimity stretches for at least 1600 to 1700 years and probably more like 1800 years until the 1830's. Since the church up until that point, whether Eastern Orthodox, Nestorian, Roman Catholic, Protestant, dissenting, evangelical, Lutheran, all preached the same message on this point, then we need to ask ourselves, why should we listen to contrary voices, especially since the New Testament, as I showed in my previous book, also unequivocally teaches the same message, once you free it from the shackles of modern dispensationalist doctrine and understand it in its original Jewish context. Jesus and the apostles in the New Testament repeatedly warned us that in the last days there will be false teachers and prophets in the church that will seduce many, and that in the last days people will listen to the doctrines of demons, hearing only what they want to hear, that which 'tickles their ears'.

As I said in my last book, the idea of the Pre-Tribulation rapture, with its intense focus on the details of the end times and the antichrist, and yet obliviating the core practical message of the New Testament and the apostolic teaching on the matter, teaching that believers will escape this suffering, is a message that really does 'tickle the ears' of a comfort loving, complacent, and sleeping church. It is the eschatological version of the 'prosperity' gospel, the 'health and wealth' seduction, and it is at least as dangerous, a false teaching. Now, I know that many sincere believers hold to the Pre-Tribulation position - as indeed do many to the prosperity gospel - but that is irrelevant to the core issue - those who believed ancient heresies such as Arianism and the like were also sincere, but that did not make their heretical doctrines any the less dangerous. I am going to go so far as to say, as a theologian, that we should use the label heresy for the Pre-Tribulation rapture teaching at least (and we should look long and hard - and fast given the times we live in - at the dispensationalist teaching that it is rooted in; Jesus said you shall know a tree by its fruit, and if the fruit of a hermeneutical approach is a heresy, a false teaching utterly contrary to the word of God and the apostolic teaching..........).

Why so strong a term, you may ask? Well, a heresy was a teaching so false that it will likely lead its hearers away from salvation and away from truth. Now, the Pre-Tribulation rapture might not be in the league of, say, a denial of the Trinity, or of the true nature of Christ, core doctrines of the faith, yet in a very straightforward, practical way, it is at least as dangerous to people's salvation in the last days. You see, if a teaching on any other topic so systematically contradicted and subverted the meat and bones message of Jesus and the New Testament on a subject, we would not hesitate to call it heresy. I was tempted to say that if anyone taught something that subverted Jesus' teaching on sexuality or on the sanctity of life or the exclusivity of Jesus being the only way to the Father, we would call it heresy, but given the way the church is today, I can't really say that with confidence - another sign of the apostasy that is paving the way for the Antichrist, but I digress. Jesus and the apostles repeatedly warned that the church would go through the Tribulation, that only those who 'endure to the end will be saved', and that the Antichrist would come upon and seduce those who 'did not love the truth', a condition that describes so much of the church today, yet we have a teaching dominating those who claim to be the most biblical that undermines and subverts all of this hard teaching by telling believers not to worry because they will effortlessly escape the worst times. The early church fathers, many of whom lived in times of extreme persecution and were martyred, saw the true import - and taught that the church needed to be prepared for the even worse Tribulation to come by righteous living and close adherence to the truth, and 'unlimited endurance' as one of them put it, but the Pre-Tribulation teaching renders such a biblically correct approach utterly null and void, just like the Pharisees' traditions and teachings nullified the commands of God. Jesus warned of the end times that 'only those who endure to the end shall be saved' and yet this false teaching says that the true believer won't need to endure to the end but shall fly to the sky and revel in heaven whilst there is hell on earth. This false teaching was widespread in the Chinese evangelical church, and it was a major contributory factor to the huge apostasy from the faith that occurred when the Communists came to power, and since apostasy means taking yourself outside of Christ, and denying him before men, that means, according to the teaching of Jesus ('those who acknowledge me before men I will acknowledge before my Father in heaven, those who deny me before men I will deny before my Father in heaven') that they are lost forever. It took the Chinese evangelical church decades to recover from this false teaching and its effects. The apostle Paul warned that the evils of that day will come upon a church that is saying 'Peace and safety', exactly what this false teaching promises, and the Western church in particular is sleeping, much of it thinking that it will escape bad times, unprepared. Since, at best, even if we include a sort of escalating run up to the last seven years of the Antichrist, the Western 'rapture believing' church will have less than a decade, then if we want to avert the effects of this pernicious doctrine of demons we have to start now and work fast and hard, otherwise millions will lose their salvation because they apostasize, utterly unprepared for the terrible persecution to come, which the early church fathers taught would include persecution and violence and betrayal within the church, among other things. This is why I think we need to harden up and use not just the term 'false teaching' but 'heresy'. Time is running out, and the implications are the eternal destiny of many in the church today.

Pastors and teachers and seminary professors, if you have been teaching this doctrine of demons, you need to repent and start teaching the truth. Pastors, you need to start preparing your flocks for great Tribulation, for it is coming, and it is coming soon. I am a trustee and a researcher for the British Pakistani Christian Association here in the UK, and I recently did a report on an asylum case where part of the persecution in Pakistan involved attacks on Christian schoolgirls for daring to eat in the street during Ramadan. At the same time, Pakistani Christians in the UK who had fled and gained asylum were reporting being attacked for precisely the same reason on the streets of the UK. I hear of a woman killed in Texas for evangelizing to Muslims, and local pastors tell me of going into the house of a Muslim on their own street and seeing pictures of the Muslim in battle dress with rocket launchers on their back in the living room. I also hear of UK pastors talking with a fellow school governor, a Muslim solicitor, who says that she is hoping that her imam doesn't order them to engage in Jihad. Surveys have shown that of 1700 mosques in the UK (and there are about 100 new ones every year) only 2 - not 200, just 2 - teach a version of Islam that is 'modernist' or 'moderate'. The situation in America is perhaps better on that front, but Muslim Brotherhood terrorist groups have infiltrated the Obama administration in sensitive and strategic posts, particularly around security and intelligence (and that has been tacitly confirmed to me by someone with top-secret clearance within the UK's anti-terror machinery, and explicitly confirmed by someone with good contacts in the highest realms of UK government and parliamentary circles).

Time is running out, and running out fast. As I was working on this book, someone I know a little, a devout Christian rescued out of satanic abuse, and very knowledgeable about the bible, as well as having a Masters in Astrophysics has started revealing something she has sat on for seven years, that if even remotely true, adds to the urgency. Some of my readers may have seen the excellent 'Star of Bethlehem' documentary about what exactly was the star of Bethlehem the wise men followed to find Jesus. She had come to the same conclusion independently using the same software she was provided with when she was at university studying Astrophysics. However, she also noted that Revelation 12 referred to two 'signs in the heavens' in explicitly astronomical terms, and so she searched for 1000's of years using the software to try and see if anything exactly matched what was described in Revelation 12, astronomically, and she found just one date, the Feast of Trumpets, 23rd September 2017. How soon the associated events on earth will occur after that is not known, but we should heed the warning God has set in the heavens since the foundation of the world for us.

Church, wake up, wake up, wake up! Pastors, wake up! Even if you have not believed or taught the heresy of a Pre-Tribulation rapture, you must start preparing your flock **NOW** before it is too late! The early church fathers have much to teach us - they did not warn of escaping the Tribulation, but of the need to prepare for it by ongoing repentance, humility, righteous living and utter fidelity to Jesus. They warned that apostasy and moral laxity in the church paved the way for the Antichrist. Are you or your congregation part of that body vulnerable to deception and the Antichrist? We need to preach this, teach this, prepare spiritually and practically for what is to come, and pay heed to what Jesus and the apostles *really* taught on the issue. Again, we can learn from the early church fathers, and a good look at the teaching of St Cyril, bishop of Jerusalem to his converts and Pseudo-Ephraim in particular will reveal the intensely practical need to prepare your flocks and people and children for what is to come.

JUST DO IT, IN JESUS NAME!

Appendix 1: Reclaiming Clement from the Clutches of Jason Hommel

Here I look at the claims of one Jason Hommel who is spectacularly creative and inane in his desperate attempt to find the Pre-Tribulation rapture in Clement's letter to the Corinthian church (and in Polycarp's letter to the Philippians - dealt with in the main body of the work), which you can read if you so wish at http://www.bibleprophesy.org/clement.htm .

Clement is writing from Rome to try and end a schism in the church in Corinth in Greece.

Hommel starts with a quote from Chapter 9. In his appeal to end the strife in the Corinthian church, Clement appeals to them to return to the compassions of God. He urges his readers to:

> '...fix our eyes on those who perfectly served his magnificent glory. Let us take Enoch, for example, who was found righteous in obedience and so was taken up and did not experience death.'

Hommel precedes this quote by asking 'Is the writer exhorting about and appealing to the truth of the pretribulation rapture in these examples? I have picked out a few important excerpts below' and follows it with 'Enoch is an example of the rapture'. If that's proof that the Pre-Tribulation rapture is being taught here, then I can find proof that President Obama is a right wing Republican!

In Chapter 11, apparently because when talking about Lot, Clement says that the Lord 'does not forsake those who hope in Him, but destines to punishment and torment those who turn aside' and that 'all those who are double-minded and those who question the power of God fall under judgement' this is also proof that Clement teaches the Pre-Trib rapture. Of course, it doesn't matter that Post-Tribulationists and plenty of other end-times positions could equally as easily say these words. Anything will do to shore-up the delusion!

Hommel also baldly asserts that because chapter 19 ends with the words 'Let us reflect how free from wrath He (God) is towards all His creation' this is a clear teaching of the Pre-Tribulation position. He cites several New Testament verses about being 'free from wrath' to 'prove' that Clement must be Pre-Trib. I systematically demolish such misinterpretations about 'not appointed to wrath' in my earlier book 'Rapture Rupture!'. This is yet another example where context goes out the window. Like Pavlovian dogs responding to a bell, brainwashed Pre-Tribbers such as Hommel see 'proof' of their position whenever anything about escaping wrath appears, no matter that the phrase is pretty much always used (I can't think of any exceptions) in the New Testament and the early church fathers to mean eternal punishment in the age to come, starting when Jesus returns. This is rather bizarre. Here is a passage that teaches that God is *currently* free from wrath against

ALL his creation, and yet it is claimed to be teaching a doctrine whose key point is that only SOME of humanity *will* undergo what is interpreted to be the wrath of God in the *future*. (I feel like beating my head against a wall in despair.)

According to Hommel, because Clement in chapter 22 quotes Psalm 32 which includes the words 'The righteous cried out, and the Lord heard him, and delivered him from all his troubles' this means that he must be teaching the rapture!

In addition, by the underlining he uses in quoting chapter 29, Hommel is clearly trying to argue that because when Clement urges abstention from evil desires 'in order that we may be shielded by His mercy from the coming judgements' he follows it with a quote from Psalm 139 that has the phrase 'If I ascend to heaven' then Clement must be teaching the Pre-Tribulation rapture! Again, apparently because chapter 39 contains the phrases 'wrath destroys a foolish man' and also says that the foolish 'will not be delivered from evil' this is teaching a Pre-Tribulation rapture.

Hommel also cites Clement 50, a passage I dealt with in the main body of the work, so I won't repeat the points made there. Because in Clement 50, Isaiah 26 is paraphrased, Hommel claims - bizarrely, but unfortunately far from uniquely - that the last few verses of Isaiah 26 are really a teaching about escaping the tribulation via the rapture. I have covered this in 'Rapture Rupture!', I believe, but put simply, this involves taking a passage to *Israel* urging them to take deliberate and specific practical action to avoid undergoing God's wrath in the last days and trying to force it to mean that largely Gentile Christians are going to be passively raptured out of the way, which is hardly sound or persuasive exegesis. Since Hommel claims that the passage explicitly teaches that the Rapture occurs before the Tribulation, let's examine it more fully *and in context*. The passage in Isaiah is at the end of several chapters that talk of how (chapter 24) God will devastate the earth and make the earth stagger and shake, leaving only a remnant, the survivors of whom will eventually after the devastation and collapse of society sing for joy and give glory to God. In that day God will punish false gods in heaven and proud rulers of Gentile nations on earth, and the light of the sun and moon will fade because the God of Israel will reign from Jerusalem. Chapter 25 is a song of praise for that time - praising God for judging the wicked but rescuing the poor from oppression and providing a great feast for them in Jerusalem and removing the cloud of gloom from the earth and destroying death forever. Chapter 26 then focuses on Judah and Jerusalem saying that 'in that day' the inhabitants will sing their own song of praise proclaiming the strength and might of Jerusalem due to God's judgement and vindication of the righteous against the enemies of Israel. They also recount their history of rebellion and discipline under God's hand, admitting they had failed to give salvation to the earth, or to bring life into the world. Then it goes on to the passage Clement alludes to and Hommel claims is the rapture and Tribulation :

> 'But those who die in the Lord will live, their bodies will rise again! Those who sleep in the earth will rise up and sing for joy! For your life-giving light will fall like dew on your people in the place of the dead!
>
> 'Go home, my people, and lock your doors! Hide yourself for a little while until the Lord's anger has passed. Look! The Lord is coming from heaven

> to punish the people of the earth for their sins. The earth will no longer hid those who have been killed. They will be brought out for all to see.'

Let us consider the events here. The chapter as a whole is set in the time when God devastates the earth but rescues Jerusalem and Judah from their enemies. The Pre-Tribulation teachers clearly (and correctly) teach that this is what happens through and at the end of the Tribulation period. The people of Jerusalem and Judah have repented with great emotion for not having brought salvation to the earth, and over the fact that their suffering has been in vain. This would fit very well with other prophecies such as Revelation 1 and Zechariah 12-14 which teach that before the coming of the Messiah to battle for Jerusalem, the Jewish people will recognize they have missed the true Messiah, Jesus, whom they killed, and repent with great emotion, which again are clearly placed by Pre-Tribulation teachers as being at the end of the Tribulation. It is in this context that Isaiah 26 places the resurrection of the believing dead. This is accompanied by the command to God's people who are living to do something practical - to go home, lock their doors and hide for 'a little while' or 'a moment' until the Lord's anger has passed. At this same time the righteous dead will be made alive for all to see. In other words, this can't be any 'secret rapture' but is the moment of resurrection when the LORD comes from heaven to punish the wicked. Thus, this is the Second Coming and the battle of Armageddon and is the moment of the resurrection. How on earth, then can this be a description of a Pre-Tribulation rapture and then the Tribulation? Once again, desperate Pre-Tribbers completely ignore context.

Furthermore, it is true that Clement does link Isaiah 26 with a passage about resurrection from Ezekiel (doubtless this rings the Pre-Tribulation Pavlovian bell because the resurrection is a feature of 'the rapture'), but if we look at the context then it too hardly matches the Pre-Tribulation position, since that teaches that the rapture is primarily for the Gentile church, and is not for Israel. Clement is talking about all the dead Old Testament saints who will be resurrected, and the Ezekiel passage he paraphrases here is from Ezekiel 37, which talks about the Resurrection specifically of Israel; this, combined with the fact that Clement says the Old Testament saints will be 'revealed' - a public event - when Christ's kingdom 'comes to us' - indicates that Clement is teaching that this event happens at the visible return of Jesus; in other words, he is taking the classic Post-Tribulation position that all the early church fathers assumed.

Hommel then goes on to make the extraordinary claim that the following passage in Chapter 56 is teaching the Pre-Tribulation rapture :

> '...,. 'Six times will he rescue you from distress, and in the seventh evil will not touch you. In famine he will rescue you from death, and in war he will release you from the power of the sword. From the scourge of the tongue he will hide you, and you will not be afraid when evils approach. You will laugh at the unrighteous and the wicked, and of the wild beasts you will not be afraid, for wild beasts will be at peace with you. Then you will know that your house will be at peace, and the tent in which you dwell will not fail. And you will know that your seed will be many, and your children will be like the grass of the fields. And you will come to the grave like ripe

> wheat harvested at the proper time, or like a heap on the threshing floor gathered together at the right time.' You see, dear friends, what great protection there is for those who are disciplined by the Master; because he is a kind Father, he disciplines us in order that we may obtain mercy through his holy discipline.'

Hommel justifies his claim that this is Pre-Tribulation rapture teaching as follows :

> 'The repeated references to being "hid", and "delivered" and "gathered together" and "protected" all indicate a pretribulation rapture. Hiding is a theme of Isaiah 26:20, which he just paraphrased, and the rapture, being hid in heaven, hid in the bridal chamber at the wedding.....'

Once again, he can get away with this only be ignoring context, including the very passage from Clement he has just quoted. He carefully starts his quotation in the middle of the chapter, and indeed in the middle of a bible quote, for Clement here is quoting from Job 5.17-26. Chapter 56 is all about praying for those who have been involved in some sin, that they will repent, urging such people to accept God's correction because it unites them with the will of God. It goes on to cite several bible passages about the goodness of God's correction of the righteous, and then starts to cite the passage from Job. The bits that Hommel oh so carefully misses out read as follows :

> 'And again it says : 'Blessed is the man whom the Lord has reproved; do not reject the correction of the Lord Almighty. For he causes pain, and he makes well again; he has wounded, and his hands have healed. Six times will he rescue you....' etc, etc

Thus Hommel has deliberately (and deceitfully) started his quote at the point where he could just about get away with claiming it is teaching the rapture, when the context makes crystal clear it is not. Even if we ignore all this wider context, just looking at the quote shows that the being 'hidden' and 'delivered' and 'gathered together' and 'protected' are all about being protected *in the midst of evil,* not being completely removed from evil into heaven. After all the passage goes on to talk of having children, which is hardly applicable to raptured saints in heaven now, is it? Furthermore, the bible passage Clement is quoting is from Job, who was disciplined by tribulation but came out in the end purified in faith. And the final comment of Clement alone would clearly indicate this cannot be about being zapped up to heaven, but rather about the cleansing power of divine discipline. The protection is not from suffering, but from the final suffering of being rejected by God at judgement day, which is why he speaks as he does about repentance now, not about the timing of some mythical rapture event.

In the very next chapter, Clement directly appeals to those who he says had initiated the schism / revolt, and this too Hommel claims is really talking about the Pre-Tribulation rapture, and not just that, but he believes Clement is actually preaching against Post-Tribulation teaching! Read the passage and ask how on earth he does that, and afterwards, I'll show you. Chapter 57 starts :

> 'You, therefore, who laid the foundation of the revolt, must submit to the elders and accept discipline leading to repentance, bending the knees of

> your heart. Learn how to subordinate yourselves, laying aside the arrogant and proud stubbornness of your tongue. For it is better for you to be found small but included in the flock of Christ than to have a pre-eminent reputation and yet be excluded from His hope. For thus says the all-virtuous Wisdom : 'Listen! I will bring forth for you a saying of my spirit, and I will teach you my word. Because I called and you did not obey, and because I held out words and you paid no attention, but ignored my advice and disobeyed my correction, I therefore will laugh at your destruction, and will rejoice when ruin comes upon you, and when confusion suddenly overtakes you, and catastrophe arrives like a whirlwind, or when tribulation and distress come upon you. At that time, when you call upon me, I will not listen to you. Evil men will seek me but will not find me, for they hated wisdom, and did not choose the fear of the Lord, nor did they desire to pay attention to my advice, but mocked my correction. Therefore they will eat the fruit of their own way, and will be filled with their own ungodliness....'

Following on from his absurd claim that 'resurrection and judgement' really means 'Pre-Trib rapture and Tribulation', Hommel then claims that the revolt mentioned here is doubting the resurrection (or rapture), and that Clement is saying that the fate of those who doubt the rapture will be that 'they will lose or miss the hope, and be cast into tribulation'. The "blessed hope" is the rapture: Titus 2:13 "Looking for that blessed hope, and the glorious appearing of the great God and our Saviour Jesus Christ".' Aside from the fact that, as I demonstrated in 'Rapture Rupture!', Titus 2.13 gives no support at all for the doctrine of a separate rapture event - quite the opposite in fact - notice the sneaky slide here. 'Hope' suddenly becomes 'the Blessed Hope' so he can try and claim that Clement is talking about the rapture. Hommel claims that 'confusion suddenly' overtaking the rebellious and the ensuing 'tribulation and distress' that comes upon them is actually the Tribulation; he does this by subtly changing 'sudden confusion' to 'sudden destruction' and claiming that this is really a quote or allusion to Paul's teaching in 1 Thessalonians 5.2-3 (another passage I deal with in 'Rapture Rupture!' and show means the opposite of what Pre-Tribulationists claim). He then concludes as follows :

> 'And Clement's last line, "they shall eat the fruits of their own way" is such an appropriate rebuke to those who deny the pretribulation rapture. They, who teach we must endure the tribulation, will certainly have to endure it themselves.'

Nice rhetoric, but here are the facts. Once again, Hommel maintains this position by carefully ending the quote at the point where it would become crystal clear if he quoted more fully, that the passage is talking about something very different to the issue of Rapture timing and the Tribulation (not to mention, as we shall see, giving a rather different reference for the 'hope of the elect' to what Hommel claims). The passage Clement is quoting is from Proverbs chapter 1, and it continues:

> '..... 'their own ungodliness. Because they wronged infants, they will be slain, and a searching enquiry will destroy the ungodly. But the one who

hears me will dwell safely, trusting in hope, and will live quietly, free from fear of all evil'.

'Let us, therefore, obey his most holy and glorious name, thereby escaping the threats which were spoken by Wisdom long ago against those who disobey, that we may dwell safely, trusting in his most holy and majestic name. Accept our advice and you will have nothing to regret. For as God lives, and as the Lord Jesus Christ lives, and the Holy Spirit (who are the faith and hope of the elect), so surely will the one who with humility and constant gentleness has kept without regret the ordinances and commandments given by God be enrolled and included among the number of those who are saved through Jesus Christ, through whom is the glory to him for ever and ever. Amen.'

So not only is the hope of the elect not the rapture, but rather the Holy Spirit, it becomes clear that the issue can't be the timing of the rapture, since at issue is moral behaviour and ceasing to rebel against the leadership God has ordained. What will save is not belief in the Pre-Tribulation rapture, as Hommel claims, but righteous and humble and gentle and obedient living, and what we are being saved from is not the Tribulation, but rather eternal punishment. In short, Clement is talking about salvation and righteousness, not end time minutiae.

How Hommel ends his diatribe is telling. His delusion is so strong that even though he has to tacitly admit that Clement is not really teaching modern Pre-Tribulation rapture doctrines, yet he still manages to turn it around to vindication of his own position - in his eyes at least - by the tried and tested Pre-Tribulation self-delusion tactic of assuming their position to 'prove' it - in this case by the usual method of conflating 'tribulation' and 'wrath of God' and thus projecting his own delusion back onto a passage that talks of something totally different to what he claims :

'Admittedly, the doctrine of the pretribulation rapture is never mentioned explicitly IN MODERN TERMS, but it is very strongly implied by the many examples provided of deliverance and salvation for Godly people, and the overwhelming evidence is that tribulation and wrath is stored up for those who have rejected God and scorned the doctrine of the resurrection and return of Jesus. In fact, it might be said that Clement's letter so strongly makes the point that tribulation comes to those who reject God, that he was being inconsistent with the examples of tribulation and martyrdom that came to the Apostles who died. But Clement did mention the Apostles, and martrydom, and he conclusively shows that such tribulations came from only an ungodly source, that of wicked men. This, therefore, seems to be Clement's proof that tribulation from ungodly men is different from the wrath of God that is stored up and is to come, and therefore, the experience of martyrdom for the Apostles is no proof that Christians are appointed to endure the great tribulation to come. Thanks Clement, I'll have to remember that great pretrib rapture argument the next time some post tribber starts telling me that the tribulations the Apostles faces means that I'll have to go through the tribulation to come!'

Now that is strong delusion indeed, but unfortunately, as this and my previous work have shown, this is - although extreme - all too typical of the delusion that animates Pre-Tribulation attempts to force both the Bible and the early Church fathers to fit their end-times heresy. May God awake us His church from our heresy induced-stupour before it is too late.

Appendix 2 : The Confusion of Pastor Bob and the Five Doves Website

As we have seen, it is an all too common tactic for Pre-Tribulationists to use arguments that try and inflate the evidence, whether deliberately or not, by basically assuming that any reference to a literal Millennium or some concept that they think 'only' Pre-Tribulationist positions can explain is evidence that the writers must have been Pre-Tribulationists. We have seen how the Pre-Trib Research Centre subtly hints at this, and wistfully wonders what would have happened if the Roman Catholic church had not suppressed the development of apparently inevitable 'Pre-Tribulation' teaching. However, some proponents are a lot more direct and strident, and I came across one that exemplified the confusion and self-contradiction at the heart of such attempts. This was someone called 'Pastor Bob', an American Methodist minister who proclaimed how he had gone through much of the early church fathers and so was qualified to pass judgement on the ignoramuses and deceivers who said there was no evidence of a belief in the Pre-Tribulation rapture before the 1830's. You can read it here - http://www.fivedoves.com/letters/may2015/pastorbob531-3.htm - and it is an excellent example of the psychological phenomena known as 'projection' where you ascribe to others - particularly opponents - the very characters or foibles that you yourself are displaying or engaging in. A quick look shows that the website seems to be for anyone - or certainly lots of people - to write all their 'revelations' on the end times, and has articles still up that proclaim that the symbol of Barack Obama during his 08 election campaign secretly had 666 in it, and how a website contributor being given 'angel' money somehow was the key to understanding that Obama was the Antichrist and that therefore the rapture was going to be 2008! At least they are honest enough to leave the articles up nearly seven years later! There are also articles saying that Revelation 12 and 13 and astronomical signs in the heavens show the date of birth of the Antichrist, and that it is 4th of August, the birth day of Obama. I am by no means a fan of Obama, but they don't seem to give up (this was an article this year, long after the rapture in 2008 claims). This month (August 2015) there are articles claiming the Pre-Tribulation rapture will happen in September 2015. They don't learn, it seems, and also, isn't it funny how people who are so insistent on the necessity of the Pre-Tribulation rapture on the basis of 'imminence' somehow seem to know the signs to be able to proclaim when an event whose whole rational is to be unknowable in timing will happen? The words 'irony' and 'deception' come to mind here. But anyway, back to Pastor Bob's contributions.

He writes fairly prolifically on the Pre-Trib rapture, condemning anyone who differs in interpretation as having an 'agenda of dishonesty, distraction, deceit and deception', apparently because ' The wealth of evidence heretofore has been conclusively on the side of the Pre-Tribulation rapture'. You can find an index to his writings here http://jesusisthewaythetruththelife.com/node/22 . He seems convinced the rapture is going to be on the Jewish / Biblical Feast of Trumpets, and so every year he starts whipping up expectations that this September could be the time..... His articles are full of the usual dispensationalist rhetoric along with a smattering of 'Hebrew Roots' language, of which this is a fair sample:

> You can allow yourself to believe the truth of "The Theme of the Bride" and the "Feasts of the Lord" or let the Scripture-torturers lead you by the nose through their contortions, lies, deceptions and deceit. Hundreds of articles, books, internet posts, blogs, attack the Pre-Tribulation Rapture, often disingenuously attempting to offer a credible case......... have persuaded millions without so much as an honest look at the Hebrew Roots of the Bible.....
>
> In my next post, I will list the events of the Hebrew calendar that are directly associated with Tishri 1, or the 'Feast of Trumpets'. This collateral information provides additional insightful information that offers a cohesive, coherent, consistent, and comprehensive understanding of the Blessed Hope!

His arguments are full of the usual 'vital church-Israel separation' and 'only we take the bible prophecy literally' and the 'imminence proves the rapture' circular reasoning, including articles like http://www.fivedoves.com/letters/aug2014/pastorbob831-5.htm where he waxes on about how he has 'used every computer Bible software program on my computer, running various algorithm searches, combining every combination of key words possible, running searches on nearly sixty sets of parameters, that specifically says the Church will go through the Tribulation. I ran various levels, from the most simple to extremely complex. I have three "free" Bible software programs, and four "very expensive" Bible software programs on my computer hard drive. I conducted mathematical algorithm word and phrase studies over the course of two days in my hot attic office.' Sounds impressive, doesn't it?

He goes on to say 'I have actually discovered dozens of additional passages which I did not have in my Pre-Tribulational binders, that I have accumulated over the past few decades on God's theme of deliverance. The fact is there is even more than I expected in the way of Biblical passages that infer, corroborate, or support the Pre-Tribulational Rapture.' Infer, corroborate, or support are rather, shall we say, elastic words, as we shall see in the one example he later cites. After saying his opponents had studied the propaganda methods of Hitler's Nazi Germany, he goes on:

> 'I even resorted to try taking the position of "Devil's Advocate" ...... thinking that I just might find some Bible passages that said we are going to go through the Wrath of the Tribulation. They simply do not exist. There is not a single passage or verse, not one! God did not put a single verse in His Word to discomfort us into believing that we would see any part of that fearful seven years of Tribulation.'

Have you noticed the significant element of circular reasoning here - of assuming what he is seeking to prove. For example, you can search for the word 'church' in Revelation, and not find it in any section describing the Tribulation, and can, hey presto!, make comments like Pastor Bob does. There are many references to the 'saints' going through the Tribulation, but because he already believes these are not the church, he can ignore them as being 'Tribulation saints', a separate group. (I showed in 'Rapture Rupture!' how this line of argument is false, and you could use the same argument to say that some of the letters of Paul were teaching a Pre-Tribulation rapture and 'Tribulation saints' using the same basic argument, which is clearly absurd. There is actually a very simple explanation for why and when Revelation switches between the terms 'saints' and 'churches'.) Similarly, remember all those loads of new supporting Scriptures he claimed to have found? He only quoted one (one long already used by many other Pre-Tribulationists), 1 Thessalonians 1.10. He quotes one line, and can only make it 'support' his position by explaining how it means what he thinks with 6 extra lines of argument, and doesn't even consider that the basic Pre-Tribulation notions he uses to 'prove' his case might have a different, and better explanation.

Anyway, going back to the original article I found, it comes towards the end of a rather ramblingly long series Pastor Bob did called 'Pre-Tribulation Truth' (he digresses a lot with folksy stories about Roman Catholicism, JW's, why moderns prefer short sermons, and conspiratorial takes on current affairs, not that that is necessarily wrong). The first article in the series starts by attacking some people who taught that the 'Secret Rapture' only started in the 1830's with the founder of the Brethren and a Scottish girl
(http://www.fivedoves.com/letters/mar2015/pastorbob329-2.htm) and it concludes:

> In the next post, I will continue with the case that *the Pre-Tribulation Rapture began with the Apostle Paul and was the generally accepted view point for the next 250 years of the early Christian Church.* Its broad acceptance went into decline when the Roman Catholic Church through Augustine began to allegorize Scripture and to spiritualize the plain sense reading of the Biblical text. The Roman Catholic Church and Augustine had the most to gain by attacking the Pre-Tribulation Rapture teaching. In the mean time, comfort one another with the Apostle Paul's words and edify one another. The "Blessed Hope" is your greatest promise on the horizon. (underlining in the original).

That next article - http://www.fivedoves.com/letters/apr2015/pastorbob45-1.htm opens bombastically with:

> **To correct the facts in the origin of the Pre-Tribulation Rapture, first one has to recognize that it did not begin with Margaret MacDonald or John Nelson Darby. Anyone that states that is either ignorant of the historical facts or is an unabashed deceiving liar. My initial post of this series exposed this fundamental lie, which every anti-Pre-Trib critic hang their hat on. Shame on them for not doing their research.** (bold in the original)

He spends a lot of time talking about his time at college and in blustering rhetoric such as:

> It's one thing to state one's opinion for not believing in the Pre-Tribulation Rapture; however, to arrogantly call the Pre-Tribulation Rapture a lie, is to

> posit a position that you cannot prove, even in a court of law, unless you are God or His anointed spokesperson. I will remind you that there are Pre-Trib theologians who in addition to having earned doctorates in Theology are holders of doctor of Law degrees as well.

He goes on to claim that there are likely 100 or more examples of Pre-Tribulation rapture teaching before the 1700's:

> As best I can suggest, and it would strictly be a guess on my part, but from the time of the Apostle John to Morgan Edwards in the 1700's, we know of upwards of 100 or more individuals that believed and taught the Pre-Tribulation Rapture view; a fact ascertained by their writings.

He provides at least 250 'proofs' from Scripture, but these are mostly rehashes of the standard dispensationalist arguments I have refuted in my previous books, or ones that are based not directly on scripture passages but on dispensationalist interpretations that are not at all obvious or straightforward, with - as could be expected - a lot of circular reasoning of the usual type, presuming the very concepts he is trying to prove. He says that together they paint 'a beautiful picture through type, and shadow, the "diamond and nuggets" as I refer to them as, that only a loving God could have placed within the New Testament.' In other words it is only by taking a primarily indirect and possibly allegorical approach that this alleged literalist can provide the '100's' of supporting scriptures he claims. He also goes through extraordinary exegetical gymnastics to try and claim in his 17th post (http://www.fivedoves.com/letters/june2015/pastorbob614-2.htm) that 2 Peter 3 teaches a Pre-Tribulation Rapture, despite admitting initially that the passage 'veils the doctrine'. He claims that when Peter talks about God not wanting anyone to perish, he is not talking of salvation, but of escaping the Tribulation, an absolutely outrageous claim that I have never seen any other Pre-Tribulation peddler try and make.

However, we will focus on what he says about the alleged teaching of the Pre-Tribulation rapture in church history, which he does at http://www.fivedoves.com/letters/apr2015/pastorbob412-1.htm . There is the usual listing of church fathers supposedly teaching a Pre-Tribulation rapture, including two that I have not covered in the main body of this book, namely Tatian and Coracion, the latter of whom I have not been able to find any evidence of at all - maybe a spelling issue, although given the imaginary evidence we have seen, I wouldn't rule out him not existing at all. Regardless of this, Pastor Bob goes on to do something he does repeatedly - switching mindlessly between 'Premillenial' belief systems, and 'Pre-Tribulation' beliefs. For example:

> This segment has taken us back to the first and second-century Christian Church in Asia Minor. The proof that the early Christian community was Pre-Millennial and Pre-Tribulation has been determined by historical evidence and early Church leaders and their writings. I have named 16 Pre-Millennial scholars above, church leaders, bishops, for which we have documents written by or attributed to those named church leaders.

In actual fact, he listed them without any evidence at all for most of them that they taught anything like a Pre-Tribulation rapture, and the few that he did, he had pretty much copied and pasted from other sites, using the false claims we have seen were false in the main body of this work. These fathers appear all to have been Pre-Millennial, but that's it. I don't think Pastor Bob is aware of his flip-flop here, at least I hope not, or else his continuous charges of deliberate deception to his opponents would blatantly be projection of the worst kind. Anyway, on the basis of this non-evidence, he goes on to urge his readers:

> Keep the point of this study clear in your memory: The Pre-Tribulation Rapture is not a late 19th century-church belief, it was an early belief doctrine of the first-century church..... It never began with Margaret MacDonald or John Nelson Darby. Those who teach to the contrary about Margaret MacDonald or John Nelson Darby are either ignorant of the facts and history or simply lie in Satan's choir.

Similarly, in this article - http://www.fivedoves.com/letters/apr2015/pastorbob412-2.htm he similarly confuses the issue, by saying:

> The list of Pre-Millennial teachers spans centuries and the Anti-Pre-Tribulation would prefer that you not know the truth.

And again in post 13 - http://www.fivedoves.com/letters/may2015/pastorbob517-2.htm :

> After 12 posts in this series you would think the low-information folks would have owned up to their errors and repent of their lies and disinformation. Whenever I read a post or article on the Rapture topic, the first mention of Margaret MacDonald and Charles Nelson Darby, I immediately delete it. This is the hallmark of another moron who does not know of what they speak or write, because it simply reveals their ignorance [lack of knowledge].

He then goes on essentially to argue that most of the evidence of the alleged ongoing teaching of the Pre-Tribulation rapture through church history has been lost, but they really did teach it, honest!

> As I have shown in this series, a history of the Rapture is much more sophisticated and varied than one might initially think. That comes as a result of the deceivers that blame it on MacDonald and Darby. The Pseudo-Ephraem document, Brother Dolcino, and Morgan Edwards could very well fit into some form of a Pre-Tribulation Rapture doctrine. We can't forget the fact that most preachers do not leave a permanent record of their teachings. From Paul's day to ours, the vast majority of sound preachers have been common men as opposed to scholars. Typically, they are not writers and do not publish books. In the record of Church history, we have only a tiny glimpse into what was really happening, and that glimpse is based on the pittance that has survived of the little that was ever recorded.

(Notice how he is rather vague about the figures - they 'could very well' 'fit into some form of a Pre-Tribulation Rapture doctrine. Given that Pseudo-Ephraem taught a Post-Trib position, and Brother Dolcino seems to have been a violent cult leader who thought he would join Elijah and Enoch, and taught that the Antichrist would be killed before Jesus returned and that then he and his followers would preach the gospel to the world, and the that Morgan Edwards taught a Mid-Tribulation position, such woolliness is warranted.)

> From all the surviving documents from the period between 100 AD and 360 AD, the Early Church was Pre-Tribulational, and it wasn't until we got to Saint Augustine where allegoricalism widely replaced the earlier view.

Here we have yet another bait and switch. It is true that a more allegorical approach became prominent about the time of Augustine, but it was Pre-Millennialism that these views replaced, not Pre-Tribulation rapture teaching. We then come to the post that I originally found, number 15 out of 19 (http://www.fivedoves.com/letters/may2015/pastorbob531-3.htm) where Pastor Bob's confusions are most evident. He starts out:

> It goes without saying that I have presented more than enough evidence and witnesses of the Pre-Tribulation Rapture well before Margaret MacDonald and Charles Nelson Darby. This post will conclude what for most of you may seem to be boring ancient church history given where we are today.
>
> I have on my computer seven different Bible software packages, and one of them has the 38-volume set of the writings of the Early Church Fathers edited by church historian Philip Schaff....I have for this study read more than 30% of the nearly 20,000 pages in the 38-volume reference work. That's probably ten times as much as I used the seminary library bound set of the Early Church Fathers. I don't like to belabor the subject since we will never convince the morons and ignorant that constantly use the pat statement that MacDonald and Darby originated this doctrine on the Pre-Tribulation Rapture.
>
> I do like to be comprehensive and thorough when I posit a position. ..... I will offer some of the recorded remarks of some of the Patristic period scholars and their views on what so many ignore.

As we have seen and will see, it would actually have been good if Pastor Bob had been just a bit more comprehensive and thorough in terms of logic and consistency. He goes on to do the usual 'hand waving' about the Roman Catholic 'Institution' (he refuses to call it a church):

> The names that I note in this post are all men who were active church leaders before the Roman Catholic Institution snuffed out the belief in the Pre-Tribulation or Millennialism doctrines. I noted them by name as part of a list in a previous post.

He then goes on to note that Papias was 'a proponent of a literal millennium' which is true enough, but as to how that demonstrates an early belief in a Pre-

Tribulation rapture, on that Pastor Bob says not a word. Similarly, he cites the Epistle of Barnabas and its belief in the Millennium. Again, nothing on the rapture. Ditto with Justin Martyr (accompanied by lots of quotes from various scholars, often themselves Pre-Tribulationist, all distracting from the point that not a word is said about a rapture). Similarly he talks about Irenaeus, in particular his belief in the literal future fulfilment of the promise of the land to Abraham. Like all too many dispensationalists, Pastor Bob seems to think that if any element of their complex schema is found in an early church father, it can be presented as evidence to imply support for any and every part of dispensationalism. They also seem to go on the basis that the positions taken are unique to dispensationalism. So for instance, I am anything but a dispensationalist, but I too believe in a literal fulfilment of the promise to Abraham. To an unwary and trusting reader with little knowledge, especially someone already seeded with dispensationalist indoctrination, this can seem convincing. For instance, he says:

> It is notable how closely Irenaeus ' understanding is to that of many Pre-Millennialists today. Such is an indicator that the early church fathers came to this conclusion of a Pre-Millennial event by their own study of the Word of God in circulation with the 1st and 2nd century church.

Again, no mention of the Rapture. Further, he goes on to say:

> Our fifth name in this list of early church fathers that taught, believed, and considered closely to those views held today by Pre-Millennial Tribulation Rapture scholars and believers. His name was Tertullian. We learn of Tertullian's pre-millennialism through his debate against the heretic Marcion (cira. 207-212 AD). Shirley Jackson Case summarizes Irenaeus ' millennial view: "This period of millennial bliss corresponds to the seventh day of rest following the six days of creation described in Genesis. During this time the earth is marvelously fruitful. Jerusalem is magnificently rebuilt, and the righteous joyfully become accustomed to the new life of incorruption. After this preliminary regime of bliss has passed, a final judgment of all the world is instituted, and the new heaven and the new earth are revealed. In this final state of blessedness the redeemed shall live in the presence of God, world without end."

Again, notice the sleight of hand - he uses the term 'Pre-Millennial Tribulation Rapture', to try and give the impression that he is 'proving' a Pre-Tribulation rapture, but he is doing nothing of the sort. It is well known that the early church fathers held to what is called 'Classic' or 'Historical' Pre-Millennialism, and that term is used precisely to distinguish it from modern dispensationalist Pre-Millennialism, but of course, he can count on most of his readers not to know that fundamental fact. I will pass over the fact that his next paragraph starts : 'My sixth early church father that was a Millennialist is none other than Tertullian.' Oops. More padding, although I am sure it is not deliberate.

Again, he covers Hippolytus of Rome, with lots of scholarly quotes about his belief in a Millennium, but nothing on the Rapture. He does the same sleight of hand and equivocation in his next 'proof'.

> The eighth on my list is Lactantius (cira 250-317 AD), he also wrote of a literal millennium. ..... An interesting thing about Lactantius is that he supplies more details about the Millennium: "Then they who shall be alive in their bodies shall not die, but during those thousand years shall produce an infinite multitude, and their offspring shall be holy, and beloved by God, but they who shall be raised from the dead shall preside over the living as judges". According to Lactantius, resurrected saints shall coexist with mortals. He also includes the idea of Satan being bound for the thousand year period and the existence of pagan nations to be ruled over by the righteous. Even if one wants to disagree with me that the Apostle Paul originated the doctrine of the Pre-Tribulation Rapture, this early church father, Lactantius, wrote and taught it at least 1,500 years before Margaret MacDonald or Charles Nelson Darby.

This is another example of the pattern so common in Pre-Tribulationists of emphasizing something that 'fits' their own view, trying to make it support much more than it should. Because the Pre-Tribulationist position sells itself (or protects itself in the minds of its adherents by telling them this) on the grounds that only it literally and satisfactorily explains things, and one of the big things in their schema is the mortals who survived the Tribulation who repopulate the earth, whilst the resurrected in the Pre-Trib rapture church remains resurrected, thus when they see a teaching from the early church that appears to agree with them they grab it, without looking at the exact details. As I show in the body of this work, there are significant contradictions to a Pre-Trib dispensationalist understanding even at points like this where the early church fathers might *seem* to be singing off the same song sheet as todays Dispensationalists. Notice also the switch. Lactantius wrote of a literal millennium, discussed in detail. But then suddenly, this is evidence that Lactantius 'wrote and taught of it [Pre-Tribulation rapture] at least 1500 years before Margaret MacDonald and Charles Nelson Darby.' He wrote and taught no such thing! Now, there are two ways of interpreting this disingenuousness on the part of Pastor Bob. Either this is quite deliberate, in which case he is a deceiver of just the type he accuses his opponents, or else he isn't aware of this illegitimate equating of the two positions; he so desperately believes in a Pre-Trib position that he doesn't see the weakness of his allegedly 'thorough and comprehensive' position. But then, wouldn't that mean that here we have more projection where he is 'ignorant' or worse, because deliberately or not, he is systematically twisting and distorting the evidence, using dishonest rhetoric worthy of the Nazi propagandists he compares his opponents to.

I laughed out loud at the 9th example, because he doesn't even notice that the very quote he uses disproves his position because he quotes the early church father on the Millennium where he is talking about the church that has endured and suffered under the Antichrist (for more detail see Appendix 5, and the section on Commodianus in the main body of the work). Here is his full quote:

> The ninth of the early church fathers not previously mentioned in this series was a man by the name of Commodianus of North Africa and he wrote about 240 AD. He also spoke of a literal Millennium. He writes, "they shall come also **who overcame cruel martyrdom under**

> **Antichrist,** and they themselves live for the whole time, and receive blessings because they have suffered evil things; and they themselves marrying, beget for a thousand years".

The irony of his next comment is delicious:

> What the dishonest folks of today reveal is their ignorance, or bias, [lack of knowledge], and their predisposition to undercut the Pre-Tribulation Rapture doctrine, for whatever their reasons be. Since most of the earliest church Fathers either taught a literal millennium (though clearly differing on details) or were silent on the matter, how did amillennialism become the predominant view of the Church from the fourth century on? .....
>
> Through adducing different sources and theories as to details, the earliest church fathers clearly taught Pre-Millennialism! Anyone who tells you differently is either a liar or not familiar with the Early Church Fathers by Philip Schaff. This is not something that just anyone has in their personal library. Its 38 hardbound large volumes numbering just shy of 20,000 pages is the definitive resource on the literature of the early church outside of the Bible.
>
> The evidence that I have presented in this series of posts provides one of the most comprehensive studies on the truth concerning the Pre-Millennial Rapture Truth in the period long before Margaret MacDonald or Charles Nelson Darby. The dishonest deceivers can no longer lie and get away with their lies of claiming the Pre-Tribulation Rapture did not exist before the late 1800's. It's a gigantic scam and dishonest rendering of the evidence. I noticed that they haven't changed their facts at their Pre-Wrath Rapture babble. They just continue to proclaim their same old set of lies.

Whilst I can't comment on the honesty or otherwise of the particular opponents Pastor Bob is denouncing, he has based this entire post on a fundamentally dishonest argument, whether he realizes it or not, and it is all to do with his predisposition to see the Pre-Tribulation Rapture doctrine where it just does not exist, and he seems - I hope, because otherwise his dishonesty is deliberate and all the more deplorable - completely unaware that he continually and illegitimately switches between Pre-Millennialism and Pre-Tribulation doctrines. Once or twice could just be a trip of the keyboard and the mind, but this..... is something else entirely. He has produced one of the most comprehensive examples of the self-deception inherent in the position he is trying to prove. He ends saying he has proved the antiquity of the 'Pre-Millennial Rapture Truth'. Well, technically, my position that he so despises is exactly that - I believe in a Rapture, and I am Pre-Millennial. But then he switches to saying 'The dishonest deceivers can no longer lie and get away with their lies of claiming the Pre-Tribulation Rapture did not exist before the late 1800's' while himself teaching the most terribly deceptive false equivocations. His judgement of opponents exactly applies to him and his work. His claims are indeed 'a gigantic scam and dishonest rendering of the evidence' and it could equally be said of him and anyone who cites him that 'They just continue to proclaim their same old set of lies.'

On the basis of this monumental deception - even if it is self-deception - he goes on to press his point in the next post
http://www.fivedoves.com/letters/june2015/pastorbob67-1.htm .

> The nay-sayers continued to beat the drum that you and I will go through the Biblical Tribulation. The host of one web site says there is no one verse in the Bible that says there will be a Pre-Tribulation Rapture. And yet, they will deny the hundreds of pieces of evidence that I have shared previously that paints a beautiful picture through type, and shadow, the "diamond and nuggets" as I refer to them as, that only a loving God could have placed within the New Testament. I do not believe it was placed there as some sort of a bad joke to simply deceive or trick us. Unfortunately, their fruits are all too obvious from what trees they bloom.

Uh, well, since most of his 'hundreds of pieces of evidence' have turned out to be a flimsy sham, falsehoods themselves, his comments about fruits and 'bad jokes' that 'deceive' are particularly ironic - or apposite, depending on your point of view. He then does some handwaving by referring to something else, which suggests, deep down, he knows the flimsiness of his position:

> I would also remind you that for thousands of years we did not have any historical proof, not even a single piece or stitch of evidence to confirm the fact that the Biblical Exodus of the Jews occurred either. The story of crossing the Red Sea seemed to have been a fable, a myth written as propaganda to encourage a persecuted people. The church even tried to allegorize the Red Sea event via various contrived stories to somehow defend God's Word. The Word of God does not need defending, it is Truth. Nonetheless, over the centuries the church painted itself into a corner, and as usual, only God could "deliver" a solution. In 2000, Dr. Lennart Moller published his book 'The Exodus Case', in which the Exodus crossing of the Red Sea was revealed. The book contains around 500 color photographs, many of the debris laying on the bottom of the land-bridge beneath the Red Sea at Yom Suph, and so much more. You can watch the archived 2-part program interview of Dr. Lennert Moller with the late J.R. Church and Gary Stearman of the television program "Prophecy in the News". Simply Google "The Exodus Case".

(I will only comment here that as a theologian I am dubious about the kinds of work he refers to here, which claims that the real Mt Sinai is in Saudi Arabia, not the Sinai, although I don't rule it out outright).

> I have said all this simply as a reminder to note the fact that, if there isn't a single verse, and I would most fervently disagree, that we have, not just a "crumb trail" if you like, that confirms God's Word in Proverbs 25:2, "It is the glory of God to conceal a thing: but the honor of kings is to search out a matter". We have a battle plan laid out before our eyes! The Bible is overflowing with evidence that declares the Pre-Tribulation Rapture! One would have to be blind not to see the grand design of God's plan of removing His Bride/Church. If not blind, then obtuse! These "out to lunch" folks needn't eat your lunch in the interim waiting period which

> can be filled with trepidation and anxiety as well as excitement for some. Their fear-mongering should be of no concern for those of you "In Christ" because you are covered by His Grace!

'Eat your lunch', I should explain, is Pastor Bob's euphemism for 'steal your joy', one which he uses elsewhere. This 'battle plan' laid out before Pastor Bob's eyes is a battle plan, but it is the deception of the enemy, sent to delude him and people like him into not preparing for what Jesus, the apostles, and the early church fathers warned us must come, as the main body of this work has proven. This is the enemy's brilliant deception operation, that he gets those who believe most fervently that they are following their own Commanders agenda when they are doing precisely the opposite. His just about final comment in this post is:

> I can't stress enough the importance that you share the Good News with everyone you can possibly reach. Even if I am wrong about Rosh HaShanah 2015, this does not change the long-term outcome. It simply confirms that the Hebrew "Idiom" that no one knows the day or hour of His coming. I have noted numerous times the words of HIlton Sutton who said, "when the bombs are descending, the saints will be ascending!"

Firstly, it is especially ironic, given that he condemns the 'dubious date-setting' of a church father who believed the end of the world would be a few hundred years after his time in the previous post, that he now sets a date far more specific for the alleged 'no sign, could happen any time' rapture. And I don't care what Hilton Sutton, whoever he is, said. A far more accurate couplet would be 'When Jesus to Jerusalem is descending, the saints to his side will be ascending'.

Appendix 3 : John 14 and the early church fathers – a Heavenly Home?

Many, although not all, Pre-Tribulationists believe John 14.1-3 is about the rapture, partly because none of the other 'rapture' passages say that those raptured go to heaven, something that is indispensible to their position. Therefore it is not surprising that they seek to find in the early church fathers interpretations to back up their view that John 14.1-3 is an end-times passage. For example, see http://www.pre-trib.org/articles/view/john-141-3-the-fathers-house-are-we-there-yet . This article is a more scholarly one, trying to claim that John 14.1-3 really is talking about a rapture of believers to heaven. It starts by saying that for this to be true, then the passage has to refer to heaven as the final destination of believers, whom Jesus says he will take to be with him. Rather than starting with exegesis they start by claiming that the passage was interpreted as heaven by several early church fathers.

(And, although I don't cover it in detail in this appendix, when the article does talk about exegesis of the passage, it is very atomized, and when it does talk about context, it is quite weak, having to make arguments from silence, claiming that Jesus' original talk to the disciples had eschatological context, but that all of that had been - conveniently - unrecorded by John. It notes that although John's gospel has very little eschatological material in it, the few other verses appear in the middle of a non-eschatological context (in John 5 and 6). However, in these passages there is a strong link, reasons why the topic should appear, from the actual real context of the text. In John 5 Jesus is talking about resurrection and his God-given authority to raise people from the dead, which he will do at the last day, and in John 6, in the middle of a debate with some of the Jews over the fact that the Father draws disciples to him and that he is the bread of life, he repeatedly mentions the last day in just the same context - his ability to raise his disciples up on the last day, even though they may die physically. It then claims that - quite probably correctly - the best fit of John's account with the Passover / Last Supper celebration would place John 14 after the traditional singing of Psalm 115-118 at the end of the Passover celebration. It claims this shows eschatological context because near the end of Psalm 118 is this: 'Blessed is he who comes in the name of the Lord. From the house of the Lord we bless you' and that because of this it is not 'grasping at straws' to claim eschatological context, but I think that is exactly what it is. First of all, although Jesus did mention this passage a few days earlier, when he said Jerusalem would not see him again until it said of him 'Blessed is he who comes in the name of the Lord', in the context of Psalm 118 and the Passover, this was not particularly eschatological. In my earlier book, I showed that actually looking at the context as the Holy Spirit has given it in the text, rather than making claims for probably imaginary 'missing discourse' showed that the passage was not talking about the return of Jesus, but the way that Jesus' death and resurrection and giving of the Holy Spirit would produce a new spiritual temple in which the disciples would dwell and function as priests. The only other time Jesus uses the term 'my Father's House' in John's gospel was a reference to the Temple in Jerusalem. If the linkage with Psalm 118 is correct, this further supports my interpretation, because the Psalm, after talking of victory over enemies, despite hard times and being chastened by the Lord, talks of opening the gates of righteousness which is probably a reference to the gates of the Temple. It then talks of how the stone that the builders rejected has become the capstone, which exactly fits the context. Within 24 hours, the priests would have Jesus arrested, falsely convicted and crucified and laid in the grave - the 'builders' of the Temple rejected the true Temple. Then there is a plea for the Lord to save us (which is what Jesus' death and resurrection did), then the declaration 'Blessed is he who comes in the name of the Lord', and finally - aside from a couple of concluding exclamations of praise - the Psalm says: *The Lord is God, and he has made his light shine on us. With boughs in hand, join in the festal procession up to the horns of the altar.* In other words, the culmination is not especially eschatological per se, but is a reference to the Temple. Jesus and his death and resurrection is the way that Jesus' has made his light shine on us, and given the way that Jesus repeatedly refers to his own death through John's gospel in paradoxical fashion as his 'glorification', it is highly likely that Psalm 118 was indeed a launching point for Jesus in John 14, not to talk about his return at the very end, but about how through his death and resurrection, a new Temple would fulfil the meaning of Psalm 118 - he would be rejected, but would be the capstone of the new spiritual Temple, based in his body, of whom his disciples would partake. In John 2, after referring to the Temple as 'my Father's House', he had talked of his own body as the Temple, and just moments before, in the Synoptic gospels, he had invited his disciples to eat the bread saying 'Take, eat, this is my body, given for many'. And in the final analysis, since Jesus saw his own resurrection as the opening event of the last days, there can be an eschatological import to these words without them having to refer specifically to Jesus' return. His resurrection, as Paul tells us, was the firstfruits of the resurrection to come, and it was the start of the Age to come breaking into this age, as Hebrews tells us.)

Back to the early church fathers and John 14. The article starts out on the topic by saying:

> Everyone likes to appeal to the early church fathers when their views are in agreement with them! As pretribulation rapturists, we have not had the most pleasant experience in this realm of exegesis. Due to the lack of corroboration for a pretribulational rapture from the early church fathers, some have cast aspersion on our view of the rapture. In reply, we have argued that patristic interpretation is not necessarily a sure guide to correct theology. The early fathers were clearly wrong on a number of issues (e.g. baptismal regeneration, allegorical hermeneutics, the value of asceticism, etc.). Nevertheless, they were also right on a number of issues, due to the fact that oral transmission of traditional interpretation was still only a generation or two removed from the apostles. At the very least, it would be interesting to see whether the early Christian writers understood John 14:1-3 as being eschatological and the "Father's house" as a reference to heaven. If the apostles had understood the reference to be both eschatological and

> heavenly, then we would expect the early fathers to reflect this understanding. In fact, we do find that the extant writings of the early fathers viewed this passage as having an eschatological orientation and the "Father's house" as a reference to heaven. At least five ante-nicene fathers make reference to John 14:1-3 in their writings.

As we have seen in the main body of this work, Pre-tribulationists certainly haven't had 'the pleasant experience in this realm' since they have no support whatsoever for the first 1000 years plus of church history, and indeed a unanimous contradiction of their position, which is why they must clutch at straws like this one, seeking out fragments that could comport to their position. The footnote to this section is also revealing:

> By the way, I believe there is a perfectly good reason why many of the ante-nicene fathers seem to support a posttrib rapture. I believe they reasoned, based on their experience, that the imperial Roman persecution they were facing must surely have been the eschatological rise of antichristian Rome in the tribulation period. Believing they were in the tribulation period, they obviously could not believe in a pretribulation rapture! We might be tempted to think the same thing, were we to have gone through that horrible experience. This is a perfectly good example of the kind of eisegesis that results from interpreting Scripture based on one's experience. We, too, must exercise great caution in interpreting Biblical prophecy based on geopolitical conditions we observe in the world.

He 'believes' there is a good reason why the church fathers 'seem' to support a post-trib rapture. This guy is desperate! He does not give a shred of evidence for his position, but this is just his desperate rationale to try and escape the force of the witness of the early church. Firstly, the apostles were also under Roman persecution in the end times, and even more fundamentally important, if this was the reason why they held 'Post-trib' positions, then why did the message not vary between those inside the Roman Empire, and those who were outside it, whether in location or time, and why did the message not vary between those early church fathers who were undergoing Imperial Roman persecution and those who spoke when Imperial Rome was Christian and the persecutions had long ended?

Anyway, he goes on to cite passages from the church fathers where John 14.1-3 is alluded to or quoted. He does so with little or no comment, in many cases. But if we read them in context, do they actually support his claims? He starts with this quote from Papias:

> As the presbyters say, then those who are deemed worthy of an abode in heaven shall go there, others shall enjoy the delights of Paradise, and others shall possess the splendor of the city; for everywhere the Saviour will be seen, according as they shall be worthy who see Him. But that there is this distinction between the habitation of those who produce an hundredfold, and that of those who produce sixty-fold, and that of those who produce thirty-fold; for the first will be taken up into the heavens, the second class will dwell in Paradise, and the last will inhabit the city; and that on this account the Lord said, 'In my Father's house are many

> mansions:' for all things belong to God, who supplies all with a suitable dwelling-place, even as His word says, that a share is given to all by the Father, according as each one is or shall be worthy. And this is the couch in which they shall recline who feast, being invited to the wedding.

He makes no comment and just leaves it as it is. But this is yet another example of a Pre-Tribulation proponent assuming his position to 'prove' it. In the Pre-Tribulation schema, the church is raptured to heaven and heaven alone, the Wedding of the Lamb occurs for seven years, but then the church returns with Jesus for the final full manifestation of the kingdom of God. Then after a 1000 years, and a final rebellion, there is a new heavens and earth, and the heavenly Jerusalem come down. Have a look at the passage again. Does it really fit with a scenario where the believers are in heaven only? The passage is talking about the varying rewards of the righteous and refers to believers living in heaven, in Paradise, and in the city, and Jesus will be seen everywhere. The passage specifically says that this multiple location situation is why Jesus said 'in my Father's house are many mansions'. The only time this can apply to is Revelation 21-22, which is not only after the visible return of Jesus, but also after his 1000 year millennium age. To use this to claim the early church fathers believed the John 14 passage could refer to heaven only, in the sense that Pre-Tribulationists require, is absurd. I can only think that because the passage mentions being invited to 'the wedding', the writer is concluding and trying to imply that this must be the wedding of Jesus as depicted in Pre-Tribulation interpretation, in heaven whilst earth goes through the Tribulation, but he seems to forget, like all Pre-Tribulationists seem to, that Revelation describes the Wedding at precisely the wrong end of the Tribulation for their position, at the moment Jesus returns to earth, and so, given that all the early church fathers were Post-Tribulational, then the best interpretation is that any wedding in this passage is at or after Jesus' return, which exactly fits the reference to both heavens / paradise and 'the city' - of Jerusalem. The quote ends in the middle of the fragment of Papias that we have, conveniently, because the rest of the passage provides context that further undermines the 'heaven only' interpretation, but rather talks about how progress in righteousness or faith results in gradations of reward in that age to come:

> The presbyters, the disciples of the apostles, say that this is the gradation and arrangement of those who are saved, and that they advance through steps of this nature; and that, moreover, they ascend through the Spirit to the Son, and through the Son to the Father; and that in due time the Son will yield up His work to the Father, even as it is said by the apostle, *For He must reign till He has put all enemies under His feet. The last enemy that shall be destroyed is death* (1 Corinthians 15:25-26). For in the times of the kingdom the just man who is on the earth shall forget to die. *But when He says all things are put under Him, it is manifest that He is excepted which did put all things under Him. And when all things shall be subdued unto Him, then shall the Son also Himself be subject unto Him that put all things under Him, that God may be all in all* (1 Corinthians 15:27-28).

This is about the rewards in the Kingdom to come when it fully comes on earth, not some disembodied rapture to heaven. If you want to check out the passage for yourself, you can view it here - http://www.newadvent.org/fathers/0125.htm .

The writer then turns to Irenaeus, saying:

> Irenaeus (ca. 130-202) - Against Heresies, Book III, Ch. XIX.3 - Irenaeus describes the future day of the Christian's resurrection as a day when the believer will be caught up to the mansions in the Father's house in heaven:
>
> "Wherefore also the Lord Himself gave us a sign, in the depth below, and in the height above, which man did not ask for, because he never expected that a virgin could conceive, or that it was possible that one remaining a virgin could bring forth a son, and that what was thus born should be 'God with us,' and descend to those things which are of the earth beneath, seeking the sheep which had perished, which was indeed His own peculiar handiwork, and ascend to the height above, offering and commending to His Father that human nature (hominem) which had been found, making in His own person the first-fruits of the resurrection of man; that, as the Head rose from the dead, so also the remaining part of the body-[namely, the body] of every man who is found in life-when the time is fulfilled of that condemnation which existed by reason of disobedience, may arise, blended together and strengthened through means of joints and bands by the increase of God, each of the members having its own proper and fit position in the body. For there are many mansions in the Father's house, inasmuch as there are also many members in the body."

See http://www.newadvent.org/fathers/0103319.htm for the original quote and the wider context. This passage comes at the end of a chapter in 'Against Heresies' arguing that Jesus was not a mere man, the son of Joseph, but very God incarnated in human flesh through the virgin Mary. Notice how the article writer prejudges the matter, indoctrinating his readers to see this as a reference to heaven when it actually says nothing of the sort. Notice that 'Wherefore' at the start. In modern English we would say 'For that reason' or 'So'. This means it is part of a wider argument. The start of that paragraph reads:

> For as He became man in order to undergo temptation, so also was He the Word that He might be glorified; the Word remaining quiescent, that He might be capable of being tempted, dishonoured, crucified, and of suffering death, but the human nature being swallowed up in it (the divine), when it conquered, and endured [without yielding], and performed acts of kindness, and rose again, and was received up [into heaven]. He therefore, the Son of God, our Lord, being the Word of the Father, and the Son of man, since He had a generation as to His human nature from Mary – who was descended from mankind, and who was herself a human being – was made the Son of man (Isaiah 7:13). Wherefore also the Lord Himself gave us a sign....

The focus is on the way Jesus came down to earth, took on humanity and was tempted, and then formed in Himself the redeemed 'new man' that all true believers participate in. It may well be that there is a reference to the second coming, but the prime focus is on the relation of Jesus and his 'body', the bride, the church. However, its primary reference looks like it is to the growth of the church and the maturity of the believers ('blended together and strengthened through means of joints and bands by the increase of God, each of the members having its own proper and fit position in the body'). He mentions the 'Father's house' and its many mansions primarily in reference to the body of Christ, as the final sentence of the chapter makes clear:

> For there are many mansions in the Father's house, inasmuch as there are also many members in the body.

No reference to heaven whatsoever. The writer of this article has just invented it, lock, stock and barrel, because he is indoctrinated into the Pre-Trib belief system that John 14 must refer to the rapture. As a point of interest, Irenaeus use of the verse from John 14.1-3 fits rather well with the contextual interpretation of the passage I gave in my last book. In it, I argued that the primary reference was to the spiritual Temple, the church, the body of believers, however you want to put it, that Jesus' death and resurrection would effect. This is precisely the main focus of Irenaeus' argument during which he quotes John 14.1-3. But no heaven mentioned in relation to John 14 whatsoever.

The writer then turns to Tertullian, with three quotes. The first is as follows:

> On the Resurrection of the Flesh, XLI - Tertullian sees in John 14:1-3 an eschatological coming at the time of the resurrection to take believers to heaven.
>
> "'For we know;' he [Paul] says, 'that if our earthly house of this tabernacle were dissolved, we have a house not made with hands, eternal in the heavens;' in other words, owing to the fact that our flesh is undergoing dissolution through its sufferings, we shall be provided with a home in heaven. He remembered the award (which the Lord assigns) in the Gospel: 'Blessed are they who are persecuted for righteousness' sake, for theirs is the kingdom of heaven.' Yet, when he thus contrasted the recompense of the reward, he did not deny the flesh's restoration; since the recompense is due to the same substance to which the dissolution is attributed, - that is, of course, the flesh. Because, however, he had called the flesh a house, he wished elegantly to use the same term in his comparison of the ultimate reward; promising to the very house, which undergoes dissolution through suffering, a better house through the resurrection. Just as the Lord also promises us many mansions as of a house in His Father's home."

You can find the full document here - http://www.newadvent.org/fathers/0316.htm - this quote is from chapter 41. Now I'll be blunt, this quote shows exactly the kind of deception and distortion of the church fathers that made me so angry and caused me to write this book. That last sentence ends with a full stop, but in the original it is a semicolon, and there is a reason the quote ends oh-so conveniently in the middle of a sentence. The article author, one George A Dunn of Shasta Bible College either is a terrible scholar, or he has to have known at some level the fundamental dishonesty of what he was doing. He stops the quote just at the very point that Tertullian goes on to say that it is possible that this is talking about this world, not the next, and more to the point, then goes on to make it quite clear that the rapture is after the Tribulation and the Antichrist - and indeed, I have quoted this very chapter when we discussed Tertullian in the body of this work. Here is the rest of the quote that shows the real context, and shows that whatever Tertullian thought of the nature and location of the 'Father's home', this passage cannot with any ounce of integrity at all be used to support a Pre-Tribulation rapture:

> Just as the Lord also promises us many mansions as of a house in His Father's home (John 14:2); although this may possibly be understood of the domicile of this world, on the dissolution of whose fabric an eternal abode is promised in heaven, inasmuch as the following context, having a manifest reference to the flesh, seems to show that these preceding words have no such reference [Authors note - remember this refers back to the original quote from Paul in 2 Corinthians]. For the apostle makes a distinction, when he goes on to say, For in this we groan, earnestly desiring to be clothed upon with our house which is from heaven, if so be that being clothed we shall not be found naked; 2 Corinthians 5:2-3 which means, before we put off the garment of the flesh, we wish to be clothed with the celestial glory of immortality. Now the privilege of this favour awaits those who shall at the coming of the Lord be found in the flesh, and who shall, owing to the oppressions of the time of Antichrist, deserve by an instantaneous death, which is accomplished by a sudden change, to become qualified to join the rising saints; as he writes to the Thessalonians: For this we say unto you by the word of the Lord, that we which are alive and remain unto the coming of the Lord shall not prevent them which are asleep. For the Lord Himself shall descend from heaven with a shout, with the voice of the archangel, and with the trump of God: and the dead in Christ shall rise first: then we too shall ourselves be caught up together with them in the clouds, to meet the Lord in the air: and so shall we ever be with the Lord (1 Thessalonians 4:15-17).

You can't put any kind of Pre-Tribulation spin on that, which is why the quote ends when it does, leaving the unwary reader deeply deceived about the true teaching of this chapter from Tertullian. He then turns to a quote from another of Tertullian's works:

> Scorpiace, Antidote for the Scorpion's Sting, Ch. VI - In a passage describing the rewards that await the Christian martyr, Tertullian likens the martyr to an athlete who endures pain and suffering in order to win the prize. The awarding of that prize takes place in the future in the Father's house:
>
> "Suits for injuries lie outside the racecourse. But to the extent that those persons deal in discoloration, and gore, and swellings, he will design for them crowns, doubtless, and glory, and a present, political privileges, contributions by the citizens, images, statues, and-of such sort as the world can give-an eternity of fame, a resurrection by being kept in remembrance.

> The pugilist himself does not complain of feeling pain, for he wishes it; the crown closes the wounds, the palm hides the blood: he is excited more by victory than by injury. Will you count this man hurt whom you see happy? But not even the vanquished himself will reproach the superintendent of the contest for his misfortune. Shall it be unbecoming in God to bring forth kinds of skill and rules of His own into public view, into this open ground of the world, to be seen by men, and angels, and all powers? - to test flesh and spirit as to steadfastness and endurance? - to give to this one the palm, to this one distinction, to that one the privilege of citizenship, to that one pay? - to reject some also, and after punishing to remove them with disgrace? You dictate to God, forsooth, the times, or the ways, or the places in which to institute a trial concerning His own troop (of competitors) as if it were not proper for the Judge to pronounce the preliminary decision also. Well now, if He had put forth faith to suffer martyrdoms not for the contest's sake, but for its own benefit, ought it not to have had some store of hope, for the increase of which it might restrain desire of its own, and check its wish in order that it might strive to mount up, seeing they also who discharge earthly functions are eager for promotion? Or how will there be many mansions in our Father's house, if not to accord with a diversity of deserts?"

Firstly, I will leave aside the irony of trying to support the concept of a Pre-Tribulation rapture whose purpose is allegedly to let the saints escape suffering with a passage - indeed a whole document - that talks in detail about the suffering of the saints in God's plans, or economies, or - dare I say it - 'dispensations' and about how good martyrdom is, the very martyrdom that the Pre-Tribulation rapture is supposed to shelter pampered modern Western Christians from.

Secondly, do you see any mention of heaven - specifically heaven as opposed to a reward in the new earth to come? I don't. Go to http://www.newadvent.org/fathers/0318.htm to read the full context - this quote comes from the middle of chapter 6. Tertullian actually goes on to say that post-salvation sin would cause people to be lost unless God gave them the way out of martyrdom, as this 'baptism of blood' renders them clean to enter heaven. The martyrdom of love renders them fit for heaven - a worldview completely different to the 'God loves his bride too much to suffer' rubbish we get from the Pre-Tribbers. We are called to be like Jesus, the suffering Servant, not Jesus the pampered of his Papa. For real taste of the message of this work by Tertullian, see this quote from chapter 9:

> Thus, by allotting this very betrayal, now to the apostles, now to all, He pours out the same destruction upon all the possessors of the name, on whom the name, along with the condition that it be an object of hatred, will rest. **But he who will endure on to the end– this man will be saved**. By enduring what but persecution–betrayal–death? For to endure to the end is nought else than to suffer the end. And therefore there immediately follow, The disciple is not above his master, nor the servant above his own lord; because, seeing the Master and Lord Himself was steadfast in suffering persecution, betrayal and death, much more will it be

> the duty of His servants and disciples to bear the same, that they may not seem as if superior to Him, or to have got an immunity from the assaults of unrighteousness, since this itself should be glory enough for them, to be conformed to the sufferings of their Lord and Master; and, preparing them for the endurance of these, He reminds them that they must not fear such persons as kill the body only, but are not able to destroy the soul, but that they must dedicate fear to Him rather who has such power that He can kill both body and soul, and destroy them in hell.

Or there is this from the start of chapter 11, totally antithetical to the seductive softness of the Pre-Tribulation position:

> In the same manner, therefore, we maintain that the other announcements too refer to the condition of martyrdom. He, says Jesus, who will value his own life also more than me, is not worthy of me (Luke 14.26), – that is, he who will rather live by denying, than die by confessing, me; and he who finds his life shall lose it; but he who loses it for my sake shall find it (Matthew 10:39). Therefore indeed he finds it, who, in winning life, denies; but he who thinks that he wins it by denying, will lose it in hell.

I strongly recommend you follow the link and read the passage, particularly chapters 12 and 13 which talk of the Antichrist and suffering and cite many passages from Revelation and Paul's letters to the Thessalonians which Pre-Tribulationists are eager to claim support their position; however Tertullian uses them in a way that is utterly antithetical to modern Pre-Tribulationism. But the point is, not one passage hints at escape *from* persecution *to* heaven, only the need to persevere through persecution and martyrdom to attain heaven.

The final quote from Tertullian is this:

> On Monogamy, Ch. X - In this passage the "many mansions" and the "house of the ... Father" are clearly references to heaven where we will one day receive our reward after our resurrection:
>
> "But if we believe the resurrection of the dead, of course we shall be bound to them with whom we are destined to rise, to render an account the one of the other. But if in that age they will neither marry nor be given in marriage, but will be equal to angels, is not the fact that there will be no restitution of the conjugal relation a reason why we shall not be bound to our departed consorts? Nay, but the more shall we be bound (to them), because we are destined to a better estate-destined (as we are) to rise to a spiritual consortship, to recognize as well our own selves as them who are ours. Else how shall we sing thanks to God to eternity, if there shall remain in us no sense and memory of this debt; if we shall be reformed in substance, not in consciousness? Consequently, we who shall be with God shall be together; since we shall all be with the one God-albeit the wages be various, albeit there be 'many mansions', in the house of the same Father having labored for the 'one penny' of the self-same hire, that is, of eternal life; in which (eternal life) God will still less separate them whom He has conjoined, than in this lesser life He forbids them to be separated."

You can read the original at http://www.newadvent.org/fathers/0406.htm . This work is an argument that widowed Christians should not remarry. We don't really need to look at context. Once again, the author has to skew the matters and predispose his reader by stating this passage contains what are 'clearly references to heaven where we will one day receive our reward after our resurrection'. However, there is not one reference to heaven in this chapter, only to the resurrection, and indeed, it specifically talks about 'that age', meaning the age to come, after Jesus' return to earth. In other words, to use this as 'proof' he has to *assume* and indeed *impose upon the text* his belief in a Pre-Tribulation rapture-resurrection that takes people to heaven. This passage is just as compatible with a Post-Tribulation position where people get their reward in the heaven-come-to-earth environment of the Millennium and the new heavens and earth, and given Tertuallian took a definite Post-Tribulation position, there is no reason to think this passage is referring to anything other than that.

He then turns to two quotes from Origen. The first is as follows:

> Commentary on the Gospel of John. Tenth Book. 28 - Though known for his allegorical interpretations, Origen did sometimes interpret literally. He appears to have done so here, interpreting the Father's house and the many mansions in terms of the eschatological feast in the kingdom of heaven:
>
> "Now, those who believe in Him are those who walk in the straight and narrow way, which leads to life, and which is found by few. It may well be, however, that many of those who believe in His name will sit down with Abraham and Isaac and Jacob in the kingdom of heaven, the Father's house, in which are many mansions."

This comes right near the very end of the commentary on the Gospel of John, from chapter 28. You can read book 10 of the commentary here - http://www.newadvent.org/fathers/101510.htm . However, I want you to notice a particular sleight of hand that is going on here. The passage never mentions 'heaven' per se. It mentions 'the kingdom of heaven' which is not the same thing. Indeed, most Pre-Tribulationist thought says the same thing - that 'the kingdom of heaven' ultimately refers to the rule of heaven on earth in the Millennium, so it is rather disingenuous for this writer to be claiming that a reference to 'my Father's House' and 'many mansions' are in any way a support for the uniquely Pre-Tribulation position that the John 14 passage specifically refers to heaven, just because it mentions the 'kingdom of heaven', and especially since it links the Father's house and it's many mansions to sitting down with Abraham, Isaac and Jacob, a reference specifically to a feast on earth when Jesus returns.

The second quote is as follows:

> De Principiis. Ch. XI On Counter Problems. 6 - Here, Origen's view of what becomes of the soul after death may seem a bit strange. Nevertheless, he clearly sees the "Father's house" as a reference to heaven and the "mansions" as other-worldly spheres leading to the Father's House.
>
> "I think, therefore, that all the saints who depart from this life will remain in some place situated on the earth, which holy Scripture calls paradise, as

> in some place of instruction, and, so to speak, class-room or school of souls, in which they are to be instructed regarding all the things which they had seen on earth, and are to receive also some information respecting things that are to follow in the future, as even when in this life they had obtained in some degree indications of future events, although 'through a glass darkly,' all of which are revealed more clearly and distinctly to the saints in their proper time and place. If any one indeed be pure in heart, and holy in mind, and more practiced in perception, he will, by making more rapid progress, quickly ascend to a place in the air, and reach the kingdom of heaven, through those mansions, so to speak, in the various places which the Greeks have termed spheres, i.e., globes, but which holy Scripture has called heavens; in each of which he will first see clearly what is done there, and in the second place, will discover the reason why things are so done: and thus he will in order pass through all gradations, following Him who has passed into the heavens, Jesus the Son of God, who said, 'I will that where I am, these may be also.' And of this diversity of places He speaks, when He says, 'In My Father's house are many mansions.'"

Now this, truly, smacks of desperation. On the Pre-Tribulation Research Centre there are numerous articles with passages on how Origen was the prime instigator of all sorts of unhelpful beliefs and approaches, quite correctly. It was not for nothing that one of his nicknames is 'the father of heresy'. This passage smacks of heavy Gnostic influence, and indeed, as Origen openly alludes to, Greek pagan philosophical influence. How on earth a passage that claims John 14.1-3 is a reference to many spheres or globes in which dead saints sit and learn and ascend one to another in any way is 'proof' of a church tradition that justifies the Pre-Tribulation rapture is beyond me, but such is the elasticity (desperation?) of this 'scholars' mind, that he has somehow managed it, in his own mind, at least. I will say nothing more except that you can read the wider context of this passage in this link here: http://www.newadvent.org/fathers/04122.htm .

Finally, the writer turns to Cyprian - see http://www.newadvent.org/fathers/050702.htm for the original context.

> Treatise II, On the Dress of Virgins. 23. Though we would probably disagree with Cyprian's view on celibacy, he nevertheless clearly viewed both the "Father's house" and the "mansions" as references to our future abode in heaven:
>
> "The first decree commanded to increase and to multiply; the second enjoined continency. While the world is still rough and void, we are propagated by the fruitful begetting of numbers, and we increase to the enlargement of the human race. Now, when the world is filled and the earth supplied, they who can receive continency, living after the manner of eunuchs, are made eunuchs unto the kingdom. Nor does the Lord command this, but He exhorts it; nor does He impose the yoke of necessity, since the free choice of the will is left. But when He says that in His Father's house are many mansions, He points out the dwellings of the

> better habitation. Those better habitations you are seeking; cutting away the desires of the flesh, you obtain the reward of a greater grace in the heavenly home."

All I will point out here is that 'the heavenly home' need not mean 'heaven' per se, much like the other passages where 'kingdom of heaven' does not mean heaven. In fact, in the New Testament, the term 'heavenly' is most often used to describe something that belongs to or comes from heaven. Just use www.biblegateway.com to search for the term 'heavenly' with either the KJV or NIV and you will find over 20 results, the majority of whom have the meaning of something 'from heaven'. The passage in Cyprian actually goes on to quote one of these very passages, and indeed, the work has 10 references to 'heavenly' in general, and arguably each one of them - virtually all, in any case - has this meaning of 'from heaven'. Thus, 'heavenly home' is at least as likely to mean 'a home *from* heaven' here as it is to mean 'a home *in* heaven'. Here is the rest of the passage to provide the context:

> Those better habitations you are seeking; cutting away the desires of the flesh, you obtain the reward of a greater grace in the heavenly home. All indeed who attain to the divine gift and inheritance by the sanctification of baptism, therein put off the old man by the grace of the saving layer, and, renewed by the Holy Spirit from the filth of the old contagion, are purged by a second nativity. But the greater holiness and truth of that repeated birth belongs to you, who have no longer any desires of the flesh and of the body. Only the things which belong to virtue and the Spirit have remained in you to glory. It is the apostle's word whom the Lord called His chosen vessel, whom God sent to proclaim the heavenly command: *The first man, says he, is from the earth, of earth; the second man is from heaven. Such as is the earthy, such are they also who are earthy; and such as is the heavenly, such also are the heavenly. As we have borne the image of him who is earthy, let us also bear the image of Him who is heavenly* (1 Corinthians 15:47). Virginity bears this image, integrity bears it, holiness bears it, and truth. Disciplines which are mindful of God bear it, retaining righteousness with religion, steadfast in faith, humble in fear, brave to all suffering, meek to sustain wrong, easy to show mercy, of one mind and one heart in fraternal peace.

Adam was from and of the earth, and so too Jesus was and is from and of heaven, whether he was on earth or is in heaven now, or will be on earth in the future. 'Heavenly' does not mean the same as 'heaven' per se, and a promise of a 'heavenly home' does not provide any sure justification for thinking it refers to a home *in* heaven, rather than a home *from* heaven, and the context of the use of 'heavenly' both in Scripture and in this passage from Cyprian strongly leans the other way - that it refers to something 'of' or 'from' heaven.

Think about these quotes for a moment that allegedly show these church fathers understood John 14.1-3 as meaning believers would go to heaven. Consider how very weak they are - how this author has only managed to claim that they do refer to heaven by in some cases claiming they say something they emphatically don't, in another case by ignoring that the primary reference is to the body of Christ, which fits the context of John 14.1-3, and in another by dishonestly cutting off a quote mid-sentence so that readers don't read the real context which disproves his thesis. I am not a betting man, but if this is the best he can do, when even those he quotes don't say what he claims, I am willing to bet that there are other interpretations out there in the early church fathers. Consider this, when he makes his concluding claim that - in his mind at least - justifies him to go on and claim John 14.1-3 really is referring to heaven:

> So we see that, from the earliest years following the death of the apostle John, through the mid third century, the promise of John 14:1-3 was seen in terms of a future coming to receive believers to heaven. The ante-nicene fathers did not think that this promise had been fulfilled either in Christ's own resurrection or in the coming of the Holy Spirit at Pentecost. And since the promise was seen as something to be fulfilled in conjunction with the believer's bodily resurrection, they clearly were not thinking in terms of multiple comings being fulfilled at individual Christians' deaths, much less of a spiritual coming at the salvation of each individual Christian, but of a future day when all believers will be raised to receive their rewards.

In fact, not one of those early church fathers cited actually said that John 14.1-3 was a future coming to receive believers to heaven. Origen applied it in one passage to the feast of the future kingdom, on earth - as indeed does Papias - and in another to a wildly esoteric interpretation that has dead believers ascending towards heaven via stages of increased understanding. Cyprian mentions 'a heavenly home' but context suggests he meant 'from heaven', not 'in heaven'. Irenaeus focuses mainly on the body of Christ in applying the passage, less on the resurrection, and in any case, says nothing of heaven in relation to the resurrection anyway, and with Tertullian one quote is dishonestly cut off mid-sentence to avoid quoting the context that disproves the articles claims, a second doesn't mention heaven and is in fact antithetical to the very reasoning of Pre-Tribulation rapture, and the third also doesn't mention heaven, but *does* mention the age to come. In short, Mr Gunn's sweeping conclusions, even if he restrained himself to just the five fathers he quoted, are based on an evidence that is at best incredibly weak, and at worst completely non-existent, made-up and based on out and out deception in one case. Not one of them saw John 14.1-3 'in terms of a future coming to receive believers to heaven'. The wider conclusion that '*The ante-nicene fathers did not think that this promise had been fulfilled either in Christ's own resurrection or in the coming of the Holy Spirit at Pentecost*' is even more unmerited. The final sentence that 'since the promise was seen as something to be fulfilled in conjunction with the believer's bodily resurrection, they clearly were not thinking in terms of multiple comings being fulfilled at individual Christians' deaths, much less of a spiritual coming at the salvation of each individual Christian, but of a future day when all believers will be raised to receive their rewards' is true enough in and of itself, but proves nothing, since it is at least as equally true of the Post-Tribulation that I hold and all the early church fathers held. Thus, his historical basis for feeling justified in going on to exegete - or should that be eisegete - John 14.1-3 in terms of a Pre-Tribulation rapture to heaven is utterly unfounded.

Appendix 4 : Irenaeus – a Dispensationalist out of time?

In the case of Irenaeus, there is one more rhetorical trick pulled off by some Pre-Tribulationists and Dispensationalists in a desperate attempt to try and find some basis for their position in the early church fathers, and that is to use a quote from Irenaeus' work 'Against Heresies' in which he mentions 'Dispensations'. A primary example of this is found at http://watch.pair.com/rapture.html where the author opens by saying:

> 'The assault on the pre-Tribulation rapture is part and parcel of a larger attack on the dispensational divisions of Scripture. Within this doctrinal framework, God's dealings with Israel were interrupted by the Church Age and will resume for seven years following the removal of the Church from earth. This doctrine is foundational to classic Pauline Dispensationalism, which was expounded by early Church fathers such as Irenaeus of Lyons (120-202 A.D.) in Book V of his treatise Against Heresies'

By 'classic Pauline Dispensationalism' he appears to mean that since he is so convinced that Paul taught dispensationalism, the early Church fathers must also have expounded on it. But the only 'evidence' he can find that all the early church fathers taught it is this one quote in Irenaeus. He then gives a big long quote that includes the classic passage that we have seen is misinterpreted to mean a Pre-Tribulation rapture. It at least has the merit of being a long quote somewhat in context, but he bolds the relevant section whilst leaving in regular text the immediate context that we have seen shows it cannot mean a Pre-Trib rapture, and omits the next chapter that clearly shows the church in the Tribulation. If we examine the rest of the quote, he also omits several other bits. Now, no-one can realistically cite a whole text, but in this case, whether deliberately or not, I think it contributes to unjustified claims about the significance of the text. For instance the passage omits several bits between the start in chapter 28 and the finish in chapter 32, notably the bits that teach that tribulation is necessary for those who are saved (hardly supportive of a Pre-Tribulation position).

To illustrate the way the gaps function, let me quote first from the article as it quotes Irenaeus but putting in which chapter they are from:

"For as the Lord 'went away in the midst of the shadow of death,' where the souls of the dead were, yet afterwards arose in the body, and after the resurrection was taken up [into heaven], it is manifest that the souls of His disciples also, upon whose account the Lord underwent these things, shall go away into the invisible place allotted to them by God, and there remain until the resurrection, awaiting that event; then receiving their bodies, and rising in their entirety, that is bodily, just as the Lord arose, they shall come thus into the presence of God. 'For no disciple is above the Master, but every one that is perfect shall be as his Master. As our Master, therefore, did not at once depart, taking flight [to heaven], but awaited the time of His resurrection prescribed by the Father, which had been also shown forth through Jonas, and rising again after three days was taken up [to heaven]; so ought we also to await the time of our resurrection prescribed by God and foretold by the prophets, and so, rising, be taken up, as many as the Lord shall account worthy of this [privilege]... (chapter 31, para 2, which is the last)

> "And these things are borne witness to in writing by Papias, the hearer of John, and a companion of Polycarp, in his fourth book; for there were five books compiled ... by him. And he says in addition, 'Now these things are credible to believers.' And he says that, 'when the traitor Judas did not give credit to them, and put the question, `How then can things about to bring forth so abundantly be wrought by the Lord?' the Lord declared, `They who shall come to these [times] shall see.' When prophesying of these times, therefore, Esaias says: 'The wolf also shall feed with the lamb, and the leopard shall take his rest with the kid; the calf also, and the bull, and the lion shall eat together; and a little boy shall lead them. The ox and the bear shall feed together, and their young ones shall agree together; and the lion shall eat straw as well as the ox. And the infant boy shall thrust his hand into the asp's den, into the nest also of the adder's brood; and they shall do no harm, nor have power to hurt anything in my holy mountain.' And again he says, in recapitulation, 'Wolves and lambs shall then browse together, and the lion shall eat straw like the ox, and the serpent earth as if it were bread; and they shall neither hurt nor annoy anything in my holy mountain, saith the Lord... (Chapter 33, para 4)
>
> Inasmuch, therefore, as the opinions of certain [orthodox persons] are derived from heretical discourses, they are both ignorant of God's dispensations, and of the mystery of the resurrection of the just, and of the [earthly] kingdom which is the commencement of incorruption, by means of which kingdom those who shall be worthy are accustomed gradually to partake of the divine nature (capere Deum); and it is necessary to tell them respecting those things, that it behoves the righteous first to receive the promise of the inheritance which God promised to the fathers, and to reign in it, when they rise again to behold God in this creation which is renovated, and that the judgment should take place afterwards. For it is just that in that very creation in which they toiled or were afflicted, being proved in every way by suffering, they should receive the reward of their suffering; and that in the creation in which they were slain because of their love to God, in that they should be revived again; and that in the creation in which they endured servitude, in that they should reign. For God is rich in all things, and all things are His. It is fitting, therefore, that the creation itself, being restored to its primeval condition, should without restraint be under the dominion of the righteous; and the apostle has made this plain in the Epistle to the Romans, when he thus speaks: "For the expectation of the creature waiteth for the manifestation of the sons of God. For the creature has been subjected to vanity, not willingly, but by reason of him who hath subjected the same in hope; since the creature itself shall also be

delivered from the bondage of corruption into the glorious liberty of the sons of God." (Chapter 32, paragraph 1)

Sneaky! Notice the out of sequence quotes - the end of chapter 31, then a jump to chapter 33, and then the start of chapter 32. Does anyone smell a rat here? We will come back to this, but I want to go on and show how something similar is done in the final quotes, which go as follows :

> Thus, then, the promise of God, which He gave to Abraham, remains stedfast. For thus He said: 'Lift up thine eyes, and look from this place where now thou art, towards the north and south, and east and west. For all the earth which thou seest, I will give to thee and to thy seed, even for ever.' And again He says, 'Arise, and go through the length and breadth of the land, since I will give it unto thee; 'and [yet] he did not receive an inheritance in it, not even a footstep, but was always a stranger and a pilgrim therein. (chapter 32, paragraph 2)
>
> "And in the Apocalypse John saw this new [Jerusalem] descending upon the new earth. For after the times of the kingdom, he says, "I saw a great white throne, and Him who sat upon it, from whose face the earth fled away, and the heavens; and there was no more place for them." And he sets forth, too, the things connected with the general resurrection and the judgment, mentioning "the dead, great and small." "The sea," he says, "gave up the dead which it had in it, and death and hell delivered up the dead that they contained; and the books were opened. Moreover," he says, "the book of life was opened, and the dead were judged out of those things that were written in the books, according to their works; and death and hell were sent into the lake of fire, the second death." Now this is what is called Gehenna, which the Lord styled eternal fire. "And if any one," it is said, "was not found written in the book of life, he was sent into the lake of fire." And after this, he says, "I saw a new heaven and a new earth, for the first heaven and earth have passed away; also there was no more sea. And I saw the holy city, new Jerusalem, coming down from heaven, as a bride adorned for her husband." "And I heard," it is said, "a great voice from the throne, saying, Behold, the tabernacle of God is with men, and He will dwell with them; and they shall be His people, and God Himself shall be with them as their God. And He will wipe away every tear from their eyes; and death shall be no more, neither sorrow, nor crying, neither shall there be any more pain, because the former things have passed away." Isaiah also declares the very same: 'For there shall be a new heaven and a new earth; and there shall be no remembrance of the former, neither shall the heart think about them, but they shall find in it joy and exultation." Now this is what has been said by the apostle: "For the fashion of this world passeth away." To the same purpose did the Lord also declare, "Heaven and earth shall pass away.' When these things, therefore, pass away above the earth, John, the Lord's disciple, says that the new Jerusalem above shall [then] descend, as a bride adorned for her husband; and that this is the tabernacle of God, in which God will dwell with men. Of this Jerusalem the former one is an image-that Jerusalem of the former earth in which the righteous

> are disciplined beforehand for incorruption and prepared for salvation. (Chapter 35, paragraph 2)

Notice how there is no '....' to indicate missed text. This might, I suppose, be an honest oversight, but still, it leaves the impression that the passages immediately follow on from each other. Why might that be? Well, the omission is from the second half of Chapter 32, paragraph 2 to the first sentence of chapter 35 paragraph 2, and what they cover rather undermines most Dispensational teaching. There may be exceptions to this, but most Dispensationalists teach that the promises of land to Abraham were specifically for the Jews, with the church having a separate celestial destiny, reigning with Jesus from heaven, whilst the Jews are among those who populate the earth in the Millennium, until the new heavens and earth and the descent of the heavenly Jerusalem. This is the impression given, or at least allowed by the juxtaposition of these two passages. However, in the omitted sections Irenaeus starts by using detailed verses from the Old and New Testament to teach that the church will inherit the promise of the land because they (too?) are the 'seed of Abraham' (you can examine all this yourselves at http://www.earlychristianwritings.com/text/irenaeus-book5.html). He goes on to explain in detail why Jesus and the church will be reunited in the physical kingdom and bliss of the promised Millennium, and then cites Papias in support (the misplaced passage we noted earlier) before going on to apply various other Old Testament prophecies to the church during the Millennium. In addition, Dispensationalists believe that the resurrection of the just is the rapture that happens before the Tribulation and the saints gain their reward in heaven, but in chapter 34, Irenaeus explicitly places the resurrection of the just at the start of the Millennium kingdom, citing both Old and New Testament passages to support it. Chapter 35 paragraph 1, as we saw in the main body of the text, is even more explicit, saying *'For all these and other words were unquestionably spoken in reference to the resurrection of the just, which takes place after the coming of Antichrist, and the destruction of all nations under his rule; in [the times of] which [resurrection] the righteous shall reign in the earth, waxing stronger by the sight of the Lord: and through Him they shall become accustomed to partake in the glory of God the Father, and shall enjoy in the kingdom intercourse and communion with the holy angels, and union with spiritual beings; and [with respect to] those whom the Lord shall find in the flesh, awaiting Him from heaven, and who have suffered tribulation, as well as escaped the hands of the Wicked one.'*

Paragraph 2 starts with the following quote that is omitted from the article:

> Now all these things being such as they are, cannot be understood in reference to super-celestial matters; "for God," it is said, "will show to the whole earth that is under heaven thy glory." But in the times of the kingdom, the earth has been called again by Christ [to its pristine condition], and Jerusalem rebuilt after the pattern of the Jerusalem above, of which the prophet Isaiah says, "Behold, I have depicted thy walls upon my hands, and thou art always in my sight," And the apostle, too, writing to the Galatians, says in like manner, "But the Jerusalem which is above is free, which is the mother of us all." He does not say this with any thought of an erratic Aeon, or of any other power which departed from the

> Pleroma, or of Prunicus, but of the Jerusalem which has been delineated on [God's] hands. And in the Apocalypse John saw this new [Jerusalem] descending upon the new earth.....

Firstly, this shows that the argument is a refutation of 'supercelestial' interpretations of these passages, which is Irenaeus' term for interpretations that have the church in heaven, not on earth, during the Millennium, which is a classic Dispensationalist interpretaton (again, there may now be versions which don't hold this). Moreover, it gives a huge clue as to Irenaeus' real motivations - contrary to the 'Irenaeus was purposing to teach dispensationalism' claim, he was focused on refuting particular Gnostic heresies of his day. No wonder the article so carefully omits even parts of the very paragraphs it quotes, because they utterly disprove the deceptive claims of the article writer. (And I wouldn't bother with much of the rest of the site either, full of wild anti-Zionism and often anti-semitic conspiracies about modern US political figures and early Medieval French kings! This is very far from the usual approach of Dispensationlists who are usually philo-Semites, but the article is the fullest exposition I could find of claims that Irenaeus taught Dispensationalism.)

With this in mind, let us go back to the suspicious re-ordering of the paragraphs in the earlier part of the seemingly long and 'in context quote' in this article. Go back up and look at those paragraphs and the order, and you will see what the author is trying to dishonestly do. First he claims that Irenaeus teaches about the modern concepts of the dispensations of Israel vs the Church and that the church will be raptured out of the way at the end of the church age, 7 years before the return of Jesus. Then he quotes chapter 28 paragraph three, where it talks about the ending of the 6000th year (when Jesus will come again to inaugurate the Millennium, according to Irenaeus), skips the next paragraph about tribulation being necessary for those being saved to be purified for the Millennium, then quotes chapter 29 paragraph one with the alleged 'rapture' quote, conveniently skips the rest of chapter 29 and the bulk of chapter 30 which talk in detail about how the church should identify the antichrist, which strongly implies the church needs to know this information because it will be around - again, antithetical to the Dispensational position - to land again in the middle of paragraph 4, carefully omitting the following passage which makes explicit why there is a need to know about how to identify the name of the Antichrist : '*But he indicates the number of the name now, that when this man comes we may avoid him, being aware who he is: the name, however, is suppressed, because it is not worthy of being proclaimed by the Holy Spirit.*'

The quotes then omit chapter 31 paragraph 1 which shows that the purpose of the argument was against Gnostic beliefs, and skips the first part of paragraph 2, which show the real purpose was to combat 'supercelestial beliefs' about people going to heaven rather than waiting to be resurrected here on earth: *'If, then, the Lord observed the law of the dead, that He might become the first-begotten from the dead, and tarried until the third day "in the lower parts of the earth; " then afterwards rising in the flesh, so that He even showed the print of the nails to His disciples, He thus ascended to the Father;-[if all these things occurred, I say], how must these men not be put to confusion, who allege that "the lower parts" refer to this world of ours, but that their tuner man, leaving the body here, ascends into the super-celestial place?'* Without citing this text, the author can just about carry off the implication that the rest of paragraph two is really about people being raptured to heaven. When we include it, it becomes clear that the passage in Irenaeus cannot be talking about rapture, but rather the ordinary death of believers and their situation until the resurrection. It does not teach, as the article writer clearly wants us to believe, that resurrected Christians go to heaven at the rapture, but rather that just as Jesus had to wait in the place of the dead for his resurrection body, so too dead Christians have to wait until they are resurrected.

Then comes the really deceitful sucker punch. The article then leaps to quote the end of chapter 33, which says that of 'these things' Papias, the hearer of John, testified to in his written works. In its original context, Papias was only affirming the Millennium, as taught by John, which Irenaeus had described in the bit that this quote has leapt over. By this deception, the article writer falsely can claim that it was the teaching on a Pre-Tribulation rapture (which we have already seen he has falsified by carefully cropped quotes) that was endorsed in a chain going back to the apostle John and was widespread in the early church. What is more, he carefully fails to quote the very last part of chapter 33, in which Irenaeus notes that some people interpreted the passage about Edenic peace in the animal kingdom as being allegorical descriptions of barbarian pagans coming to Christ, but counters by saying *'But although this is [true] now with regard to some men coming from various nations to the harmony of the faith, nevertheless in the resurrection of the just [the words shall also apply] to those animals mentioned.'* Including this would make clear that the teaching in view that Papias endorsed was not a separate rapture, because here Irenaeus is teaching the 'resurrection of the just' (aka the rapture) happens not as a gateway to heaven, but rather at the start of the Millennium, so deceitfully the article omits it, before jumping back to the start of chapter 32 with its opening words: *'Inasmuch, therefore, as the opinions of certain [orthodox persons] are derived from heretical discourses, they are both ignorant of God's dispensations, and of the mystery of the resurrection of the just, and of the [earthly] kingdom which is the commencement of incorruption'*. By ignoring the context and Irenaeus' usage of the word 'dispensation' (which we will deal with shortly), this proves to be immensely useful, because it can be used to say that people today who are orthodox Christians but don't accept dispensationalism can be said to be similar to those in Irenaeus' day who were deemed orthodox and yet had opinions 'derived from heretical discourses'. The arguments of anyone challenging dispensationalism can be dispensed with as being from people *'ignorant of God's dispensations and of the mystery of the resurrection of the just'*. Given that dispensationalists are indoctrinated into a view that holds that the 'mystery' is that of the Pre-Trib rapture teaching, then this seems to them to fit just perfectly their views, and any dispensationalist reader can go away confident that his or her basic position was that of the early fathers, totally unaware of the whole suite of deceptive selective and out of order quotes that has been called upon to pull this impose this false impression on them.

The term 'dispensation' used in that last quote is the last example in Book 5, the last book of 'Against Heresies'. The question then becomes, in what way does Irenaeus use the term 'dispensation' and does it match the usage of modern day

Dispensationalists at all, or is it completely different? Now, I don't have space here to go through each usage in detail, but I will give some brief summaries, along with the links to the full text so you can check it out for yourself. We start with Book 1 in which Irenaeus starts outlining the views of the heretics that this work is designed to refute and expose as falsehood - see http://www.earlychristianwritings.com/text/irenaeus-book1.html . There are 13 uses of the word 'dispensation' and virtually all of them are references to his opponents' belief that a special dispensation had to be made to give Jesus an 'animal body' (remember that the Gnostics believed that the physical world and flesh was evil, so the perfect Son of God in a physical body and being physically resurrected was a big problem for them to 'solve'). However, there were two exceptions, in a passage from Chapter 10 I shall quote in full, because it contains an early creed, and because it shows just how careful the church was to preserve the teaching of the apostles (contrary to the implications of the Dispensationalists, who as we have seen, try and say that the early fathers were confused and unsure in what they transmitted concerning the Tribulation and the church):

> The Church, though dispersed through our the whole world, even to the ends of the earth, has received from the apostles and their disciples this faith: [She believes] in one God, the Father Almighty, Maker of heaven, and earth, and the sea, and all things that are in them; and in one Christ Jesus, the Son of God, who became incarnate for our salvation; and in the **Holy Spirit, who proclaimed through the prophets the dispensations of God,** and the advents, and the birth from a virgin, and the passion, and the resurrection from the dead, and the ascension into heaven in the flesh of the beloved Christ Jesus, our Lord, and His [future] manifestation from heaven in the glory of the Father "to gather all things in one," and to raise up anew all flesh of the whole human race, in order that to Christ Jesus, our Lord, and God, and Saviour, and King, according to the will of the invisible Father, "every knee should bow, of things in heaven, and things in earth, and things under the earth, and that every tongue should confess" to Him, and that He should execute just judgment towards all; that He may send "spiritual wickednesses," and the angels who transgressed and became apostates, together with the ungodly, and unrighteous, and wicked, and profane among men, into everlasting fire; but may, in the exercise of His grace, confer immortality on the righteous, and holy, and those who have kept His commandments, and have persevered in His love, some from the beginning [of their Christian course], and others from [the date of] their repentance, and may surround them with everlasting glory.
>
> As I have already observed, the Church, having received this preaching and this faith, although scattered throughout the whole world, yet, as if occupying but one house, carefully preserves it. She also believes these points [of doctrine] just as if she had but one soul, and one and the same heart, and she proclaims them, and teaches them, and hands them down, with perfect harmony, as if she possessed only one mouth. For, although the languages of the world are dissimilar, yet the import of the tradition is

> one and the same. For the Churches which have been planted in Germany do not believe or hand down anything different, nor do those in Spain, nor those in Gaul, nor those in the East, nor those in Egypt, nor those in Libya, nor those which have been established in the central regions of the world. But as the sun, that creature of God, is one and the same throughout the whole world, so also the preaching of the truth shines everywhere, and enlightens all men that are willing to come to a knowledge of the truth. Nor will any one of the rulers in the Churches, however highly gifted he may be in point of eloquence, teach doctrines different from these (for no one is greater than the Master); nor, on the other hand, will he who is deficient in power of expression inflict injury on the tradition. For the faith being ever one and the same, neither does one who is able at great length to discourse regarding it, make any addition to it, nor does one, who can say but little diminish it.
>
> It does not follow because men are endowed with greater and less degrees of intelligence, that they should therefore change the subject-matter [of the faith] itself, and should conceive of some other God besides Him who is the Framer, Maker, and Preserver of this universe, (as if He were not sufficient for them), or of another Christ, or another Only-begotten. But the fact referred to simply implies this, that one may [more accurately than another] bring out the meaning of those things which have been spoken in parables, and accommodate them to the general scheme of the faith; and explain [with special clearness] **the operation and dispensation of God connected with human salvation**; and show that God manifested longsuffering in regard to the apostasy of the angels who transgressed, as also with respect to the disobedience of men; and set forth why it is that one and the same God has made some things temporal and some eternal, some heavenly and others earthly; and understand for what reason God, though invisible, manifested Himself to the prophets not under one form, but differently to different individuals; and show **why it was that more covenants than one were given to mankind; and teach what was the special character of each of these covenants;** and search out for what reason "God hath concluded every man in unbelief, that He may have mercy upon all'.....

The bits in bold highlight the relevant bits. Notice that these dispensations are neither defined nor delineated in the manner of modern day dispensationalists, and indeed a key is the different nature of specifically *covenants*, which is not necessarily the same as modern day concepts of 'dispensations'. This is important, because other Pre-Tribulationists claim that there is a dispensational pattern akin to modern day dispensationalism in Irenaeus and several other of the early church fathers both before and after. The claim is that they taught a pattern of four dispensations - from Adam to Noah (or Abraham), Noah or Abraham to Moses, Moses to Christ, and then Christ onwards. We shall go on to see how the term is used in later books and find out if this is the way Irenaeus used the term.

In book 2 - see http://www.earlychristianwritings.com/text/irenaeus-book2.html - Irenaeus goes on to expose inconsistencies and contradictions in the teaching of the heretics he opposes, and the word 'dispensation' appears only five times. In each case the use of the term is used in relation to the creation of the physical world, and in refuting the views of those Gnostic heretics who believed that created matter was evil.

In book 3 - http://www.earlychristianwritings.com/text/irenaeus-book3.html - the term appears 34 times. In over a third of them, 12 times, he is again referring to particular teachings of the Gnostic heretics he is refuting, usually using the term 'the dispensational Jesus' to refer to their teaching that the heavenly Christ descended on the 'animal' Jesus at the baptism in the Jordan. It is true that sometimes he uses the term consistent with the ways that modern Dispensationalists do - we have the 'legal' or 'Mosaic dispensation' or 'dispensation of the law', along with '*new dispensation of liberty, the covenant, through the new advent of His Son*'. However, he also uses the term in other ways, for instance for different aspects of the character of Jesus, calling the faces of the cherubim (who had four faces) *'images of the dispensation of the Son of God'* (ch 11.8) or a more general 'dispensations of God' or 'dispensation of God' - the singular and plural suggesting that there is no clearly defined set of dispensations in the way modern Dispensationalists have. After all, all non-dispensational interpretations of the bible acknowledge differences in the way God dealt with humanity during the time of the Law and of Christ, so just because Irenaeus does the same doesn't prove he was dispensational in the modern understanding of the term. The emphasis in several places was not on the nature of the different dispensations, but the fact that the same God was behind them all (see eg ch 12, para15), because the views Irenaeus was confronting held that a different deity was involved in sending Christ than the one who created the world or gave the law. In fact, in that paragraph (15 of chapter 12), Irenaeus cuts across another classic Dispensationalist teaching, because he is noting that Jesus' three apostles, Peter, James and John, all scrupulously obeyed the Mosaic law even in what dispensationalists call 'the church age'. Another interesting thing to note is that there is a strong focus on the new dispensation that came with Jesus starting at his advent, contrary to modern dispensationalist views which tend to see the key point as being variously the cross, the resurrection, the ascension or the Pentecost birth of the church at the outpouring of the Holy Spirit (or in the cases of some hyper-dispensationalists, even later events such as Acts 28 - Jewish rejection of the gospel made complete, in their view). Irenaeus also uses the term to refer to true Christian church or doctrine (ch 16.8) and seems to see the coming of the Spirit as a predestined dispensation that is one with the incarnation of Jesus (ch 17.4). He also refers to a specific 'dispensation of suffering' of Jesus on the cross that the Gnostic heresy denied. In chapters 22 to 24 Irenaeus teaches that there is one whole dispensation of man bound up in Jesus and the Virgin Mary undoing the damage to the human race done by Adam and Eve. All this is very different to the rigid and set language of modern Dispensational schemes.

It is much the same in book 4 - http://www.earlychristianwritings.com/text/irenaeus-book4.html with about 38 uses of the word. I rather suspect that the translators of the text I link to were dispensationalists because of some of the chapter titles and edits they use, such as the explanatory brackets in the first example, in Preface paragraph 4, where Irenaeus says the heretics always *'come to this at last, that they blaspheme the Creator, and disallow the salvation of God's workmanship, which the flesh truly is; on behalf of which I have proved, in a variety of ways, that the Son of God accomplished the whole dispensation [of mercy], and have shown that there is none other called God by the Scriptures except the Father of all, and the Son, and those who possess the adoption.'* But even if the phrase 'dispensation of mercy' is correctly understood by them, it doesn't mean that this is the same as modern day Dispensationalist understandings where this would be the Christian or church dispensation after Jesus – the focus is on the physical body being the workmanship of God and able to be saved. Again, Irenaeus can use the term of '*the whole dispensation of God'* which the heretics deny (ch 1 para 1), or of an action or experience of Jesus '*the dispensation of his Suffering'* which the heretics had rejected in book 3 (chapter 5 para 5) – again very different from the rigid usage of modern dispensationalism where it has to mean a specific age or era, not an action. In chapter 11.3 he talks not in terms of the Adamic or Abrahamic or Mosaic dispensations of modern teaching, but rather a more general 'Old Testament Dispensation'. In chapter 20 para 6, the prophets were held to have seen *'the advent of the Lord, and that dispensation which obtained from the beginning, by which He accomplished the will of the Father with regard to things both celestial and terrestrial;'* which tends to cut across modern dispensationalist notions of separate earthly and heavenly matters, and of multiple dispensations – instead the coming of Jesus was a dispensation that had 'obtained from the beginning'. I can't resist quoting paragraph 7 at length because it contains one of the most wonderful quotes from the early church about the relation of God and man: *'And for this reason did the Word become the dispenser of the paternal grace for the benefit of men, for whom He made such great dispensations, revealing God indeed to men, but presenting man to God, and preserving at the same time the invisibility of the Father, lest man should at any time become a despiser of God, and that he should always possess something towards which he might advance; but, on the other hand, revealing God to men through many dispensations, lest man, failing away from God altogether, should cease to exist.* For the glory of God is a living man; and the life of man consists in beholding God. *For if the manifestation of God which is made by means of the creation, affords life to all living in the earth, much more does that revelation of the Father which comes through the Word, give life to those who see God.'* Paragraphs 10 and 11 effectively define dispensations as something of God's work that is seen, as opposed to the face of God the Father which is not seen, concluding that the Word of God '*points out to men the various forms (species), as it were, of the dispensations of the Father, teaching us the things pertaining to God.'* Chapter 20 paragraph 3 has several mentions of dispensations, but here too the emphasis was on the unity of faith between the patriarchs and the church, not the differences; again rather different to the emphasis of classic Dispensationalism.

'Dispensations' are used of the work of the kingdom generally in 21 para 1, and I could go on listing the many uses of the word that are not used in the Dispensationalist way, but I would draw your attention particularly to chapter 28 para 2 which reads: *'For as, in the New Testament, that faith of men [to be placed] in God has been increased, receiving in addition [to what was already revealed] the Son of God, that man too might be a partaker of God; so is also our walk in life required to be more circumspect, when we are directed not merely to abstain from evil actions, but even from evil thoughts, and from idle words, and empty talk, and scurrilous-language: thus also the punishment of those who do not believe the Word of God, and despise His advent, and are turned away backwards, is increased; being not merely temporal, but rendered also eternal. For to whomsoever the Lord shall say, "Depart from me, ye cursed, into everlasting fire," these shall be damned for ever; and to whomsoever He shall say, "Come, ye blessed of my Father, inherit the kingdom prepared for you for eternity," these do receive the kingdom for ever, and make constant advance in it; since there is one and the same God the Father, and His Word, who has been always present with the human race, by means indeed of various dispensations, and has wrought out many things, and saved from the beginning those who are saved, (for these are they who love God, and follow the Word of God according to the class to which they belong,) and has judged those who are judged, that is, those who forget God, and are blasphemous, and transgressors of His word.'* The reason I quote this in full is because although it talks about the 'various dispensations' of the Word of God (Jesus) who has always been present with the human race, yet people of all dispensations are judged at the Matthew 25 judgement seat of Christ, as shown by the quotes 'Come, you blessed of my father...' etc, which is very inconsistent with the teaching of the Dispensationalists, who limit who the judgement in Matthew 25 refers to very tightly. Finally, I direct your attention to the start of chapter 36 para 2, which reads: '*Whom these men did therefore preach to the unbelievers as Lord, Him did Christ teach to those who obey Him; and the God who had called those of the former dispensation, is the same as He who has received those of the latter. In other words, He who at first used that law which entails bondage, is also He who did in after times [call His people] by means of adoption. For God planted the vineyard of the human race when at the first He formed Adam and chose the fathers; then He let it out to husbandmen when He established the Mosaic dispensation: He hedged it round about, that is, He gave particular instructions with regard to their worship....'* If Irenaeus had really been holding to a strict dispensationalist scheme like Dispensationalists like to suggest, in which there was a specific Adamic or Patriarchal dispensation, we would expect him to use the term here, since he describes a particular period between the time of Adam and the giving of the Mosaic law, but he uses no such term - he only uses it of the Mosaic one, simply designating the 'former' and the 'latter' dispensations.

Thus we can see from the first four books that to get from Irenaeus any kind of modern classic Dispensationalist scheme you have to be *extremely* selective in which uses of 'dispensation' you focus on, and ignore many that cut across modern Dispensationalist positions. However, things get very interesting when we come back to book 5 because pretty much every use of the term 'dispensation' - see http://www.earlychristianwritings.com/text/irenaeus-book5.html - occurs in one context only, that of the redemption, salvation or resurrection of the physical body, as exemplified in the fact that Jesus was made incarnate in a human body, or God as creator of the physical world. If we exclude its use in title headings, there are 14 examples of the term 'dispensation', and if we exclude a couple of usages which might still prove the general point - two uses in chapter 17 para 4 that talk of 'the dispensation of a tree', meaning Jesus' suffering and death on a cross (they still kind of fit because they are talking about the physical nature of Jesus' sufferings, contrary to the Gnostic heretics beliefs) - every example has in its immediate context reference to God as creator of the physical world, God's attitude of blessing toward the physical human race, or to the incarnation of Jesus as a means of redeeming the human race. In each case, it is specifically the heretics disbelief in the goodness of the physicality of God's creation that is being refuted when the term 'dispensation' is used, and so it proves in the very final example that we started with, which is supposed to prove Irenaeus taught a full-panoply Dispensational Pre-Trib rapture position. We have already seen how the immediate context shows that isn't the case, and if we examine the context, we find that just like the rest of book 5, the context of the term 'dispensation' is an affirmation of the physical body through the 'resurrection of the just' as well as an earthly kingdom, not an example of a dispensational division of the ages, let alone a detailed application to the end times and the timing of the rapture.

To summarize then, the only way the author of this article can claim Irenaeus taught the Pre-Trib rapture and Dispensationalism is by a deceptive disordering of the material he quotes, accompanied by very carefully selected editing points, both of which have to have on some level been deliberately dishonest - unless he was copying someone else, he has to have known he was cutting out material contradictory to his declared position. More generally, claims that Irenaeus taught a modern day strict dispensationalist schema fail because of the rich variety of ways in which he uses the term 'dispensation', and specifically because in book 5 his use of the term is for something else entirely.

So if someone tells you that Irenaeus taught a Dispensational scheme like those of today, they are at best not being coherent or consistent with the whole truth, at worst.... they are lying to you, so challenge them to provide detailed, in context evidence and test it well. And I rather suspect the same will apply to other church fathers that are supposed to hold to more or less modern 'Dispensationalist' teaching.

Appendix 5 : Commodianus' 'Carmen Apologeticum' on the end times.

I here simply lift the translation of this work from the website of the translator from the Latin, Darius Matthew Klein (http://christianlatin.blogspot.co.uk/2008/08/excerpt-from-commodianus-carmen.html). You will find it highly detailed about the end times, somewhat reminiscent of modern popular end times teaching, but with considerable differences in detail - Nero is said to return from exile or the dead, and be one of several oppressors in the last days, culminating in the Antichrist. I won't give any comment, except to highlight in bold all the parts that speak against Dispensational or Pre-Tribulation interpretations, whether it is where the text indicates that there is a continuity between the church when Commodianus wrote and those who will encounter the end times, or that the saints endure the persecution ordained by God at the same time as the events of Daniel's final week happen in Israel, or where expressions that might be called 'imminence' are linked to a description of what must happen before Jesus returns, or where the resurrection of the righteous (the rapture) is placed after the time of the Antichrist, at Jesus return, or indeed the very climax of the passage when the ultimate end is a united people of God, completely contrary to the Dispensational teaching of a strict division between the Jews and the church. Here is the relevant passage, lines 785 to 1083:

And with the fulfillment of six thousand years shall these things come to pass. **I hope indeed that we are already on the farther shore by that time.** For at that time, a man of the sun, revived in agony, will arise once more. Recalling what had taken place beforehand, he shall rejoice in God. Because he is incorruptible, he shall be cognizant of the prophecies of the previous age which he had heard while in the flesh. Amazed that such glory could come forth before a mere human being, he shall say: "I see exactly what is, just as I heard it before." And all who will be lifted from Hell will likewise cry: "Just as we heard in former times, behold! this is now what we see." All suffering will take leave of the body, and every wound as well. There shall be no anxiety, but always joy. Each nation believes intuitively that there is One: One Who will be perpetually reborn into the generations of eternity.

But certain persons shall cry out: "At what point can we be certain that these things shall come about?" Accept it as truth, I say, from the few signs by which other signs shall multiply. **For many signs of the fulfillment of the terrible destruction will come to be**, and our seventh persecution shall begin. **Already it knocks at the gate**: the sword of the Goths will presently cross the river, and they shall break in. King Apollyon, he of the dire name, shall be with them. **He shall use his armies the spread the persecution of the holy ones. He shall proceed to Rome with many thousands of tribes; and by the decree of God will he take captive a portion of those subdued by him. And many of the nobility, having been led captive, shall weep. When they see that they have been**

vanquished by the barbarian, they shall blaspheme the God of the Heavens. Still, the nations that are shall continue to nurture the Christians. Filled with joy, they shall seek them as brothers, desisting from worshipping vain idols and luxuries. They shall persecute and enslave the nobility. Those who persecuted the beloved ones shall perpetrate these evils: and within five months, those under the rule of the enemy shall be slain.

Meanwhile, Cyrus shall arise. It shall be his will to terrorize his enemies and liberate the nobility. He who had been put in command of the kingdom, and was known for a long time to have been preserved in his body for many years, shall return from the dead. It has already been revealed to us that this is Nero, who had flogged Peter and Paul in the city. From hidden places at the very end of the world shall he return, since he was reserved for these things. The nobility shall marvel that he is hated: for when he appears they will think that he is almost like a god.

The exact time of his coming, which will be in the middle of the week, shall be prophesied by Elijah at the appointed time. And when Nero has completed his time, the Unspeakable One shall succeed him. Him shall both the Jews and Romans worship. But there shall be another coming from the East whom they await. **Nevertheless they shall wax savage with Nero in slaughtering us. Thus when Elijah prophesies in Judea,** and baptizes the appropriate populace in the name of Christ (concerning whom Elijah in outrage shall pray against their receiving rain, inasmuch as so many of them shall choose not to believe), then the heavens shall be closed, nor shall they moisten the earth with their dew. And in a rage shall the prophet turn the rivers into blood. The land shall become sterile, it shall not be moistened with spring waters, and famine shall come about. There shall be, moreover, a plague over all the world. Because Elijah shall do these things, the tormented Judeans shall contrive many false charges against him after they have provoked the nobility to rise in wrath against him by calling him the enemy of the Romans. Then the nobility, taking note of these things, will hasten to beseech Nero with prayers and iniquitous gifts: "Take this enemy of the people, by whom our gods are condemned rather than worshiped, away from the affairs of men." **And Nero, entirely possessed by madness induced by the prayers of the nobility, shall seize the Eastern prophets in a public vehicle. And when he is satisfied that they are Jews, he shall burn them first. Thereafter he shall turn to the churches, in whose martyrdom a tenth part of the city - seven thousand all in all - shall perish.** On the fourth day of the persecution the Lord shall bear those denied graves into the heavens. He shall only revive those made immortal from death. And their enemies shall look up and behold them going through the heavens.

But they shall not be terrified, but shall instead wax fierce, **executing the people of Christ with all of their hatred. The Most High shall harden these disgraceful ones in their hearts, just as he once hardened Pharaoh's ears. Then the hard and wicked monarch Nero, formerly exiled, shall order the Christian populace to be expelled from the city. Two Caesars shall participate with him in this, with whom he shall persecute the Christian populace with dire madness. They shall order the judges to issue edicts throughout the land, so that they can compel Christians to abandon the**

name of Christ. And in the event that any should be able to evade them, they shall order all to go forth crowned that they should place offerings of incense before idols. If any of the faithful refuse to take part in the spectacle, he shall die a blessed death. But if not, he merely becomes one of the crowd. At that time there shall be no day of peace, nor offering to Christ. Blood shall flow everywhere, which I shrink from describing. Fear shall prevail, hands shall fail, and hearts shall tremble: many shall be the deaths fit to impose upon the martyrs. For a long time shall the despised victims be sought over the sea, over the lands, through the islands, and in their hiding places, before they have been led forth to their deaths.

Nero shall do these things for three and one-half years - thus he shall fulfill his appointed time. But a fatal revenge shall be exacted for his crimes. The city and its people will be handed over along with him; and his rule, filled as it was with wickedness, shall be taken away. For he had oppressed for so long a time all of the people by imposing evil tribulations. With the downfall of Nero, a king will again arise from the East with four other nations. As many nations, moreover, as are willing to bring him assistance shall he thus invite into the city with him. And thus he shall be exceptionally powerful, and he shall fill the sea with many thousands of ships. And if anyone shall go against him, that one shall be cut down with the sword. He shall subdue and capture Tyre and Sidon, that the nations on the borders may faint with terror. Henceforth pestilence, wars, famine, and announcements of sad tidings shall all come at once. And so all of the peoples shall be confounded.

Meanwhile a trumpet blares forth from Heaven, the sound of which shakes all in their very bowels. At that time a fiery chariot, drawn by four horses, shall be seen among the stars, and a running torch shall announce a conflagration to the nations. The entire Euphrates River shall be dried, so that the way is prepared for the king and the nations with him. Persians, Medes, Chaldeans, and Babylonians shall come. They shall be mighty and agile men, incapable of knowing pain. When this one arises and begins to come, Nero will be confounded, and with him the nobility, at the very sight of him. The three Caesars will go out to fight against him - but he shall slay them and hand them over to the vultures to be eaten. And their armies shall be compelled to worship the victor. When they return to the city with their minds so altered, they will despoil the temples and whatever else is in the city. They will seize the men and slaughter them with great bloodshed. And when the city is at last laid bare by fire, they will destroy it, leaving no vestige whatsoever to remain. The hearts of the authorities shall melt at this destruction, nor will they be able to ascertain at what time they themselves shall be overthrown. She [Babylon?] indeed rejoices while the whole earth groans. Nor can a retribution worthy of such oppressors be found anywhere on Earth. She who once considered herself eternal [Babylon again?] now mourns, she whose tyrants are now judged by the Most High. At the very end, when Rome burns, will the time be ripe. But fitting forms of recompense will eventually come about for those deserving.

Nevertheless, the victor shall continue on to Judea, he whom the Judeans had observed conquering Rome. He shall make many signs so that they can believe in him. For he was iniquitously sent to seduce them. But a voice believed to come from the Most High rebukes him from the very heavens. A man from Persia will call himself immortal - as Nero for us, so shall this one be for the Jews. These are the two of whom there have been prophecies throughout the generations, who shall appear in the final age. Nero is the destroyer of the city, but this latter shall lay waste to the entire earth. But concerning him I may only hint darkly of a few things, which themselves ought to be read secretly.

Meanwhile he will displease the Jews and the other nations, and they will murmur amongst themselves that he fraudulently deceived them. With wailing voices they will cry as one to the heavens, that the true God will come to their aid from on high. Then the almighty God, in order to end all the things which I have described, will lead forth a populace that had been hidden for a long time. They had been Jews, hidden on the further side of the Persian river [Euphrates?], whom God had wished to tarry there until the end. Captivity had compelled them there, who were fully half of the twelve tribes. There is no dishonesty amongst them, nor any hatred. The child does not die before the parents; there is no bewailing over the dead, nor any mourning, as there customarily is amongst us. There they await the life to come. They eat no animal flesh, but only vegetables, since to eat as much involves no shedding of blood. They exist with their bodies intact, the course of their lives dictated by justice. Impious powers are not engendered in them, nor do illnesses of any kind ever draw near to them. **For they are sincerely obedient to the law which we also follow in order to live in purity.** Only death and toil can be found amongst them, but other afflictions are absent.

This people who now live beyond the borders [i.e., of the Roman Empire] shall be the people that go forth. When the river has dried up, they will once more seek the land of Judea. And when the Lord comes to fulfill His promises to them, they will exult in His presence throughout their journey. All of the lands will become fertile before them, all things will rejoice; the beasts themselves will be glad to receive the saints; springs will well up in every place as if of their own volition. The people of the Most High go forth in fear of the Lord. The clouds shall make shade for them, lest they be harassed by the sun. And should they become fatigued, the mountains will prostrate themselves before them. An angel of Him Who is on high shall be sent before them, who shall preside over their peaceful army in its passage. With no effort shall they go forward with light steps, and they shall lay waste to all whom they cross, just like passing lions. No nation will be able to resist them if they should wage war against them - for God shall be with them. They will cast out the peoples, and overthrow their cities. By the permission of God they will deprive all of the colonies of their gold and silver, that they might grow rich by such depredations. And thus they shall chant hymns to their upright God along the way. Presently they shall draw near to the city of their holy ancestral land; and that fearsome tyrant will become terrified. He shall flee from that great army into a northern land. He shall vanquish to populace there and from them raise another army which shall fight as if for its own territory. But when they draw near, the army of God will cause the rebels to lie prostrate after a single battle waged by the angels. The wicked king and the false prophets, seized at the same time, shall be cast down; they shall endure the punishments of Hell while still living. **His principal commanders and ambassadors, being wicked like their master, shall be**

demoted to the station of slaves. The saints, meanwhile, shall enter into their holy estates, which, having been promised to them, they take with unending rejoicing. They will beseech God to bring their dead back to life, which He Himself had once promised with regards to the first resurrection.

At that time God shall grow angered at his enemies, and the appointed day will at last come upon the wicked. Then He shall commence to judge the world with fire. He shall bypass the pious while He lets fire fall upon the impious. Scarcely a few shall remain who can tell of such events. Whosoever is reserved to live shall escape only to be slaves unto the just.

After the persecution and ghastly slaughter of the holy ones, the dreadful day of burning shall be imminent. Lo! A loud trumpet shall sound, reverberating across the sky in all directions. It shall terrify an entire world as it falls to ruin. The sun shall withdraw straightaway, and a likeness of the night shall suddenly come to be. And God shall exclaim: "How long did you believe I would tolerate you?" After He has given this signal, destruction shall pour forth from the sky, thunder shall come down, and a rush of lightning shall descend with a terrific noise. From the stars shall come more lightning yet again - a fiery storm held back for so many ages shall rage. Disaster shall come with a great clamor, and the agitated earth shall tremble. None of the human race shall be able to predict for how long they might escape it. The stars of the heavens shall fall, and the heavenly bodies shall be judged by us: the inhabitants of the heavens shall be disturbed while the destruction of the age is accomplished. At that time there shall be no aid, and any outcry will be in vain. There will be no ship to deliver a man, nor any hiding place. None whom they had heretofore worshipped, as if great, shall come forth to provide assistance: every man, no matter how vexed, shall be left to his own devices. **The only help will come to those who were known to Christ, for whom there shall be safety. But for the remainder there shall only be death-bearing punishments. A portion of the unbelievers shall be only lightly scorched, and so preserved; and thereby they and their kind can bewail their lot on the last day.**

Wherever men turn, there the fiery power burns. The universe itself, formerly so delighted with itself, shall be consumed by fire from its very essence. And all lightning and storms of the heavens which I have described are the accumulated rage of the ages pouring forth. Thus fire, thunder, and all the evils of maelstrom shall boil over. The heavens themselves shall be taken up into the shadow of death. The quaking earth shall first release the destruction enclosed within it, then the thunder will overturn the lowest walls and foundations of the world just as if it were casting dust into the wind. Cliffs shall crumble and stones shall fall; all the houses shall be obliterated, every city of the fatherland shall be laid low. Nothing whatsoever shall remain as a vestige. Who will be able to bear so much noise, so much uproar, so great a ruination - or to look upon such wreckage? What shall the wretched mother do for her sweet little one? What will it profit the father to clutch his son to his breast? Woe to those who flee before the Lord! **The quarreling prophets who knew not Christ, whose once-happy lot shall also be judged, shall now bewail themselves. They shall prostrate themselves on the ground, lowing like cattle, while the blessed heavenly palace shall begin to shine on**

the Christian brothers. Then the eternal light of the supernal life shall wash clean the man, and whoever was humble shall now seem to be a celestial god. Angels of the eternal effulgence will descend with Him; graves will be broken open, bodies will rise up from the slime. But whatever is marked by corruption will be carried by Hell's savage guardians into the abyss. Here there will be living Jews: and He shall lift them up that they might see the glory of Him Whom they crucified. But at last he shall arise from the depths that He might be a witness of those miserable ones, He Who was killed by them. How much money do you now count, you who cunningly laid snares by bribing soldiers to be silent? Concerning you, envious nation, we now declaim. We shall conquer you, Judea, when the just rejoice and the damned are burned in Hell. God shall say to them: "Go back down!" And whoever did not believe shall go out into the shadow of death; likewise will it be for those who were capable of attaining to more, but chose only the things of this world instead. The remainder of those who opposed Christ will make a headlong descent into Hell. **With regards to the holy ones, there shall forever after by one holy multitude from the two peoples [i.e., from among the Jew and the Gentiles shall come the single holy Christian populace]. This shall be the greater end: and God has judged that it should remain so for eternity.**

Appendix 6 : Hildegaard of Bingen on the Antichrist.

This medieval saint was an impressive individual indeed. Just the basic summary on the Wikipedia page about her is impressive:

> Hildegard of Bingen.... (1098 - 17 September 1179), also known as Saint Hildegard and Sibyl of the Rhine, was a German Benedictine abbess, writer, composer, philosopher, Christian mystic, visionary, and polymath.
>
> Hildegard was elected magistra by her fellow nuns in 1136; she founded the monasteries of Rupertsberg in 1150 and Eibingen in 1165. One of her works as a composer, the Ordo Virtutum, is an early example of liturgical drama and arguably the oldest surviving morality play. She wrote theological, botanical, and medicinal texts, as well as letters, liturgical songs, and poems....

And a couple of years ago she was officially given the title 'Doctor of the Church' by the Roman Catholic church. I do not know whether she was one of the relative few in the Medieval period to have maintained a Pre-Millennial position, but she was absolutely crystal clear in taking a Post-Tribulation position. I have not found the original full writings to check, but found the following very extensive (and sometimes repetitive) quote comes from the webpage http://www.unitypublishing.com/prophecy/AntichristbySaints.htm , and since it has proved to be entirely accurate in its quotes of earlier church fathers, I think we can be confident this is accurate too, despite its unfortunate habit of not citing exactly where its quotes come from. (You should understand that in the Medieval period both 'Turk' and 'Mohammedan' are terms for what we today would call 'Muslims'.) I will simply quote in full, because further comment is probably not necessary:

> When the great ruler (the Great Monarch who is to rule Europe after the collapse of Communism) exterminates the Turks almost entirely, one of the remaining Mohammedans will be converted, become a priest bishop and cardinal, and when the new pope is elected (immediately before Antichrist) this cardinal will kill the pope before he is crowned, through jealousy, wishing to be pope himself; then when the other cardinals elect the next pope this cardinal will proclaim himself Anti-pope, and two-thirds of the Christians will go with him. He, as well as Antichrist, are descendants of the tribe of Dan.
>
> An unchaste woman will conceive an unchaste son. The wicked serpent who deceived Adam will influence this child in such as way that nothing good or virtuous will enter him; nor under the circumstances will it even be possible for any good to be in him
>
> The mark (of Antichrist) will be a hellish symbol of Baptism, because thereby a person will be stamped as an adherent of Antichrist and also of

the Devil in that he thereby gives himself over to the influence of Satan. Whoever will not have this mark of Antichrist can neither buy nor sell anything and will be beheaded.

He will win over to himself the rulers, the mighty and the wealthy, will bring about the destruction of those who do not accept his faith and, finally, will subjugate the entire earth.

The streets of Jerusalem, will then shine in the brightest gold with the blood of Christians which will flow like water. Simultaneously Antichrist will try to increase his wonders. His executioners will work such miracles when they torment the Christians that the people will think Antichrist is the true God. The executioners will not permit the Christians to win the martyrs' crown easily for they will endeavour to prolong their pain until they renounce their faith. Yet some will receive a special grace from God to die during the torments.

Antichrist will make the earth move, level mountains, dry up rivers, produce thunder and lightning and hail, remove the leaves from the trees and return them again to the trees, make men sick and cure them, exorcise devils, raise the dead to life. He will appear to be crucified and rise from the dead. All in all, Christians will be astounded and in grievous doubts while the followers of Antichrist will be confirmed in their false faith.

Finally, when he shall have converted all his plans into action, he will gather his worshippers about him and tell them that he will presently ascend toward Heaven. However, at the moment of the ascension a bolt of lightning will overwhelm and annihilate him. The planned ascent into heaven will have been prepared by the artful employment of ingenious devices, and the moment at which the event was to have taken place, leading to his destruction, will produce a cloud that will spread an unbearable odour. Through this many people will again come to their senses and to understanding.

Then the people should prepare for the last judgment, the day of which is indeed veiled in secrecy and obscurity, but not far distant."

Enoch and Elijah [for the rest of the quote I will leave the original spelling of Henoch and Elias where they are used] are being instructed by God in a mysterious manner in paradise. God shows them the works of men as though they could see these with natural eyes. The two men are therefore, much wiser than all wise men put together. The same force which removed Henoch and Elias from the earth will bring them back in a storm wind at the time when the Antichrist will spread his false doctrine. As long as they will dwell amongst men they will always be refreshed after 40 days. They have the mission from God to resist the Antichrist and lead the erring back to the road of salvation. Both men, distinguished by age and stature, will speak to men: `This accursed one is sent by the devil in order to lead men into error. We have been preserved by God at a secreted place, where we did not experience the suffering of men. We are now sent by God in order to oppose the heresy of this destroyer. Look, if we resemble you in stature and age.' And because the testimony of both shall agree they will be believed. All will follow these two aged men and renounce heresy. They will visit all cities and towns where previously the Antichrist had sown his heresy, and through the power of the Holy Ghost will work genuine miracles. All the people will be greatly astonished at them. Henoch and Elias will confuse the followers of Satan with thunder strokes, and destroy them and fortify the Christians in faith. Therefore, the Christians will hurry to martyrdom, which the son of evil will prepare for them like to a banquet, so that the murderers will grow tired of counting the dead on account of their great numbers; for their blood will run like rivers. Henoch and Elias have been taught much wisdom and knowledge in Paradise while awaiting their return to earth. God will instruct them every forty days while they are on earth. They will receive exceptional graces and powers from God to use against Antichrist. Enoch and Elias will be instructed by God in a most secret manner in paradise. God reveals to them the actions and condition of men that they may regard them with the eyes of compassion. Because of those special preparation, these two holy men are more wise than all the wise men on the earth taken together. God will give them the task of opposing antichrist and of bringing back those who have strayed from the way of salvation. Both of these men will say to people: "This accursed one has been sent by the devil to lead men astray and into error; we have been preserved by God in a hidden place where we did not experience the sorrows of men but God has now sent us to combat the heresy of this son of perdition. They will go into all cities and villages where previously antichrist had broadcasted his heresies and by the power of the Holy Spirit will perform wonderful miracles so that all nations will greatly marvel at them. This as to a wedding feast, Christians will hasten to death by martyrdom which the son of perdition will have prepared for them in such numbers that those murderers will be unable even to count the slain, then the blood of these martyrs will fill the rivers

When the fear of God has been disregarded everywhere, violent and furious wars will take place. A multitude of people will be slaughtered and many cities will be transformed into. heaps of rubbish.

The Son of Corruption and Ruin will appear and reign for only a short time, towards the end of the days of the world's duration; the period which corresponds to the moment when the sun has disappeared beyond the horizon; that is to say he shall come at the last days of the world. He will not be Satan himself, but a human being equalling and resembling him in atrocious hideousness. His mother, a depraved woman possessed by the devil, will live as a prostitute in the desert. She will declare that she is ignorant as to the identity of his father, and will maintain that her son was presented to her by God in a supernatural manner, as was the Child of the Blessed Virgin. She will then be venerated as a saint by deceived people.

Antichrist will come from a land that lies between two seas, and will practise his tyranny in the East. After his birth false teachers and doctrines will appear, followed by wars, famines, and pestilence. His mother will seldom let any one see him, and yet by magic art, she will manage to gain the love of the people for him.

He will be raised at different secret places and will be kept in seclusion until full grown. When he has grown to full manhood he will publicly announce a hostile doctrine on religion. He will attract the people to himself by granting them complete exemption from the observance of all divine and ecclesiastical commandments, by forgiving them their sins and requiring of them only their belief in his divinity. He will spurn and reject baptism and the gospel. He will open his mouth to preach contradiction. He will say, `Jesus of Nazareth is not the son of God, only a deceiver who gave himself out as God; and the Church, instituted by him is only superstition'. The true Christ has come in his person. He will say, `I am the Saviour of the world'. Especially will he try to convince the Jews that he is the Messiah sent by God and the Jews will accept him as such. His doctrine of faith will be taken from the Jewish religion and seemingly will not differ much from the fundamental doctrine of Christianity for he will teach that there is one God who created the world, who is omniscient and knows the thoughts of man and is just, who rewards the obeyers of his commands and the trespassers he chastises, who raises all from the dead in due time. This God has spoken through Moses and the Prophets, therefore the precepts of the Mosaic laws are to be kept, especially circumcision and keeping the Sabbath, yet by his moral laws he will try to reverse all order on earth. Therefore he is called in Holy Writ the `Lawless One'. He will think that he can change time and laws. He will discard all laws, morals and religious principles, to draw the world to himself. He will grant entire freedom from the commandments of God and the Church and permit everyone to live as his passions dictate. By doing so he hopes to be acknowledged by the people as deliverer from the yoke and as the cause of prosperity in the world.

Religion he will endeavour to make convenient. He will say that you need not fast and embitter your life by renunciation as the people of former times did when they had no sense of God's goodness. It will suffice to love God. He will let the people feast to their heart's content so that they will pity the unfortunate people of former centuries. He will preach free love and tear asunder family ties. He will scorn everything holy, and he will ridicule all graces of the Church with devilish mockery. He will condemn humility and foster proud and gruesome dogmas. He will tear down that which God has taught in the Old and New Testament and he will maintain that sin and vice are not sin and vice. Briefly he will declare the road to Hell is the way to Heaven......

After having passed a licentious youth among very perverted men, and in a desert, she being conducted by a demon disguised as an angel of light, the mother of the son of perdition will conceive and give birth without knowing the father. In another land, she will make men believe that her birth was some miraculous thing, seeing that she had not appointed a spouse, and she will ignore that, she will say, how the infant she had brought into the world had been formed in her womb, and the people will regard it as a saint and qualified to the title.

The son of perdition is this very wicked beast who will put to death those who refuse to believe in him; who will associate with kings, priests, the great and the rich; who will mistake the humility and will esteem pride; who will finally subjugate the entire universe by his diabolic means.

He will gain over many people and tell them: "You are allowed to do all that you please; renounce the fasts; it suffices that you love me; I who am your God."

He will show them treasures and riches, and he will permit them to riot in all sorts of festivities, as they please. He will oblige them to practice circumcision and other Judaic observances, and he will tell them: "Those who believe in me will receive pardon of their sins and will live with me eternally."

He will reject baptism and evangelism, and he will reject in derision all the precepts the Spirit has given to men of my part.

Then he will say to his partisans, "Strike me with a sword, and place my corpse in a proper shroud until the day of my resurrection." They will believe him to have really given over to death, and from his mortal wound he will make a striking semblance of resuscitation.

After which, he will compose himself a certain cipher, which he will say is to be a pledge of salute; he will give it to all his servitors like the sign of our faith in heaven, and he will command them to adore it. Concerning those who, for the love of my name, will refuse to render this sacrilegious adoration to the son of perdition, he will put them to death amidst the cruellest torments.

But I will defend my two Witnesses, Enoch and Elias, whom I have reserved for those times. Their mission will be to combat the man of evil and reprimand him in the sight of the faithful whom he has seduced. They will have the virtue of operating the most brilliant miracles, in all the places where the son of perdition has spread his evil doctrines. In the meanwhile, I will permit this evildoer to put them to death; but I will give them in heaven the recompense of their travails.

Later, however, after the coming of Enoch and Elias, the Antichrist will be destroyed, and the Church will sing forth with unprecedented glory, and the victims of the great error will throng to return to the fold."

The Man of Sin will be born of an ungodly woman who, from her infancy, will have been initiated into occult sciences and the wiles of the demon. She will live in the desert with perverse men, and abandon herself to crime with so much the greater ardor, as she will think she is authorized thereby to by the revelations of an angel. And thus, in the fire of burning concupiscence she will conceive the Son of Perdition, without knowing by what father. Then she will teach that fornication is permitted, declaring herself holy and honoured as a saint.

But Lucifer, the old and cunning serpent, will find the fruit of her womb with his infernal spirit and entirely possess the fruit of sin.

Now when he shall have attained the age of manhood, he will set himself up as a new master and teach perverse doctrine. Soon he will revolt against the saints; and he will acquire such great power that in the madness of his pride he would raise himself above the clouds; and as in the beginning Satan said: "I will be like unto the most high", and fell; so in those days, he will fall when he will say in the person of his son, "I am the Saviour of the World!"

He will ally himself with the kings, the princes and the powerful ones of the earth; he will condemn humility and will extol all the doctrines of pride. His magic art will feign the most astonishing prodigies; he will disturb the atmosphere, command thunder and tempest, produce hail and horrible lightning. He will move mountains, dry up streams, reanimate the withered verdure of forests. His arts will be practiced upon the elements, but chiefly upon man will he exhaust his infernal power. He will seem to take away health and restore it. How so? By sending some possessed soul into a dead body, to move it for a time. But these resurrections will be of short duration.

At the sight of these things, many will be terrified and will believe in him; and some, preserving their primitive faith, will nevertheless court the favour of the Man of Sin or fear his displeasure. And so many will be led astray among those who, shutting the interior eye of their soul, will live habitually in exterior things.

After the Antichrist has ascended a high mountain and been destroyed by Christ, many erring souls will return to truth, and men will make rapid progress in the ways of holiness."

Nothing good will enter into him nor be able to be in him. For he will be nourished in diverse and secret places, lest he should be known by men, and he will be imbued with all diabolical arts, and he will be hidden until he is of full age, nor will he show the perversities which will be in him, until he knows himself to be full and superabundant in all iniquities.

He will appear to agitate the air, to make fire descend from heaven, to produce rainbows, lightning, thunder and hail, to tumble mountains, dry up streams, to strip the verdure of trees, of forests, and to restore them again. He will also appear to be able to make men sick or well at will, to chase out demons, and at times even to resuscitate the dead, making a cadaver move like it was alive. But this kind of resurrection will never endure beyond a little time, for the glory of God will not suffer it.

Ostensibly he will be murdered, spill his blood and die. With bewilderment and consternation, mankind will learn that he is not dead, but has awakened from his death=sleep.

From the beginning of his course many battles and many things contrary to the lawful dispensation will arise, and charity will be extinguished in men. In them also will arise bitterness and harshness and there will be so many heresies that heretics will preach their errors openly and certainly; and there shall be so much doubt and incertitude in the Catholic faith of Christians that men shall be in doubt of what God they invoke, and many signs shall appear in the sun and moon, and in the stars and in the waters, and in other elements and creatures, so that, as it were in a picture, future events shall be foretold in their portents.

Then so much sadness shall occupy men at that time, that they shall be led to die as if for nothing. But those who are perfect in the Catholic faith will await in great contrition what God wills to ordain. And these great tribulations shall proceed in this way, while the Son of Perdition shall open his mouth in the words of falsehood and his deceptions, heaven and earth shall tremble together. But after the fall of the Antichrist the glory of the Son of God shall be increased.

As soon as he is born, he will have teeth and pronounce blasphemies; in short, he will be a born devil. He will emit fearful cries, work miracles, and wallow in luxury and vice. He will have brothers who are also demons incarnate, and at the age of twelve, they will distinguish themselves in brilliant achievements. They will command an armed force, which will be supported by the infernal legions.

After the Son of Perdition has accomplished all of his evil designs, he will call together all of his believers and tell them that he wishes to ascend into heaven.

At the moment of his ascension, a thunderbolt will strike him to the ground, and he will die.

The mountain where he was established for the operation of his ascension, in an instant will be covered with a thick cloud which emits an unbearable odour of truly infernal corruption... At the sight of his body, the eyes of great number of persons will open and they will be made to see their miserable error.

After the sorrowful defeat of the Son of Perdition, the spouse of my Son, who is the Church, will shine with a glory without equal, and the victims of the error will be impressed to re-enter the sheepfold.

As to the day, after the fall of Antichrist, when the world will end, man must not seek to know, for he can never learn it. That secret the Father has reserved for Himself.

After Enoch and Elias suffer physical death the spirit of life will reawaken them raise them up into the clouds and the rejoicing of that man's

> followers (antichrist) will change into fear, sorrow and dismay. Then the son of corruption will gather together a large group of people in order that his glory can be openly shown forth. He will attempt to walk through the heavens so that any remnant of the catholic faith that might remain throughout the world might completely disappear. In the sight of crowds standing around and listening he will order the high strata of the sky to lift him up during his ascension into heaven and the words of my loyal servant Paul will be fulfilled and these are the words which Paul who is full of the spirit of truth says" and the lord Jesus will slay him with the breath of his mouth and will destroy him with his glorious appearance at his coming..." "...when the son of corruption ascends on high through diabolical trickery he will be thrust down again by divine power. The fumes of sulphur and pitch will consume him such that the crowds standing nearby will flee into the mountains for protection. Such abject fear will seize all who see and hear these things that they will reject the devil and his spiritual son antichrist and be converted to the true faith by baptism.
>
> The son of perdition will come when the day declines and the sun sinks, that is when the time arrives and the world loses its stability.

I suspect that this is a composite quote taken from different places in Hildegards writings, hence the repetitious nature of the long quote. Even if we disregard issues such as the monstrous appearance of the Antichrist, and his origin, there are still some things relevant to us here. In the light of other church fathers' teaching that it is apostasy and immorality in the church that pave the way for the Antichrist, a number of the facets of the Antichrist as described here are particularly fascinating - namely the way he makes religion 'convenient' (prosperity gospel and seeker-friendly churches, perhaps, as well as general laxity), and preaches free love and tearing apart family ties. In the light of modern technology, her claims that the Antichrist will perform signs and wonders by 'ingenious devices' including lightning bolts from heaven (satellites and lasers?) and the like, suddenly takes on an all too great plausibility. What is clear is that she taught that the church would be so badly persecuted that even after many are restored by the teaching of Enoch and Elijah, there will be very few true Christians left by the end of the time of the Antichrist, something Jesus also taught in the gospels about the Tribulation.

Appendix 7 : Fraudulent misrepresentation of Seventeenth Century Puritans and their contemporaries

Although I have only really covered up to the first part of the Middle Ages, Pre-Tribulationists regularly claim as their own later writers in the century or two leading up to the undisputed Pre-Tribulationalism of Darby and McDonald in the 1830's. It wouldn't surprise me if there were one or two relatively late precursors, but I decided to have a brief look at some of their claims, which can be found in a short article - http://www.pre-trib.org/data/pdf/Ice-HistoryoftheRaptureU1.pdf by Thomas Ice in which he has extracted from a much longer and supposedly more rigorous academic study http://www.pre-trib.org/data/pdf/Watson-PretribulationalRapt.pdf by a Dr. William Watson, Professor of History, Colorado Christian University.

Before we start, I want to examine one separate quote you see fairly often in articles such as this: http://www.evidenceunseen.com/theology/eschatology/a-pretribulational-rapture/ .

> Scholar Paul Benware writes,
>
> As early as 1687, Peter Jurieu, in his book Approaching Deliverance of the Church (1687), taught that Christ would come in the air to rapture the saints and return to heaven before the battle of Armageddon. He spoke of a secret rapture prior to His coming in glory and judgment at Armageddon...

Grant Jeffery mentions him several times, for instance in his book 'Heaven: The Mystery of Angels'

> 'The first Calvinist reformer to begin to see the truth about what would later be termed the Rapture was a French clergyman in Rotterdam. In 1687, Peter Jurieu, known as the 'Goliath of the Protestants' wrote a book on *The Accomplishment of the Scriptural Prophecies or The Approaching Deliverance of the Church.* (p49) ..... He says, 'There is a first coming of Christ, and it may be a first resurrection..... Who can be certain that this coming of Christ, to establish His Kingdom upon Earth, shall not be in that matter, with the voice of an arch-angel, and in great magnificence and Glory? Who can prove that at that first coming of Christ He shall not raise some of the dead, as St John seems expressly to have fore-told....Our Lord should for a short space come down from Heaven to establish a Kingdom for a thousand years, and to give His seal to the Conversion of all the nations, by some glorious Apparition, returning back to Heaven immediately after' (Gaps in original Geffrey quote).

> Peter Jurieu continues his argument against those who deny the possibility of the 'clandestine coming of Christ' for His Church. He says that their denial is based on 'a false supposition; viz, that there shall be no other coming of Christ, but for the last and final judgement, which is not true: the Coming of Christ here spoken of, is to settle the Peace, and Glory, and Kingdom of His Church; and we may be certain that this meant in almost all of the Passages, where the coming of Christ is spoken of.' (p50)

This work was written in 1996. I don't know if you've noticed, but each quote exactly fits a Post-Tribulation rapture, although Jeffrey seems to disguise this. Jurieu is obviously referring to 1 Thessalonians 4, combined with 'the First resurrection' in Revelation, but the 'short space' in which Jesus comes down from heaven, in Jurieu's view, is what we would call his second coming, not any separate rapture. He returns to heaven leaving the church to rule for 1000 years. Similarly with the last actual quote - Jeffrey leaves his readers with the impression that something like a secret rapture is being discussed here, a 'clandestine coming of Christ' for His church, but again, if you actually read the quote, he is referring to a coming that is separate from the Final Judgement at the very end of all things - in other words, a Pre-Millennial coming of Jesus, not a Pre-Tribulation coming of Jesus. To be fair, Jeffrey does not explicitly say anything in this work about Jurieu teaching a Pre-Trib rapture, but claims he was the first to 'begin to see the truth about... the Rapture' thus giving a misleading impression to those of his readers already conditioned by their belief system to see at least compatability with a Pre-Trib position in the words he quoted.

It appears Jeffrey made even stronger, and completely false, claims in his earlier 1992 book 'Apocalypse: The Coming Judgement of Nations' p92-3, and to his credit, it is Thomas Ice who tells the truth on this issue, in the following article: http://www.bbc.edu/barndollar/barndollar_history_rapture.pdf . He says:

> Pretribulationist Paul Benware has made the following claims about other preDarby pre-trib rapturists:
>
> As early as 1687, Peter Jurieu, in his book Approaching Deliverance of the Church (1687), taught that Christ would come in the air to rapture the saints and return to heaven before the battle of Armageddon. He spoke of a secret Rapture prior to His coming in glory and judgment at Armageddon. . . . It is clear that these men believed that this coming will precede Christ's descent to the earth and the time of judgment. The purpose was to preserve believers from the time of judgment.
>
> The problem with claiming Jurieu as a pretribulationist is that when one looks up the original documents that Benware refers to for support from Grant Jeffrey, they do not mention a "secret" rapture and the judgment mentioned is the second coming, not the tribulation–contra Jeffrey. Jurieu actually says, *And St. John saith, that the Saints shall reign with Christ a thousand years. I would not be too confident, that this ought to be understood of a visible descent and abode of Christ upon earth; yea, I do not believe it probable. But to me it seems very Evident, that this Reign shall begin with some miraculous appearance of our Lord in his Glory.*

> *After which he shall go back to Heaven, and from thence govern this victorious Church. Mr. J. Mede, and others after him, would make this reign of Christ for a thousand years.* Mr. Jeffrey may have been confused by Jerieu's statement that Christ would return to heaven after his coming to the earth. This is not a pre-trib rapture statement; instead it is the commonly held view by historicist premillennialists of the day that was championed by Joseph Mede, the father of English premillennialism. Mede held that Christ would return to earth, then rapture and resurrect believers, but during the millennium Christ would reign from heaven, ruling the world through the church on earth. This is not a pre-trib rapture at all, but a two-state second coming where believers are raptured into the air at the second coming of Christ in order to miss the conflagration of judgment that will take place on the unbelieving world.
>
> Jue says that, *"Jurieu was a committed millenarian, heavily influenced by Mede."* "*One criticism leveled against Jerieu's commentary claimed that it was simply 'unoriginal,'*" notes Jue. *"Gottfried Wilhelm Leibniz observed that Jurieu was basically reproducing Mede's interpretations.*" Neither Mede nor Jurieu taught any form of pretribulationism.

I only wish Ice had shown the same diligence and commitment to checking the truth of claims by his fellow Pre-Tribulationists in the article we turn to examine now (see the links at the start of this appendix). We will start with the first quote from Thomas Ice's article:

> Robert Maton (1607-1653) in Israel's Redemption (1642) says, "why shall the elect onely be gathered together and the rest left behind... they shall be left, either to perish in that great destruction, which shall come upon all Nations that fight against the Jewes, whom our Saviour shall then redeem: Or to bee eye-witnesses of Gods wonders in all Countreys at that time."

Notice those dots between 'behind' and 'they shall be left. I smelt a rat as soon as I saw this, and it looks very much like I was right to do so. Somebody, somewhere, has been very naughty indeed, whether deliberately or not. Mr Ice might have just been copying from Dr Watson, but unless there has been some extremely radical altering of editions of Robert Maton's work and thought, then even his longer quote seems less than honest, if it is meant to be presented proof of a Pre-Tribulation rapture belief which it looks like it might because of the bits in bold. That quote is:

> When our Saviour comes to reign over all the earth, he comes not alone, but brings all the Saints with him. ...why shall the Saints come with him, but because they have a share in this Kingdome...why shall the elect onely be gathered together and the rest **left behind**...they shall be left, because the good Angels cannot at once assemble them to the place of Judgement, and the Elect to meete the Lord in the Aire, if these things were to be done at the same particular time. And therefore, as I suppose, they shall **be left, either to perish in that great destruction, which shall come upon all Nations that fight against the Jewes**, whom our Saviour shall then

> redeem: Or to **bee eye-witnesses of Gods wonders** in all Countreys at that time. (bold in original)

So, firstly, I googled a phrase from the passage and got at least the last part of Ice's original quote. I found it in a 1652 book by Robert Maton, whereas according to Dr Watson, the quotes are taken from a book published in 1642. I searched for that, and although it is on google books it hasn't been digitized, or at least not made available. However, the book I found the quote from 10 years later seems to consist of the entire text of the original work for the purposes of a point by point rebuttal of a critic, and is called 'Christ's Personal Reigne on earth, One Thousand years with His saints' - along with the usual plethora of subtitles normal for books of this era. So I started searching back and found the first part of the quote Ice used, although I didn't find the earlier bits that Dr Watson cited, which suggests they were so far earlier in the work they were in another *chapter* (I only searched to the start of the chapter the original quote was in). To be fair, it should be said that Dr Watson was studying more than just the Pre-Tribulation rapture, such as Pre-Millennialms and a belief in the restoration of Jews, but on the other hand he *does* precede his quote of Maton by saying:

> Maton believed the resurrection would happen before Christ's coming with his saints to rule on earth, and that the ungodly would be "left behind" to experience the wrath of God in the last days:

Quite frankly Dr Watson is using exactly the same deceptive tactics as we have seen used over and over again by Pre-Tribulationists - spinning quotes before they are even quoted. He says Maton believed the resurrection would happen before Christ's coming with his saints to rule on earth, implying some considerable time, and that the ungodly would be 'left behind' - using the iconic Pre-Trib rapture phrase ,to experience the 'wrath of God' - another iconoic Pre-Trib phrase in the last days (notice the plural).

However if you read the *full* quote in the original, then the impression that here we have some substantive time period between the resurrection and the return of Jesus akin to a Pre-Tribulation rapture is scotched completely:

> To this also may be added that in Matth 24.31 which shewes that when the Sonne of man descends, *He shall send his Angels with a great sound of a Trumpet, and they shall gather together his elect from the four windes, from one end of the heaven to the other* at which time *two shall be in the field, the one shall be taken and the other left; two women shall be grinding at the Mill, the one shall be taken and the other left;* and as Saint Mark records *two men shall be in one bed, the one shall be taken and the other left.* But if our Saviour at his coming shall presently give sentence on all that are not written in the Booke of life if he shall make no stay on earth before he undertakes this businesse, then why shall the elect onely be gathered together, and the rest left behind? Seeing that great Assise is to be held chiefly for the condemnation of ungodly men who doubtless are not to be left, that the evill Angels may fetch them, for they shall be partakers with them of that judgement, and therefore will be as unwilling to appeare before that barre, as they. Neither is it likely, that they shall be left, because

> the good Angels cannot at once assemble them to the place of judgement, and the elect to meet the Lord in the aire, if these things were to be done at the same particular time. And therefore as I suppose, they shall be left, either to perish in that general destruction, which shall come upon all Nations that fight against the Jewes, whom our Saviour shall then redeeme; or to be eye-witnesses of God's wonders in all countries at that time.

Notice not just that Maton is placing the rapture where Jesus did - after the Tribulation - but also how the detailed arguments as to why the wicked are 'left behind' rely on the return of Jesus and the rapture happening at the same time. In other words, this is clearly a Post-Tribulation statement, only all the bits that showed that were on-so-conveniently taken out in the quotes, which means that Dr Watson's apologies in his introductory comments ring rather hollow:

> My apologies for quoting in length so many passages from these primary sources, but it was to avoid accusations that anything was taken out of context or that my own interpretations were imposed upon the sources.

For a history professor that is pretty shabby handling of source material, which should be elementary, my dear Dr Watson. If there is any more doubt about what Maton meant, then his words at this point in his second work where he is replying to his critic, one Mr Petrie, should remove every possible room for misunderstanding (p301):

> The righteous shall be caught up to meete with Christ, and to come along with him to the earth. And **not to stay with him in the aire, or to be carried up to heaven from thence**; as hath been shewed already more than once. And therefore this is but a trifling argument.

You can't really put it more clearly than that. Mr Ice is, to put it bluntly, lying, whether he knows it or not, when he claims this passage proves a belief in a Pre-Tribulation rapture was held before Darby and the 1820's or 30's.

For the next quote, I also looked for the original writing online (The personal Reign of Christ upon Earth, John Archer 1642) so I could check the original, and wasted a lot of time because there were websites saying it was available on websites that didn't actually have it. Anyway, here it is in the fuller quotes from Dr Watson:

> That same year John Archer also expected a resurrection before the return of Christ:
>
> Christ shall come from heaven...that is, Christ shall visibly appeare, which is not spoken of as the Day of the last Judgement. For it is the Time of the Israelites great trouble, after the first conversion to Christianity. ... First, He will raise up the Saints, which are dead before this his coming...this resurrection is not at the Worlds end,...that they should rule with him in his kingdom...that they should sit as kings, and rule the Tribes of Israel, which cannot be meant of Heaven, for that is the Fathers Kingdome, and Christs Kingdom ends when the world ends. ...they should rule with him in his Kingdom...our Raigning with Christ...

> Archer clearly has the return of Christ with his saints a period of time after the resurrection of those saints:
>
> The first thing that Christ will doe, when he comes from Heaven to set up his Kingdom, he will raise up all Saints who are dead before his coming, therefore he is said to come with all his Saints (Zach 14.5). For surely, as Christ had a middle State betwixt his Resurrection and Ascension for forty days; so shall his Saints have who dye before his coming from Heaven; ... but they shall have a middle state betwixt glory and mortality...yet he said then to come from Heaven, although he had come before, therefore he must have gone to heaven again...God hath approved somewhat proper and peculiar to every Age of his Church and people; ...and in this place they are kept till this Kingdome of Christ come...

Notice all those ellipses - those ... between sentence fragments. Well, as you would expect, I am highly suspicious, especially after the last case, that a similar oh-so-convenient editing has been done here, but of course, I cannot prove it. However, what I do think is telling is that even with these quotes as we have them, they apply at least as well, if not better, to a Post-Tribulation scenario, despite a certain amount of spin. You see, in the previous work of Maton we looked at, there was lots I didn't quote, but they made it quite clear that when he talked of a major time difference between the resurrection of the elect and that of the wicked, Maton was talking about the resurrection or rapture of the elect at the visible second coming of Jesus at the start of the Millennium, and that of the wicked at the end of the Millennium, and this appears to be exactly what Archer is referring to here, despite Dr Watson's apparent editing and what looks like attempts to spin it to give the impression it is talking about a rapture separate to the visible return of Jesus. Go and have a look at the first quote again. Christ appears visibly from heaven (can't be a secret rapture, fits with Second coming), but it isn't spoken of as the Last Day of judgement (which it isn't, because that comes 1000 years later). This visible return of Jesus is the Time of the Isrealites great trouble, when they turn to Christ. If you were already indoctrinated in a Pre-Trib position, then the nudge at the start that this is about a 'resurrection before the return of Christ', the fact we have the time of Israel's trouble which is always placed as post-rapture in the Pre-Trib thought world, and the quotes about a resurrection of the saints 'not at the world's end' would make you think that this is talking about a Pre-Trib rapture, but I would place good money on the 'resurrection not at the world's end' is simply a reiteration of the ancient and biblical distinction between the resurrection of the righteous at Jesus' visible return, and the general resurrection at the end of the Millennium. All those ellipses and short sentence fragments are great flashing warning lights that something is being hidden here, and the second quote is just the same.

There is the nudging comment from Dr Watson that here Archer 'clearly has the return of Christ with his saints a period of time after the resurrection of those saints' which is true, but a period of time can range from a minute to a thousand years. This passage too fits a Post-Trib rapture at least as well as the Pre-Trib position. After all, consider the end of the previous quote - it has argued that the saints will rule as Kings with Christ over the tribes of Israel (and given the ellipses, this could even just mean just the apostles do this - 12 apostles, 12 tribes), and that this can't be in heaven, because this is the Fathers kingdom, and Christ's kingdom ends when the world ends (and all is handed back to the Father after death is ended). I rather suspect that in those glaring gaps we would find that Archer is arguing that these saints are reigning in the Millenium between the resurrections, in Christ's kingdom. But regardless, if we just accept what is quoted, coming back to the second quote it proves that Archer can't be claiming that the dead saints are raised to heaven. Why? Well this quote starts out that:

> The first thing that Christ will doe, when he comes from Heaven to set up his Kingdom, he will raise up all Saints who are dead before his coming, therefore he is said to come with all his Saints (Zach 14.5).

Now, from what has been quoted before, this can't be a resurrection of the dead Saints to heaven, because that is the Father's Kingdom and this passage is about what Christ will do in setting up his own Kingdom, plus in a Pre-Trib scenario, how can the rapture be Christ coming to set up his own kingdom when the reality is that it is the start of the kingdom of the Antichrist. The only scenario that then fits is a Post-Trib position, *especially* since the passage starts by saying that the *first thing* Christ will do when he comes *from* heaven to set up his Kingdom is to raise the dead saints, not that he does this *before* he returns from heaven to set up his Kingdom. The rest of the quote says:

> For surely, as Christ had a middle State betwixt his Resurrection and Ascension for forty days; so shall his Saints have who dye before his coming from Heaven; ...but they shall have a middle state betwixt glory and mortality...yet he said then to come from Heaven, although he had come before, therefore he must have gone to heaven again...God hath approved somewhat proper and peculiar to every Age of his Church and people; ...and in this place they are kept till this Kingdome of Christ come...

Here's the problem: I don't know what exactly Archer was trying to argue, particularly with all those gaps in the quote, but if Watson is trying to spin this as evidence of a belief in a Pre-Trib rapture position where the saints dwell in heaven for seven years, it just won't work. Jesus had a middle state between his Resurrection and Ascension to heaven where he had a resurrected body and *stayed on earth.* In the Pre-Trib position, any 'intermediate state' would not be on earth, but would be in heaven. The pattern doesn't work, because in that scenario the resurrection and ascension of the saints happens in one event without any intermediate state. I suspect that what Archer is talking about in between all those gaps is the souls of the Saints being kept in some disembodied but possibly conscious state between their death and the rapture / resurrection at Jesus' return - that would explain the phrases about a 'middle state betwixt glory and mortality' and 'in this place they are kept till this Kingdome of Christ come'. Similarly, the blatant sentence fragment 'yet he said then to come from Heaven, although He had come before, therefore he must have gone to heaven again' does not have to mean a Pre-Trib 'dip and out' scenario where Jesus dips in to the atmosphere to the rescue the saints, yo-yo's back to heaven, only to return with the saints again. Rather, it fits just as well if you understand that Jesus' first coming was from Heaven, he returned there at his ascension, and will come from there again. I don't know that is what is being said, because this is blatantly not even a whole sentence, but I suspect it, given the highly suspicious way this quote is cut up. I am not sure exactly what the 'God hath approved somewhat proper and peculiar to every Age of His church and people' is meant to prove, unless it is that Archer is teaching some form of Dispensationalism, and again the fact that this is blatantly just a fragment of a sentence sets my alarm bells ringing loudly, particularly given the misbehaviours of Dr Watson and Mr Ice in the previous case where I could check the original before they got out their dishonest dispensationalist scissors and started cutting.

I should note that Ice skipped the next writer quoted by Dr Watson, because as even Dr Watson admitted, it was blatantly and unequivacally Post-Tribulation, talking about the persecution and tribulation of the church before Jesus' return, and - irony of ironies - actually quotes Justin Martyr and Lactantius as proof, the very same who Pre-Tribbers try and claim said the opposite. No wonder Ice skipped it! I should also note that Dr Watson cites several earlier writers, and again there is a similar pattern - small sentence fragments and the strongest suspicion in my mind that the conclusions are utterly unwarranted. For instance, he quotes mostly short fragments from various works of one Thomas Draxe, only one of which I have been able to find online (and that one the least useful for checking up on). I am particularly suspicious about the following quote and conclusion:

> Draxe exhorted us to "watch and pray, that we may be accompted (sic) worthy to escape all these things that shall come." He apparently believed in a partial rapture only of those worthy.

The reason is that it seems to me to be a typical case of assuming a Pre-Trib position to claim this as proof. You see, this verse from the bible is repeatedly claimed by Pre-Tribbers as proof of their position, even though as I showed in my previous book, in context it is no such thing. Given what I have seen so far, I am on the whole rather more impressed with these Puritan era writers' exegetical abilities and fidelity to the contextual understanding of Scripture than those of modern Pre-Tribbers. I have learned to be especially suspicious of sweeping conclusions by Pre-Tribbers such as Dr Watson makes here from very flimsy quotes. I suspect that there is the motive and the will to try and stretch anything to try and produce any form of separate rapture. I could be wrong, of course, but I would want a heck of a lot more contextual evidence before my suspicions on this conclusion were to be in any degree mollified. I am even more suspicious when later on there is a similar quote which screams out 'Post-Trib' to me:

> In a later work of 1615 Draxe warned that we should "make ourselves ready against that day, that we may bee accounted worth to escape al those things that shall come upon the world, and to stand before the Sonne of Man." He concluded by asking God, "after we have suffered a while, and made our selues ready, bring vsvnto, and translate vs into, thine euerlasting Kingdome of glory."

Suffering a while and being deemed worthy to stand before the Sonne of Man (from a bible passage that previously said only those who endure to the end will be saved)? That doesn't sound at all like Pre-Trib to me.

My suspicions are further aroused when even after admitting that a writer appears to be Post-Trib, Dr Watson still tries to muddy the water and spin things in an echo of the 'oh the early church fathers were confused and incoherent' tactic we have seen concerning the early church fathers, as he does here:

> Joseph Mede believed in two resurrections, but they were before and after the millennium, however his 1627 comment on 1 Thessalonians 4:14-18 used the same illustration on his "first resurrection" as did Darby on the rapture. He connected it to Noah's family lifted up away from the death and suffering on earth....... Although he seems to suggest a post-tribulation rapture, he does give a bit of time between the rapture and return to earth of the saints. Note also his word usage, that those "translated into the air" would "be preserved during the conflagration of the earth":
>
> After this, our gathering together unto Christ at His coming...The saints being translated into the air...and they may be preserved during the conflagration of the earth, and the works thereof: 2 Pet. 3.10. that as Noah and his family were preserved from the deluge by being lifted up above the waters in the ark, so should the saints at the conflagration be lifted up in the clouds, unto their ark, Christ, to be preserved there from the deluge of fire, wherein the wicked shall be consumed.

I think this is sneaky rhetoric indeed, with 'seems to suggest a Post-Tribulation rapture' when the matter is as clear as day. That is a bit like saying that this and my previous work 'Although he seems to suggest that the Pre-Trib rapture position has problems, he uses the same bible passages as Pre-Trib proponents' - putting doubt-implying qualifiers where there should be none and trying to clutch at any straw, however small or fantastic, that gives any kind of 'wiggle room' for squeezing in some element of Pre-Tribulationism. Why should using the same bible passage / illustration as Darby be something that should be highlighted, if not to distract from the clear and firm Post-Tribulational stance Joseph Mede took and so to try and blunt the impact of the clear message he spoke?

I shall try and be more concise with the rest, otherwise this appendix will turn into a book all on its own, just like this whole book was originally going to be an appendix.

> Ephraim Huit (Hewitt), founder the first church in Connecticut in 1639, believed "the comming of the Son of Man in the Cloudes" would save the elect from "trials" and allow the Jews regain their role in God's plan:
>
> "deliverance from outward trials is expressed by the Lords coming in the clouds...in the deliverance of his Church, from Egypt, and preservation in the wildernesse is described by his riding on the heavens...
>
> "Secondly, this coming of the Son of Man in the clouds is...some memorable event, not long before the general judgement, whereof it was a foregoing signe, and must therefore teach some other appearance.

> "Thirdly, upon this comming of the Son of Man in the cloudes, the kingdom is given to the Iewes...but upon the Incarnation of our Lord, the kingdom was taken from the Iewes, and given to the Romanes...
>
> "the summoning of the Elect by the sound of a trumpet...but this trumpet is heard only by the Elect, so that to me it seems to intend some voice, and call of the Lord, whereof the reprobates are incapable:
>
> "our Lord Mat 24.30. & his beloved disciple Iohn Rev 1.7. do couple this coming of the Son of man in the Cloudes with that holy wailing of the Iewes in their conuersion...Zac 12.10."

Again, notice the implicit spin in Dr Watson's introductory comments, most probably quite sincere (and remember he was looking for more than just Pre-Tribulation positions), because to a Pre-Tribber, the Son of Man coming in the clouds to save the elect from trials means a Pre-Trib rapture, as does 'allowing the Jews to regain their role in God's plan', which they believes happens after the rapture, during the Tribulation. But the actual quotes don't really bear this out. First of all, the footnote says that these few fragments have been extracted from a whole four pages of the original document, which leaves me wondering again about all those gaps and what is in them. Secondly, notice how these five quotes better fit a Post-Tribulation scenario. The first does mention Jesus delivering people from outward trials - that fits a Post-Trib situation where the church has been persecuted and decimated, and even more so when the second part of that quote links 'riding in the heaven's' with the church being preserved in the *wilderness*, <u>not</u> in heaven. The second could fairly fit a Post-trib position as well, since the general judgement is usually held by these authors to be that at the end of the Millennium, which would explain the 'some other appearance' (although again, I am highly suspicious given that there is that strategically placed elipse). Even if it did refer to say, the Matthew 25 judgement, or Huit was an Amillennialist, then it would indeed be a 'memorable event, not long before the general judgement'. I also note that many of the early church fathers believed that the sign of the Son of Man preceded the Son of Man, so perhaps this is something similar, the sight of the coming of the Son of Man in clouds of glory precedes his touching down on earth and being seen on the judgement throne. The third quote is problematic for Pre-Tribulationists, for in their scenario, the Jews prophetic clock starts ticking and they receive back an earthly kingdom at the point that the Tribulation starts, but this explicitly places their being given the kingdom only when Jesus returns in clouds of glory, which better fits a Post-Trib Millennial understanding. The fourth quote can fit a Post-Trib scenario just as easily as any other scenario, and the final quote actually far better fits a Post-Trib scenario, because Jesus coming 'on the clouds of heaven' is how 1 Thessalonians 4 describes the rapture, yet here the same is explicitly linked to Matthew 24.30 which says it happens 'after the Tribulation'. But Watson gives us more, telling us that:

> Huit went on to imply a partial resurrection prior to the "general judgement and resurrection."
>
> "In the days of affliction the Lord stands for the defense of his Church. ... these things cannot be meant by the generall judgement and resurrection.

> First the children of Daniel's people onely are delievered, the Iews onely are capable of this rising again, who in the generall judgement have no preeminence.
>
> Secondly, this time is a great time of trouble even to them that rise to life, but the state unto which the godly do arise in the generall judgement, is replenished with rest and peace.
>
> Thirdly, in this resurrection many shall arise but not all...but in the generall judgement even all shall arise how profane so ever they be

Now a 'partial resurrection prior to the general judgement and resurrection' is the teaching of the early church fathers (and the bible) in an explicitly Post-Trib scenario, as I have shown in this and my previous books - 'the resurrection of the righteous' - although admittedly Huit here seems to think it is not just for the righteous. Secondly, the quote starts out with something that on the face of it is antithetical to Pre-Tribulationism - the Lord stands for the defence of his Church in the days of affliction - he would have no need to if he had raptured them up to heaven out of the way - and again, a rather suspicious gap there. We don't know how long it is, or what 'these things' refers back to. It is true that Huit's focus is solely on what he believes to be Jewish resurrections (but that assumes that this is what he means, because notice he talks of the Jews being 'delivered' and that could be what 'this rising again' refers to. The quote starting 'secondly' does not really fit a Pre-Trib rapture scenario, because by definition all those who are raptured get rest and peace.

I was also singularly unimpressed with how the quotes from Elizabeth Avery ('Scripture-Prophecies Opened') seem to have been spun, if they were meant to show some sort of precursor to a Pre-Tribulation rapture which I think they may have been:

> Elizabeth Avery in 1647 understood the woman of Revelation 12, who was taken by the two wings of an eagle to safety in the wilderness, to be the true Church rescued from the persecution of the false church. She also understood passages where God would gather his people from around the world (commonly understood as Jews gathered to Israel) and gather them to himself: 'he will gather all his from all places whither they have been led captives, as well as out of this Land, which doth more evidently appear to be spiritual Babylon then any other place...the great Tribulation which shall befall the Church of God immediately before her deliverance out of Babylon...and her deliverance likewise temporally from the bondage of the creature, the hateful enemies of God; and so the Church shall be secured in that chamber spoken of in Isai 26, and the wildernesse (Revel 12). As well in a temporal sense as in a spiritual, which is a place of safety...which God will provide as a restingplace for the Saints: which I say is an undoubted truth, in respect of the judgements of God which are coming on the earth, an utter destruction of the wicked by Sword, Pestilence and Famine.

Aside from those gaps marked by '....' - which we don't know are legitimately placed or not - what needs to be emphasised here is that the church is definitely not described as having been rescued to heaven, but rather locked into their houses, or out in the wilderness (again, I'm not surprised Ice skipped this one when he was claiming the Pre-Trib rapture was taught in this period). What I really don't like is the spin in the next comment:

> Avery supports this gathering of saints as a separate event than the actual return of Christ, and from the same passages as did Darby and later Dispensationalists:

Since 'gather of saints as a separate event than the actual return of Christ' is a mainstay of the Pre-Trib position, despite this quote not supporting such a position at all, I think this, while technically true, is something of a 'dog-whistle' phrase to try and bedazzle unwary and 'scholar-awed' readers into thinking there is some semblance of Pre-Trib rapture when there isn't, especially when he goes on to say that she is using the 'same passages as did Darby and later Dispensationalists'. Think about it. If she used the same passages as Darby and later dispensationalists to support a position totally contrary to theirs, then surely that shows against the Pre-Trib position, not support for it - but again, that will be lost on an unwary or already indoctrinated reader.

> Whereas the saints do expect a dissolution of all things at the last days, when the Son of man shall come in the clouds of heaven with power and great glory, and all the Saints with him in like manner, who shall be gathered together by the sound of a trumpet, as in 1 Cor 15. And 1 Thess 4 and 5 Chap. ... 1 Pet 3.Where it is said, that the day shall come as a thief in the night...those that are risen at the coming of Christ, with those who are risen from the dead, shall be caught up into the clouds, to meet the Lord in the air...and accordingly do expect Christ coming in glory spiritually, and all his Saints with him. ...thoughts concerning the state of the Saints departed, with those who shall, before the glorious manifestation of Jesus Christ in the flesh...

Firstly, there is no sign in the first parts of the quote that this is a separate event to the return of Jesus. She links the rapture with the 'dissolution of all things at the last days', a dissolution which does not happen before the Tribulation, but after. Not only are those many gaps ringing alarm bells again, so is the fact that the last few quotes are tiny partial sentence fragments, which in the last case is a fragment that doesn't actually make sense because of lack of sufficient context. Not only that, but these sentence fragments use phrases which I call 'Pavlovian signals' to Pre-Tribulationists who have been conditioned to associate them solely with the Pre-Trib position - 'thief in the night' 'meet the Lord in the air', and the last nonsensical fragment is cut in such a way as to leave possible the interpretation that it refers to a separate rapture 'before the glorious manifestation of Jesus Christ in the flesh', but I'll bet the context would show otherwise. The other thing is that to the unwary reader, it would seem that all these sections and fragments are from one sustained passage, that they are all close by each other, but a look at the footnote reveals that they come from very widely spread page numbers - so of those four gaps, one has to contain 6 pages of material, and another no less than 11 pages. Now that, when combined with the tiny sentence fragments really does set alarm bells ringing with me! So much for 'lengthy quotes' to provide 'context'!

Despite this, Dr Watson obviously thinks this is sufficient basis for this sweeping conclusion (which again may be well be technically correct - and yet.....):

> An expectation that the Saints would be taken out of tribulation and protected from the wrath of Antichrist was common in the seventeenth century. Lady Mary Cary believed that "enlargements shall come for the Saints, and they being delivered from the rage of the Beast, shall be preserved wholly from his fury..."

Now it is true that he doesn't say explicitly that this taking out of tribulation and protection was by means of a heavenly rapture I suspect that this is the impression that will be left with unwary readers (and that last sentence fragment with no context doesn't fill me with confidence, either).

I was also singularly unimpressed with the spin put on this quote:

> Peter Sterry, another member of the Westminster Assembly of Divines, in 'The Clouds in which Christ Comes' (1648) seems to describe as a pre-tribulation rapture:
>
> This second Coming of Christ, is, as the dayes of Noah. The Lord Jesus in the Spirit shall be both Ark and Flood: An Ark to those which are taken into Christ, lifting them high above all miseries toward Heaven; And [illegible] carrying away insensible Persons, and Scorners [illegible] ing Woe.

Notice once again the weasel-words 'seems to describe a pre-tribulation rapture'. The trouble is that this passage is just as valid in a Post-Tribulation position. Notice also that it does not say that they were taken *to* or *into* heaven, but that they were lifted '*toward* heaven' but only above 'all miseries', meaning the judgements and woes coming at the very end to unbelievers. Given that Jesus is describe as being simultaneously both Ark and Flood, and that the ark was lifted up 'toward heaven' (but not *into* heaven) above the destruction only to immediately fall back to the earth from which it came at the end of the flood of judgement, it would not surprise me in the least if Peter Sterry was in fact post-Tribulationist. You can apparently get a copy of this sermon on Amazon, so if you want to find out for sure.....

Ice quotes Watson about Nathaniel Homes, but gets it wrong as rather confusingly Watson starts by citing Joseph Mede (even though his footnote says it was Nathaniel Homes - incorrectly, as far as I can see because I couldn't find any part of this part of this in Homes, although there were some passages that were close. You can look for yourself in; there's a nice page turning edition here - https://archive.org/details/resurrectionreve00homerich or if your browser doesn't support that you can just use google books - the title is 'The Resurrection Revealed: Or, The Dawning of the Day-star'). Here is the initial quote I had trouble with:

Nathaniel Homes is another seventeenth century author who used the word "rapture" for the event in 1 Thessalonians 4. He cited Joseph Mede who wrote twenty six years earlier:

> The resurrection of those which slept in Christ, and the rapture of those which shall be left alive, together with them into the aire, should be at one and the same time: For the words in 1 Thess 4. v.16,17...may admit a great distance of time... Everyone (or, all mankind) shall rise in their order, Christ the first fruits...afterwards, they that are Christs at his coming... notes a distance of time of above a thousand and a halfe of yeers... Suppose this rapture of the Saints into the aire, be to translate them to heaven, ...the rapture of the Saints into the clouds, to be for their present translation into heaven. ...this our gathering together unto Christ at his coming (so the Apostle calls this rapture, 2 Thess.2.1.) wee shall from henceforth never lose his presence, but always enjoy it, partly on earth, during his reign of the thousand yeers, and partly in heaven, when wee shall be translated thither.

Firstly, let's just take the quote as it is. There's those gaps again, along with at least five sentence fragments. So, the first quote seems solid enough, but it applies just as easily to a Post-Trib understanding. After that I start getting downright suspicious. 'For the words in 1 Thess 4.16-17 - unspecified gap, then 'may admit a great distance of time'. I would bet that the 'great distance of time' is totally out of context and would be more like the 'distance of time about a thousand and a halfe of yeers' that comes later. Then more fragments, including the hypothetical 'Suppose this rapture... be to translate them to heaven' - all very fishy. But even then, the end quote kind of gives the game away - where it talks about a gathering to Christ at his second coming where we will be with him always, firstly on earth during the 1000 years, then in heaven later on - exactly the wrong way round for a Pre-Trib position. And then I managed to find the document these quotes are from, and boy was I right. Not just a rat, but a swarm of rats. I found the real deal, ironically enough, through an article on the Five Doves website I slated in an earlier appendix. The article there had several quotes, correctly noting that Joseph Mede was exploring different options, as a good academic should, although it incorrectly claimed one of those options was a Pre-Trib rapture, and then linked to the full work, which was a letter Mede wrote in response to a question about what we would call 'the rapture' from a Sam Meddes. You can read the full details for yourself about a third of the way down
http://quod.lib.umich.edu/e/eebo/A50522.0001.001/1:72?rgn=div1;view=fulltext - letter number 22.

The question Mr Mede was asked was this:

> They that then are found alive shall be caught up in the air? and ever be with the Lord; I mean the godly: But if there shall be a 1000 years reign on earth, what need they be caught up in the air, and how ever be with the Lord from thenceforth, if they and their posterity after them continue for the space of a 1000 years subject to mortality?

After apologizing that ill health had delayed his answer, he replied as follows, and I quote in full context, to show the real meaning, with the bits Dr Watson has quoted in **bold** (I should add that in the original text there were some problems with ancient Greek letters, so wherever you see <> there is a Greek word there):

> I will therefore, as well as I can, propound what I had before conceived might be answered to such an Objection; wherein you shall also perceive in part wherein I differ from the Lutheran.
>
> 1. **Therefore, It is not needful that the Resurrection of those which slept in Christ, and the Rapture of those which shall be left alive together with them into the Aire, should be at one and the same time: For the words** <> and <>, first and then or afterwards, **may admit a great distance of time,** as 1 Cor. 15. 23. **Every one (or, all mankind) shall rise in their order, Christ the first-fruits (that is, first,)** <> afterwards **they that are Christ's, at his coming.** Here <>, afterwards, **notes a distance of time of above a thousand and a half of years,** as we find by experience. **Suppose therefore this Rapture of the Saints into the Aire be to translate them to Heaven;** yet it might be construed thus, The dead in Christ (that is, for Christ, namely, the Martyrs) shall rise first; afterwards, <>, (viz. a thousand years after) we which are alive and remain shall together with them be caught up in the clouds, and meet the Lord in the Aire, and so (from thenceforth) we shall ever be with the Lord. Thus Tertullian seems to understand it, who interprets <>, or as it is in ver. 14. <>, of Martyrs; namely, such as die *propter Christum*, for Christ, by means of Christ, through Christ, for Christ's sake; taking <> as noting the cause or means of their death. So Piscator expounds the like speech, Apoc. 14. 13. Blessed are the dead which die <> *id est, propter Dominum*, for the Lord; Beza, *qui Domini causâ moriuntur*, which die for the Lord's sake.
>
> 2. If thus to restrain <>, or <> seem not so fully to answer the Apostle's scope and intention, which seems to be a general consolation to all that die in the faith, a fruition of Christ: then may we give it the largest sense, and yet say, That it is not needful that the Resurrection of those which died in Christ should be all at once or altogether; but the Martyrs first, in the First resurrection; then (after an appointed time) the rest of the dead in the Last resurrection; afterward, when the Resurrection shall be thus compleat, those which remain alive at Christ's coming shall together with those which are risen be caught up into the clouds, to meet the Lord in the Aire, and from thenceforth be eternally with him. And so the reason why those which Christ found alive at his coming were not instantly translated should be in part, that they might not prevent the dead, but be consummate with them.
>
> 3. Both these Interpretations suppose **the Rapture of the Saints into the Clouds to be for their present translation into Heaven.** But suppose that be not the meaning of it; for the words, if we weigh them well, seem to imply it to be for another end, namely, To do honour unto their Lord

and King at his return, and to attend upon him when he comes to judge the World: Those (saith the Text) which sleep in Iesus, will God bring with him; he saith not, carry away with him. Again, They and those which are alive shall be caught up together in the clouds, to meet the Lord in the Aire; to meet the Lord's coming hither to Iudgment; not to follow him returning hence, the Iudgment being finished. Besides, it is to be noted, that although in the Hebrew notion the Aire be comprehended under the name of Heaven, yet would not the Apostle here use the word Heaven, but the word [Aire,] as it were to avoid the ambiguity, lest we might interpret it of our translation into Heaven.

If this be the meaning, then are those words [We shall ever be with the Lord] thus to be interpreted; After **this our gathering together unto Christ at his coming, (so the Apostle calls this Rapture, 2 Thess. 2. 1.) we shall from henceforth never lose his presence, but always enjoy it, partly on earth, during his reign of a 1000 years, and partly in Heaven, when we shall be translated thither.** For it cannot be concluded, because the Text saith, the Saints after their rapture on high should thenceforth be ever with the Lord; Ergò, they shall from thenceforth be in Heaven; for no Heaven is here mentioned. If they must needs be with Christ there where they are to meet him, it would rather follow, they should be ever with him in the Aire, than in Heaven; which I suppose none will admit. And otherwise the Text will afford no more for Heaven than it will for Earth; nay, the words [he shall bring them with him] make most for the latter.

I will add this more, namely, what may be conceived to be the cause of this Rapture of the Saints on high to meet the Lord in the Clouds, rather than to wait his coming to the Earth. What if it be, that they may be preserved during the Conflagration of the earth and the works thereof, 2 Pet. 3. 10. that as Noah and his family were preserved from the Deluge by being lift up above the waters in the Ark; so should the Saints at the Conflagration be lift up in the Clouds unto their Ark, Christ, to be preserved there from the deluge of fire, wherein the wicked shall be consumed? There is a Tradition of the Iews founding this way, which they ascribe unto one Elias a Iewish Doctor, whose is that Tradition of the duration of the World, and well known among Divines, {I have removed some Latin text that seems to be about years, here}. He lived under the second Temple about the first times of the Greek Monarchy; so that it is no device of any latter Rabbies, but a Tradition anciently received amongst them whilst they were yet the Church of God. I will transcribe it, because it hath something remarkable concerning the 1000 years: It sounds thus.

The Hebrew words are in Gemara Sanhedrin, <> The Tradition of the house of Elias. The just whom God shall raise up (viz. in the First Resurrection) shall not be turned again to dust. Now if you ask, How it shall be with the just in those Thousand years wherein the Holy Blessed God shall renew his world, whereof it is said (Esa. 2. 11.) And the Lord alone shall be exalted in that day; you must know, that the Holy Blessed

> God will give them the wings as it were of Eagles, to fly upon the face of the waters: whence it is said (Psal. 46. 3.) Therefore shall we not fear, when the Earth shall be changed. But perhaps you will say, it shall be a pain and affliction to them. Not at all, for it is said (Esa. 40. 31.) They that wait upon the Lord, shall renew their strength, they shall mount up with wings as Eagles.

I will be blunt. I am disgusted. There is no two ways about it – those 'quotes' can only have been out and out deception. Dr Watson had to have known the utter dishonesty of what he was doing (unless he was only copying quotes from someone else, which would be another form of academic dishonesty, since he claimed at the start to have waded through all original material). He has taken fragments and longer quotes from completely different paragraphs in a work discussing different interpretations of the same Scriptures or concepts, and strung them together to make out Mede was taking a position which he never held. Mede only considered a gap between the raising of the dead and the rapture of the living as a theoretical possibility, and wasn't even considering a Pre-Tribulation position at that. Rather, he was talking of the martyrs being resurrected at Jesus' second coming, and the rest of the righteous being raptured at the end of the Millennium, but Dr Watson has so radically edited and shredded the words to give the impression that something like a Pre-Tribulation concept is being taught here.

Even putting this aside, there would still be cause for concern, because there are a number of arguments Mede uses which powerfully undermine any kind of Pre-Tribulation argument at all, but which Dr Watson has skilfully avoided by sneaky scissor work. In particular I refer to these passages:

> Besides, it is to be noted, that although in the Hebrew notion the Aire be comprehended under the name of Heaven, yet would not the Apostle here use the word Heaven, but the word [Aire,] as it were to avoid the ambiguity, lest we might interpret it of our translation into Heaven.

Furthermore, the end of Dr Watson's selective quote, which was edited to try and make it seem to support a Pre-Trib rapture, but in fact even cut out of context is at odds with such an interpretation, as I showed above, is in fact immediately followed by an even more powerful refutation of the necessary core of the Pre-Trib concept:

> For it cannot be concluded, because the Text saith, the Saints after their rapture on high should thenceforth be ever with the Lord; Ergò, they shall from thenceforth be in Heaven; **for no Heaven is here mentioned**. If they must needs be with Christ there where they are to meet him, it would rather follow, they should be ever with him in the Aire, than in Heaven; which I suppose none will admit. **And otherwise the Text will afford no more for Heaven than it will for Earth; nay, the words [he shall bring them with him] make most for the latter**.

I think that says it all really. Anyway, Dr Watson continues:

> Using a classic Pre-Tribulation argument, Homes wondered why the saints would be raptured into the aire, instead of meeting Christ when he arrives on earth:

> What may be conceived to be the cause of this rapture of the Saints on high to meet the Lord in the clouds, rather then to wait his coming to the earth. What if it bee, that they may be preserved during the conflagration of the earth, and the works thereof, 2 Pet.3.10. That as Noah, and his family were preserved from the deluge, by being lift up above the waters in the Ark, so should the Saints at the conflagration bee lift up in the clouds unto their Ark, Christ, to be preserved there from the Deluge of fire, wherein the wicked shall be consumed?

Even putting aside what we have already discovered about the context of the letter in which this passage originally appears, I would note that just this passage proves nothing at all in regards to a Pre-Trib rapture, because in this the saints rise in the air to escape not the Tribulation, but the 'conflagration of the earth', something that happens specifically at the visible return of Jesus to earth. This passage was by Mede originally, but quoted by Homes. Describing this as a 'classic Pre-Tribulation argument' when in the original setting they are anything but is problematic, but does Homes himself use the quote in any way to promote something like a Pre-Tribulation rapture? The answer is an unequivocal NO. Here is the lead up to this passage, and it is during interpretation of 2 Peter3 and the 'great conflagration', which as we have already noted, is something that happens at the end of the Tribulation, at the visible return of Jesus. Homes says:

> That we may have the full intent of the Apostle in this text, note that v14 {of 2 Peter 3}, ("Seeing ye look for such things, be diligent that ye be found of him in peace, without spot and blameless.') suggests a query that must be answered' viz. What is the place and state of the *saints* in the time of this burning? We answer; that the Lord can miraculously keep his people in this fire, as he did the three children in the fiery oven, and the Israelites in Goshen, whilst fiery judgements were spread over all the land of Egypt round about. Respecting these and similar preservations it is said 'We went through fire and water, but thou broughtest us into a place of refreshing. And it is promised for the future 'When thou passest through the fire thou shlat not be burned, &c. I am thy saviour, that gave Egypt for thy ranson'. He can carry them through this fire, by taking them up into the air at his coming, according to 1 Thess. iv, 17 - "We which are alive and remain, shall be caught up together with them in the clouds to meet the Lord in the air." On which words learned Mr Mede hath this: 'I will add what may be conceived..... ' etc

Again, this is unequivocal. The rapture is definitively linked with the 2 Peter 3 'conflagration' that only happens at the return of Jesus after the Tribulation. Once again, Dr Watson has spun things by anachronistically claiming that Homes uses a 'classic Pre-Tribulationist' argument, when that same argument was used by Homes and many others to assert a Post-Tribulationist position. The latter was the dominant position, as it had been for the entirety of preceding church history, whereas 'PreTribulationism, well, we've yet to see a sign of it, so how can this be a 'classic Pre-Tribulationist' argument specifically? I think I have to say it: 'My dear Dr Watson, Mr Homes fires you for failing at elementary context!' Moving on:

> Homes wrote of a dual resurrection, "Blessed & holy is he that hath part in the first resurrection," which would occur at "a Resurrection...of the deceased beleevers...intimating that the bringing in of the Jewes at the Resurrection of all things would be a very great and glorious businesse..."

As we have seen, a dual resurrection is a classic Post-Trib position right back to the earliest church, so I am not sure what significance this point is meant to have. What is also slightly troubling is the quotes. To a casual reader, one would expect that all is set out in order in one passage, but in fact the first quote about the 'first resurrection' is from P310, and the rest come from a short passage much earlier, on p56-7. However, in this case I don't think Dr Watson has materially distorted any teaching of Mr Mede, although he does appear to have substituted 'Resurrection of all things' for 'restitution of all things'. He goes on:

> Homes believes the rapture and the calling of the Jews would happen simultaneously:
>
> The likeliest maine time to make out the true meaning of this Text ["they will look upon him whom they have pierced and mourn" Zachariah 12:10] is the time of the general Call, and conversion of the Jewes yet to come, at the beginning of the Restitution of all things. ...this coming is meant of a coming after his Ascension, and yet before the ultimate day of doome...a future thing...it is not intended of his last Act that ever hee will doe, which is the ultimate judgement. BEHOLD implies some eminent coming, and none more eminent than this, for the RESTITUTION OF ALL THINGS. ... HEE cometh...IN the clouds. ...this coming shall not bee so obscure, as his Incarnation...but he shall come conspicuous and glorious visibly to all upon the earth... Zechary the Prophet, and John the Apostle both prophesie in the aforesaid places of one and the same personal appearance of Christ visibly to the eyes of men on earth after his Ascension. But this cannot be understood of his appearance at the ultimate day of judgement, because they speak of his pouring out of grace, and giving repentance to the families of the Jewes...

Seven gaps, and several sentence fragments only two or three words long? Am I suspicious? You bet! But even before searching for the original context, I have to ask, so what? Pretty much all of this as it stands fits a Post-Trib scenario. The work is quoting Revelation 1.7 and Zechariah 12.10,and places them at the start of the Restitution of all things, which happens when Jesus visibly returns (I wonder if somehow Watson is mixing up the biblical 'restitution of all things', with the Pre-Tribulationist concept of Israel's 'prophetic clock' starting again re Daniel 9's 70 weeks). The 'ultimate day of doome' can be understood as the day of General Judgement at the end of the Millennium, so that would fit a Post-Trib scenario. The coming is not 'obscure', which rules out a 'secret rapture'. Whilst, as best I can tell, there is no *really* creative editing here, because there is nothing that I can find that is 'out of order' and the quotes come from only a couple of pages, (although there were a couple of phrases that appear in the quote that didn't when I looked the passages up, and a few small gaps where there are no ellipses in the quote, but I suspect that may simply be because Watson is using a different edition to the one I found - and by the way, the google books version has missed out a couple of pages at the start of the longer passage), still it is instructive to read the whole passage unabridged, because it makes it more clear that Homes is taking an explicitly Post-Trib position, and the gaps in the quote disguise that for Watson's readers quite, although not entirely, successfully, as we have seen. The first and key thing to note is the chapter title in which this passage appears: The Personal Appearing of Christ **To** His Church **At** her Restauration on Earth (emphasis mine). That pretty much rules out a Pre-Tribulation position right there, because such a postition has the personal 'appearing' of Christ to his church seven years before her Restoration on earth. He then goes on to say:

> Our position therefore will contain these two particulars: I. That Christ shall then at least *appear* visibly in person, more or less. II. That the saints under him shall sensibly, and properly, reign over the whole earth. In order to establish these we shall bring forward a few different passages of Scripture; not in the order in which they occur, but so places, as that they may best throw light on one another.

He then goes on to quote Zechariah 12.10 (the mourning of the inhabitants of Jerusalem and Judah for the 'one they have pierced'. He argues that it cannot be the - in his view - few Jews who followed Christ in the New Testament period, and goes on to say:

> Those that would avoid the force of this text for the point of Christ's personal appearing at the great future restauration, must of necessity make it relate, either to the time of Christ's passion, or to the time of the last judgement; but to neither of them will it *fully* answer.

After explaining why, we come to where our passage starts:

> The likeliest time therefore t o make out the true and full meaning of this text is, the period of the general call and conversion of the Jews yet to come; as will more plainly appear from the next section, which is another quotation of this same place.
>
> Revelation i, 7

He then quotes Revelation 1.7 and briefly shows the context in which it quotes Zechariah 12.10 means it must speak of Christ, and goes on:

> It is still more evident, that the *coming* here named cannot be meant of Christ's firt coming in the flesh, because it is prophesied so many years after his ascension : it must relate to that coming spoken of Acts i, 11 - 'This same Jesus, which is taken up from you into heaven, shall so come, in like manner as ye have seen him go into heaven;' - spoken when the '*cloud* received Him.' His disciples had just asked of him 'whether at that time he would restore the kingdom to Israel;' and he left his angels to give them this answer.
>
> Every word almost of this text intimates, that this coming is meant of a time after his ascension, and yet before the ultimate day of doom. 'Behold! He cometh' - implies a future thing, now, and after his ascension; and

> some *eminent* coming. 'He cometh with *clouds'* that is, *in* the clouds; as the Greeks in the same manner say, *a man WITH armour,* for *a man IN armour.* The meaning doubtless is, that this coming of Christ shall not be so obscure as at his incarnation, or as his coming among the disciples after his resurrection; but he shall come conspicuous and gloriously visible to all upon the earth. His people *now* see him with the eye of *faith;* but they do not behold him *visibly:* then however 'every eye shall see him' which must needs signify more than a sight by faith: for faith and sight are so distinct that the Apostle makes them opposite. It is questionable, wehter eery eye, that is said here to see him, shall first see him by faith: for *every eye* must see him, and *all kindreds of the earth* shall mourn. Surely his enemies, whom he destroys at his coming, shall not see him by faith!

After a brief paragraph on that point of faith versus sight, Homes goes on:

> On the other hand this text cannot be understood of the ultimate day of judgement: First, because it is the same with Zechariah i, 10; and therefore the same reasons prevail, which are noticed under that head. Secondly, because this is set here, as the main and general proposition of the book of the Revelation; of which the subject therefore is, to set forth Christ *to come* and set up his Church into a most glorious estate on earth, before the day of judgement, (as we have seen abundantly.) and to make her reign with him on earth. Thirdly, it were very incongruous for John, in the last clause of verse 6, to applaud Christ's *dominon* as to continue *for ever,* (that is, while times and ages last, as the Greek imports) and in the first clause of the very next verse to say, he cometh to make an *end* of his dominion. For the ultimate day of judgement is the last act of Christ's dominion; which he then lays down, that God may be all in all.
>
> Thus then observer, that Zechariah and John both prophesied in the aforesaid places of one and the same personal appearance of Christ. This, from the whole tenor and time of the vision to John, must be subsequent to his asencsion: but it cannot be understood of the ultimate general judgement, because they both speak of his *pouring out grace on, and giving repentance to, the families of the Jews,* and of his *dominion, to continue thence for many ages;* Therefore the said visible appearance of Christ is yet to be *before* the ultimate day of judgement. (All italics in the original)

He then goes on to discuss Matthew 24.30, showing it deals with the same event. Now, in the original cut up quote, there was just about room to give the impression of some event between the ascension and the second coming, but the full context makes it clear that Homes was talking about an event between the ascension and the final judgement at the end of the Millennium. The next quote is yet another dishonest handling of the text and another example of spin so great as to make a gyroscope blush:

> After pages of arguments as to why numerous prophetic events could not have yet occurred, Homes *implies* a pre-trib rapture and *explicitly states* a pre-mil scenario, that there would be a (italics mine)

> "first Resurrection, wherein all the Saints rise; so that the ruine of Babylon, and the raising of the Saints immediately concurre with the sorrow of the one, and the triumph of the other."

Even without looking at the context here, there is a major problem I spotted - this seems to say that the ruin of Babylon (false church or religion? - certainly in a Pre-Trib scenario, anyway) and the resurrection of the saints happen simultaneously, to the sorrow of Babylon, and the triumph of the saints. The trouble is that in a Pre-Trib scenario the resurrection of the saints occurs and is usually depicted as a time of rejoicing for 'Babylon' because her chief enemies have disappeared. In a Pre-Trib scenario the ruin and sorrow of Babylon does not occur for another seven years after the rapture, at the point of Jesus' visible return - hardly simultaneous. And when we look at the context (p246 of Homes' book), this is made clear - once again, the quote is started and finished at just the point where it is possible to spin this as a Pre-Trib scenario (and even that only 'implicitly') expertly excising away the context that would demonstrate that this is a clearly Post-Tribulation interpretation. Oh, and one more thing. You would get the impression that this discussion comes *after* the previous quote, but in fact it comes just before, at the end of the *preceding* chapter, which I think is telling. It comes in a discussion of Revelation chapters *eighteen and nineteen* - after the Tribulation, which again, Watson has oh-so-conveniently forgotten to mention to his readers:

> Nor verses 11-19 {of chapter 18 - ed} viz 'the *mourning* of the merchants over her destruction;' neither verse 20, the *rejoicing* of the holy apostles and prophets over it, mentioned again also in the first seven verses of the nineteenth chapter. In which the last passage, the coupling with the judgement on the great Whore the declaration that 'the marriage of the Lamb is come, and his wife hath made herself ready' clearly relates to the first resurrection, wherein all the saints, rise; so that the ruin of Babylon, and the raising of the saints, immediately concur with the sorrow of the one, and the triumph of the other. Once more, from the eighth verse of the nineteenth chapter to the end of the chapter is not fulfilled; viz of the glory of the Church, of the glorious appearance of Christ, and of the corporal destruction of all whatsoever that take part against him and his Church.

You cannot get much more systematically Post-Trib than that - no wonder Dr Watson can't even quote an entire sentence. This is out and out dishonesty and lying, and it offends me both as a scholar and a Christian, and makes me bloody angry - it is exactly this kind of thing that made me want to set out the lies of these false teachers who are deceiving the church wantonly and systematically with the demonic doctrines. One or two misinterpretations is one thing, but a doctrine that relies on such complete and utter distortion of the truth over and over again can only come from the devil, the father of lies.

Since Dr Watson's document goes on for 55 pages, and we have only reached the middle of page 9, I will now deal only with those quoted by Mr Ice and not spend too much time looking at context, if I can help it.... (the old adage here has been proven true, that a lie goes around the world before the truth has time to put its boots on – it has taken a great deal of time and text to examine context and expose the lies that are usually achieved by shredding passages to small fragments and skating over them). It is possible that there may actually be one or two Pre-Darby examples in Dr Watson's work that genuinely do have elements of a nascent 'Pre-Tribulation' rapture, but the signs thus far have not been good. The next such quote from Ice is:

> James Durham (1622-1658) in A Commentarie upon the Book of the Revelation (1658) says, "1. Antichrist Rome's destruction, her people lament, but the Saints sing 'Alleluja' 2. Preparation for the Bride (Church): the first resurrection, 'clothed in fine linen' 3. The Lambs order and army... after the Lambs marriage...a flourishing Church, able to send out Armies... not only Angels and Saints glorified; but such of the Church, as are arrayed..."

Now, aside from those oh so suspicious gaps and partial sentence fragments, ask yourself what is there in this order, assuming it is accurate, that contradicts or disproves a Post-Tribulation position, and necessitates a Pre-Tribualation one? This is exactly the order of events in Revelation 18 and 19 in a Post-Tribulation scenario-destruction of Babylon / Antichrist, Preperation for the Bride / Church, the first resurrection 'clothed in fine linen' (surely in a Pre-Trib scenario this should be first, right back in around Revelation 4?) and the Lamb and His army coming down *after* their marriage where they are united (in the air as Jesus descends). My response to this is simply, 'So what. It in no way proves what you claim, and if anything disproves it and supports the position you are opposing'.

Next quote:

> John Birchensha (c 1630s-1681) in The History of the Scripture (1660) says, "The dead shall be raised,... some of them which did slay them, shal behold them when they ascend into heaven in a Cloud,... A tenth part... will leave the great Whore; partly abhorring her cruelties, partly seeing the mighty wonders of God in raising the dead, and partly foreseeing the judgements ready to fall upon the Babylonish and Papal Empire. And...the Lord will put it into their hearts of the Jews (having seen the sign of the Sonne of Man in Heaven, and being convinced that their Messiah is come) to imbodie, in order to a journie into their owne Land. ... All Nations shal be brought against Jerusalem to battle; for Wars wil be among the Turks, as wel as among those who are called Christians; and the spoile shal be divided in the midst of Jerusalem: and the City shall be taken, and the houses spoiled, and the women defiled... But the Heathen shal not long possesse the Holy City: For now the Lord wil come to give his Saints possession of their own Land: And he wil come with All his Saints..."

Again, my response is 'So what?'. And again, lots of highly suspicious gaps and sentence fragments all over the place. I assume the gaps and orders are there to try and present an order that goes 'Rapture' – Babylon (and therefore those leaving 'must' be 'Tribulation Saints'?) and then the end, Armageddon and so on. But there are some serious problems. Firstly, in most Pre-Trib rapture thought, the eyes of unbelievers cannot see the saints as they are raptured, nor the 'clouds of glory' with which Christ descends - they just know that people have disappeared leaving driverless cars and little piles of clothes all over the place, leaving the governments to blame 'UFO's or whatever. So given Watson's track record, I would bet a lot of money on there being some form of creative editing to give a false impression and hide a Post-Tribulation belief system. Next quote:

> William Sherwin (1607-1687) in Eirenikon: or a Peaceable consideration of Christ's Peaceful Kingdom on Earth (1665) says, "the Saints...jointly at the sounding of that last Trumpet at the end of the world shall be changed in a moment, at the twinkling of an eye...be rapt up to meet Christ in the air... the end of the fourth Monarchy...which agree with the times of the seventh Trumpet... Christ by a change before, in an instant delivers the faithful then alive, from that temporal destruction, and the ruine of the Antichrist... The examples of the Flood in Noahs time, and the destruction of Sodom and Gomorrah in Lots time are instances... he will raise all his people that then sleep in the grave, to raign on earth with him, till the great multitude of their fellow-members be come in. This Doctrine many of the ancient Fathers acknowledged ...Justine Martyr...Irenaeus... Tertullian...even Augustine sometime held it, though by the subtlety of Satan, forgeinglyes to asperse the Millenary opinion, and stirring men up to foist in offensive errours...in these latter times hath again discovered it, after so many hundred years of its lying hid for the most part in the Church, to be a doctrine really embraced by his faithful people [who] will doubtless certainly know, that upon their rapture to meet Christ, they shall be perfected in glory evermore in heaven."

Again, loads of suspicious gaps and short sentence fragments, with most of them quoting what I call the 'Pre-trib Pavlovian phrases', and the bits that echo modern Dispesnationalist' thoughts about the history of the Millennium in the church - which I basically agree with. But, anything that actually shows a distinct 'Pre-Trib' position as opposed to 'Post-Trib'? Nope. It explicitly describes the rapture and the 'last Trumpet' as being 'at the end of the world', not 'some time before the end of the world'. If we take the quotes at face value, then it happens at 'the end of the fourth Monarchy' (meaning Daniel's four empires, I suspect). In a Pre-Trib scenario the fourth empire is revived and goes right past the rapture for seven years, so this doesn't fit. The bit about Jesus 'in an instant' delivering 'the faithful then alive, from that temporal desctruction and the ruine of the Antichrist' also fits a Post-Trib scenario. For a Pre-Trib scenario it would have to talk about avoiding the plagues, the wrath, and the *reign* of the Antichrist, not his *ruin*. As we have seen just such a purpose for the rapture was widespread at that time - in *explicitly Post-Trib scenarios*. The interesting one is 'he will raise all his people that then sleep in the grave, to reign on earth with him, till the great multitude of their fellow-members be come in'. To a Pre-Tribber indoctrinated in their scenario would think - raise the Christians to reign in heaven, till the Tribulation saints are come in, but that doesn't work, because the quote actually says 'to reign *on earth* with him', so in the section about others being 'come in' it must refer to people *during* the Millennium. What's the betting very explicitly Post-Trib material would be found in all those conveniently closely edited gaps? Next:

> John Mason (1646-1694) in The Midnight Cry (1691) says "'Watch therefore, for you know not the Day, nor the hour, when the Son of man cometh'... why the doctrine of Christ's Kingdom hath met with so cold a reception, especially when the time of the End draws near... they who live in the daily expectation of the coming of Christ, are the most lively zealous Christians. When 'the times of the Gentiles shall be fulfilled' Christ... will reign here upon earth... there will be a Tribulation. This goes before the Destruction of Babylon, it comes on the Protestant Churches, Repent Quickly... Immediately after this, the Sun is darkened... This is an Overthrow...of the fourth great Empire, the Papal Empire, the Popes having the Fag-end of the Roman Empire... the Destruction of Mystical Babylon. Then comes the Conversion of the Jews: the appearance of the Son of Man, the Tribes mourning...'then shall two be in the Field, the one shall be taken, and the other left.'"

Well, you probably know what I am going to say - lots of gaps, short sentence fragments - alarm bells! Also, 'dog-whistle' Pre-Trib phrases such as 'you know not the day nore the hour', 'times of the Gentiles fulfilled' 'one taken, one left' and the concept I have found Pre-Tribbers use over and over to cast aspersions on the spirituality of their opponents 'they who live in daily expectation of the coming of Christ, are the most lively, zealous Christians' which is probably true enough, but doesn't require a Pre-Trib rapture, despite what their indoctrination about 'imminence' and the Pre-Trib rapture stamps into them. But taking the quote as it is on face value, there are problems. In the Pre-Trib scenario, 'the times of the Gentiles are fulfilled' before the Tribulation and the rapture, but here it only happens when 'Christ... will reign here upon earth'. Yes, it then says 'there will be a Tribulation' but that is right after one of those all too convenient gaps. Want to bet that in the gap we would find text that shows that this is not the chronological order the original writer had in mind? I certainly wouldn't bet against you, particularly because the question then arises: why the need to warn that the Tribulation falls on Protestant churches, and that they need to repent quickly, if this really were saying the true church escapes the Tribulation by a rapture event? Then comes the end of the age, but notice that it is only in the context of the visible second coming after the tribulation that the iconic Pre-Trib rapture concept of 'two in a field, one taken, the other left' is used. Convincing as proof of a Pre-Trib rapture being taught? Uh, no, a thousand times no! Next quote:

> Thomas Beverly (no dates) in The Dead Raised First (1691) says, "there must be...a space of Time between the Time of the Saints dead in Christ [martyrs] Rising first, who Answer to the Saints of the First Resurrection; and the Saints chang'd, who Answer to the Partakers of the First Resurrection; and the Time of these Chang'd Saints being Caught up... Both of these Saints Live and Reign with Christ a thousand years."

Wow, only two gaps, and whole sentences! Looks promising, until we notice that the passage limits the first resurrection only to the martyrs. We have seen this before, and in that scenario the first resurrection was Post-Trib, and the rest of the saints were raised after the *Milllennium* with the rest of the dead, 1000 years later. True, this can't be the same here, if we take the quote at face value, because both these saints live and reign with Christ a thousand years. But even then, let's look at this. That first gap - looks particularly suspicious to me, on reflection. Also, a 'space of time' is remarkably flexible. It could be a second, a minute, a year, seven years, a thousand years.... How long is a piece of string? Even a Post-Trib scenario will have some space of time, however small between the dead being raised and the living being changed, so what does this passage prove, exactly? Not a lot, when it comes down to a battle between Pre and Post-trib. Next quote:

> Sam Petto (no dates) in The Revelation Unvailed (1693) says, "The Rise or first State of this Kingdom, will be speedily after the Resurrection of the Witnesses, and the first conversion of the Jews. Rev.11.12,15. and before the Thousand Years begin. This is the Kingdom of Stone, Dan.2.34,45. Whose beginning will be small, and its way unpeaceable and troublesome, conflicting with Enemies, yet prevailing against and breaking of them, v.45."

No gaps - promising, but, why on earth Ice decided this was proof of a Pre-Tribulation position, I have absolutely no idea, as it is not referring to the Rapture at all, but only to the conversion of the Jews, the resurrection of the two Witnesses of Revelation and the Millennium. The only thing I can think of is he uses it because the word 'Resurrection' appears before the conversion of the Jews, but since that is explicitly about the Witnesses.... well the words lame, weak, straw clutching, desperate and dishonest all come to my mind at this point. And finally:

> Anonymous tract in A Short Survey of the Kingdom of Christ here on Earth with his Saints (1699) says, "those saints that are then alive shall not prevent the rising of the Saints that were dead at the coming of Christ...for the dead in Christ shall be raised first; then the Saints alive in the Body, in this mortal state, shall be changed...in the twinkling of an eye, less than a moment, raise all the dead Saints, and change all the Saints then alive into an incorruptible immortal state... They shall be caught up in the Clouds to meet the Lord in the Air...in this appearing of Christ. but here it's another sight of Christ, viz. as their Judg: for so he will be to the Sinner and ungodly, when he shall come the second time in the Clouds of Heaven... coming to enter upon his Kingdom here on Earth, with all his Saints in a glorified State, after having received their gloried bodies, and after meeting their Lord in the air], prepared for this great Assize and Judgment of the World."

Well, those old friends - the gaps and the suspiciously closely edited sentence fragments - have turned up again. The key here is in the gap between 'meet the Lord in the Air' and 'in this appearing of Christ. but here it's another sight of Christ, viz as their Judg:' That short end of sentence fragment rings alarm bells especially loud for me. As it stands, it is made to read as if this is referring to a separate 'appearing' to the rapture described repeatedly in the earlier fragments. However, the following context makes it clear that this is not about difference in timing, but a difference in the viewers - this time, how the ungodly view and experience the return of Jesus. Plus, given that in a Pre-Trib scenario the rapture itself is supposed to be invisible to unbelievers, even if it's effects aren't, then the unbelievers having 'another sight of

Christ' is problematic, to say the least. It is also problematic that the iconic rapture notion of Jesus 'coming in the Clouds' appears in both the putative 'Pre Trib Rapture' that Ice is trying to prove was taught here, and the second coming of Christ. Like I said before, the gap edits are suspiciously closely cut, and I have a lot more time for the biblical fidelity of these Puritan era writers than I do for these modern dispensationalist approaches.

Like I said, it is possible that genuine 'Pre-Trib' elements might appear later on in Watson's work, but given the way he has repeatedly and deceptively edited quotes to turn passages that are in context clearly Post-Tribulation into alleged hints of 'Pre-Tribulationism', I will bet that if they exist at all, they will be *very* few and far between, and certainly won't justify the sweeping statements and claims of support that are repeatedly made about the writers of this period. Now, if such lies, distortions are used by those who claim to be Christians and scholars, who are supposed to be fair under academic norms, and not underhand according to the command of the New Testament, we have to ask: what is the true nature of the doctrine they are using the native language of hell to defend? It certainly can't be truth, or they would not need to use lies and deceptions and underhandedness to defend it. It can only come from the Father of lies, Satan himself. There needs to be some serious repenting on the part of many people from the Pre-Tribulation research centre and the Pre-Tribulation crowd, because some of them have to have known what they were doing, and even lies believed and told unwittingly have to be repented of, especially among those who are pastors, teachers in the church and seminary professors - teachers of the teachers. This is part of the deception and the false teachers that Jesus and the apostles warned us about, and these false teachers that masquerade and present themselves as true teachers must be exposed for what they are and the lies must expunged from the church at the greatest possible speed, because, as I have said in both this and my previous book, if they are allowed to stand, they will lead to untold numbers of Christians losing their salvation in the all-too rapidly approaching Tribulation and being lost for eternity.

Appendix 8 : It's the UFO's wot dun it, honest – because the 'Queen of Heaven' says so and related issues

This is going to be a bit of a random and rambling appendix, which could well upset one or two theological applecarts among some readers. Whilst researching this book I came across this page - http://www.bibleprobe.com/rapture.htm . I don't know what to make of the site itself. It bills itself as a Non-Denominational site for Christians and Messianic Jews, which sounds very evangelical, yet it has numerous articles defending certain Roman Catholic practices and doctrines, and yet also has links to sites of groups such as the Worldwide Church of God, or some splinter of it (this body was a cult, but there has been a large split, with significant portions of the group coming back to a basically evangelical position and away from the false doctrines of the original group). Anyway, this page was talking about the rapture in a rather confused way. It eventually seems to come out for some kind of Pre-Tribulation rapture, even though at the start it seems to deny there is evidence for it. Anyway, what struck me was that in support they quoted from an alleged appearance of the Virgin Mary in Bayside New York. They apparently believe that although most visions of Mary are false, this one is true because it 'stands out with consistent messages that are in line with Scripture'. When I was a teenager, there was at least one apparent appearance of Mary that I - rightly or wrongly - thought the same of (in Israel), so I wouldn't necessarily have a problem with that per se, but the cynical part of me wonders if the sole criteria for them judging it biblical is the fact that it teaches a Pre-Tribulation rapture in the bit that they quote:

> Here is what was told to the woman Veronica by Our Lady at Bayside about the Rapture:
>
> "I give you great grace of heart, My children, to know that many shall be taken from your earth before the great Chastisement.... Many of your news media's shall state that they have been carried off by flying saucers. Oh no, My children! They were carried off into a supernatural realm of the Eternal Father to await the return of My Son upon earth." - Our Lady, December 7, 1976 (http://www.tldm.org/Directives/d45.htm)

The reason this perked my interest is that I have long been aware - since my teenage years, in fact - of a considerable amount of speculation and indeed flat out assertion amongst many Pre-Tribulationists that the governments of the world would explain all the missing Christians who had been raptured out of there by saying 'UFO's took them away'. It is a repeated theme in much popular Pre-Trib thought, and you sometimes even get people claiming to have had revelations from God about it, such as here - http://aliensrevealed.blogspot.co.uk/2009/08/rapture-and-satanic-lie.html . Plus it all tends to get tangled up in the rising obsession with speculative esoteric beliefs about end-time demon-human hybrids that seems to parallel the rise in interest in UFO's in general in the world. For one example of this kind of approach that I mean, see the interview recorded here - https://www.raptureready.com/terry/ufo.html . (By the way, if you want a really fantastic, well grounded and comprehensive book on the issue of UFO's, Alien encounters and the Bible, may I recommend 'Alien Intrusion' by Gary Bates.) What interests me is that as a rule, those who believe most fervently in the Pre-Tribulation rapture and the idea that the world will blame UFO's for the rapture disappearances tend to be militantly anti-Catholic, and yet here is this alleged appearance of the Virgin Mary saying exactly the same thing!

Now, you might be asking why I, who am so hostile to the Pre-Tribulation rapture, might raise this. Well, remember in an earlier appendix where I quoted Hildegard of Bingen to the effect that the Antichrist would do a good proportion of his signs and wonders by 'ingenious devices' - technology in other words? I have found out that there is some technology out there that in the right conditions can imitate a 'rapture event'. If we have millions of Christians out there who believe in a Pre-Tribulation rapture, and then find that some totally unexpected people have disappeared (blatant non-Christians, for instance), but that they have been left behind, that could truly mess with their faith. Speculative in the extreme, I know, but if any kind of such a fake rapture were to come into play, then claims of 'the UFO's did it' might well be used to great effect, especially if the goal is to unite all of humanity into some kind of one world religion, and one world government.

The other related matter that I think very interesting is something I found out whilst reading very conservative Catholic websites, including the alleged visions and words of Jesus, Mary and other saints that we referred to at the start of this appendix. There are some remarkable parallels and similarities between the views of these 'ultra-Catholics' and the alleged visions of Mary etc, and the views of what we might call 'ultra-Protestants' or fundamentalists, and I am talking about something beyond the to be expected convergence of views on societal issues such as abortion, sexual immorality and homosexuality and general moral breakdown, modernism in the church, humanism, naturalism in science and the like.

For instance, for many in the fundamentalist churches, the Vatican 2 council is a big deal. They believe it to be a trick, in which the Roman Catholic church pretends reform and pretends to change and reach out to other churches, only to suck them in. The interesting thing is that conservative Roman Catholics, in a mirror image, will warn that the Vatican 2 council was a Satanic deception that introduced Protestant heretical ideas into the Catholic church.

But even more to the point is how closely the views of a good many conservative Catholics, closely track that of Protestant fundamentalists in many details about the end times. Indeed, the messages believed to be from Mary in the website we started out with, whilst still resolutely Catholic - with penance, Hail Mary's, Rosary's and sacraments and medallions, and Mary as Co-Mediatrix and so on - warn of a great apostasy in the church, a coming one world government with a one world religion - indeed a false church, the 'church of man' in which the Antichrist will be enthroned in the Vatican, no less, and remarkably, his opponents are said to be small bands of Catholics, Orthodox and Protestants in every nation. That is probably not what fundamentalist rapture-believing Christians would expect from alleged visions of Mary! Something to think about. I should make it clear that I am not endorsing or asserting these visions are truly as they present themselves, but I am presenting the parallels in thought, because it is highly likely that true allies in the end times - when, as Jesus taught, Christian turns against Christian - might not be who you expect them to be.

Appendix 9 – Help! So what do I do about it?

So, if you have believed up until now that you will escape the Great Tribulation, or if you have been complacent about the end times, no doubt there are a million questions, worries, fears going through your mind. First, don't panic! Be very concerned, yes, but don't panic and give way to fear, but rather, have faith. Jesus in the gospels warned us what was coming, and that it would be a fearful time for all, but he warned us not to fill us with fear, but that we might be prepared for what is to come.

The first and most important preparation of all is spiritual. You need to understand what is at stake. Both the New Testament and the early church fathers warn us that 'only those who endure to the end will be saved'. Praying a sinners prayer at some point in the past does not save you. It does not mean you will get into heaven no matter what. The message of the New Testament and the early church fathers is that all the time of your faith will avail you nothing if you fall in the last hour. That's why it is important to face the reality now. In our own strength, we cannot stand, and we - I as much as any - need to stand only in God's power. I am no masochist, but pampered, at ease, used to comfort. We all together need to seek God's face, seek his strength not for an easy life, but to face what is to come. Jesus is looking for those who will be faithful unto death for Him, just as He was for us. Not works, but faithfulness in confession and lifestyle. Jesus warned that even doing miracles in His name was no guarantee, but living for and with Jesus in righteousness, in relationship, and not denying him is the key to eternal life; in other words persistence in doing good and giving ultimate allegiance to none other, no matter the cost.

You need to get this message about the true teaching of the New Testament and the church fathers out. If you are a pastor, then you need to start preparing your flock for tribulation and persecution. If you are in a church environment that teaches the lie of a Pre-Tribulation rapture, you will need to ask God for boldness and wisdom and grace in teaching the truth. I can tell you from experience that you will likely get a lot of flack from some quarters, because people really don't like their comfort-cocoons being popped. Remember that the false prophets of old always said 'Peace, Peace', and that disaster won't come upon the people of God. Perhaps you could remind them of Jesus' warnings of deception in the church in the last days, and suggest gently that an idea that is less than 200 years old might not be the best candidate for biblical truth on the matter. If you are in a church that doesn't really talk much about the return of Jesus, then similarly pray for wisdom and grace, and start winsomely and judiciously pointing to the very practical warnings Jesus and the apostles gave about the last days. If it is a church that has the attitude of 'We don't know, but it will all pan out in the end', well, it could be a church that is wearied with endless frenetic focus on the end times, but remind them that we should not idly ignore the very practical warnings Jesus gave, especially when he gave them with warnings of saints losing their salvation and being lost for all eternity.

If you feel unable to articulate arguments, particularly in environments where there is constant reinforcement by means of circular argument, you could buy and give to pastors and leaders one of my books on the topic. There is my first work, 'Rapture Rupture!' which systematically destroys the with the alleged 'irrefutable proofs' of the rapture from the late Tim LaHaye, and many other common arguments, focusing on particular issues and arguments in the debate.. If they are adamant that the early church fathers taught the Pre-Tribulation rapture, then of course this one would be the one to give them or point them to. I have also written 'The Rapture Trap' which covers much of the same ground as 'Rapture Rupture', but much more, including the theological developments behind the secret rapture doctrine. It has what one early reader and church leader called the best discussion of biblical covenants he has ever seen. It also has a highly detailed look at all 'day of the Lord' and related language through the entire bible, and generally tracks the biblical teaching in order rather than using the bible to counter particular arguments, the method of my first book. Now, I realize that for many potential readers, big, detailed works might put them off, so I have also written a short, clear book called 'Rapture Reality Check' that deals with just three key bible passages - Matthew 24, 1 Thessalonians 4-5 and 2 Thessalonians 1-2 - plus a key teaching from Jesus in a verse from Luke 21. I should also have relevant material on my website www.natlewis.co.uk that you can direct people to. Now, I know there is some self-interest here, given that buying my books means pennies for me, but it is the message that is important, so any other sound and well argued book that teaches the truth on the issue, buy and give them that, by all means; however, I don't think you will find many as thorough and incisive as mine, and as a theologian, my main books are ideal for church leaders and seminarians, thinkers and other people of influence.

The other thing to do will be to spiritually and mentally prepare your children - your own or your church's - for the persecution and tribulation that is to come. One of the things I hope to do is to produce some Sunday School material that will in part be about helping to do that, as well as dealing with the pressures and attacks on their faith that children of today are facing.

We also need to reach out in love to those who don't know Jesus, because in the last days, Jesus warns, things will get so bad that if they were not cut short for the sake of the elect, no-one would survive. As well, stand with Israel, not blindly - for she is not perfect - but faithfully, because God loves her and has called her by name. Don't be daunted by the anti-Semitic de-legitimization or the claims of genocide or widespread human rights abuses or war crimes that are so prevalent. I can tell you as a human rights worker that a great many of the accusations are utterly unwarranted and certainly disproportionate, particularly compared to the relative lack of outrage about many other situations that are far worse. Also, don't forget your already badly persecuted brothers and sisters in other countries such as Iraq, Sudan, Pakistan and the like. Speak up for them, and urge your political representatives to fight to remove the blockages for them to get to relative safety in the West. For more about Pakistani Christians in particular, see http://www.britishpakistanichristians.co.uk/ .

Finally, many readers, particularly in the US, might be wondering, should you become - if you are not already - preppers, and stock up on food, water, emergency supplies, prepare hideouts and the like? Well, first and foremost to be prepared, we need to stock up on faith, hope, love, joy, peace, faithfulness, self-control, sound thinking, holiness, the Holy Spirit and obedience, and steadfast reliance on Jesus. Any other kind of prepping will be of little value without these. That said, the biblical proverb 'The prudent see danger and take refuge, but the simple keep going and pay the penalty' (Proverbs 22.3) rather applies. If great trouble comes, then Western society is too reliant on a quick and easy - and easily interruptible - food supply, along with other amenities. More to the point, the bible makes it quite clear that in the time of the Antichrist, anyone who does not take his mark of damnation will not be able to buy or sell. What is more, Jesus warned any local disciples at that time to flee into the mountains or wilderness of Judah, and the early church fathers applied this more generally, consistently teaching that the trouble and persecution - massacre, even - would be greatest in the cities and that the true church would be forced to live out in hills and caves, relying on the plants of the wild for food. So prayerfully consider preparations, but don't let it consume you and rob you of the opportunities and callings God has for you now. Don't be selfish - don't make it all about protecting me and mine - but rather recognize the need to be islands of divine stability and peace in troubled times for those around you. As to the practicalities, I am not an expert, but rather a comfortable stay-at-home, rely on convenience kind of guy, and I know I have to do something here too. I also know that there are lots of products out there - if you look you will find all sorts of videos and pitches, fear mongering, saying that only they have the answer, the bullet-proof plan that everyone else has missed. Again, prayerful wisdom is in order, and faith in God, even amidst prudent preparations. What I do know is that at least one solid church leader I know here in the UK has started stocking up on food, and he says dried food is simple and best. In these days of ecology and conservation, I suspect we can learn from some of those in the green movement who have aimed at living off the grid, and there are also types of agriculture to consider known as aquaphonics which can be conducted in cities or residences or outhouses. The Israelis also have a lot of great technology in agriculture, medicine and renewable energy. I also suggest that getting churches out on hikes might serve more than a social purpose, it might start acclimatizing people to life in nature, however gently. There is also a course out there which I have not taken, but which a Christian leader whose judgement I trust recommends highly called the Omega Program - which you can find here - http://www.omegaprogramme.com/. I have read the companion book 'End Time Survivor', some of which I thought very good, but some rather off beam; however it doesn't cover practicalities, more an interpretation of the bible's teaching on the end times. There is also said to be a book come out by influential author Carl Gallups on similar issues called 'Be Thou Prepared'. I have no idea what it is like, but it might be worth a look. The author is a pastor and ex- policeman: http://www.amazon.com/Be-Thou-Prepared-Equipping-Persecution/dp/1935071319 .

But above all, back to the first point, spiritual preparation is something we all need to focus on, for the sake of our souls and families, if nothing else, but above all for the sake of Jesus' name and glory. He died for you. Don't throw it away at the last hurdle, however high it may be, but look to the promises given to those who overcome and endure (Revelation 2-3), and take heed to Jesus' warnings for those who don't endure to the end, and for whom those times come 'like a thief in the night'. I suspect that there are going to be pre-shocks before the final worst period. Don't ignore those warnings and sink back into worldly pre-occupation and worries and desires, but keep your eyes fixed on Jesus who suffered for you, for the joy set before him, and set yourself to do the same with the help of His Spirit, to the glory of our heavenly Father and his Messiah. Amen.

Great News for Imperfect people in Terrible Times

(I have lightly adapted the following from my website, www.natlewis.co.uk because I think it provides a template for preaching the gospel in light of the true end times message of the bible we have discovered in the earlier parts of this book. I think it should be useful in light of the fact that right from the start of the church, teaching for new disciples included material on how to face the end times and spot end times deception, and we should do the same.)

Jesus called the message he proclaimed about himself and the Kingdom of God 'good news'. The core message is 'God is love', and Jesus brings - and indeed is - good news for all who will receive him. If you are anything like me, there are all sorts of things in your life that you know are not the best, habits, actions, words, thoughts, whether it be addictions or anxiety and depression, or anger, or even just arrogant independence in living apart from God. If you don't think any of these apply to you, then you are lying to yourself! These all ultimately stem - whether directly or indirectly - from lack of faith in God, both by you as an individual, and society around you. This is what the bible calls sin, and it makes it quite clear that every single human being is infected by this moral disease - every single human in history, except, that is, Jesus of Nazareth. Right from our fore-father and fore-mother, Adam and Eve, the bible says, we have all 'fallen short of the glory of God' and his perfect standards by sinning, or falling short of the mark (and as God's representatives delegated to have authority over much of creation, the natural world is also broken by human sin and causes misery - is in bondage to decay as the apostle Paul puts it in Romans). God's standards may be perfect, but he is not - thankfully - a perfectionist, or at least, he has been very creative with his perfectionism, if He is a perfectionist. As a God who is perfectly just and holy, for all sin there must be punishment, but humans are not able to bear such a punishment. Therefore, right from the start of history, God has promised, in ever increasing detail, to send a man who is the perfect representative of God, a God-man, if you will, who would be able to rescue us from this dilemma and condemnation - Jesus Christ. He was untouched by the stain of sin, whilst suffering the effects of living in a sinful world and remaining perfect in word, thought and deed, even in the face of extreme temptation, and finally willingly taking up the just punishment for our sins. For those who will make allegiance to Jesus by declaring his divine lordship and confessing their sinfulness before God and believing or trusting in Jesus and the work he did by suffering for us on the cross, Jesus offers the reward for his perfect righteousness that he put aside to bear our just punishment in one of the most shameful, painful and degrading deaths possible - both physically and spiritually. God then vindicated him and rewarded him by raising him from the dead several days later, giving him a resurrected body with super-natural powers untouched by the death and decay of this sinful age. This is a downpayment, or 'firstfruits' of what God promises for those who make their allegiance to Jesus.

This is great news. However, there is a dark down side, and an unbelievably fantastic destiny on the other side of that dark valley. The down side is that we are called to be disciples of Jesus. Really believing and making allegiance to Jesus means being one who follows Jesus, and models him, and Jesus' way is one of victory and resurrection, but only through suffering in one form or another. Jesus also warned that because 'the world' - meaning human society and government systems that oppose God's will and law and purpose - hated him, it would also hate and persecute those who were truly his disciples. As the apostle Paul puts it we 'have to go through many tribulations to enter the kingdom of God'. Jesus and his apostles repeatedly warned that in the very last days this opposition would intensify - that there would be an increase in wickedness and selfishness, an increase in violent opposition, and an increase in abandoning the true law and faith and doctrine of God, including in the church that professes to follow Jesus (and this last factor will make it even more difficult for those who wish to stay true to the teaching of Jesus and the bible). This situation of violence and wickedness and laxness or worse in the church will pave the way for a grand deception, a false Messiah who will promise peace, but at a huge price; this is the one also known as the anti-Christ. Despite early appearances of goodness, he will come to demand allegiance, and oppress those who refuse to give it to him, particularly those who follow Jesus. In the days before his return, Jesus taught, the times would be absolutely terrible - and not just for those who seek to follow God. The battle lines will be drawn, and there will be no middle ground - choices must be made, either for or against Jesus and his ways and his true church.

But giving and maintaining allegiance to Jesus in the last days will be an absolute necessity, no matter what we face, because Jesus said 'only those who endure to the end will be saved'. Saved from what, you ask. Well, remember the just punishment that God delivers? Ultimately, our sinfulness is against Him, the eternal God and Creator to whom all allegiance is justly due, and the punishment will match the stature of the one wronged. Jesus said of judgement day 'Those who deny me before men, I will deny before my Father in heaven' (in other words, will end up in Hell), 'but those who acknowledge me before men, I will also acknowledge before my Father' (in other words an eternal welcome into the heavenly kingdom). Deliberately denying and persisting in denying the suffering Saviour in the face of suffering demonstrates lack of faith and not truly being a disciple of Jesus the crucified. Jesus also asked of his return whether he 'will find faith in the earth?' That can also be translated as 'faithfulness'. When Jesus returns, just as God vindicated Jesus after his tremendous suffering, so God will vindicate his church, Jesus 'bride' - or at least such as have remained faithful in suffering like Jesus did. They will be fit for each other, and fit for the full expression of the Kingdom of God that currently only is found in partial and hidden form in this age. God is not looking for perfection in a legalistic way, but he is looking for faithfulness, one that is expressed in righteous (not perfect) living and in fidelity to Jesus. Although it will appear the easy option, giving allegiance to the anti-Christ by taking his mark is to doom yourself to damnation for eternity.

You will hear preachers say all sorts of things that run counter to this message. The bible warns that in the last days, people in the church will gather to themselves teachers who tell them what they want to hear, using the memorable phrase 'having their ears tickled'. Such siren preachers will talk about 'living your best life now' and about financial wealth and blessings above all else, the so-called 'Prosperity Gospel', and whilst I don't want to deny God's willingness to bless materially for the furthering of his kingdom when He chooses, the whole tenor of much of this preaching is in complete opposition to the pattern of teaching in the New Testament. There is also a particular teaching that is immensely popular in the evangelical 'bible-believing' church and believed to be 'biblical', but is anything but. It's called 'the rapture', and it is really a form of prosperity gospel, ironically often held by those who are ardently against the regular form. Don't listen to such seducing sermonizers, no matter how sincere they are, or how they are reputed to be 'biblical'. What they are teaching is little short of heresy, because again, it is completely contrary to the pattern of teaching in the New Testament about the last days. Their teaching says that the church will escape the suffering of the last days when Jesus and the apostles taught precisely the opposite.

When I was researching my book on the subject, 'Rapture Rupture', I found that the New Testament and the early church fathers consistently taught a number of things about the last days. Along with the terrible times, the abandonment of God's law and the persecution of God's people, both Israel and the true church and an increase of wickedness, they also taught that to remain strong in the faith, Christians should not give up meeting together, and also that the key to remaining ready for Jesus' return was not about looking for some kind of escape, but living spiritually alert and righteously, because it is righteous living that enables us to escape the dissolution that will blind people to the times and the need for holiness. For those, Jesus' return will be like 'a thief in the night', and taken unawares, they will be excluded from the kingdom. As Jesus warned, in that day, 'Many will say Lord, Lord,... but I will say to them 'Away from me you workers of lawlessness, I never knew you'.' People who have done miracles in Jesus name will be cast out because they did not live righteously in communion with him.

For those of you reading this who have never given allegiance to Jesus, then it is time you made your choice. It is time to face up to this choice while you are still breathing, for when you are dead it is too late, and no-one knows when their own end will come. However, Jesus made it quite clear that in the time before he returns there will be death in abundance. In fact, he taught that no-one would be left alive if he didn't come early to save his own. It is a matter of the heart, in which you acknowledge what Jesus has done for you, taking your punishment so that you could gain paradise and eternity with Him. It is a matter of giving allegiance to Jesus as rightful Lord. The exact words are not vital, but generally a prayer like this is a good guide :

'Father God, I acknowledge that I am a sinner, and that I have lived a life apart from You, and in rebellion against your laws. I believe that you sent your Son, Jesus, to die for my sin. I am sorry for my sins and I submit to Jesus as my Lord and Saviour. Take away my sin and come into my heart by your Holy Spirit, in Jesus name, Amen.'

This is not some insurance policy, something you can pray, and then live your life as before. Unfortunately, much of the evangelical church has got this desperately wrong. They urge people to just 'say the prayer' and you will be saved, but that is again, very different to what the bible teaches, and there are many professing Christians who need to pay attention. Just because you have 'said the prayer' does not mean your salvation is guaranteed. Fidelity to Jesus and living (however imperfectly) according to his laws are evidence of saving faith. Denying Jesus and abandoning allegiance to him is a way to put yourself out of the Kingdom, and persistently unholy living risks the same. That is why the early church was so big on repentance and holy living, and so should we be. Paul said 'Examine yourself to see if you are in the faith', a warning we all need to heed from time to time, and even more so as the last days loom ahead. So, there is good news, but there is also a warning for those who don't yet believe, and those who think that they do. 'If you think you stand', said Paul, 'take heed, lest you fall'.

Maintaining allegiance to Jesus in the face of the forces that are preparing for the anti-Christ will be hard, the seductions and intimidations many, but it is worth enduring to the end, for that is the only way we will be saved, as Jesus said. Any teaching, however revered or believed in as biblical, that gets in the way of preparing for that reality is a demonic delusion, a snare that should be repudiated, and it is something that the church of Jesus Christ, and in particular the professing evangelical church urgently needs to do now, and to step up to stand alongside their suffering brothers and sisters, abandoning the apathy and remembering Jesus' criteria on judgement day - helping suffering brothers and sisters who imitate the suffering Saviour. Broad is the gate and wide is the way that leads to destruction, and unfortunately much of the Western evangelical church is embracing that way and encouraging others to race down that road too. May God have mercy on our souls and give us true endurance that leads to salvation.

Other books by Nathanael Lewis

Rapture Rupture! The Big Lie Behind 'Left Behind' Exposed

In the world of end-times writing, tables of 'proofs' contrasting the 'rapture' and the second coming of Jesus are rife. In this work, an evangelical theologian dissects a typical example from perhaps the most prominent and prosperous Rapture-teacher of modern times, Tim Lahaye, author of the famous Left Behind series of novels. He shows how in each and every case the 'proofs' show precisely the opposite, including how the only consistent way to take the 'blessed hope' as the rapture is to engage in out and out heresy in the same verse of scripture. He also shows how dispensationalism is an idolatrous prism that distorts Scripture and explains how Paul gets the order of the resurrection / rapture from Jesus' own teaching. As well, he addresses false concepts or interpretations that are touted as rapture proofs such as 'imminence' and 'not under wrath'.

A massively expanded second edition will cover a great many more false arguments, as well as showing who and what the 'Restrainer' is in 2 Thessalonians and why the restraint is lifting now, the nature of the final judgement, and how Isaiah 24-6 is the source for much New Testament teaching on the End times. Do you dare face up to the question: have you been deceived?

The Rapture Trap : How the Heresy of the Pre-Tribulation rapture can send people to hell

The rapture is Satan's theological end times horror story to trap evangelicals, says this theological work: it is actually a salvation issue in one sense, according to Jesus. This is not some one verse slasher tale, but a detailed theological look at the issue. It examines the core concepts and fundamental flaws in dispensationalism, the theology behind 'Rapture' teaching, in particular how it directly contradicts Paul's teaching in Romans. It also has a highly praised chapter on the nature of covenant in the bible, and a highly detailed examination of almost all the key 'end times' phrases in the bible. As well as dealing with Matthew 24-5, including who Jesus was talking about when he refers to the 'least of my brethren' (not Jews), it also has a number of chapters deconstructing the dispensationalist concept of 'imminence'. It also looks at the bible's teaching on the necessity of suffering for sanctification, and much, much more, including a detailed look at the structure of Revelation and God's last days anger and ending with a look at what the New Testament really teaches about salvation and judgement day, plus a detailed examination of 'the abomination of desolation'. If you want to find out how what you believe about the rapture can be an issue of eternal salvation, this is the book for you.

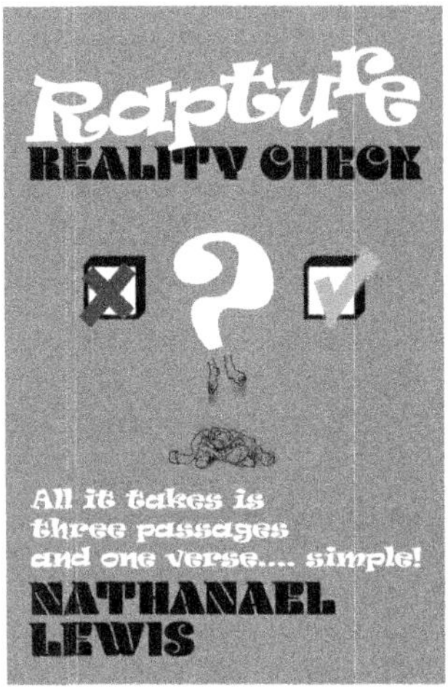

Rapture Reality Check : All it takes is three passages and one verse.... simple!

In all the myriad of complexities about the rapture, evangelical theologian Nathanael Lewis cuts to the heart of the matter by examining just three key passages, and one absolutely key bible verse in a short, popular level but scholarly rigorous work. Cutting aside layers of man-made theological encrustation, he takes us back to the pure message of the New Testament and the twelve Apostles and shows that there is just one simple answer to this much debated question - and shows why in practice your eternal destiny might even be determined by what you believe on this seeming merely theoretical question. A must read for those who want the truth short and quick.

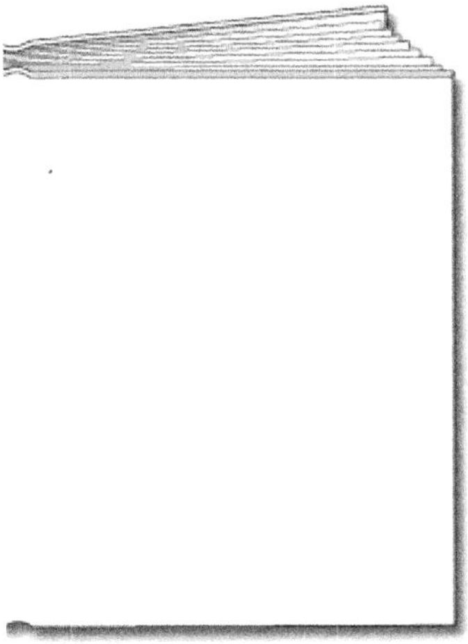

The Genesis of Geology

This short but penetrating work tackles a key issue of our time and sets it in a wider context. How do we understand the record of the rocks on which we exist, and how has that understanding come about? Exploding many myths along the way, it tracks the debate all the way back to ancient Greece and Rome, tells how it was that the church ended up wedded to a pagan scientific philosophy that hampered scientific progress for centuries, how the founder of modern geology is on the verge of becoming a

Catholic saint, and how a key idea of his turned out to be catastrophically wrong, plus how Darwin was groomed by a devious geologist for maximum effect in a vicious political powerplay that has shaped today's understanding of the history of the world. Fraud, revolutionary politics, fossils and a dastardly 30 year plan all feature. Who knew that investigating dry rocks and fossil ideas could reveal such a story?

The Christmas Ghost of Pagan Past

Enter a world of strange allies - Islamic terrorists, conspiracy theorists, druids, atheists and fundamentalist Jewish Christians who all sing the same song about Christmas. Discover a strange world where lies become truth and truth becomes lies, where the self-described opponents of paganism end up pushing a pagan lie, where surprising truths are suppressed by blinded ideologues who should most welcome them. Find out how a strange mythology veils the truth about why December 25th really became the date of Christmas. Find out if you've been deceived into shooting down your own side, into making alliances with enemies and making enemies of allies and friends in an intellectual mystery. Who done it, who made December 25th Jesus' birthday? and why? It's not what you think, not how you think, not why you think. Do you dare discover the truth?

If you want to keep up to date with Nathanael Lewis's writings, music and so on, sign up for updates at www.natlewis.co.uk . You can also contact him at nat@melodyofthemind.com

Printed in Great Britain
by Amazon

23757437R00169